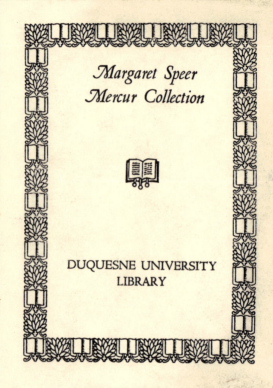

Wm H. Mercer,

Pittsburgh,

Pa.

𝕽𝖎𝖛𝖊𝖗𝖘𝖎𝖉𝖊 𝕰𝖉𝖎𝖙𝖎𝖔𝖓

THE WRITINGS OF
OLIVER WENDELL HOLMES

IN FOURTEEN VOLUMES
VOLUME X.

OUR HUNDRED DAYS
IN EUROPE

BY

OLIVER WENDELL HOLMES

BOSTON AND NEW YORK
HOUGHTON, MIFFLIN AND COMPANY
The Riverside Press, Cambridge

The Riverside Press, Cambridge, Mass., U. S. A.
Electrotyped and Printed by H. O. Houghton & Co.

To

MY DAUGHTER AMELIA

(MRS. TURNER SARGENT)

MY FAITHFUL AND DEVOTED COMPANION

THIS OUTLINE OF OUR SUMMER EXCURSION

IS AFFECTIONATELY DEDICATED.

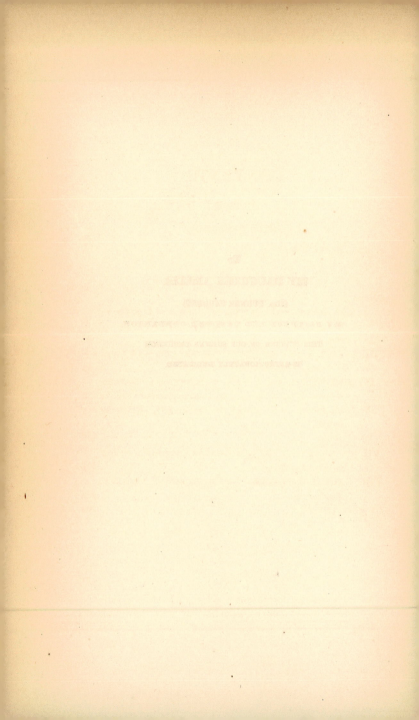

CONTENTS.

INTRODUCTORY.

PAGE

A PROSPECTIVE VISIT 1

OUR HUNDRED DAYS IN EUROPE.

CHAPTER

   I. THE VOYAGE. — LIVERPOOL. — CHESTER. — LONDON. —
      EPSOM 9

  II. EPSOM. — LONDON. — WINDSOR 38

 III. LONDON. — ISLE OF WIGHT. — CAMBRIDGE. — OXFORD.
      — YORK. — EDINBURGH 65

 IV. STRATFORD-ON-AVON. — GREAT MALVERN. — TEWKES-
      BURY. — BATH. — SALISBURY. — STONEHENGE . . 90

  V. STONEHENGE. — SALISBURY. — OLD SARUM. — BEMER-
      TON. — BRIGHTON 113

 VI. LONDON 135

 VII. BOULOGNE. — PARIS. — LONDON. — LIVERPOOL. — THE
      HOMEWARD PASSAGE 161

VIII. GENERAL IMPRESSIONS. — MISCELLANEOUS OBSERVA-
      TIONS 182

GENERAL INDEX 209

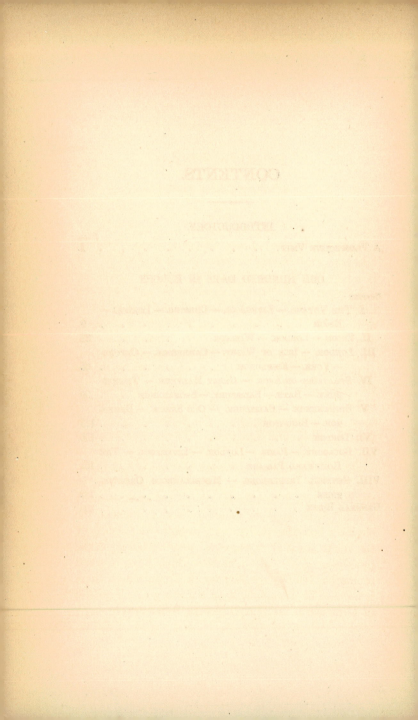

INTRODUCTORY.

A PROSPECTIVE VISIT.

———•———

AFTER an interval of more than fifty years, I propose taking a second look at some parts of Europe. It is a Rip Van Winkle experiment which I am promising myself. The changes wrought by half a century in the countries I visited amount almost to a transformation. I left the England of William the Fourth, of the Duke of Wellington, of Sir Robert Peel; the France of Louis Philippe, of Marshal Soult, of Thiers, of Guizot. I went from Manchester to Liverpool by the new railroad, the only one I saw in Europe. I looked upon England from the box of a stage-coach, upon France from the coupé of a diligence, upon Italy from the cushion of a carrozza. The broken windows of Apsley House were still boarded up when I was in London. The asphalt pavement was not laid in Paris. The Obelisk of Luxor was lying in its great boat in the Seine, as I remember it. I did not see it erected; it must have been an exciting scene to witness, the engineer standing underneath, so as to be crushed by the great stone if it disgraced him by falling in the process. As for the dynasties which have overlaid each other like Dr. Schliemann's Trojan cities, there is no need of moralizing over a history which instead of Finis is constantly ending with What next?

With regard to the changes in the general conditions of society and the advance in human knowledge,
think for one moment what fifty years have done! I
have often imagined myself escorting some wise man
of the past to our Saturday Club, where we often have
distinguished strangers as our guests. Suppose there
sat by me, I will not say Sir Isaac Newton, for he has
been too long away from us, but that other great man,
whom Professor Tyndall names as next to him in intellectual stature, as he passes along the line of master minds of his country, from the days of Newton to
our own, — Dr. Thomas Young, who died in 1829.
Would he or I be the listener, if we were side by
side? However humble I might feel in such a presence, I should be so clad in the grandeur of the new
discoveries, inventions, ideas, I had to impart to him
that I should seem to myself like the ambassador of
an Emperor. I should tell him of the ocean steam-
ers, the railroads that spread themselves like cobwebs
over the civilized and half-civilized portions of the
earth, the telegraph and the telephone, the photograph
and the spectroscope. I should hand him a paper with
the morning news from London to read by the electric
light, I should startle him with a friction match, I
should amaze him with the incredible truths about
anæsthesia, I should astonish him with the later conclusions of geology, I should dazzle him by the fully
developed law of the correlation of forces, I should
delight him with the cell-doctrine, I should confound
him with the revolutionary apocalypse of Darwinism.
All this change in the aspects, position, beliefs, of
humanity since the time of Dr. Young's death, the
date of my own graduation from college!

I ought to consider myself highly favored to have

lived through such a half century. But it seems to me that in walking the streets of London and Paris I shall revert to my student days, and appear to myself like a relic of a former generation. Those who have been born into the inheritance of the new civilization feel very differently about it from those who have lived their way into it. To the young and those approaching middle age all these innovations in life and thought are as natural, as much a matter of course, as the air they breathe; they form a part of the inner framework of their intelligence, about which their mental life is organized. To men and women of more than threescore and ten they are external accretions, like the shell of a mollusk, the jointed plates of an articulate. This must be remembered in reading anything written by those who knew the century in its teens; it is not likely to be forgotten, for the fact betrays itself in all the writer's thoughts and expressions.

The story of my first visit to Europe is briefly this: my object was to study the medical profession, chiefly in Paris, and I was in Europe about two years and a half, from April, 1833, to October, 1835. I sailed in the packet ship Philadelphia from New York for Portsmouth, where we arrived after a passage of twenty-four days. A week was spent in visiting Southampton, Salisbury, Stonehenge, Wilton, and the Isle of Wight. I then crossed the Channel to Havre, from which I went to Paris. In the spring and summer of 1834 I made my principal visit to England and Scotland. There were other excursions to the Rhine and to Holland, to Switzerland and to Italy, but of these I need say nothing here. I returned in the packet ship Utica, sailing from Havre, and reaching New York after a passage of forty-two days.

A few notes from my recollections will serve to re-call the period of my first visit to Europe, and form a natural introduction to the experiences of my second. I take those circumstances which happen to suggest themselves.

After a short excursion to Strasbourg, down the Rhine, and through Holland, a small steamer took us from Rotterdam across the Channel, and we found ourselves in the British capital.

The great sight in London is — London. No man understands himself as an infinitesimal until he has been a drop in that ocean, a grain of sand on that sea-margin, a mote in its sunbeam, or the fog or smoke which stands for it; in plainer phrase, a unit among its millions.

I had two letters to persons in England: one to kind and worthy Mr. Petty Vaughan, who asked me to dinner; one to pleasant Mr. William Clift, con-servator of the Hunterian Museum, who asked me to tea.

To Westminster Abbey. What a pity it could not borrow from Paris the towers of Notre Dame! But the glory of its interior made up for this shortcoming. Among the monuments, one to Rear Admiral Charles Holmes, a descendant, perhaps, of another namesake, immortalized by Dryden in the "Annus Mirabilis" as

"the Achates of the general's fight."

He accompanied Wolfe in his expedition which re-sulted in the capture of Quebec. My relative, I will take it for granted, as I find him in Westminster Abbey. Blood is thicker than water, — and warmer than marble, I said to myself, as I laid my hand on the cold stone image of the once famous Admiral.

To the Tower, to see the lions, — of all sorts. There I found a "poor relation," who made my acquaintance without introduction. A large baboon, or ape, — some creature of that family, — was sitting at the open door of his cage, when I gave him offence by approaching too near and inspecting him too narrowly. He made a spring at me, and if the keeper had not pulled me back would have treated me unhandsomely, like a quadrumanous rough, as he was. He succeeded in stripping my waistcoat of its buttons, as one would strip a pea-pod of its peas.

To Vauxhall Gardens. All Americans went there in those days, as they go to Madame Tussaud's in these times. There were fireworks and an exhibition of polar scenery. "Mr. Collins, the English PAGANINI," treated us to music on his violin. A comic singer gave us a song, of which I remember the line,

" You 'll find it all in the agony bill."

This referred to a bill proposed by Sir Andrew Agnew, a noted Scotch Sabbatarian agitator.

To the opera to hear Grisi. The king, William the Fourth, was in his box; also the Princess Victoria, with the Duchess of Kent. The king tapped with his white-gloved hand on the ledge of the box when he was pleased with the singing. — To a morning concert and heard the real Paganini. To one of the lesser theatres and heard a monologue by the elder Mathews, who died a year or two after this time. To another theatre, where I saw Liston in Paul Pry. Is it not a relief that I am abstaining from description of what everybody has heard described?

To Windsor. Machinery to the left of the road. Recognized it instantly, by recollection of the plate in "Rees's Cyclopedia," as Herschel's great telescope. — Oxford. Saw only its outside. I knew no one there, and no one knew me. — Blenheim, — the Titians best remembered of its objects on exhibition. The great Derby day of the Epsom races. Went to the race with a coach - load of friends and acquaintances. Plenipotentiary, the winner, "rode by P. Connelly." So says Herring's picture of him, now before me. Chestnut, a great "bullock" of a horse, who easily beat the twenty-two that started. Every New England deacon ought to see one Derby day to learn what sort of a world this is he lives in. Man is a sporting as well as a praying animal.

Stratford-on-Avon. Emotions, but no scribbling of name on walls. — Warwick. The castle. A village festival, "The Opening of the Meadows," a true exhibition of the semi-barbarism which had come down from Saxon times. — Yorkshire. "The Hangman's Stone." Story told in my book called the "Autocrat," etc. York Cathedral. — Northumberland. Alnwick Castle. The figures on the walls which so frightened my man John when he ran away from Scotland in his boyhood.

Berwick-on-Tweed. A regatta going on; a very pretty show. Scotland. Most to be remembered, the incomparable loveliness of Edinburgh. — Sterling. The view of the Links of Forth from the castle. The whole country full of the romance of history and poetry. Made one acquaintance in Scotland, Dr Robert Knox, who asked my companion and myself to breakfast. I was treated to five entertainments in Great Britain: the breakfast just mentioned; lunch with

Mrs. Macadam, — the good old lady gave me bread, and not a stone; dinner with Mr. Vaughan; one with Mr. Stanley, the surgeon; tea with Mr. Clift, — for all which attentions I was then and am still grateful, for they were more than I had any claim to expect. Fascinated with Edinburgh. Strolls by Salisbury Crag; climb to the top of Arthur's Seat; delight of looking up at the grand old castle, of looking down on Holyrood Palace, of watching the groups on Calton Hill, wandering in the quaint old streets and sauntering on the sidewalks of the noble avenues, even at that time adding beauty to the new city. The weeks I spent in Edinburgh are among the most memorable of my European experiences. To the Highlands, to the Lakes, in short excursions; to Glasgow, seen to disadvantage under gray skies and with slippery pavements. Through England rapidly to Dover and to Calais, where I found the name of M. Dessein still belonging to the hotel I sought, and where I read Sterne's "Preface Written in a Désobligeante," sitting in the vehicle most like one that I could find in the stable. From Calais back to Paris, where I began working again.

All my travelling experiences, including a visit to Switzerland and Italy in the summer and autumn of 1835, were merely interludes of my student life in Paris. On my return to America, after a few years of hospital and private practice, I became a Professor in Harvard University, teaching Anatomy and Physiology, afterwards Anatomy alone, for the period of thirty-five years, during part of which time I paid some attention to literature, and became somewhat known as the author of several works in prose and verse which have been well received. My prospective visit will not be a professional one, as I resigned my office in 1882, and am no longer known chiefly as a teacher or a practitioner.

BOSTON, *April*, 1886.

OUR HUNDRED DAYS IN EUROPE.

I.

I BEGIN this record with the columnar, self-reliant capital letter to signify that there is no disguise in its egoisms. If it were a chapter of autobiography, this is what the reader would look for as a matter of course. Let him consider it as being such a chapter, and its egoisms will require no apology.

I have called the record *our* hundred days, because I was accompanied by my daughter, without the aid of whose younger eyes and livelier memory, and especially of her faithful diary, which no fatigue or indisposition was allowed to interrupt, the whole experience would have remained in my memory as a photograph out of focus.

We left Boston on the 29th of April, 1886, and reached New York on the 29th of August, four months of absence in all, of which nearly three weeks were taken up by the two passages, one week was spent in Paris, and the rest of the time in England and Scotland.

No one was so much surprised as myself at my undertaking this visit. Mr. Gladstone, a strong man for his years, is reported as saying that he is too old to travel, at least to cross the ocean, and he is younger than I am, — just four months, to a day, younger. It is true that Sir Henry Holland came to this country, and travelled freely about the world, after he was eighty years old; but his pitcher went to the well once too often, and met the usual doom of fragile articles. When my friends asked me why I did not go to Europe, I reminded them of the fate of Thomas Parr. He was only twice my age, and was getting on finely towards his two hundredth year, when the Earl of Arundel carried him up to London, and, being feasted and made a lion of, he found there a premature and early grave at the age of only one hundred and fifty-two years. He lies in Westminster Abbey, it is true, but he would probably have preferred the upper side of his own hearth-stone to the under side of the slab which covers him.

I should never have thought of such an expedition if it had not been suggested by a member of my family that I should accompany my daughter, who was meditating a trip to Europe. I remembered how many friends had told me I ought to go; among the rest, Mr. Emerson, who had spoken to me repeatedly about it. I had not seen Europe for more than half a century, and I had a certain longing for one more sight of the places I remembered, and others it would be a delight to look upon. There were a few living persons whom I wished to meet. I was assured that I should be kindly received in England. All this was tempting enough, but there was an obstacle in the way which I feared, and, as it proved, not without good reason. I doubted whether I could possibly breathe in a narrow state-room. In certain localities I have found myself liable to attacks of asthma, and, although I had not had one for years, I felt sure that I could not escape it if I tried to sleep in a state-room.

I did not escape it, and I am glad to tell my story about it, because it excuses some of my involuntary social shortcomings, and enables me to thank collectively all those kind members of the profession who trained all the artillery of the pharmacopœia upon my troublesome enemy, from bicarbonate of soda and Vichy water to arsenic and dynamite. One costly contrivance, sent me by the Reverend Mr. Haweis, whom I have never duly thanked for it, looked more like an angelic trump for me to blow in a better world than what I believe it is, an inhaling tube intended to prolong my mortal respiration. The best thing in my experience was recommended to me by an old friend in London. It was Himrod's asthma cure, one of the many powders, the smoke of which when burning is inhaled. It is made in Providence, Rhode Island, and I had to go to London to find it. It never failed to give at least temporary relief, but nothing enabled me to sleep in my state-room, though I had it all to myself, the upper berth being removed. After the first night and part of the second, I never lay down at all while at sea. The captain allowed me to have a candle and sit up in the saloon, where I worried through the night as I best might. How could I be in a fit condition to accept the attention of my friends in Liverpool, after sitting up every night for more than a week; and how could I be in a mood for the catechizing of interviewers, without having once lain down during the whole return passage? I hope the reader will see why I mention these facts. They explain and excuse many things; they have been alluded to, sometimes with exaggeration, in the newspapers, and I could not tell my story fairly without mentioning them. I got along well enough as soon as

I landed, and have had no return of the trouble since
I have been back in my own home.   I will not adver-
tise an assortment of asthma remedies for sale, but I
assure my kind friends I have had no use for any one
of them since I have walked the Boston pavements,
drank, not the Cochituate, but the Belmont spring
water, and breathed the lusty air of my native north-
easters.

My companion and I required an attendant, and we
found one of those useful androgynous personages
known as *courier-maids*, who had travelled with
friends of ours, and who was ready to start with us
at a moment's warning.   She was of English birth,
lively, short-gaited, serviceable, more especially in
the first of her dual capacities.   So far as my wants
were concerned, I found her zealous and active in
providing for my comfort.

It was no sooner announced in the papers that I was
going to England than I began to hear of preparations to welcome me.   An invitation to a club meeting
was cabled across the Atlantic.   One of my countrywomen who has a house in London made an engagement for me to meet friends at her residence.   A reverend friend, who thought I had certain projects in
my head, wrote to me about lecturing: where I should
appear, what fees I should obtain, and such business
matters.   I replied that I was going to England to
spend money, not to make it; to hear speeches, very
possibly, but not to make them; to revisit scenes I had
known in my younger days; to get a little change of
my routine, which I certainly did; and to enjoy a
little rest, which I as certainly did not, at least in
London.   In a word, I wished a short vacation, and
had no thought of doing anything more important than

rubbing a little rust off and enjoying myself, while at the same time I could make my companion's visit somewhat pleasanter than it would be if she went without me. The visit has answered most of its purposes for both of us, and if we have saved a few recollections which our friends can take any pleasure in reading, this slight record may be considered a work of super-erogation.

The Cephalonia was to sail at half past six in the morning, and at that early hour a company of well-wishers was gathered on the wharf at East Boston to bid us good-by. We took with us many tokens of their thoughtful kindness; flowers and fruits from Boston and Cambridge, and a basket of champagne from a Concord friend whose company is as exhilarating as the sparkling wine he sent us. With the other gifts came a small tin box, about as big as a common round wooden match box. I supposed it to hold some pretty gimcrack, sent as a pleasant parting token of remembrance. It proved to be a most valued daily companion, useful at all times, never more so than when the winds were blowing hard and the ship was struggling with the waves. There must have been some magic secret in it, for I am sure that I looked five years younger after closing that little box than when I opened it. Time will explain its mysterious power.

All the usual provisions for comfort made by sea-going experts we had attended to. Impermeable rugs and fleecy shawls, head-gear to defy the rudest north-easters, sea-chairs of ample dimensions, which we took care to place in as sheltered situations as we could find, — all these were a matter of course. Everybody stays on deck as much as possible, and lies wrapped up and spread out at full length on his or her sea-chair, so that the deck looks as if it had a row of mummies on exhibition. Nothing is more comfortable, nothing, I should say, more indispensable, than a hot-water bag, — or rather, *two* hot-water bags; for they will burst sometimes, as I found out, and a passenger who has become intimate with one of these warm bosom friends feels its loss almost as if it were human.

Passengers carry all sorts of luxuries on board, in the firm faith that they shall be able to profit by them all. Friends send them various indigestibles. To many all these well-meant preparations soon become a mockery, almost an insult. It is a clear case of *Sic(k) vos non vobis*. The tougher neighbor is the gainer by these acts of kindness; the generosity of a sea-sick sufferer in giving away the delicacies which seemed so desirable on starting is not ranked very high on the books of the recording angel. With us three things were best: grapes, oranges, and especially oysters, of which we had provided a half barrel in the shell. The "butcher" of the ship opened them fresh for us every day, and they were more acceptable than anything else.

Among our ship's company were a number of family relatives and acquaintances. We formed a natural group at one of the tables, where we met in more or less complete numbers. I myself never missed; my companion, rarely. Others were sometimes absent, and sometimes came to time when they were in a very doubtful state, looking as if they were saying to themselves, with Lear, —

> " Down, thou climbing sorrow,
> Thy element 's below."

As for the intellectual condition of the passengers, I should say that faces were prevailingly vacuous, their owners half hypnotized, as it seemed, by the monotonous throb and tremor of the great sea-monster on whose back we were riding. I myself had few thoughts, fancies, emotions. One thing above all struck me as never before, — the terrible solitude of the ocean.

> " So lonely 't was that God himself
> Scarce seemed there to be."

Whole days passed without our seeing a single sail. The creatures of the deep which gather around sailing vessels are perhaps frightened off by the noise and stir of the steamship. At any rate, we saw nothing more than a few porpoises, so far as I remember.

No man can find himself over the abysses, the floor of which is paved with wrecks and white with the bones of the shrieking myriads of human beings whom the waves have swallowed up, without some thought of the dread possibilities hanging over his fate. There is only one way to get rid of them: that which an old sea-captain mentioned to me, namely, to keep one's self under opiates until he wakes up in the harbor where he is bound. I did not take this as serious advice, but its meaning is that one who has all his senses about him cannot help being anxious. My old friend, whose beard had been shaken in many a tempest, knew too well that there is cause enough for anxiety.

What does the reader suppose was the source of the most ominous thought which forced itself upon my mind, as I walked the decks of the mighty vessel?

Not the sound of the rushing winds, nor the sight of the foam-crested billows; not the sense of the awful imprisoned force which was wrestling in the depths below me. The ship is made to struggle with the elements, and the giant has been tamed to obedience, and is manacled in bonds which an earthquake would hardly rend asunder. No! It was the sight of the *boats* hanging along at the sides of the deck, — the boats, always suggesting the fearful possibility that before another day dawns one may be tossing about in the watery Sahara, shelterless, fireless, almost foodless, with a fate before him he dares not contemplate. No doubt we should feel worse without the boats; still they are dreadful tell-tales. To all who remember Géricault's Wreck of the Medusa, — and those who have seen it do not forget it, — the picture the mind draws is one it shudders at. To be sure, the poor wretches in the painting were on a raft, but to think of fifty people in one of these open boats! Let us go down into the cabin, where at least we shall not see them.

The first morning at sea revealed the mystery of the little round tin box. The process of *shaving*, never a delightful one, is a very unpleasant and awkward piece of business when the floor on which one stands, the glass in which he looks, and he himself are all describing those complex curves which make cycles and epicycles seem like simplicity itself. The little box contained a reaping machine, which gathered the capillary harvest of the past twenty-four hours with a thoroughness, a rapidity, a security, and a facility which were a surprise, almost a revelation. The idea of a guarded cutting edge is an old one; I remember the "Plantagenet" razor, so called, with the comblike row of blunt teeth, leaving just enough of the edge free to do its work. But this little affair had a blade only an inch and a half long by three quarters of an inch wide. It had a long slender handle, which took apart for packing, and was put together with the greatest ease. It was, in short, a lawn-mower for the masculine growth of which the proprietor wishes to rid his countenance. The mowing operation required no glass, could be performed with almost reckless boldness, as one cannot cut himself, and in fact had become a pleasant amusement instead of an irksome task. I have never used any other means of shaving from that day to this. I was so pleased with it that I exhibited it to the distinguished tonsors of Burlington Arcade, half afraid they would assassinate me for bringing in an innovation which bid fair to destroy their business. They probably took me for an agent of the manufacturers; and so I was, but not in their pay nor with their knowledge. I determined to let other persons know what a convenience I had found the "Star Razor" of Messrs. Kampf, of New York, without fear of reproach for so doing. I know my danger, — does not Lord Byron say, "I have even been accused of writing puffs for Warren's blacking"? I was once offered pay for a poem in praise of a certain stove polish, but I declined. It is pure good-will to my race which leads me to commend the Star Razor to all who travel by land or by sea, as well as to all who stay at home.

With the first sight of land many a passenger draws a long sigh of relief. Yet everybody knows that the worst dangers begin after we have got near enough to see the shore, for there are several ways of landing, not all of which are equally desirable. On Saturday,

May 8th, we first caught a glimpse of the Irish coast, and at half past four in the afternoon we reached the harbor of Queenstown. A tug came off, bringing newspapers, letters, and so forth, among the rest some thirty letters and telegrams for me. This did not look much like rest, but this was only a slight prelude to what was to follow. I was in no condition to go on shore for sight-seeing, as some of the passengers did.

We made our way through the fog towards Liverpool, and arrived at 1.30, on Sunday, May 9th. A special tug came to take us off: on it were the American consul, Mr. Russell, the vice-consul, Mr. Sewall, Dr. Nevins, and Mr. Rathbone, who came on behalf of our as yet unseen friend, Mr. Willett, of Brighton, England. Our Liverpool friends were meditating more hospitalities to us than, in our fatigued condition, we were equal to supporting. They very kindly, however, acquiesced in our wishes, which were for as much rest as we could possibly get before any attempt to busy ourselves with social engagements. So they conveyed us to the Grand Hotel for a short time, and then saw us safely off to the station to take the train for Chester, where we arrived in due season, and soon found ourselves comfortably established at the Grosvenor Arms Hotel. A large basket of Surrey primroses was brought by Mr. Rathbone to my companion. I had set before me at the hotel a very handsome floral harp, which my friend's friend had offered me as a tribute. It made melody in my ears as sweet as those hyacinths of Shelley's, the music of whose bells was so

> "delicate, soft, and intense,
> It was felt like an odor within the sense."

At Chester we had the blissful security of being unknown, and were left to ourselves. Americans know Chester better than most other old towns in England, because they so frequently stop there awhile on their way from Liverpool to London. It has a mouldy old cathedral, an old wall, partly Roman, strange old houses with overhanging upper floors, which make sheltered sidewalks and dark basements. When one sees an old house in New England with the second floor projecting a foot or two beyond the wall of the ground floor, the country boy will tell him that "them haouses was built so th't th' folks upstairs could shoot the Injins when they was tryin' to git threew th' door or int' th' winder." There are plenty of such houses all over England, where there are no "Injins" to shoot. But the story adds interest to the somewhat lean traditions of our rather dreary past, and it is hardly worth while to disturb it. I always heard it in my boyhood. Perhaps it is true; certainly it was a very convenient arrangement for discouraging an untimely visit. The oval lookouts in porches, common in our Essex County, have been said to answer a similar purpose, that of warning against the intrusion of undesirable visitors. The walk round the old wall of Chester is wonderfully interesting and beautiful. At one part it overlooks a wide level field, over which the annual races are run. I noticed that here as elsewhere the short grass was starred with daisies. They are not considered in place in a well-kept lawn. But remembering the cuckoo song in "Love's Labour 's Lost," "When daisies pied . . . do paint the meadows with delight," it was hard to look at them as unwelcome intruders.

The old cathedral seemed to me particularly mouldy, and in fact too high-flavored with antiquity. I could

not help comparing some of the ancient cathedrals
and abbey churches to so many old cheeses. They
have a tough gray rind and a rich interior, which
find food and lodging for numerous tenants who live
and die under their shelter or their shadow, — lowly
servitors some of them, portly dignitaries others, humble holy ministers of religion many, I doubt not, —
larvæ of angels, who will get their wings by and by.
It is a shame to carry the comparison so far, but it is
natural enough; for Cheshire cheeses are among the
first things we think of as we enter that section of the
country, and this venerable cathedral is the first that
greets the eyes of great numbers of Americans.

We drove out to Eaton Hall, the seat of the Duke
of Westminster, the many-millioned lord of a good
part of London. It is a palace, high-roofed, marble-
columned, vast, magnificent, everything but homelike,
and perhaps homelike to persons born and bred in such
edifices. A painter like Paul Veronese finds a palace
like this not too grand for his banqueting scenes.
But to those who live, as most of us do, in houses of
moderate dimensions, snug, comfortable, which the
owner's presence fills sufficiently, leaving room for a
few visitors, a vast marble palace is disheartening and
uninviting. I never get into a very large and lofty
saloon without feeling as if I were a weak solution of
myself, — my personality almost drowned out in the
flood of space about me. The wigwam is more homelike than the cavern. Our wooden houses are a
better kind of wigwam; the marble palaces are artificial caverns, vast, resonant, chilling, good to visit,
not desirable to live in, for most of us. One's individuality should betray itself in all that surrounds
him; he should *secrete* his shell, like a mollusk; if he

can sprinkle a few pearls through it, so much the better. It is best, perhaps, that one should avoid being a duke and living in a palace, — that is, if he has his choice in the robing chamber where souls are fitted with their earthly garments.

One of the most interesting parts of my visit to Eaton Hall was my tour through the stables. The Duke is a famous breeder and lover of the turf. Mr. Rathbone and myself soon made the acquaintance of the chief of the stable department. Readers of Homer do not want to be reminded that *hippodamoio*, horse-subduer, is the genitive of an epithet applied as a chief honor to the most illustrious heroes. It is the last word of the last line of the Iliad, and fitly closes the account of the funeral pageant of Hector, the tamer of horses. We Americans are a little shy of confessing that any title or conventional grandeur makes an impression upon us. If at home we wince before any official with a sense of blighted inferiority, it is by general confession the clerk at the hotel office. There is an excuse for this, inasmuch as he holds our destinies in his hands, and decides whether, in case of accident, we shall have to jump from the third or sixth story window. Lesser grandeurs do not find us very impressible. There is, however, something about the man who deals in horses which takes down the spirit, however proud, of him who is unskilled in equestrian matters and unused to the horse-lover's vocabulary. We followed the master of the stables, meekly listening and once in a while questioning. I had to fall back on my reserves, and summoned up memories half a century old to gain the respect and win the confidence of the great horse-subduer. He showed us various fine animals, some in their stalls, some outside of them.   Chief of all was the renowned Bend Or, a Derby winner, a noble and beautiful bay, destined in a few weeks to gain new honors on the same turf in the triumph of his offspring Ormonde, whose acquaintance we shall make by-and-by.

The next day, Tuesday, May 11th, at 4.25, we took the train for London.   We had a saloon car, which had been thoughtfully secured for us through unseen, not unsuspected, agencies, which had also beautified the compartment with flowers.

Here are some of my first impressions of England as seen from the carriage and from the cars. — How very English!   I recall Birket Foster's Pictures of English Landscape, — a beautiful, poetical series of views, but hardly more poetical than the reality. How thoroughly England *is groomed!*   Our New England out-of-doors landscape often looks as if it had just got out of bed, and had not finished its toilet. The glowing green of everything strikes me: green hedges in place of our rail-fences, always ugly, and our rude stone-walls, which are not wanting in a certain look of fitness approaching to comeliness, and are really picturesque when lichen-coated, but poor features of landscape as compared to these universal hedges.   I am disappointed in the trees, so far; I have not seen one large tree as yet.   Most of those I see are of very moderate dimensions, feathered all the way up their long slender trunks, with a lop-sided mop of leaves at the top, like a wig which has slipped awry.   I trust that I am not finding everything *couleur de rose;* but I certainly do find the cheeks of children and young persons of such brilliant rosy hue as I do not remember that I have ever seen before.   I am almost ready to think this and that child's face has been colored from a pink saucer. If the Saxon youth exposed for sale at Rome, in the days of Pope Gregory the Great, had complexions like these children, no wonder that the pontiff exclaimed, Not *Angli*, but *angeli!* All this may sound a little extravagant, but I am giving my impressions without any intentional exaggeration. How far these first impressions may be modified by after-experiences there will be time enough to find out and to tell. It is better to set them down at once just as they are. A first impression is one never to be repeated; the second look will see much that was not noticed before, but it will not reproduce the sharp lines of the *first proof*, which is always interesting, no matter what the eye or the mind fixes upon. "I see men as trees walking." That first experience could not be mended. When Dickens landed in Boston, he was struck with the brightness of all the objects he saw, — buildings, signs, and so forth. When I landed in Liverpool, everything looked very dark, very dingy, very massive, in the streets I drove through. So in London, but in a week it all seemed natural enough.

We got to the hotel where we had engaged quarters, at eleven o'clock in the evening of Wednesday, the 12th of May. Everything was ready for us, — a bright fire blazing and supper waiting. When we came to look at the accommodations, we found they were not at all adapted to our needs. It was impossible to stay there another night. So early the next morning we sent out our courier-maid, a dove from the ark, to find us a place where we could rest the soles of our feet. London is a nation of something like four millions of inhabitants, and one does not feel easy without he has an assured place of shelter. The dove flew all over the habitable districts of the city, — inquired at as many as twenty houses. No roosting-place for our little flock of three. At last the good angel who followed us everywhere, in one shape or another, pointed the wanderer to a place which corresponded with all our requirements and wishes. This was at No. 17 Dover Street, Mackellar's Hotel, where we found ourselves comfortably lodged and well cared for during the whole time we were in London. It was close to Piccadilly and to Bond Street. Near us, in the same range, were Brown's Hotel and Batt's Hotel, both widely known to the temporary residents of London.

We were but partially recovered from the fatigues and trials of the voyage when our arrival pulled the string of the social shower-bath, and the invitations began pouring down upon us so fast that we caught our breath, and felt as if we should be smothered. The first evening saw us at a great dinner-party at our well-remembered friend Lady Harcourt's. Twenty guests, celebrities and agreeable persons, with or without titles. The tables were radiant with silver, glistening with choice porcelain, blazing with a grand show of tulips. This was our "baptism of fire" in that long conflict which lasts through the London season. After dinner came a grand reception, most interesting, but fatiguing to persons hardly as yet in good condition for social service. We lived through it, however, and enjoyed meeting so many friends, known and unknown, who were very cordial and pleasant in their way of receiving us.

It was plain that we could not pretend to answer all the invitations which flooded our tables. If we had attempted it, we should have found no time for anything

else.   A secretary was evidently a matter of immediate necessity.   Through the kindness of Mrs. Pollock,
we found a young lady who was exactly fitted for the
place.   She was installed in the little room intended
for her, and began the work of accepting with pleasure and regretting our inability, of acknowledging the
receipt of books, flowers, and other objects, and being
very sorry that we could not subscribe to this good
object and attend that meeting in behalf of a deserving charity, — in short, writing almost everything for
us except autographs, which I can warrant were always
genuine.   The poor young lady was almost tired out
sometimes, having to stay at her table, on one occasion, so late as eleven in the evening, to get through
her day's work.   I simplified matters for her by
giving her a set of formulæ as a base to start from,
and she proved very apt at the task of modifying each
particular letter to suit its purpose.

From this time forward continued a perpetual round
of social engagements.   Breakfasts, luncheons, dinners, teas, receptions with spread tables, two, three,
and four deep of an evening, with receiving company
at our own rooms, took up the day, so that we had
very little time for common sight-seeing.

Of these kinds of entertainments, the breakfast,
though pleasant enough when the company is agreeable, as I always found it, is the least convenient of
all times and modes of visiting.   You have already
interviewed one breakfast, and are expecting soon to
be coquetting with a tempting luncheon.   If one had
as many stomachs as a ruminant, he would not mind
three or four serious meals a day, not counting the
tea as one of them.   The luncheon is a very convenient affair: it does not require special dress; it is

informal; it is soon over, and may be made light or heavy, as one chooses. The afternoon tea is almost a necessity in London life. It is considered useful as "a pick me up," and it serves an admirable purpose in the social system. It costs the household hardly any trouble or expense. It brings people together in the easiest possible way, for ten minutes or an hour, just as their engagements or fancies may settle it. A cup of tea at the right moment does for the virtuous reveller all that Falstaff claims for a good sherris-sack, or at least the first half of its "twofold operation:" "It ascends me into the brain; dries me there all the foolish and dull and crudy vapors which environ it; makes it apprehensive, quick, forgetive, full of nimble, fiery and delectable shapes, which delivered over to the voice, the tongue, which is the birth, becomes excellent wit."

But it must have the right brain to work upon, and I doubt if there is any brain to which it is so congenial and from which it brings so much as that of a first-rate London old lady. I came away from the great city with the feeling that this most complex product of civilization was nowhere else developed to such perfection. The octogenarian Londoness has been in society, — let us say the highest society, — all her days. She is as tough as an old macaw, or she would not have lasted so long. She has seen and talked with all the celebrities of three generations, all the beauties of at least half a dozen decades. Her wits have been kept bright by constant use, and as she is free of speech it requires some courage to face her. Yet nobody can be more agreeable, even to young persons, than one of these precious old dowagers. A great beauty is almost certainly thinking how she looks

while one is talking with her; an authoress is waiting
to have one praise her book; but a grand old lady,
who loves London society, who lives in it, who understands young people and all sorts of people, with her
high-colored recollections of the past and her grand-
maternal interests in the new generation, is the best
of companions, especially over a cup of tea just strong
enough to stir up her talking ganglions.

A breakfast, a lunch, a tea, is a circumstance, an
occurrence, in social life, but a dinner is an event.
It is the full-blown flower of that cultivated growth
of which those lesser products are the buds. I will
not try to enumerate, still less to describe, the various entertainments to which we were invited, and
many of which we attended. Among the professional
friends I found or made during this visit to London,
none were more kindly attentive than Dr. Priestley,
who, with his charming wife, the daughter of the late
Robert Chambers, took more pains to carry out our
wishes than we could have asked or hoped for. At his
house I first met Sir James Paget and Sir William
Gull, long well known to me, as to the medical profession everywhere, as preëminent in their several de-
partments. If I were an interviewer or a newspaper
reporter, I should be tempted to give the impression
which the men and women of distinction I met made
upon me; but where all were cordial, where all made
me feel as nearly as they could that I belonged where
I found myself, whether the ceiling were a low or a
lofty one, I do not care to differentiate my hosts and
my other friends. *Fortemque Gyan fortemque Cloan-
thum*, — I left my microscope and my test-papers at
home.

Our friends, several of them, had a pleasant way of

sending their carriages to give us a drive in the Park, where, except in certain permitted regions, the common numbered vehicles are not allowed to enter. Lady Harcourt sent her carriage for us to go to her sister's, Mrs. Mildmay's, where we had a pleasant little "tea," and met one of the most agreeable and remarkable of those London old ladies I have spoken of. For special occasions we hired an unnumbered carriage, with professionally equipped driver and footman.

Mrs. Bloomfield Moore sent her carriage for us to take us to a lunch at her house, where we met Mr. Browning, Sir Henry and Lady Layard, Oscar Wilde and his handsome wife, and other well-known guests. After lunch, recitations, songs, etc. House full of pretty things. Among other curiosities a portfolio of drawings illustrating Keeley's motor, which, up to this time, has manifested a remarkably powerful *vis inertiæ*, but which promises miracles. In the evening a grand reception at Lady Granville's, beginning (for us, at least) at eleven o'clock. The house a palace, and A—— thinks there were a thousand people there. We made the tour of the rooms, saw many great personages, had to wait for our carriage a long time, but got home at one o'clock.

English people have queer notions about iced-water and ice-cream. "You will surely die, eating such cold stuff," said a lady to my companion. "Oh, no," she answered, "but I should certainly die were I to drink your two cups of strong tea." I approved of this "counter" on the teacup, but I did not think either of them was in much danger.

The next day Rev. Mr. Haweis sent his carriage, and we drove in the Park. In the afternoon we went to our Minister's to see the American ladies who had been presented at the drawing-room. After this, both of us were glad to pass a day or two in comparative quiet, except that we had a room full of visitors. So many persons expressed a desire to make our acquaintance that we thought it would be acceptable to them if we would give a reception ourselves. We were thinking how we could manage it with our rooms at the hotel, which were not arranged so that they could be thrown together. Still, we were planning to make the best of them, when Dr. and Mrs. Priestley suggested that we should receive our company at their house. This was a surprise, and a most welcome one, and A—— and her kind friend busied themselves at once about the arrangements.

We went to a luncheon at Lansdowne House, Lord Rosebery's residence, not far from our hotel. My companion tells a little incident which may please an American six-year-old: "The eldest of the four children, Sibyl, a pretty, bright child of six, told me that she wrote a letter to the Queen. I said, 'Did you begin, Dear Queen?' 'No,' she answered, 'I began, Your Majesty, and signed myself, Your little humble servant, Sibyl.'" A very cordial and homelike reception at this great house, where a couple of hours were passed most agreeably.

On the following Sunday I went to Westminster Abbey to hear a sermon from Canon Harford on A Cheerful Life. A lively, wholesome, and encouraging discourse, such as it would do many a forlorn New England congregation good to hear. In the afternoon we both went together to the Abbey. Met our Beverly neighbor, Mrs. Vaughan, and adopted her as one of our party. The seats we were to have were full, and we had to be stowed where there was any place that would hold us. I was smuggled into a stall, going through long and narrow passages, between crowded rows of people, and found myself at last with a big book before me and a set of official personages around me, whose duties I did not clearly understand. I thought they might be mutes, or something of that sort, salaried to look grave and keep quiet. After service we took tea with Dean Bradley, and after tea we visited the Jerusalem Chamber. I had been twice invited to weddings in that famous room: once to the marriage of my friend Motley's daughter, then to that of Mr. Frederick Locker's daughter to Lionel Tennyson, whose recent death has been so deeply mourned. I never expected to see that Jerusalem in which Harry the Fourth died, but there I found myself in the large panelled chamber, with all its associations. The older memories came up but vaguely; an American finds it as hard to call back anything over two or three centuries old as a sucking-pump to draw up water from a depth of over thirty-three feet and a fraction. After this A—— went to a musical party, dined with the Vaughans, and had a good time among American friends.

The next evening we went to the Lyceum Theatre to see Mr. Irving. He had placed the Royal box at our disposal, so we invited our friends the Priestleys to go with us, and we all enjoyed the evening mightily. Between the scenes we went behind the curtain, and saw the very curious and admirable machinery of the dramatic spectacle. We made the acquaintance of several imps and demons, who were got up wonderfully well. Ellen Terry was as fascinating as ever. I remembered that once before I had met her and Mr. Irving behind the scenes. It was at the Boston Theatre, and while I was talking with them a very heavy piece of scenery came crashing down, and filled the whole place with dust. It was but a short distance from where we were standing, and I could not help thinking how near our several life-dramas came to a simultaneous *exeunt omnes.*

A long visit from a polite interviewer, shopping, driving, calling, arranging about the people to be invited to our reception, and an agreeable dinner at Chelsea with my American friend, Mrs. Merritt, filled up this day full enough, and left us in good condition for the next, which was to be a very busy one.

In the Introduction to these papers, I mentioned the fact that more than half a century ago I went to the famous Derby race at Epsom. I determined, if possible, to see the Derby of 1886, as I had seen that of 1834. I must have spoken of this intention to some interviewer, for I find the following paragraph in an English sporting newspaper, "The Field," for May 29th, 1886: —

"The Derby has always been the one event in the racing year which statesmen, philosophers, poets, essayists, and *littérateurs* desire to see once in their lives. A few years since Mr. Gladstone was induced by Lord Granville and Lord Wolverton to run down to Epsom on the Derby day. The impression produced upon the Prime Minister's sensitive and emotional mind was that the mirth and hilarity displayed by his compatriots upon Epsom race-course was Italian rather than English in its character. On the other hand, Gustave Doré, who also saw the Derby for the first and only time in his life, exclaimed, as he gazed with horror upon the faces below him, *Quelle scène brutale!* We wonder to which of these two impressions Dr. Oliver Wendell Holmes inclined, if he went last Wednesday to Epsom! Probably the well-known, etc., etc. — Of one thing Dr. Holmes may rest finally satisfied: the Derby of 1886 may possibly have seemed to him far less exciting than that of 1834; but neither in 1834 nor in any other year was the great race ever won by a better sportsman or more honorable man than the Duke of Westminster."

My desire to see the Derby of this year was of the same origin and character as that which led me to re-visit many scenes which I remembered. I cared quite as much about renewing old impressions as about getting new ones. I enjoyed everything which I had once seen all the more from the blending of my recol-lections with the present as it was before me.

The Derby day of 1834 was exceedingly windy and dusty. Our party, riding on the outside of the coach, was half smothered with the dust, and arrived in a very deteriorated condition, but recompensed for it by the extraordinary sights we had witnessed. There was no train in those days, and the whole road between London and Epsom was choked with vehicles of all kinds, from four-in-hands to donkey-carts and wheel-barrows. My friends and I mingled freely in the crowds, and saw all the "humours" of the occasion. The thimble-riggers were out in great force, with their light, movable tables, the cups or thimbles, and the "little jokers," and the coachman, the sham gentle-man, the country greenhorn, all properly got up and gathered about the table. I think we had "Aunt Sally," too, — the figure with a pipe in her mouth, which one might shy a stick at for a penny or two and win something, I forget what. The clearing the course of stragglers, and the chasing about of the

frightened little dog who had got in between the thick
ranks of spectators, reminded me of what I used to
see on old "artillery election" days.

It was no common race that I went to see in 1834.
"It is asserted in the columns of a contemporary that
Plenipotentiary was absolutely the best horse of the
century." This was the winner of the race I saw so
long ago. Herring's colored portrait, which I have
always kept, shows him as a great, powerful chestnut
horse, well deserving the name of "bullock," which
one of the jockeys applied to him. "Rumor credits
Dr. Holmes," so "The Field" says, "with desiring
mentally to compare his two Derbies with each other."
I was most fortunate in my objects of comparison.
The horse I was about to see win was not unworthy
of being named with the renowned champion of my
earlier day. I quote from a writer in the "London
Morning Post," whose words, it will be seen, carry
authority with them: —

"Deep as has hitherto been my reverence for Plenipotentiary, Bay Middleton, and Queen of Trumps
from hearsay, and for Don John, Crucifix, etc., etc.,
from my own personal knowledge, I am inclined to
award the palm to Ormonde as the best three-year-old
I have ever seen during close upon half a century's
connection with the turf."

Ormonde, the Duke of Westminster's horse, was
the son of that other winner of the Derby, Bend Or,
whom I saw at Eaton Hall.

Perhaps some coeval of mine may think it was a
rather youthful idea to go to the race. I cannot help
that. I was off on my first long vacation for half a
century, and had a right to my whims and fancies.
But it was one thing to go in with a vast crowd at five

and twenty, and another thing to run the risks of the excursion at more than thrice that age. I looked about me for means of going safely, and could think of nothing better than to ask one of the pleasantest and kindest of gentlemen, to whom I had a letter from Mr. Winthrop, at whose house I had had the pleasure of making his acquaintance. Lord Rosebery suggested that the best way would be for me to go in the special train which was to carry the Prince of Wales. First, then, I was to be introduced to his Royal Highness, which office was kindly undertaken by our very obliging and courteous Minister, Mr. Phelps. After this all was easily arranged, and I was cared for as well as if I had been Mr. Phelps himself. On the grand stand I found myself in the midst of the great people, who were all very natural, and as much at their ease as the rest of the world. The Prince is of a lively temperament and a very cheerful aspect, — a young girl would call him "jolly" as well as "nice." I recall the story of "Mr. Pope" and his Prince of Wales, as told by Horace Walpole. "Mr. Pope, you don't love princes." "Sir, I beg your pardon." "Well, you don't love kings, then." "Sir, I own I love the lion best before his claws are grown." Certainly, nothing in Prince Albert Edward suggests any aggressive weapons or tendencies. The lovely, youthful-looking, gracious Alexandra, the always affable and amiable Princess Louise, the tall youth who sees the crown and sceptre afar off in his dreams, the slips of girls so like many school misses we left behind us, — all these grand personages, not being on exhibition, but off enjoying themselves, just as I was and as other people were, seemed very much like their fellow-mortals. It is really easier to feel at home with the highest people in the land than with the awkward commoner who was knighted yesterday. When "My Lord and Sir Paul" came into the Club which Goldsmith tells us of, the hilarity of the evening was instantly checked. The entrance of a dignitary like the present Prince of Wales would not have spoiled the fun of the evening. If there is any one accomplishment specially belonging to princes, it is that of making the persons they meet feel at ease.

The grand stand to which I was admitted was a little privileged republic. I remember Thackeray's story of his asking some simple question of a royal or semi-royal personage whom he met in the courtyard of an hotel, which question his Highness did not answer, but called a subordinate to answer for him. I had been talking some time with a tall, good-looking gentleman, whom I took for a nobleman to whom I had been introduced. Something led me to think I was mistaken in the identity of this gentleman. I asked him, at last, if he were not So and So. "No," he said, "I am Prince Christian." . You are a Christian prince, anyhow, I said to myself, if I may judge by your manners.

I once made a similar mistake in addressing a young fellow-citizen of some social pretensions. I apologized for my error.

"No offence," he answered.

Offence indeed! I should hope not. But he had not the "*manière de prince*," or he would never have used that word.

I must say something about the race I had taken so much pains to see. There was a preliminary race, which excited comparatively little interest. After this the horses were shown in the paddock, and many of our privileged party went down from the stand to look at them. Then they were brought out, smooth, shining, fine-drawn, frisky, spirit-stirring to look upon, — most beautiful of all the bay horse Ormonde, who could hardly be restrained, such was his eagerness for action. The horses disappear in the distance. — They are off, — not yet distinguishable, at least to me. A little waiting time, and they swim into our ken, but in what order of precedence it is as yet not easy to say. Here they come! Two horses have emerged from the ruck, and are sweeping, rushing, storming, towards us, almost side by side. One slides by the other, half a length, a length, a length and a half. Those are Archer's colors, and the beautiful bay Ormonde flashes by the line, winner of the Derby of 1886. "The Bard" has made a good fight for the first place, and comes in second. Poor Archer, the king of the jockeys! He will bestride no more Derby winners. A few weeks later he died by his own hand.

While the race was going on, the yells of the betting crowd beneath us were incessant. It must have been the frantic cries and movements of these people that caused Gustave Doré to characterize it as a brutal scene. The vast mob which thronged the wide space beyond the shouting circle just round us was much like that of any other fair, so far as I could see from my royal perch. The most conspicuous object was a man on an immensely tall pair of stilts, stalking about among the crowd. I think it probable that I had as much enjoyment in forming one of the great mob in 1834 as I had among the grandeurs in 1886, but the last is pleasanter to remember and especially to tell of.

After the race we had a luncheon served us, a com-

fortable and substantial one, which was very far from
unwelcome. I did not go to the Derby to bet on the
winner. But as I went in to luncheon, I passed a
gentleman standing in custody of a plate half covered
with sovereigns. He politely asked me if I would
take a little paper from a heap there was lying by the
plate, and add a sovereign to the collection already
there. I did so, and, unfolding my paper, found it
was a blank, and passed on. The pool, as I afterwards learned, fell to the lot of the Turkish Ambassador. I found it very windy and uncomfortable on the
more exposed parts of the grand stand, and was glad
that I had taken a shawl with me, in which I wrapped
myself as if I had been on shipboard. This, I told
my English friends, was the more civilized form of
the Indian's blanket. My report of the weather does
not say much for the English May, but it is generally
agreed upon that this is a backward and unpleasant
spring.

After my return from the race we went to a large
dinner at Mr. Phelps's house, where we met Mr.
Browning again, and the Lord Chancellor Herschell,
among others. Then to Mrs. Cyril Flower's, one of
the most sumptuous houses in London; and after that
to Lady Rothschild's, another of the private palaces,
with ceilings lofty as firmaments, and walls that might
have been copied from the New Jerusalem. There
was still another great and splendid reception at Lady
Dalhousie's, and a party at Mrs. Smith's, but we
were both tired enough to be willing to go home after
what may be called a pretty good day's work at enjoying ourselves.

We had been a fortnight in London, and were now
inextricably entangled in the meshes of the golden
web of London social life.

II.

The reader who glances over these papers, and, finding them too full of small details and the lesser personal matters which belong naturally to private correspondences, turns impatiently from them, has my entire sympathy and good-will. He is not one of those for whom these pages are meant. Having no particular interest in the writer or his affairs, he does not care for the history of "the migrations from the blue bed to the brown" and the many Mistress Quicklyisms of circumstantial narrative. Yet all this may be pleasant reading to relatives and friends.

But I must not forget that a new generation of readers has come into being since I have been writing for the public, and that a new generation of aspiring and brilliant authors has grown into general recognition. The dome of Boston State House, which is the centre of my little universe, was glittering in its fresh golden pellicle before I had reached the scriptural boundary of life. It has lost its lustre now, and the years which have dulled its surface have whitened the dome of that fragile structure in which my consciousness holds the session of its faculties. Time is not to be cheated. It is easy to talk of perennial youth, and to toy with the flattering fictions which every ancient personage accepts as true so far as he himself is concerned, and laughs at as foolish talk when he hears them applied to others. When, in my exulting immaturity, I wrote the lines not unknown to the reading public under the name of "The Last Leaf," I spoke of the possibility that I myself might linger on the old bough until the buds and blossoms

of a new spring were opening and spreading all around
me. I am not as yet the solitary survivor of my literary contemporaries, and, remembering who my few
coevals are, it may well be hoped that I shall not be.
But I feel lonely, very lonely, in the pages through
which I wander. These are new names in the midst
of which I find my own. In another sense I am very
far from alone. I have daily assurances that I have
a constituency of known and unknown personal
friends, whose indulgence I have no need of asking.
I know there are readers enough who will be pleased
to follow me in my brief excursion, *because I am myself*, and will demand no better reason. If I choose
to write for them, I do no injury to those for whom
my personality is an object of indifference. They will
find on every shelf some publications which are not
intended for them, and which they prefer to let alone.
No person is expected to help himself to everything
set before him at a public table. I will not, therefore, hesitate to go on with the simple story of our
Old World experiences.

Thanks to my Indian blanket, — my shawl, I mean, .
— I found myself nothing the worse for my manifold adventures of the 27th of May. The cold wind
sweeping over Epsom downs reminded me of our own
chilling easterly breezes; especially the northeasterly
ones, which are to me less disagreeable than the
southeasterly. But the poetical illusion about an
English May, —

> "Zephyr with Aurora playing,
> As he met her once a-Maying," —

and all that, received a shrewd thrust. Zephyr
ought to have come in an ulster, and offered Aurora
a warm petticoat. However, in spite of all difficul-

ties, I brought off my recollections of the Derby of
1886 in triumph, and am now waiting for the colored
portrait of Ormonde with Archer on his back, —
Archer, the winner of five Derby races, one of which
was won by the American horse Iroquois. When
that picture, which I am daily expecting, arrives, I
shall have it framed and hung by the side of Herring's picture of Plenipotentiary, the horse I saw win
the Derby in 1834. These two, with an old portrait
of the great Eclipse, who, as my engraving of 1780
(Stubbs's) says, "was never beat, or ever had occa-
tion for Whip or Spur," will constitute my entire
sporting gallery. I have not that vicious and demor-
alizing love of horse-flesh which makes it next to impossible to find a perfectly honest hippophile. But a
racer is the realization of an ideal quadruped, —

A pard-like spirit, beautiful and swift ; "

so ethereal, so bird-like, that it is no wonder that the
horse about whom those old story-tellers lied so stoutly,
— telling of his running a mile in a minute, — was
called Flying Childers.

The roses in Mrs. Pfeiffer's garden were hardly out
of flower when I lunched with her at her pretty villa
at Putney. There I met Mr. Browning, Mr. Holman Hunt, Mrs. Ritchie, Miss Anna Swanwick, the
translator of Æschylus, and other good company,
besides that of my entertainer.

One of my very agreeable experiences was a call
from a gentleman with whom I had corresponded, but
whom I had never met. This was Mr. John Bellows,
of Gloucester, publisher, printer, man of letters, or
rather of words; for he is the author of that truly
remarkable little manual, "The Bona Fide Pocket

Dictionary of the French and English Languages." To the review of this little book, which is dedicated to Prince Lucien Bonaparte, the "London Times" devoted a full column. I never heard any one who had used it speak of it except with admiration. The modest Friend may be surprised to find himself at full length in my pages, but those who know the little miracle of typography, its conciseness, completeness, arrangement, will not wonder that I was gratified to see the author, who sent it to me, and who has written me most interesting letters on the local antiquities of Gloucester and its neighborhood.

We lunched that day at Lady Camperdown's, where we were happy to meet Miss Frances Power Cobbe. In the afternoon we went by invitation to a "tea and talk" at the Reverend Mr. Haweis's, at Chelsea. We found the house close packed, but managed to get through the rooms, shaking innumerable hands of the reverend gentleman's parishioners and other visitors. It was very well arranged, so as not to be too fatiguing, and we left the cordial gathering in good condition. We drove home with Bishop and Mrs. Ellicott.

After this Sir James Paget called, and took me to a small and early dinner-party; and A—— went with my secretary, the young lady of whom I have spoken, to see "Human Nature," at Drury Lane Theatre.

On the following day, after dining with Lady Holland (wife of Sir Henry, niece of Macaulay), we went across the street to our neighbor's, Lady Stanley's. There was to be a great meeting of schoolmistresses, in whose work her son, the Honorable Lyulph Stanley, is deeply interested. Alas! The schoolma'ams were just leaving as we entered the door, and all we saw of them was the trail of their descending robes. I was very sorry for this, for I have a good many friends among our own schoolmistresses, — friends whom I never saw, but know through the kind words they have addressed to me.

No place in London looks more reserved and exclusive than Devonshire House, standing back behind its high wall, extending along Piccadilly. There is certainly nothing in its exterior which invites intrusion. We had the pleasure of taking tea in the great house, accompanying our American friend, Lady Harcourt, and were graciously received and entertained by Lady Edward Cavendish. Like the other great houses, it is a museum of paintings, statues, objects of interest of all sorts. It must be confessed that it is pleasanter to go through the rooms with one of the ladies of the household than under the lead of a liveried servant. Lord Hartington came in while we were there. All the men who are distinguished in political life become so familiar to the readers of "Punch" in their caricatures, that we know them at sight. Even those who can claim no such public distinction are occasionally the subjects of the caricaturist, as some of us have found out for ourselves. A good caricature, which seizes the prominent features and gives them the character Nature hinted, but did not fully carry out, is a work of genius. Nature herself is a remorseless caricaturist, as our daily intercourse with our fellow men and women makes evident to us, and as is curiously illustrated in the figures of Charles Lebrun, showing the relations between certain human faces and those of various animals. Hardly an English statesman in bodily presence could be mistaken by any of "Punch's" readers.

On the same day that we made this quiet visit we attended a great and ceremonious assembly. There were two parts in the programme, in the first of which I was on the stage *solus*, — that is, without my companion; in the second we were together. This day, Saturday, the 29th of May, was observed as the Queen's birthday, although she was born on the 24th. Sir William Harcourt gave a great dinner to the officials of his department, and later in the evening Lady Rosebery held a reception at the Foreign Office. On both these occasions everybody is expected to be in court dress, but my host told me I might present myself in ordinary evening dress. I thought that I might feel awkwardly among so many guests, all in the wedding garments, knee-breeches and the rest, without which I ventured among them. I never passed an easier evening in any company than among these official personages. Sir William took me under the shield of his ample presence, and answered all my questions about the various notable personages at his table in a way to have made my fortune if I had been a reporter. From the dinner I went to Mrs. Gladstone's, at 10 Downing Street, where A—— called for me. She had found a very small and distinguished company there, Prince Albert Victor among the rest. At half past eleven we walked over to the Foreign Office to Lady Rosebery's reception.

Here Mr. Gladstone was of course the centre of a group, to which I was glad to add myself. His features are almost as familiar to me as my own, for a photograph of him in his library has long stood on my revolving bookcase, with a large lens before it. He is one of a small circle of individuals in whom I have had and still have a special personal interest. The

year 1809, which introduced me to atmospheric existence, was the birth-year of Gladstone, Tennyson, Lord
Houghton, and Darwin. It seems like an honor to
have come into the world in such company, but it is
more likely to promote humility than vanity in a common mortal to find himself coeval with such illustrious
personages. Men born in the same year watch each
other, especially as the sands of life begin to run low,
as we can imagine so many damaged hour-glasses to
keep an eye on each other. Women, of course, never
know who are their contemporaries.

Familiar to me as were the features of Mr. Gladstone, I looked upon him with astonishment. For he
stood before me with epaulets on his shoulders and
a rapier at his side, as military in his aspect as if he
had been Lord Wolseley, to whom I was introduced
a short time afterwards. I was fortunate enough to
see and hear Mr. Gladstone on a still more memorable
occasion, and can afford to leave saying what were my
impressions of the very eminent statesman until I
speak of that occasion.

A great number of invitations had been given out
for the reception at Lady Rosebery's, — over two
thousand, my companion heard it said. Whatever
the number was, the crowd was very great, — so great
that one might well feel alarmed for the safety of any
delicate person who was in the *pack* which formed itself at one place in the course of the evening. Some
obstruction must have existed *a fronte*, and the *vis a
tergo* became fearful in its pressure on those who were
caught in the jam. I began thinking of the crushes
in which I had been caught, or which I had read and
heard of: the terrible time at the execution of Holloway and Haggerty, where some forty persons were

squeezed or trampled to death; the Brooklyn Theatre and other similar tragedies; the crowd I was in at the unveiling of the statue on the column of the Place Vendome, where I felt as one may suppose Giles Corey did when, in his misery, he called for "more weight" to finish him. But there was always a *deus ex machina* for us when we were in trouble. Looming up above the crowd was the smiling and encouraging countenance of the ever active, always present, always helpful Mr. Smalley. He cleared a breathing space before us. For a short time it was really a formidable wedging together of people, and if a lady had fainted in the press, she might have run a serious risk before she could have been extricated. No more "marble halls" for us, if we had to undergo the *peine forte et dure* as the condition of our presence! We were both glad to escape from this threatened asphyxia, and move freely about the noble apartments. Lady Rosebery, who was kindness itself, would have had us stay and sit down in comfort at the supper-table, after the crowd had thinned, but we were tired with all we had been through, and ordered our carriage. *Ordered our carriage!*

> "I can call spirits from the vasty deep." . . .
> *But will they come when you do call for them?*"

The most formidable thing about a London party is getting away from it. "C'est le *dernier* pas qui coute." A crowd of anxious persons in retreat is hanging about the windy door, and the breezy stairway, and the airy hall.

A stentorian voice, hard as that of Rhadamanthus, exclaims, —

"Lady Vere de Vere's carriage stops the way!"

If my Lady Vere de Vere is not on hand, and that

pretty quickly, off goes her carriage, and the stern
voice bawls again, —

"Mrs. Smith's carriage stops the way!"

Mrs. Smith's particular Smith may be worth his
millions and live in his marble palace; but if Mrs.
Smith thinks her coachman is going to stand with his
horses at that door until she appears, she is mistaken,
for she is a minute late, and now the coach moves on,
and Rhadamanthus calls aloud, —

"Mrs. Brown's carriage stops the way!"

Half the lung fevers that carry off the great people
are got waiting for their carriages.

I know full well that many readers would be disappointed if I did not mention some of the grand places
and bring in some of the great names that lend their
lustre to London society. We were to go to a fine
musical party at Lady Rothschild's on the evening of
the 30th of May. It happened that the day was Sunday, and if we had been as punctilious as some New
England Sabbatarians, we might have felt compelled
to decline the tempting invitation. But the party was
given by a daughter of Abraham, and in every Hebrew household the true Sabbath was over. We were
content for that evening to shelter ourselves under the
old dispensation.

The party, or concert, was a very brilliant affair.
Patti sang to us, and a tenor, and a violinist played
for us. How we two Americans came to be in so favored a position I do not know; all I do know is that
we were shown to our places, and found them very
agreeable ones. In the same row of seats was the
Prince of Wales, two chairs off from A——'s seat.
Directly in front of A—— was the Princess of Wales,
"in ruby velvet, with six rows of pearls encircling

her throat, and two more strings falling quite low;" and next her, in front of me, the startling presence of Lady de Grey, formerly Lady Lonsdale, and before that Gladys Herbert. On the other side of the Princess sat the Grand Duke Michael of Russia.

As we are among the grandest of the grandees, I must enliven my sober account with an extract from my companion's diary: —

"There were several great beauties there, Lady Claude Hamilton, a queenly blonde, being one. Minnie Stevens Paget had with her the pretty Miss Langdon, of New York. Royalty had one room for supper, with its attendant lords and ladies. Lord Rothschild took me down to a long table for a sit-down supper, — there were some thirty of us. The most superb pink orchids were on the table. The [Thane] of —— sat next me, and how he stared before he was introduced! . . . This has been the finest party we have been to, sitting comfortably in such a beautiful ball-room, gazing at royalty in the flesh, and at the shades of departed beauties on the wall, by Sir Joshua and Gainsborough. It was a new experience to find that the royal lions fed upstairs, and mixed animals below!"

A visit to Windsor had been planned, under the guidance of a friend whose kindness had already shown itself in various forms, and who, before we left England, did for us more than we could have thought of owing to any one person. This gentleman, Mr. Willett, of Brighton, called with Mrs. Willett to take us on the visit which had been arranged between us.

Windsor Castle, which everybody knows, or can easily learn, all about, is one of the largest of those huge caverns in which the descendants of the original

cave men, when they have reached the height of human grandeur, delight to shelter themselves. It seems
as if such a great hollow quarry of rock would strike a
chill through every tenant, but modern improvements
reach even the palaces of kings and queens, and the
regulation temperature of the castle, or of its inhabited portions, is fixed at sixty-five degrees of Fahrenheit. The royal standard was not floating from the
tower of the castle, and everything was quiet and
lonely. We saw all we wanted to, — pictures, furniture, and the rest. My namesake, the Queen's librarian, was not there to greet us, or I should have
had a pleasant half-hour in the library with that very
polite gentleman, whom I had afterwards the pleasure
of meeting in London.

After going through all the apartments in the castle
that we cared to see, or our conductress cared to show
us, we drove in the park, along the "three-mile walk,"
and in the by-roads leading from it. The beautiful
avenue, the open spaces with scattered trees here and
there, made this a most delightful excursion. I saw
many fine oaks, one about sixteen feet of honest girth,
but no one which was very remarkable. I wished I
could have compared the handsomest of them with one
in Beverly, which I never look at without taking my
hat off. This is a young tree, with a future before
it, if barbarians do not meddle with it, more conspicuous for its spread than its circumference, stretching
not very far from a hundred feet from bough-end to
bough-end. I do not think I saw a specimen of the
British *Quercus robur* of such consummate beauty.
But I know from Evelyn and Strutt what England
has to boast of, and I will not challenge the British
oak.

Two sensations I had in Windsor park, or forest, for I am not quite sure of the boundary which separates them. The first was the lovely sight of the *hawthorn* in full bloom. I had always thought of the hawthorn as a pretty shrub, growing in hedges; as big as a currant bush or a barberry bush, or some humble plant of that character. I was surprised to see it as a tree, standing by itself, and making the most delicious roof a pair of young lovers could imagine to sit under. It looked at a little distance like a young apple-tree covered with new-fallen snow. I shall never see the word hawthorn in poetry again without the image of the snowy but far from chilling canopy rising before me. It is the very bower of young love, and must have done more than any growth of the forest to soften the doom brought upon man by the fruit of the forbidden tree. No wonder that

" In the spring a young man's fancy lightly turns to thoughts of love,"

with the object of his affections awaiting him in this boudoir of nature. What a pity that Zekle, who courted Huldy over the apples she was peeling, could not have made love as the bucolic youth does, when

" Every shepherd tells his tale
Under the hawthorn in the dale ! "

(I will have it *love*-tale, in spite of Warton's comment.) But I suppose it does not make so much difference, for love transmutes the fruit in Huldy's lap into the apples of the Hesperides.

In this way it is that the associations with the poetry we remember come up when we find ourselves surrounded by English scenery. The great poets build temples of song, and fill them with images and symbols which move us almost to adoration; the lesser minstrels fill a panel or gild a cornice here and there, and make our hearts glad with glimpses of beauty. I felt all this as I looked around and saw the hawthorns in full bloom, in the openings among the oaks and other trees of the forest. Presently I heard a sound to which I had never listened before, and which I have never heard since : —

Coooo — coooo !

Nature had sent one cuckoo from her aviary to sing his double note for me, that I might not pass away from her pleasing show without once hearing the call so dear to the poets. It was the last day of spring. A few more days, and the solitary voice might have been often heard; for the bird becomes so common as to furnish Shakespeare an image to fit "the skipping king : "—

> " He was but as the cuckoo is in June,
>   Heard, not regarded."

For the lyric poets the cuckoo is "companion of the spring," "darling of the spring; " coming with the daisy, and the primrose, and the blossoming sweet-pea. Where the sound came from I could not tell; it puzzled Wordsworth, with younger eyes than mine, to find whence issued

> " that cry
> Which made me look a thousand ways
> In bush, and tree, and sky."

Only one hint of the prosaic troubled my emotional delight: I could not help thinking how capitally the little rogue imitated the cuckoo clock, with the sound of which I was pretty well aquainted.

On our return from Windsor we had to get ready for another great dinner with our Minister, Mr. Phelps. As we are in the habit of considering our great officials as public property, and as some of my readers want as many glimpses of high life as a decent regard to republican sensibilities will permit, I will borrow a few words from the diary to which I have often referred: —

"The Princess Louise was there with the Marquis, and I had the best opportunity of seeing how they receive royalty at private houses. Mr. and Mrs. Phelps went down to the door to meet her the moment she came, and then Mr. Phelps entered the drawing-room with the Princess on his arm, and made the tour of the room with her, she bowing and speaking to each one of us. Mr. Goschen took me in to dinner, and Lord Lorne was on my other side. All of the flowers were of the royal color, red. It was a grand dinner. . . . The Austrian Ambassador, Count Karoli, took Mrs. Phelps in [to dinner], his position being higher than that of even the Duke [of Argyll], who sat upon her right."

It was a very rich experience for a single day: the stately abode of royalty, with all its manifold historical recollections, the magnificent avenue of forest trees, the old oaks, the hawthorn in full bloom, and the one cry of the cuckoo, calling me back to Nature in her spring-time freshness and glory; then, after that, a great London dinner-party at a house where the kind host and the gracious hostess made us feel at home, and where we could meet the highest people in the land, — the people whom we who live in a simpler way at home are naturally pleased to be with under such auspices. What of all this shall I remember longest? Let me not seem ungrateful to my friends who planned the excursion for us, or to those who asked us to the brilliant evening entertainment,

but I feel as Wordsworth felt about the cuckoo, — he
will survive all the other memories.

> " And I can listen to thee yet,
> Can lie upon the plain
> And listen, till I do beget
> That golden time again.

Nothing is more hackneyed than an American's description of his feelings in the midst of the scenes and
objects he has read of all his days, and is looking
upon for the first time. To each of us it appears in
some respects in the same way, but with a difference
for every individual. We may smile at Irving's emotions at the first sight of a distinguished Englishman
on his own soil, — the ingenious Mr. Roscoe, as an
earlier generation would have called him. Our tour-
ists, who are constantly going forward and back between England and America, lose all sense of the special distinctions between the two countries which do
not bear on their personal convenience. Happy are
those who go with unworn, unsatiated sensibilities from
the New World to the Old; as happy, it may be,
those who come from the Old World to the New, but
of that I cannot form a judgment.

On the first day of June we called by appointment
upon Mr. Peel, the Speaker of the House of Commons,
and went through the Houses of Parliament. We
began with the train-bearer, then met the housekeeper,
and presently were joined by Mr. Palgrave. The
"Golden Treasury" stands on my drawing-room table
at home, and the name on its title-page had a familiar
sound. This gentleman is, I believe, a near relative
of Professor Francis Turner Palgrave, its editor.

Among other things to which Mr. Palgrave called
our attention was the death-warrant of Charles the

First. One name in the list of signers naturally fixed our eyes upon it. It was that of John Dixwell. A lineal descendant of the old regicide is very near to me by family connection, Colonel Dixwell having come to this country, married, and left a posterity, which has resumed the name, dropped for the sake of safety at the time when he, Goffe, and Whalley, were in concealment in various parts of New England.

We lunched with the Speaker, and had the pleasure of the company of Archdeacon Farrar. In the afternoon we went to a tea at a very grand house, where, as my companion says in her diary, "it took full six men in red satin knee-breeches to let us in." Another grand personage asked us to dine with her at her country place, but we were too full of engagements. In the evening we went to a large reception at Mr. Gosse's. It was pleasant to meet artists and scholars, — the kind of company to which we are much used in our æsthetic city. I found our host as agreeable at home as he was when in Boston, where he became a favorite, both as a lecturer and as a visitor.

Another day we visited Stafford House, where Lord Ronald Gower, himself an artist, did the honors of the house, showing us the pictures and sculptures, his own included, in a very obliging and agreeable way. I have often taken note of the resemblances of living persons to the portraits and statues of their remote ancestors. In showing us the portrait of one of his own far-back progenitors, Lord Ronald placed a photograph of himself in the corner of the frame. The likeness was so close that the photograph might seem to have been copied from the painting, the dress only being changed. The Duke of Sutherland, who had just come back from America, complained that the

dinners and lunches had used him up. I was fast
learning how to sympathize with him.

Then to Grosvenor House to see the pictures. I
best remember Gainsborough's beautiful Blue Boy,
commonly so called, from the color of his dress, and
Sir Joshua's Mrs. Siddons as the Tragic Muse, which
everybody knows in engravings. We lunched in clerical company that day, at the Bishop of Gloucester and Bristol's, with the Archbishop of York, the
Reverend Mr. Haweis, and others as guests. I told
A—— that she was not sufficiently impressed with
her position at the side of an archbishop; she was not
crumbling bread in her nervous excitement. The
company did not seem to remember Sydney Smith's
remark to the young lady next him at a dinner-party:
"My dear, I see you are nervous, by your crumbling
your bread as you do. *I* always crumble bread when
I sit by a bishop, and when I sit by an archbishop I
crumble bread with both hands." That evening I had
the pleasure of dining with the distinguished Mr.
Bryce, whose acquaintance I made in our own country, through my son, who has introduced me to many
agreeable persons of his own generation, with whose
companionship I am glad to mend the broken and
merely fragmentary circle of old friendships.

The 3d of June was a memorable day for us, for on
the evening of that day we were to hold our reception.
If Dean Bradley had proposed our meeting our guests
in the Jerusalem Chamber, I should hardly have been
more astonished. But these kind friends meant what
they said, and put the offer in such a shape that it was
impossible to resist it. So we sent out our cards to
a few hundreds of persons, — those who we thought
might like invitations. I was particularly desirous

that many members of the medical profession whom
I had not met, but who felt well disposed towards
me, should be at this gathering. The meeting was in
every respect a success. I wrote a prescription for as
many baskets of champagne as would be consistent
with the well-being of our guests, and such light accom-
paniments as a London company is wont to expect
under similar circumstances. My own recollections
of the evening, unclouded by its festivities, but confused by its multitudinous succession of introductions,
are about as definite as the Duke of Wellington's
alleged monosyllabic description of the battle of Waterloo. But A—— writes in her diary: "From nine
to twelve we stood, receiving over three hundred people out of the four hundred and fifty we invited." As
I did not go to Europe to visit hospitals or museums, I
might have missed seeing some of those professional
brethren whose names I hold in honor and whose writings are in my library. If any such failed to receive
our cards of invitation, it was an accident which, if I
had known, I should have deeply regretted. So far
as we could judge by all we heard, our unpretentious
party gave general satisfaction. Many different social
circles were represented, but it passed off easily and
agreeably. I can say this more freely, as the credit
of it belongs so largely to the care and self-sacrificing
efforts of Dr. Priestley and his charming wife.

I never refused to write in the birthday book or the
album of the humblest schoolgirl or schoolboy, and I
could not refuse to set my name, with a verse from
one of my poems, in the album of the Princess of
Wales, which was sent me for that purpose. It was
a nice new book, with only two or three names in it,
and those of musical composers, — Rubinstein's, I

think, was one of them, — so that I felt honored by the great lady's request. I ought to describe the book, but I only remember that it was quite large and sumptuously elegant, and that I copied into it the last verse of a poem of mine called "The Chambered Nautilus," as I have often done for plain republican albums.

The day after our simple reception was notable for three social events in which we had our part. The first was a lunch at the house of Mrs. Cyril Flower, one of the finest in London, — Surrey House, as it is called. Mr. Browning, who seems to go everywhere, and is one of the vital elements of London society, was there as a matter of course. Miss Cobbe, many of whose essays I have read with great satisfaction, though I cannot accept all her views, was a guest whom I was very glad to meet a second time.

In the afternoon we went to a garden-party given by the Princess Louise at Kensington Palace, a gloomy-looking edifice, which might be taken for a hospital or a poorhouse. Of all the festive occasions which I attended, the garden-parties were to me the most formidable. They are all very well for young people, and for those who do not mind the nipping and eager air, with which, as I have said, the climate of England, no less than that of America, falsifies all the fine things the poets have said about May, and, I may add, even June. We wandered about the grounds, spoke with the great people, stared at the odd ones, and said to ourselves, — at least I said to myself, — with Hamlet,

"The air bites shrewdly, it is very cold."

The most curious personages were some East Indians, a chocolate-colored lady, her husband, and children.

The mother had a diamond on the side of her nose, its setting riveted on the inside, one might suppose; the effect was peculiar, far from captivating. A—— said that she should prefer the good old-fashioned nose-ring, as we find it described and pictured by travellers. She saw a great deal more than I did, of course. I quote from her diary: "The little Eastern children made their native salaam to the Princess by prostrating themselves flat on their little stomachs in front of her, putting their hands between her feet, pushing them aside, and kissing the print of her feet!"

I really believe one or both of us would have run serious risks of catching our "death o' cold," if we had waited for our own carriage, which seemed forever in coming forward. The good Lady Holland, who was more than once our guardian angel, brought us home in hers. So we got warmed up at our own hearth, and were ready in due season for the large and fine dinner-party at Archdeacon Farrar's, where, among other guests, were Mrs. Phelps, our Minister's wife, who is a great favorite alike with Americans and English, Sir John Millais, Mr. Tyndall, and other interesting people.

I am sorry that we could not have visited Newstead Abbey. I had a letter from Mr. Thornton Lothrop to Colonel Webb, the present proprietor, with whom we lunched. I have spoken of the pleasure I had when I came accidentally upon persons with whose name and fame I had long been acquainted. A similar impression was that which I received when I found myself in the company of the bearer of an old historic name. When my host at the lunch introduced a stately-looking gentleman as Sir Kenelm Digby, it gave me a start, as if a ghost had stood before me. I

recovered myself immediately, however, for there was
nothing of the impalpable or immaterial about the
stalwart personage who bore the name. I wanted to
ask him if he carried any of his ancestor's "powder of
sympathy" about with him. Many, but not all, of my
readers remember that famous man's famous preparation. When used to cure a wound, it was applied to
the weapon that made it; the part was bound up so as
to bring the edges of the wound together, and by the
wondrous influence of the sympathetic powder the
healing process took place in the kindest possible manner. Sir Kenelm, the ancestor, was a gallant soldier,
a grand gentleman, and the husband of a wonderfully
beautiful wife, whose charms he tried to preserve from
the ravages of time by various experiments. He was
also the homœopathist of his day, the Elisha Perkins
(metallic tractors) of his generation. The "mind
cure" people might adopt him as one of their precur-
sors.

I heard a curious statement which was illustrated
in the person of one of the gentlemen we met at this
table. It is that English sporting men are often deaf
on one side, in consequence of the noise of the frequent discharge of their guns affecting the right ear.
This is a very convenient infirmity for gentlemen who
indulge in slightly aggressive remarks, but when they
are hit back never seem to be conscious at all of the
riposte, — the return thrust of the fencer.

Dr. Allchin called and took me to a dinner, where
I met many professional brothers, and enjoyed myself
highly.

By this time every day was pledged for one or more
engagements, so that many very attractive invitations
had to be declined. I will not follow the days one by

one, but content myself with mentioning some of the more memorable visits. I had been invited to the Rabelais Club, as I have before mentioned, by a cable message. This is a club of which the late Lord Houghton was president, and of which I am a member, as are several other Americans. I was afraid that the gentlemen who met,

"To laugh and shake in Rabelais's easy chair,"

might be more hilarious and demonstrative in their mirth than I, a sober New Englander in the superfluous decade, might find myself equal to. But there was no uproarious jollity; on the contrary, it was a pleasant gathering of literary people and artists, who took their pleasure not sadly, but serenely, and I do not remember a single explosive guffaw.

Another day, after going all over Dudley House, including Lady Dudley's boudoir, "in light blue satin, the prettiest room we have seen," A—— says, we went, by appointment, to Westminster Abbey, where we spent two hours under the guidance of Archdeacon Farrar. I think no part of the Abbey is visited with so much interest as Poets' Corner. We are all familiarly acquainted with it beforehand. We are all ready for "O rare Ben Jonson ! " as we stand over the place where he was planted standing upright, as if he had been dropped into a post-hole. We remember too well the foolish and flippant mockery of Gay's "Life is a Jest." If I were dean of the cathedral, I should be tempted to alter the J to a G. Then we could read it without contempt; for life is a gest, an achievement, — or always ought to be. Westminster Abbey is too crowded with monuments to the illustrious dead and those who have been considered so in their day to produce any other than a confused impression. When we visit the tomb of Napoleon at the Invalides, no side-lights interfere with the view before us in the field of mental vision. We see the Emperor; Marengo, Austerlitz, Waterloo, Saint Helena, come before us, with him as their central figure. So at Stratford, — the Cloptons and the John a Combes, with all their memorials, cannot make us lift our eyes from the stone which covers the dust that once breathed and walked the streets of Stratford as Shakespeare.

Ah, but here is one marble countenance that I know full well, and knew for many a year in the flesh! Is there an American who sees the bust of Longfellow among the effigies of the great authors of England without feeling a thrill of pleasure at recognizing the features of his native fellow-countryman in the Valhalla of his ancestral fellow-countrymen? There are many memorials in Poets' Corner and elsewhere in the Abbey which could be better spared than that. Too many that were placed there as luminaries have become conspicuous by their obscurity in the midst of that illustrious company. On the whole, the Abbey produces a distinct sense of being overcrowded. It appears too much like a lapidary's store-room. Look up at the lofty roof, which we willingly pardon for shutting out the heaven above us, — at least in an average London day; look down at the floor, and think of what precious relics it covers; but do not look around you with the hope of getting any clear, concentrated, satisfying effect from this great museum of gigantic funereal bricabrac. Pardon me, shades of the mighty dead! I had something of this feeling, but at another hour I might perhaps be overcome by emotion, and weep, as my fellow-countryman did at the grave of the earliest of his ancestors. I should love myself better in that aspect than I do in this cold-blooded criticism; but it suggested itself, and as no flattery can soothe, so no censure can wound, "the dull, cold ear of death."

Of course we saw all the sights of the Abbey in a hurried way, yet with such a guide and expositor as Archdeacon Farrar our two hours' visit was worth a whole day with an undiscriminating verger, who recites his lesson by rote, and takes the life out of the little mob that follows him round by emphasizing the details of his lesson, until "Patience on a monument" seems to the sufferer, who knows what he wants and what he does not want, the nearest emblem of himself he can think of. Amidst all the imposing recollections of the ancient edifice, one impressed me in the inverse ratio of its importance. The Archdeacon pointed out the little holes in the stones, in one place, where the boys of the choir used to play marbles, before America was discovered, probably, — centuries before, it may be. It is a strangely impressive glimpse of a living past, like the *graffiti* of Pompeii. I find it is often the accident rather than the essential which fixes my attention and takes hold of my memory. This is a tendency of which I suppose I ought to be ashamed, if we have any right to be ashamed of those idiosyncrasies which are ordered for us. It is the same tendency which often leads us to prefer the picturesque to the beautiful. Mr. Gilpin liked the donkey in a forest landscape better than the horse. A touch of imperfection interferes with the beauty of an object and lowers its level to that of the picturesque. The accident of the holes in the stone of the noble building, for the boys to play marbles with, makes me

a boy again and at home with them, after looking with
awe upon the statue of Newton, and turning with a
shudder from the ghastly monument of Mrs. Nightingale.

What a life must be that of one whose years are
passed chiefly in and about the great Abbey! Nowhere does Macbeth's expression "dusty death" seem
so true to all around us. The dust of those who have
been lying century after century below the marbles
piled over them, — the dust on the monuments they
lie beneath; the dust on the memories those monuments were raised to keep living in the recollection of
posterity, — dust, dust, dust, everywhere, and we ourselves but shapes of breathing dust moving amidst
these objects and remembrances! Come away! The
good Archdeacon of the "Eternal Hope" has asked us
to take a cup of tea with him. The tea-cup will be a
cheerful substitute for the funeral urn, and a freshly
made infusion of the fragrant leaf is one of the best
things in the world to lay the dust of sad reflections.

It is a somewhat fatiguing pleasure to go through
the Abbey, in spite of the intense interest no one can
help feeling. But my day had but just begun when
the two hours we had devoted to the visit were over.
At a quarter before eight, my friend Mr. Frederick
Locker called for me to go to a dinner at the Literary Club. I was particularly pleased to dine with
this association, as it reminded me of our own Saturday Club, which sometimes goes by the same name as
the London one. They complimented me with a toast,
and I made some kind of a reply. As I never went
prepared with a speech for any such occasion, I take
it for granted that I thanked the company in a way
that showed my gratitude rather than my eloquence.

And now, the dinner being over, my day was fairly begun.

This was to be a memorable date in the record of the year, one long to be remembered in the political history of Great Britain. For on this day, the 7th of June, Mr. Gladstone was to make his great speech on the Irish question, and the division of the House on the Government of Ireland Bill was to take place. The whole country, to the corners of its remotest colony, was looking forward to the results of this evening's meeting of Parliament. The kindness of the Speaker had furnished me with a ticket, entitling me to a place among the "distinguished guests," which I presented without modestly questioning my right to the title.

The pressure for entrance that evening was very great, and I, coming after my dinner with the Literary Club, was late upon the ground. The places for "distinguished guests" were already filled. But all England was in a conspiracy to do everything possible to make my visit agreeable. I did not take up a great deal of room, — I might be put into a seat with the ambassadors and foreign ministers. And among them I was presently installed. It was now between ten and eleven o'clock, as nearly as I recollect. The House had been in session since four o'clock. A gentleman was speaking, who was, as my unknown next neighbor told me, Sir Michael Hicks-Beach, a leading member, as we all know, of the opposition. When he sat down there was a hush of expectation, and presently Mr. Gladstone rose to his feet. A great burst of applause welcomed him, lasting more than a minute. His clean-cut features, his furrowed cheeks, his scanty and whitened hair, his well-shaped but not extraordinary head, all familiarized by innumerable portraits and emphasized in hundreds of caricatures, revealed him at once to every spectator. His great speech has been universally read, and I need only speak of the way in which it was delivered. His manner was forcible rather than impassioned or eloquent; his voice was clear enough, but must have troubled him somewhat, for he had a small bottle from which he poured something into a glass from time to time and swallowed a little, yet I heard him very well for the most part. In the last portion of his speech he became animated and inspiriting, and his closing words were uttered with an impressive solemnity: "Think, I beseech you, think well, think wisely, think not for a moment, but for the years that are to come, before you reject this bill."

After the burst of applause which followed the conclusion of Mr. Gladstone's speech, the House proceeded to the division on the question of passing the bill to a second reading. While the counting of the votes was going on there was the most intense excitement. A rumor ran round the House at one moment that the vote was going in favor of the second reading. It soon became evident that this was not the case, and presently the result was announced, giving a majority of thirty against the bill, and practically overthrowing the liberal administration. Then arose a tumult of applause from the conservatives and a wild confusion, in the midst of which an Irish member shouted, "Three cheers for the Grand Old Man!" which were lustily given, with waving of hats and all but Donnybrook manifestations of enthusiasm.

I forgot to mention that I had a very advantageous seat among the diplomatic gentlemen, and was felicitating myself on occupying one of the best positions in the House, when an usher politely informed me that the Russian Ambassador, in whose place I was sitting, had arrived, and that I must submit to the fate of eviction. Fortunately, there were some steps close by, on one of which I found a seat almost as good as the one I had just left.

It was now two o'clock in the morning, and I had to walk home, not a vehicle being attainable. I did not know my way to my headquarters, and I had no friend to go with me, but I fastened on a stray gentle- man, who proved to be an ex-member of the House, and who accompanied me to 17 Dover Street, where I sought my bed with a satisfying sense of having done a good day's work and having been well paid for it.

III.

On the 8th of June we visited the Record Office for a sight of the Domesday Book and other ancient objects of interest there preserved. As I looked at this too faithful memorial of an inexorable past, I thought of the battle of Hastings and all its consequences, and that reminded me of what I have long remembered as I read it in Dr. Robert Knox's "Races of Men." Dr. Knox was the monoculous Waterloo surgeon, with whom I remember breakfasting, on my first visit to England and Scotland. His celebrity is less owing to his book than to the unfortunate connection of his name with the unforgotten Burke and Hare hor- rors. This is his language in speaking of Hastings: " . . . that bloody field, surpassing far in its terrible results the unhappy day of Waterloo. From this the

Celt has recovered, but not so the Saxon. To this day he feels, and feels deeply, the most disastrous day that ever befell his race ; here he was trodden down by the Norman, whose iron heel is on him yet. . . . To this day the Saxon race in England have never recovered a tithe of their rights, and probably never will."

The Conqueror meant to have a thorough summing up of his stolen property. The Anglo-Saxon Chronicle says, — I quote it at second hand, — "So very straitly did he cause the survey to be made, that there was not a single hyde, nor a yardland of ground, nor — it is shameful to say what he thought no shame to do — was there an ox or a cow, or a pig passed by, and that was not down in the accounts, and then all these writings were brought to him." The "looting" of England by William and his "twenty thousand thieves," as Mr. Emerson calls his army, was a singularly methodical proceeding, and Domesday Book is a searching inventory of their booty, movable and immovable.

From this reminder of the past we turned to the remembrances of home; A—— going to dine with a transplanted Boston friend and other ladies from that blessed centre of New England life, while I dined with a party of gentlemen at my friend Mr. James Russell Lowell's.

I had looked forward to this meeting with high expectations, and they were abundantly satisfied. I knew that Mr. Lowell must gather about him, wherever he might be, the choicest company, but what his selection would be I was curious to learn. I found with me at the table my own countrymen and his, Mr. Smalley and Mr. Henry James. Of the other guests, Mr.

Leslie Stephen was my only old acquaintance in person; but Du Maurier and Tenniel I have met in my
weekly "Punch" for many a year; Mr. Lang, Mr.
Oliphant, Mr. Townsend, we all know through their
writings; Mr. Burne-Jones and Mr. Alma Tadema,
through the frequent reproductions of their works in
engravings, as well as by their paintings. If I could
report a dinner-table conversation, I might be tempted
to say something of my talk with Mr. Oliphant. I
like well enough conversation which floats safely over
the shallows, touching bottom at intervals with a commonplace incident or truism to push it along; I like
better to find a few fathoms of depth under the surface;
there is a still higher pleasure in the philosophical
discourse which calls for the deep sea line to reach
bottom; but best of all, when one is in the right
mood, is the contact of intelligences when they are off
soundings in the ocean of thought. Mr. Oliphant is
what many of us call a mystic, and I found a singular pleasure in listening to him. This dinner at Mr.
Lowell's was a very remarkable one for the men it
brought together, and I remember it with peculiar interest. My entertainer holds a master-key to London
society, and he opened the gate for me into one of its
choicest preserves on that evening.

I did not undertake to renew my old acquaintance
with hospitals and museums. I regretted that I could
not be with my companion, who went through the
Natural History Museum with the accomplished direc-
tor, Professor W. H. Flower. One old acquaintance I
did resuscitate. For the second time I took the hand of
Charles O'Byrne, the celebrated Irish giant of the last
century. I met him, as in my first visit, at the Royal
College of Surgeons, where I accompanied Mr. Jona-

than Hutchinson. He was in the condition so longed
for by Sydney Smith on a very hot day; namely, with
his flesh taken off, and sitting, or rather standing, in
his bones. The skeleton measures eight feet, and the
living man's height is stated as having been eight feet
two, or four inches, by different authorities. His
hand was the only one I took, either in England or
Scotland, which had not a warm grasp and a hearty
welcome in it.

A—— went with Boston friends to see "Faust" a
second time, Mr. Irving having offered her the Royal
box, and the polite Mr. Bram Stoker serving the party
with tea in the little drawing-room behind the box; so
that she had a good time while I was enjoying myself
at a dinner at Sir Henry Thompson's, where I met
Mr. Gladstone, Mr. Browning, and other distinguished
gentlemen. These dinners of Sir Henry's are well
known for the good company one meets at them, and I
felt myself honored to be a guest on this occasion.

Among the pleasures I had promised myself was
that of a visit to Tennyson, at the Isle of Wight. I
feared, however, that this would be rendered impracti-
cable by reason of the very recent death of his younger
son, Lionel. But I learned from Mr. Locker-Lampson, whose daughter Mr. Lionel Tennyson had married, that the poet would be pleased to see me at his
place, Farringford; and by the kind intervention of
Mr. Locker-Lampson, better known to the literary
world as Frederick Locker, arrangements were made
for my daughter and myself to visit him. I considered it a very great favor, for Lord Tennyson has a
poet's fondness for the tranquillity of seclusion, which
many curious explorers of society fail to remember.
Lady Tennyson is an invalid, and though nothing could

be more gracious than her reception of us both, I fear it may have cost her an effort which she would not allow to betray itself. Mr. Hallam Tennyson and his wife, both of most pleasing presence and manners, did everything to make our stay agreeable. I saw the poet to the best advantage, under his own trees and walking over his own domain. He took delight in pointing out to me the finest and the rarest of his trees, — and there were many beauties among them. I recalled my morning's visit to Whittier at Oak Knoll, in Danvers, a little more than a year ago, when he led me to one of his favorites, an aspiring evergreen which shot up like a flame. I thought of the graceful American elms in front of Longfellow's house and the sturdy English elms that stand in front of Lowell's. In this garden of England, the Isle of Wight, where everything grows with such a lavish extravagance of greenness that it seems as if it must bankrupt the soil before autumn, I felt as if weary eyes and overtasked brains might reach their happiest haven of rest. We all remember Shenstone's epigram on the pane of a tavern window. If we find our "warmest welcome at an inn," we find our most soothing companionship in the trees among which we have lived, some of which we may ourselves have planted. We lean against them, and they never betray our trust; they shield us from the sun and from the rain; their spring welcome is a new birth, which never loses its freshness; they lay their beautiful robes at our feet in autumn; in winter they "stand and wait," emblems of patience and of truth, for they hide nothing, not even the little leaf-buds which hint to us of hope, the last element in their triple symbolism.

This digression, suggested by the remembrance of

the poet under his trees, breaks my narrative, but
gives me the opportunity of paying a debt of gratitude.   For I have owned many beautiful trees, and
loved many more outside of my own leafy harem.
Those who write verses have no special claim to be
lovers of trees, but so far as one is of the poetical
temperament he is likely to be a tree-lover.   Poets
have, as a rule, more than the average nervous sensibility and irritability.   Trees have no nerves.   They
live and die without suffering, without self-questioning
or self-reproach.   They have the divine gift of silence.
They cannot obtrude upon the solitary moments when
one is to himself the most agreeable of companions.
The whole vegetable world, even "the meanest flower
that blows," is lovely to contemplate.   What if creation had paused there, and you or I had been called
upon to decide whether self-conscious life should be
added in the form of the existing animal creation, and
the hitherto peaceful universe should come under the
rule of Nature as we now know her,

        " red in tooth and claw " ?

Are we not glad that the responsibility of the decision
did not rest on us?

I am sorry that I did not ask Tennyson to read or
repeat to me some lines of his own.   Hardly any one
perfectly understands a poem but the poet himself.
One naturally loves his own poem as no one else can.
It fits the mental mould in which it was cast, and it
will not exactly fit any other.   For this reason I had
rather listen to a poet reading his own verses than
hear the best elocutionist that ever spouted recite
them.   He may not have a good voice or enunciation,
but he puts his heart and his inter-penetrative intelli-

gence into every line, word, and syllable. I should have liked to hear Tennyson read such lines as

> "Laborious orient ivory, sphere in sphere ; "

and in spite of my good friend Matthew Arnold's *in terrorem*, I should have liked to hear Macaulay read,

> " And Aulus the Dictator
> Stroked Auster's raven mane,"

and other good mouthable lines, from the "Lays of Ancient Rome." Not less should I like to hear Mr. Arnold himself read the passage beginning, —

> " In his cool hall with haggard eyes
> The Roman noble lay."

The next day Mrs. Hallam Tennyson took A——— in her pony cart to see Alum Bay, The Needles, and other objects of interest, while I wandered over the grounds with Tennyson. After lunch his carriage called for us, and we were driven across the island, through beautiful scenery, to Ventnor, where we took the train to Ryde, and there the steamer to Portsmouth, from which two hours and a half of travel carried us to London.

My first visit to Cambridge was at the invitation of Mr. Gosse, who asked me to spend Sunday, the 13th of June, with him. The rooms in Neville Court, Trinity College, occupied by Sir William Vernon Harcourt when lecturing at Cambridge, were placed at my disposal. The room I slept in was imposing with the ensigns armorial of the Harcourts and others which ornamented its walls. I had great delight in walking through the quadrangles, along the banks of the Cam, and beneath the beautiful trees which border it. Mr. Gosse says that I stopped in the second court of Clare, and looked around and smiled as if I were bestowing my benediction. He was mistaken: I smiled as if I were receiving a benediction from my dear old grand-mother; for Cambridge in New England is my mother town, and Harvard University in Cambridge is my Alma Mater. She is the daughter of Cambridge in Old England, and my relationship is thus made clear.

Mr. Gosse introduced me to many of the younger and some of the older men of the university. Among my visits was one never to be renewed and never to be forgotten. It was to the Master of Trinity, the Rev-erend William Hepworth Thompson. I hardly ex-pected to have the privilege of meeting this very dis-tinguished and greatly beloved personage, famous not alone for scholarship, or as the successor of Dr. Whe-well in his high office, but also as having said some of the wittiest things which we have heard since Vol-taire's *pour encourager les autres*. I saw him in his chamber, a feeble old man, but noble to look upon in all "the monumental pomp of age." He came very near belonging to the little group I have mentioned as my coevals, but was a year after us. Gentle, digni-fied, kindly in his address as if I had been his school-mate, he left a very charming impression. He gave me several mementoes of my visit, among them a beau-tiful engraving of Sir Isaac Newton, representing him as one of the handsomest of men. Dr. Thompson looked as if he could not be very long for this world, but his death, a few weeks after my visit, was a pain-ful surprise to me. I had been just in time to see "the last of the great men" at Cambridge, as my cor-respondent calls him, and I was very grateful that I could store this memory among the hoarded treasures I have been laying by for such possible extra stretch of time as may be allowed me.

My second visit to Cambridge will be spoken of in due season.

While I was visiting Mr. Gosse at Cambridge, A—— was not idle. On Saturday she went to Lambeth, where she had the pleasure and honor of shaking hands with the Archbishop of Canterbury in his study, and of looking about the palace with Mrs. Benson. On Sunday she went to the Abbey, and heard "a broad and liberal sermon" from Archdeacon Farrar. Our young lady-secretary stayed and dined with her, and after dinner sang to her. "A peaceful, happy Sunday," A—— says in her diary, — not less peaceful, I suspect, for my being away, as my callers must have got many a "not at 'ome" from young Robert of the multitudinous buttons.

On Monday, the 14th of June, after getting ready for our projected excursions, we had an appointment which promised us a great deal of pleasure. Mr. Augustus Harris, the enterprising and celebrated manager of Drury Lane Theatre, had sent us an invitation to occupy a box, having eight seats, at the representation of "Carmen." We invited the Priestleys and our Boston friends, the Shimminses, to take seats with us. The chief singer in the opera was Marie Roze, who looked well and sang well, and the evening went off very happily. After the performance we were invited by Mr. Harris to a supper of some thirty persons, where we were the special guests. The manager toasted me, and I said something, — I trust appropriate; but just what I said is as irrecoverable as the orations of Demosthenes on the seashore, or the sermons of St. Francis to the beasts and birds.

Of all the attentions I received in England, this was, perhaps, the least to be anticipated or dreamed

of. To be fêted and toasted and to make a speech in
Drury Lane Theatre would not have entered into my
flightiest conceptions, if I had made out a programme
beforehand. It is a singularly gratifying recollection.
Drury Lane Theatre is so full of associations with literature, with the great actors and actresses of the past,
with the famous beauties who have stood behind the
footlights and the splendid audiences that have sat
before them, that it is an admirable nucleus for remembrances to cluster around. It was but a vague spot
in memory before, but now it is a bright centre for
other images of the past. That one evening seems to
make me the possessor of all its traditions from the
time when it rose from its ashes, when Byron's poem
was written and recited, and when the brothers Smith
gave us the "Address without a Phœnix," and all
those exquisite parodies which make us feel towards
their originals somewhat as our dearly remembered
Tom Appleton did when he said, in praise of some
real green turtle soup, that it was almost as good as
mock.

With much regret we gave up an invitation we had
accepted to go to Durdans to dine with Lord Rosebery. We must have felt very tired indeed to make
so great a sacrifice, but we had to be up until one
o'clock getting ready for the next day's journey; writing, packing, and attending to what we left behind us
as well as what was in prospect.

On the morning of Wednesday, June 16th, Dr. Donald Macalister called to attend us on our second visit
to Cambridge, where we were to be the guests of his
cousin, Alexander Macalister, Professor of Anatomy,
who, with Mrs. Macalister, received us most cordially.

There was a large luncheon-party at their house, to which we sat down in our travelling dresses. In the evening they had a dinner-party, at which were present, among others, Professor Stokes, President of the Royal Society, and Professor Wright. We had not heard much talk of political matters at the dinner-tables where we had been guests, but A—— sat near a lady who was very earnest in advocating the Irish side of the great impending question.

The 17th of June is memorable in the annals of my country. On that day of the year 1775 the battle of Bunker's Hill was fought on the height I see from the window of my library, where I am now writing. The monument raised in memory of our defeat, which was in truth a victory, is almost as much a part of the furniture of the room as its chairs and tables; outside, as they are inside, furniture. But the 17th of June, 1886, is memorable to me above all the other anniversaries of that day I have known. For on that day I received from the ancient University of Cambridge, England, the degree of Doctor of Letters, "Doctor Litt.," in its abbreviated academic form. The honor was an unexpected one; that is, until a short time before it was conferred.

Invested with the academic gown and cap, I repaired in due form at the appointed hour to the Senate Chamber. Every seat was filled, and among the audience were youthful faces in large numbers, looking as if they were ready for any kind of outbreak of enthusiasm or hilarity.

The first degree conferred was that of LL. D., on Sir W. A. White, G. C. M., G. C. B., to whose long list of appended initials it seemed like throwing a perfume on the violet to add three more letters.

When I was called up to receive my honorary title, the young voices were true to the promise of the young faces. There was a great noise, not hostile nor unpleasant in its character, in answer to which I could hardly help smiling my acknowledgments. In presenting me for my degree the Public Orator made a Latin speech, from which I venture to give a short extract, which I would not do for the world if it were not disguised by being hidden in the mask of a dead language. But there will be here and there a Latin scholar who will be pleased with the way in which the speaker turned a compliment to the candidate before him, with a reference to one of his poems and to some of his prose works.

" *Juvat nuper audivisse eum cujus carmen prope primum ' Folium ultimum' nominatum est, folia adhuc plura e scriniis suis esse prolaturum. Novimus quanto lepore descripserit colloquia illa antemeridiana, symposia illa sobria et severa, sed eadem festiva et faceta, in quibus totiens mutata persona, modo poeta, modo professor, modo princeps et arbiter, loquendi, inter convivas suos regnat.*"

I had no sooner got through listening to the speech and receiving my formal sentence as Doctor of Letters than the young voices broke out in fresh clamor. There were cries of "A speech! a speech!" mingled with the title of a favorite poem by John Howard Payne, having a certain amount of coincidence with the sound of my name. The play upon the word was not absolutely a novelty to my ear, but it was good-natured, and I smiled again, and perhaps made a faint inclination, as much as to say, "I hear you, young gentlemen, but I do not forget that I am standing on my dignity, especially now since a new degree has

added a moral cubit to my stature." Still the cries
went on, and at last I saw nothing else to do than to
edge back among the silk gowns, and so lose myself
and be lost to the clamorous crowd in the mass of
dignitaries. It was not indifference to the warmth
of my welcome, but a feeling that I had no claim to
address the audience because some of its younger members were too demonstrative. I have not forgotten my
very cordial reception, which made me feel almost as
much at home in the old Cambridge as in the new,
where I was born and took my degrees, academic, professional, and honorary.

The university town left a very deep impression
upon my mind, in which a few grand objects predomi-
nate over the rest, all being of a delightful character.
I was fortunate enough to see the gathering of the
boats, which was the last scene in their annual procession. The show was altogether lovely. The pretty
river, about as wide as the Housatonic, I should
judge, as that slender stream winds through "Canoe Meadow," my old Pittsfield residence, the gaily
dressed people who crowded the banks, the flower-
crowned boats, with the gallant young oarsmen who
handled them so skilfully, made a picture not often
equalled. The walks, the bridges, the quadrangles,
the historic college buildings, all conspired to make
the place a delight and a fascination. The library of
Trinity College, with its rows of busts by Roubiliac
and Woolner, is a truly noble hall. But beyond,
above all the rest, the remembrance of King's College
Chapel, with its audacious and richly wrought roof and
its wide and lofty windows, glowing with old devices
in colors which are ever fresh, as if just from the fur-
nace, holds the first place in my gallery of Cambridge
recollections.

I cannot do justice to the hospitalities which were bestowed upon us in Cambridge. Professor and Mrs. Macalister, aided by Dr. Donald Macalister, did all that thoughtful hosts could do to make us feel at home. In the afternoon the ladies took tea at Mr. Oscar Browning's. In the evening we went to a large dinner at the invitation of the Vice-Chancellor. Many little points which I should not have thought of are mentioned in A——'s diary. I take the following extract from it, toning down its vivacity more nearly to my own standard: —

"Twenty were there. The Master of St. John's took me in, and the Vice-Chancellor was on the other side. . . . The Vice-Chancellor rose and returned thanks after the meats and before the sweets, as usual. I have now got used to this proceeding, which strikes me as extraordinary. Everywhere here in Cambridge, and the same in Oxford, I believe, they say grace and give thanks. A gilded ewer and flat basin were passed, with water in the basin to wash with, and we all took our turn at the bath! Next to this came the course with the finger-bowls! . . . Why two baths?"

On Friday, the 18th, I went to a breakfast at the Combination Room, at which about fifty gentlemen were present, Dr. Sandys taking the chair. After the more serious business of the morning's repast was over, Dr. Macalister, at the call of the chairman, arose, and proposed my welfare in a very complimentary way. I of course had to respond, and I did so in the words which came of their own accord to my lips. After my unpremeditated answer, which was kindly received, a young gentleman of the university, Mr. Heitland, read a short poem, of which the following is the title: —

LINES OF GREETING TO DR. OLIVER WENDELL HOLMES.

AT BREAKFAST IN COMBINATION ROOM, ST. JOHN'S COLLEGE, CAMBRIDGE, ENGLAND.

I wish I dared quote more than the last two verses of these lines, which seemed to me, not unused to giving and receiving complimentary tributes, singularly happy, and were so considered by all who heard them. I think I may venture to give the two verses referred to: —

> "By all sweet memory of the saints and sages
>   Who wrought among us in the days of yore ;
> By youths who, turning now life's early pages,
>   Ripen to match the worthies gone before :

> "On us, O son of England's greatest daughter,
>   A kindly word from heart and tongue bestow ;
> Then chase the sunsets o'er the western water,
>   And bear our blessing with you as you go."

I need not say that I left the English Cambridge with a heart full of all grateful and kindly emotions.

I must not forget that I found at Cambridge, very pleasantly established and successfully practising his profession, a former student in the dental department of our Harvard Medical School, Dr. George Cunningham, who used to attend my lectures on anatomy. In the garden behind the quaint old house in which he lives is a large medlar-tree, — the first I remember seeing.

On this same day we bade good-by to Cambridge, and took the two o'clock train to Oxford, where we arrived at half past five. At this first visit we were to be the guests of Professor Max Müller, at his fine residence in Norham Gardens. We met there, at dinner, Mr. Herkomer, whom we have recently had with us in Boston, and one or two others. In the evening we had music; the professor playing on the piano, his two daughters, Mrs. Conybeare and her unmarried sister, singing, and a young lady playing the violin. It was a very lovely family picture; a pretty house, surrounded by attractive scenery; schol- arship, refinement, simple elegance, giving distinction to a home which to us seemed a pattern of all we could wish to see beneath an English roof. It all comes back to me very sweetly, but very tenderly and sadly, for the voice of the elder of the two sisters who sang to us is heard no more on earth, and a deep shadow has fallen over the household we found so bright and cheerful.

Everything was done to make me enjoy my visit to Oxford, but I was suffering from a severe cold, and was paying the penalty of too much occupation and excitement. I missed a great deal in consequence, and carried away a less distinct recollection of this magnificent seat of learning than of the sister univer- sity.

If one wishes to know the magic of names, let him visit the places made memorable by the lives of the illustrious men of the past in the Old World. As a boy I used to read the poetry of Pope, of Goldsmith, and of Johnson. How could I look at the Bodleian Library, or wander beneath its roof, without recalling the lines from "The Vanity of Human Wishes"?

> " When first the college rolls receive his name,
> The young enthusiast quits his ease for fame;
> Resistless burns the fever of renown,
> Caught from the strong contagion of the gown :
> O'er Bodley's dome his future labors spread,
> And Bacon's mansion trembles o'er his head."

The last line refers to Roger Bacon. "There is a tradition that the study of Friar Bacon, built on an arch over the bridge, will fall when a man greater than Bacon shall pass under it. To prevent so shocking an accident, it was pulled down many years since." We shall meet with a similar legend in another university city. Many persons have been shy of these localities, who were in no danger whatever of meeting the fate threatened by the prediction.

We passed through the Bodleian Library, only glancing at a few of its choicest treasures, among which the exquisitely illuminated missals were especially tempting objects of study. It was almost like a mockery to see them opened and closed, without having the time to study their wonderful miniature paintings. A walk through the grounds of Magdalen College, under the guidance of the president of that college, showed us some of the fine trees for which I was always looking. One of these, a wych-elm (Scotch elm of some books), was so large that I insisted on having it measured. A string was procured and carefully carried round the trunk, above the spread of the roots and below that of the branches, so as to give the smallest circumference. I was curious to know how the size of the trunk of this tree would compare with that of the trunks of some of our largest New England elms. I have measured a good many of these. About sixteen feet is the measurement of a large elm, like that on Boston Common, which all middle-aged people remember. From twenty-two to twenty-three feet is the ordinary maximum of the very largest trees. I never found but one exceed it: that was the great Springfield elm, which looked as if it might have been formed by the coalescence from the earliest period of growth, of two young trees.   When I measured this in 1837, it was twenty-four feet eight inches in circumference at five feet from the ground; growing larger above and below.   I remembered this tree well, as we measured the string which was to tell the size of its English rival.   As we came near the end of the string, I felt as I did when I was looking at the last dash of Ormonde and The Bard at Epsom. — Twenty feet, and a long piece of string left. — Twenty-one. — Twenty-two. — Twenty-three. — An extra heartbeat or two. — Twenty-four! — Twenty-five and six inches over!! — The Springfield elm may have grown a foot or more since I measured it, fifty years ago, but the tree at Magdalen stands ahead of all my old measurements.   Many of the fine old trees, this in particular, may have been known in their younger days to Addison, whose favorite walk is still pointed out to the visitor.

I would not try to compare the two university towns, as one might who had to choose between them.   They have a noble rivalry, each honoring the other, and it would take a great deal of weighing one point of superiority against another to call either of them the first, except in its claim to antiquity.

After a garden-party in the afternoon, a pleasant evening *at home*, when the professor played and his daughter Beatrice sang, and a garden-party the next day, I found myself in somewhat better condition, and ready for the next move.

At noon on the 23d of June we left for Edinburgh, stopping over night at York, where we found close by the station an excellent hotel, and where the next morning we got one of the best breakfasts we had in our whole travelling experience.   At York we wan-

dered to and through a flower-show, and *did* the cathedral, as people *do* all the sights they see under the
lead of a paid exhibitor, who goes through his lesson
like a sleepy old professor. I missed seeing the slab
with the inscription *miserrimus*. There may be other
stones bearing this sad superlative, but there is a story
connected with this one, which sounds as if it might
be true.

In the year 1834, I spent several weeks in Edinburgh. I was fascinated by the singular beauties of
that "romantic town," which Scott called his own, and
which holds his memory, with that of Burns, as a most
precious part of its inheritance. The castle with the
precipitous rocky wall out of which it grows, the deep
ravines with their bridges, pleasant Calton Hill and
memorable Holyrood Palace, the new town and the
old town with their strange contrasts, and Arthur's
Seat overlooking all, — these varied and enchanting
objects account for the fondness with which all who
have once seen Edinburgh will always regard it.

We were the guests of Professor Alexander Crum
Brown, a near relative of the late beloved and admired
Dr. John Brown. Professor and Mrs. Crum Brown
did everything to make our visit a pleasant one. We
met at their house many of the best known and most
distinguished people of Scotland. The son of Dr.
John Brown dined with us on the day of our arrival,
and also a friend of the family, Mr. Barclay, to whom
we made a visit on the Sunday following. Among the
visits I paid, none was more gratifying to me than one
which I made to Dr. John Brown's sister. No man
could leave a sweeter memory than the author of "Rab
and his Friends," of "Pet Marjorie," and other writings, all full of the same loving, human spirit. I

have often exchanged letters with him, and I thought how much it would have added to the enjoyment of my visit if I could have taken his warm hand and listened to his friendly voice. I brought home with me a precious little manuscript, written expressly for me by one who had known Dr. John Brown from the days of her girlhood, in which his character appears in the same lovable and loving light as that which shines in every page he himself has written.

On Friday, the 25th, I went to the hall of the university, where I was to receive the degree of LL. D. The ceremony was not unlike that at Cambridge, but had one peculiar feature: the separate special investment of the candidate with the *hood*, which Johnson defines as "an ornamental fold which hangs down the back of a graduate." There were great numbers of students present, and they showed the same exuberance of spirits as that which had forced me to withdraw from the urgent calls at Cambridge. The cries, if possible, were still louder and more persistent; they must have a speech and they would have a speech, and what could I do about it? I saw but one way of pacifying a crowd as noisy and long-breathed as that which for about the space of two hours cried out, "Great is Diana of the Ephesians!" So I stepped to the front and made a brief speech, in which, of course, I spoke of the "*perfervidum ingenium Scotorum*." A speech without that would have been like that "Address without a Phœnix" before referred to. My few remarks were well received, and quieted the shouting Ephesians of the warm-brained and warm-hearted northern university. It gave me great pleasure to meet my friend Mr. Underwood, now American consul in Glasgow, where he has made himself highly esteemed and respected.

In my previous visit to Edinburgh in 1834, I was fond of rambling along under Salisbury Crags, and climbing the sides of Arthur's Seat. I had neither time nor impulse for such walks during this visit, but in driving out to dine at Nidrie, the fine old place now lived in by Mr. Barclay and his daughters, we passed under the crags and by the side of the great hill. I had never heard, or if I had I had forgotten, the name and the story of "Samson's Ribs." These are the columnar masses of rock which form the face of Salisbury Crags. There is a legend that one day one of these pillars will fall and crush the greatest man that ever passes under them. It is said that a certain professor was always very shy of "Samson's Ribs," for fear the prophecy might be fulfilled in his person. We were most hospitably received at Mr. Barclay's, and the presence of his accomplished and pleasing daughters made the visit memorable to both of us. There was one picture on their walls, that of a lady, by Sir Joshua, which both of us found very captivating. This is what is often happening in the visits we make. Some painting by a master looks down upon us from its old canvas, and leaves a lasting copy of itself, to be stored in memory's picture gallery. These surprises are not so likely to happen in the New World as in the Old.

It seemed cruel to be forced to tear ourselves away from Edinburgh, where so much had been done to make us happy, where so much was left to see and enjoy, but we were due in Oxford, where I was to receive the last of the three degrees with which I was honored in Great Britain.

Our visit to Scotland gave us a mere glimpse of the land and its people, but I have a very vivid recollec-

tion of both as I saw them on my first visit, when I
made an excursion into the Highlands to Stirling and
to Glasgow, where I went to church, and wondered
over the uncouth ancient psalmody, which I believe is
still retained in use to this day. I was seasoned to
that kind of poetry in my early days by the verses of
Tate and Brady, which I used to hear "entuned in the
nose ful swetely," accompanied by vigorous rasping of
a huge bass-viol. No wonder that Scotland welcomed
the song of Burns!

On our second visit to Oxford we were to be the
guests of the Vice-Chancellor of the university, Dr.
Jowett. This famous scholar and administrator lives
in a very pleasant establishment, presided over by the
Muses, but without the aid of a Vice-Chancelloress.
The hospitality of this classic mansion is well known,
and we added a second pleasant chapter to our previous experience under the roof of Professor Max Müller. There was a little company there before us,
including the Lord Chancellor and Lady Herschell,
Lady Camilla Wallop, Mr. Browning, and Mr. Lowell. We were too late, in consequence of the bad
arrangement of the trains, and had to dine by ourselves, as the whole party had gone out to a dinner, to
which we should have accompanied them had we not
been delayed. We sat up long enough to see them
on their return, and were glad to get to bed, after our
day's journey from Edinburgh to Oxford.

At eleven o'clock on the following day we who were
to receive degrees met at Balliol College, whence we
proceeded in solemn procession to the Sheldonian Theatre. Among my companions on this occasion were
Mr. John Bright, the Lord Chancellor Herschell, and

Mr. Aldis Wright. I have an instantaneous photograph, which was sent me, of this procession. I can
identify Mr. Bright and myself, but hardly any of the
others, though many better acquainted with their faces
would no doubt recognize them. There is a certain
sensation in finding one's self invested with the academic gown, conspicuous by its red facings, and the
cap with its square top and depending tassel, which is
not without its accompanying satisfaction. One can
walk the streets of any of the university towns in his
academic robes without being jeered at, as I am afraid
he would be in some of our own thoroughfares. There
is a noticeable complacency in the members of our
Phi Beta Kappa society when they get the pink and
blue ribbons in their buttonholes, on the day of annual
meeting. How much more when the scholar is wrapped
in those flowing folds, with their flaming borders, and
feels the dignity of the distinction of which they are
the symbol! I do not know how Mr. John Bright
felt, but I cannot avoid the impression that some in
the ranks which moved from Balliol to the Sheldonian
felt as if Solomon in all his glory was not arrayed like
the candidates for the degree of D. C. L.

After my experience at Cambridge and Edinburgh,
I might have felt some apprehension about my reception at Oxford. I had always supposed the audience
assembled there at the conferring of degrees was a
more demonstrative one than that at any other of the
universities, and I did not wish to be forced into a
retreat by calls for a speech, as I was at Cambridge,
nor to repeat my somewhat irregular proceeding of
addressing the audience, as at Edinburgh. But when
I found that Mr. John Bright was to be one of the
recipients of the degree I felt safe, for if he made a

speech I should be justified in saying a few words, if I thought it best; and if he, one of the most eloquent men in England, remained silent, I surely need not make myself heard on the occasion. It was a great triumph for him, a liberal leader, to receive the testimonial of a degree from the old conservative university. To myself it was a graceful and pleasing compliment; to him it was a grave and significant tribute. As we marched through the crowd on our way from Balliol, the people standing around recognized Mr. Bright, and cheered him vociferously.

The exercises in the Sheldonian Theatre were more complex and lasted longer than those at the other two universities. The candidate stepped forward and listened to one sentence, then made another move forward and listened to other words, and at last was welcomed to all the privileges conferred by the degree of Doctor of Civil Law, which was announced as being bestowed upon him. Mr. Bright, of course, was received with immense enthusiasm. I had every reason to be gratified with my own reception. The only "chaffing" I heard was the question from one of the galleries, "Did he come in the One-Hoss Shay?" — at which there was a hearty laugh, joined in as heartily by myself. A part of the entertainment at this ceremony consisted in the listening to the reading of short extracts from the prize essays, some or all of them in the dead languages, which could not have been particularly intelligible to a large part of the audience. During these readings there were frequent *interpellations*, as the French call such interruptions, something like these: "That will do, sir!" or "You had better stop, sir!" — always, I noticed, with the *sir* at the end of the remark. With us it would have been "Dry up!" or

"Hold on!" At last came forward the young poet of the occasion, who read an elaborate poem, "Savonarola," which was listened to in most respectful silence, and loudly applauded at its close, as I thought, deservedly. Prince and Princess Christian were among the audience. They were staying with Professor and Mrs. Max Müller, whose hospitalities I hope they enjoyed as much as we did. One or two short extracts from A——'s diary will enliven my record: "The Princess had a huge bouquet, and going down the aisle had to bow both ways at once, it seemed to me: but then she has the Guelph spine and neck! Of course it is necessary that royalty should have more elasticity in the frame than we poor ordinary mortals. After all this we started for a luncheon at All Souls, but had to wait (impatiently) for H. R. H. to rest herself, while our resting was done standing."

It is a long while since I read Madame d'Arblay's Recollections, but if I remember right, *standing* while royalty rests its bones is one of the drawbacks to a maid of honor's felicity.

"Finally, at near three, we went into a great luncheon of some fifty. There were different tables, and I sat at the one with royalty. The Provost of Oriel took me in, and Mr. Browning was on my other side. Finally, we went home to rest, but the others started out again to go to a garden-party, but that was beyond us." After all this came a dinner-party of twenty at the Vice-Chancellor's, and after that a reception, where among others we met Lord and Lady Coleridge, the lady resplendent in jewels. Even after London, this could hardly be called a day of rest.

The Chinese have a punishment which consists simply in keeping the subject of it awake, by the constant teasing of a succession of individuals employed for the purpose. The best of our social pleasures, if carried beyond the natural power of physical and mental endurance, begin to approach the character of such a penance. After this we got a little rest; did some mild sight-seeing, heard some good music, called on the Max Müllers, and bade them good-by with the warmest feeling to all the members of a household which it was a privilege to enter. There only remained the parting from our kind entertainer, the Vice-Chancellor, who added another to the list of places which in England and Scotland were made dear to us by hospitality, and are remembered as true homes to us while we were under their roofs.

On the second day of July we left the Vice-Chancellor's, and went to the Randolph Hotel to meet our friends, Mr. and Mrs. Willett, from Brighton, with whom we had an appointment of long standing. With them we left Oxford, to enter on the next stage of our pilgrimage.

IV.

It had been the intention of Mr. Willett to go with us to visit Mr. Ruskin, with whom he is in the most friendly relations. But a letter from Mr. Ruskin's sister spoke of his illness as being too serious for him to see company, and we reluctantly gave up this part of our plan.

My first wish was to revisit Stratford-on-Avon, and as our travelling host was guided in everything by our inclinations, we took the cars for Stratford, where we arrived at five o'clock in the afternoon. It had been

arranged beforehand that we should be the guests of
Mr. Charles E. Flower, one of the chief citizens of
Stratford, who welcomed us to his beautiful mansion
in the most cordial way, and made us once more at
home under an English roof.

I well remembered my visit to Stratford in 1834.
The condition of the old house in which Shakespeare
was born was very different from that in which we see
it to-day. A series of photographs taken in different
years shows its gradual transformation since the time
when the old projecting angular sign-board told all
who approached "The immortal Shakespeare was born
in this House." How near the old house came to
sharing the fortunes of Jumbo under the management
of our enterprising countryman, Mr. Barnum, I am
not sure; but that he would have "traded" for it, if
the proprietors had been willing, I do not doubt, any
more than I doubt that he would make an offer for the
Tower of London, if that venerable structure were in
the market. The house in which Shakespeare was
born is the Santa Casa of England. What with my
recollections and the photographs with which I was
familiarly acquainted, it had nothing very new for
me. Its outside had undergone great changes, but its
bare interior was little altered.

My previous visit was a hurried one, — I took but
a glimpse, and then went on my way. Now, for nearly
a week I was a resident of Stratford-on-Avon. How
shall I describe the perfectly ideal beauty of the new
home in which I found myself! It is a fine house,
surrounded by delightful grounds, which skirt the
banks of the Avon for a considerable distance, and
come close up to the enclosure of the Church of the
Holy Trinity, beneath the floor of which lie the mortal

remains of Shakespeare. The Avon is one of those narrow English rivers in which half a dozen boats might lie side by side, but hardly wide enough for a race between two rowing abreast of each other. Just here the river is comparatively broad and quiet, there being a dam a little lower down the stream. The waters were a perfect mirror, as I saw them on one of the still days we had at Stratford. I do not remember ever before seeing cows walking with their legs in the air, as I saw them reflected in the Avon. Along the banks the young people were straying. I wondered if the youthful swains quoted Shakespeare to their lady-loves. Could they help recalling Romeo and Juliet? It is quite impossible to think of any human being growing up in this place which claims Shakespeare as its child, about the streets of which he ran as a boy, on the waters of which he must have often floated, without having his image ever present. Is it so? There are some boys, from eight to ten or a dozen years old, fishing in the Avon, close by the grounds of "Avonbank," the place at which we are staying. I call to the little group. I say, "Boys, who was this man Shakespeare, people talk so much about?" Boys turn round and look up with a plentiful lack of intelligence in their countenances. "Don't you know who he was nor what he was?" Boys look at each other, but confess ignorance. — Let us try the universal stimulant of human faculties. "Here are some pennies for the boy that will tell me what that Mr. Shakespeare was." The biggest boy finds his tongue at last. "He was a writer, — he wrote plays." That was as much as I could get out of the youngling. I remember meeting some boys under the monument upon Bunker Hill, and testing their knowledge as I did that of the

Stratford boys. "What is this great stone pillar here for?" I asked. "Battle fought here, — great battle." "Who fought?" "Americans and British." (I never hear the expression British*ers*.) "Who was the general on the American side?" "Don' know, — General Washington or somebody." — What is an old battle, though it may have settled the destinies of a nation, to the game of base-ball between the Boston and Chicago Nines which is to come off to-morrow, or to the game of marbles which Tom and Dick are just going to play together under the shadow of the great obelisk which commemorates the conflict?

The room more especially assigned to me looked out, at a distance of not more than a stone's-throw, on the northern aspect of the church where Shakespeare lies buried. Workmen were busy on the roof of the transept. I could not conveniently climb up to have a talk with the roofers, but I have my doubts whether they were thinking all the time of the dust over which they were working. How small a matter literature is to the great seething, toiling, struggling, love-making, bread-winning, child-rearing, death-awaiting men and women who fill this huge, palpitating world of ours! It would be worth while to pass a week or a month among the plain, average people of Stratford. What is the relative importance in human well-being of the emendations of the text of Hamlet and the patching of the old trousers and the darning of the old stockings which task the needles of the hard-working households that fight the battle of life in these narrow streets and alleys? I ask the question; the reader may answer it.

Our host, Mr. Flower, is more deeply interested, perhaps, than any other individual in the "Shakespeare Memorial" buildings which have been erected on the banks of the Avon, a short distance above the Church of the Holy Trinity. Under Mr. Flower's guidance we got into one of his boats, and were rowed up the stream to the Memorial edifice. There is a theatre, in a round tower which has borrowed some traits from the octagon "Globe" theatre of Shake-speare's day; a Shakespeare library and portrait gallery are forming; and in due time these buildings, of stately dimensions and built solidly of brick, will constitute a Shakespearean centre which will attract to itself many mementoes now scattered about in various parts of the country.

On the 4th of July we remembered our native land with all the affectionate pride of temporary exiles, and did not forget to drink at lunch to the prosperity and continued happiness of the United States of America. In the afternoon we took to the boat again, and were rowed up the river to the residence of Mr. Edgar Flower, where we found another characteristic English family, with its nine children, one of whom was the typical English boy, most pleasing and attractive in look, voice, and manner.

I attempt no description of the church, the birth-place, or the other constantly visited and often de-scribed localities. The noble bridge, built in the reign of Henry VII. by Sir Hugh Clopton, and afterwards widened, excited my admiration. It was a much finer piece of work than the one built long afterwards. I have hardly seen anything which gave me a more strik-ing proof of the thoroughness of the old English work-men. They built not for an age, but for all time, and the New Zealander will have to wait a long while be-fore he will find in any one of the older bridges that broken arch from which he is to survey the ruins of London.

It is very pleasant to pick up a new epithet to apply to the poet upon whose genius our language has nearly exhausted itself. It delights me to speak of him in the words which I have just found in a memoir not yet a century old, as " the Warwickshire bard," "the inestimable Shakespeare."

Ever since Miss Bacon made her insane attempt to unearth what is left of Shakespeare's bodily frame, the thought of doing reverently and openly what she would have done by stealth has been entertained by psychologists, artists, and others who would like to know what were his cranial developments, and to judge from the conformation of the skull and face which of the various portraits is probably the true one. There is little doubt that but for the curse invoked upon the person who should disturb his bones, in the well-known lines on the slab which covers him, he would rest, like Napoleon, like Washington, in a fitting receptacle of marble or porphyry. In the transfer of his remains the curiosity of men of science and artists would have been gratified, if decay had spared the more durable portions of his material structure. It was probably not against such a transfer that the lines were written, — whoever was their author, — but in the fear that they would be carried to the charnel-house.

"In this charnel-house was contained a vast collection of human bones. How long they had been deposited there is not easily to be determined; but it is evident, from the immense quantity contained in the vault, it could have been used for no other purpose for many ages." "It is probable that from an early contemplation of this dreary spot Shakespeare imbibed that horror of a violation of sepulture which is observable in many parts of his writings."

The body of Raphael was disinterred in 1833 to settle a question of identity of the remains, and placed in a new coffin of lead, which was deposited in a marble sarcophagus presented by the Pope. The sarcophagus, with its contents, was replaced in the same spot from which the remains had been taken. But for the inscription such a transfer of the bones of Shakespeare would have been proposed, and possibly carried out. Kings and emperors have frequently been treated in this way after death, and the proposition is no more an indignity than was that of the exhumation of the remains of Napoleon, or of André, or of the author of "Home, Sweet Home." But sentiment, a tender regard for the supposed wishes of the dead poet, and a natural dread of the consequences of violating a dying wish, coupled with the execration of its contemner, are too powerful for the arguments of science and the pleadings of art. If Shakespeare's body had been embalmed, — which there is no reason that I know of to suppose, — the desire to compare his features with the bust and the portraits would have been much more imperative. When the body of Charles the First was examined, under the direction of Sir Henry Halford, in the presence of the Regent, afterwards George the Fourth, the face would have been recognized at once by all who were acquainted with Vandyke's portrait of the monarch, if the lithograph which comes attached to Sir Henry's memoir is an accurate representation of what they found. Even the bony framework of the face, as I have had occasion to know, has sometimes a striking likeness to what it was when clothed in its natural features. As between the first engraved portrait and the bust in the church, the form of the bones of the head and face would probably be decisive. But the world can afford to live without solving this doubt, and leave his perishing vesture of decay to its repose.

After seeing the Shakespeare shrines, we drove over to Shottery, and visited the Anne Hathaway cottage. I am not sure whether I ever saw it before, but it was as familiar to me as if I had lived in it. The old lady who showed it was agreeably communicative, and in perfect keeping with the place.

A delightful excursion of ten or a dozen miles carried our party, consisting of Mr. and Mrs. Flower, Mr. and Mrs. Willett, with A—— and myself, to Compton Wynyate, a most interesting old mansion, belonging to the Marquis of Northampton, who, with his daughter-in-law, Lady William Compton, welcomed us and showed us all the wonders of the place. It was a fine morning, but hot enough for one of our American July days. The drive was through English rural scenery; that is to say, it was lovely. The old house is a great curiosity. It was built in the reign of Henry the Eighth, and has passed through many vicissitudes. The place, as well as the edifice, is a study for the antiquarian. Remains of the old moat which surrounded it are still distinguishable. The twisted and variously figured chimneys are of singular variety and exceptional forms. Compton *Wynyate* is thought to get its name from the vineyards formerly under cultivation on the hillsides, which show the signs of having been laid out in terraces. The great hall, with its gallery, and its hangings, and the long table made from the trunk of a single tree, carries one back into the past centuries. There are strange nooks and corners and passages in the old building, and one place, a queer little "cubby-hole," has the appearance of having been a Roman Catholic chapel. I asked the master of the house, who pointed out the curiosities of the place most courteously, about the ghosts who of course were tenants in common with the living proprietors. I was surprised when he told me there were none. It was incredible, for here was every accommodation for a spiritual visitant. I should have expected at least one haunted chamber, to say nothing of blood-stains that could never be got rid of; but there were no legends of the supernatural or the terrible.

Refreshments were served us, among which were some hot-house peaches, ethereally delicate as if they had grown in the Elysian Fields and been stolen from a banquet of angels. After this we went out on the lawn, where, at Lady William Compton's request, I recited one or two poems; the only time I did such a thing in England.

It seems as if Compton Wynyate must have been written about in some novel or romance, — perhaps in more than one of both. It is the place of all others to be the scene of a romantic story. It lies so hidden away among the hills that its vulgar name, according to old Camden, was "Compton in the Hole." I am not sure that it was the scene of any actual conflict, but it narrowly escaped demolition in the great civil war, and in 1646 it was garrisoned by the Parliament army.

On the afternoon of July 6th, our hosts had a large garden-party. If nothing is more trying than one of these out-of-door meetings on a cold, windy, damp day, nothing can be more delightful than such a social gathering if the place and the weather are just what we could wish them. The garden-party of this afternoon was as near perfection as such a meeting could well be. The day was bright and warm, but not uncomfortably hot, to me, at least. The company strolled about the grounds, or rested on the piazzas, or watched the birds in the aviary, or studied rudimentary humanity in the monkey, or, better still, in a charming baby, for the first time on exhibition since she made the acquaintance of sunshine. Every one could dispose of himself or herself as fancy might suggest. I broke away at one time, and wandered alone by the side of the Avon, under the shadow of the tall trees upon its bank. The whole scene was as poetical, as inspiring, as any that I remember. It would be easy to write verses about it, but unwritten poems are so much better!

One reminiscence of that afternoon claims precedence over all the rest. The reader must not forget that I have been a medical practitioner, and for thirty-five years a professor in a medical school. Among the guests whom I met in the grounds was a gentleman of the medical profession, whose name I had often heard, and whom I was very glad to see and talk with. This was Mr. Lawson Tait, F. R. C. S., M. D., of Birmingham. Mr., or more properly Dr., Tait has had the most extraordinary success in a class of cases long considered beyond the reach of surgery. If I refer to it as a scientific *hari kari*, not for the taking but for the saving of life, I shall come near enough to its description. This operation is said to have been first performed by an American surgeon in Danville, Kentucky, in the year 1809. So rash and dangerous did it seem to most of the profession that it was sometimes spoken of as if to attempt it were a crime. Gradually, however, by improved methods, and especially by the most assiduous care in nursing the patient after the operation, the mortality grew less and less, until it was recognized as a legitimate and indeed an invaluable addition to the resources of sur-gery. Mr. Lawson Tait has had, so far as I have been able to learn, the most wonderful series of suc-cessful cases on record: namely, one hundred and thirty-nine consecutive operations without a single death.

As I sat by the side of this great surgeon, a ques-tion suggested itself to my mind which I leave the reader to think over. Which would give the most sat-isfaction to a thoroughly humane and unselfish being, of cultivated intelligence and lively sensibilities: to have written all the plays which Shakespeare has left as an inheritance for mankind, or to have snatched from the jaws of death more than a hundred fellow-creatures, — almost seven scores of suffering women, — and restored them to sound and comfortable exist-ence? It would be curious to get the answers of a hundred men and a hundred women, of a hundred young people and a hundred old ones, of a hundred scholars and a hundred operatives. My own specialty is asking questions, not answering them, and I trust I shall not receive a peck or two of letters inquiring of me how I should choose if such a question were asked me. It may prove as fertile a source of dispute as "The Lady or the Tiger."

It would have been a great thing to pass a single night close to the church where Shakespeare's dust lies buried. A single visit by daylight leaves a com-paratively slight impression. But when, after a night's sleep, one wakes up and sees the spire and the old walls full before him, that impression is very greatly deepened, and the whole scene becomes far more a reality. Now I was nearly a whole week at Stratford-on-Avon. The church, its exterior, its interior, the birthplace, the river, had time to make themselves permanent images in my mind. To effect this requires a certain amount of exposure, as much as in the case of a photographic negative.

And so we bade good-by to Stratford-on-Avon and its hospitalities, with grateful remembrances of our kind entertainers and all they did for our comfort and enjoyment.

Where should we go next? Our travelling host proposed Great Malvern, a famous watering-place, where we should find peace, rest, and good accommodations. So there we went, and soon found ourselves installed at the "Foley Arms" hotel. The room I was shown to looked out upon an apothecary's shop, and from the window of that shop stared out upon me a plaster bust which I recognized as that of Samuel Hahnemann. I was glad to change to another apartment, but it may be a comfort to some of his American followers to know that traces of homœopathy, — or what still continues to call itself so, — survive in the Old World, which we have understood was pretty well tired of it.

We spent several days very pleasantly at Great Malvern. It lies at the foot of a range of hills, the loftiest of which is over a thousand feet in height. A—— and I thought we would go to the top of one of these, known as the Beacon. We hired a "four-wheeler," dragged by a much-enduring horse and in

charge of a civil young man. We turned out of one
of the streets not far from the hotel, and found ourselves facing an ascent which looked like what I should
suppose would be a pretty steep toboggan slide. We
both drew back. "Facilis *a*scensus," I said to myself,
"sed revocare gradum." It is easy enough to get up
if you are dragged up, but how will it be to come
down such a declivity? When we reached it on our
return, the semi-precipice had lost all its terrors. We
had seen and travelled over so much worse places that
this little bit of slanting road seemed as nothing. The
road which wound up to the summit of the Beacon was
narrow and uneven. It ran close to the edge of the
steep hillside, — so close that there were times when
every one of our forty digits curled up like a bird's
claw. If we went over, it would not be a fall down a
good honest precipice, — a swish through the air and
a smash at the bottom, — but a tumbling, and a roll-
ing over and over, and a bouncing and bumping, ever
accelerating, until we bounded into the level below,
all ready for the coroner. At one sudden turn of the
road the horse's body projected so far over its edge
that A—— declared if the beast had been an inch
longer he would have toppled over. When we got
close to the summit we found the wind blowing almost
a gale. A—— says in her diary that I (meaning her
honored parent) "nearly blew off from the top of the
mountain." It is true that the force of the wind was
something fearful, and seeing that two young men
near me were exposed to its fury, I offered an arm to
each of them, which they were not too proud to accept;
A—— was equally attentive to another young person;
and having seen as much of the prospect as we cared
to, we were glad to get back to our four-wheeler and

our hotel, after a perilous journey almost comparable to Mark Twain's ascent of the Riffelberg.

At Great Malvern we were deliciously idle. We walked about the place, rested quietly, drove into the neighboring country, and made a single excursion, — to Tewkesbury. There are few places better worth seeing than this fine old town, full of historical associations and monumental relics. The magnificent old abbey church is the central object of interest. The noble Norman tower, one hundred and thirty-two feet in height, was once surmounted by a spire, which fell during divine service on Easter Day of the year 1559. The arch of the west entrance is sixteen feet high and thirty-four feet wide. The fourteen columns of the nave are each six feet and three inches in diameter and thirty feet in height. I did not take these measurements from the fabric itself, but from the guidebook, and I give them here instead of saying that the columns were huge, enormous, colossal, as they did most assuredly seem to me. The old houses of Tewkesbury compare well with the finest of those in Chester. I have a photograph before me of one of them, in which each of the three upper floors overhangs the one beneath it, and the windows in the pointed gable above project over those of the fourth floor.

I ought to have visited the site of Holme Castle, the name of which reminds me of my own origin. "The meaning of the Saxon word ' Holme ' is a meadow surrounded with brooks, and here not only did the castle bear the name, but the meadow is described as the ' Holme,— where the castle was.' " The final s in the name as we spell it is a frequent addition to old English names, as Camden mentions, giving the name Holmes among the examples. As there is no castle at the Holme now, I need not pursue my inquiries any further. It was by accident that I stumbled on this bit of archæology, and as I have a good many name-sakes, it may perhaps please some of them to be told about it. Few of us hold any castles, I think, in these days, except those *châteaux en Espagne*, of which I doubt not, many of us are lords and masters.

In another of our excursions we visited a venerable church, where our attention was called to a particular monument. It was erected to the memory of one of the best of husbands by his " wretched widow," who records upon the marble that there never was such a man on the face of the earth before, and never will be again, and that there never was anybody so miserable as she, — no, never, never, never! These are not the exact words, but this is pretty nearly what she declares. The story is that she married again within a year.

From my window at the Foley Arms I can see the tower of the fine old abbey church of Malvern, which would be a centre of pilgrimages if it were in our coun-try. But England is full of such monumental struc-tures, into the history of which the local antiquarians burrow, and pass their peaceful lives in studying and writing about them with the same innocent enthusiasm that White of Selborne manifested in studying nature as his village showed it to him.

In our long drives we have seen everywhere the same picturesque old cottages, with the pretty gardens, and abundant flowers, and noble trees, more frequently elms than any other. One day — it was on the 10th of July — we found ourselves driving through what seemed to be a gentleman's estate, an ample domain, well wooded and well kept. On inquiring to whom this place belonged, I was told that the owner was Sir

Edmund Lechmere. The name had a very familiar sound to my ears. Without rising from the table at which I am now writing, I have only to turn my head, and in full view, at the distance of a mile, just across the estuary of the Charles, shining in the morning sun, are the roofs and spires and chimneys of East Cam-bridge, always known in my younger days as Lech-mere's Point. Judge Richard Lechmere was one of our old Cambridge Tories, whose property was confis-cated at the time of the Revolution. An engraving of his handsome house, which stands next to the Vas-sall house, long known as Washington's headquarters, and since not less celebrated as the residence of Long-fellow, is before me, on one of the pages of the pleas-ing little volume, "The Cambridge of 1776." I take it for granted that our Lechmeres were of the same stock as the owner of this property. If so, he proba-bly knows all that I could tell him about his colonial relatives, who were very grand people, belonging to a little aristocratic circle of friends and relatives who were faithful to their king and their church. The Baroness Riedesel, wife of a Hessian officer who had been captured, was for a while resident in this house, and her name, scratched on a window-pane, was long shown as a sight for eyes unused to titles other than governor, judge, colonel, and the like. I was tempted to present myself at Sir Edmund's door as one who knew something about the Lechmeres in America, but I did not feel sure how cordially a descendant of the rebels who drove off Richard and Mary Lechmere would be received.

From Great Malvern we went to Bath, another place where we could rest and be comfortable. The Grand Pump-Room Hotel was a stately building, and

the bath-rooms were far beyond anything I had ever
seen of that kind. The remains of the old Roman
baths, which appear to have been very extensive, are
partially exposed. What surprises one all over the
Old World is to see how deeply all the old civilizations contrive to get buried. Everybody seems to
have lived in the cellar. It is hard to believe that
the cellar floor was once the sun surface of the smiling earth.

I looked forward to seeing Bath with a curious kind
of interest. I once knew one of those dear old English ladies whom one finds all the world over, with
their prim little ways, and their gilt prayer-books,
and lavender-scented handkerchiefs, and family recollections. She gave me the idea that Bath, a city
where the great people often congregate, was more
especially the paradise of decayed gentlewomen.
There, she told me, persons with very narrow incomes
— not *demi-fortunes*, but *demi-quart-de-fortunes* —
could find everything arranged to accommodate their
modest incomes. I saw the evidence of this everywhere. So great was the delight I had in looking in
at the shop-windows of the long street which seemed
to be one of the chief thoroughfares that, after exploring it in its full extent by myself, I went for A——,
and led her down one side its whole length and up the
other. In these shops the precious old dears could
buy everything they wanted in the most minute quantities. Such tempting heaps of lumps of white sugar,
only twopence! Such delectable cakes, two for a
penny! Such seductive scraps of meat, which would
make a breakfast nourishing as well as relishing, possibly even what called itself a dinner, blushing to see
themselves labelled threepence or fourpence ! We did

not know whether to smile or to drop a tear, as we
contemplated these baits hung out to tempt the coins
from the exiguous purses of ancient maidens, forlorn
widows, withered annuitants, stranded humanity in
every stage of shipwrecked penury. I am reminded
of Thackeray's "Jack Spiggot." "And what are
your pursuits, Jack? says I. 'Sold out when the governor died. Mother lives at Bath. Go down there
once a year for a week. Dreadful slow. Shilling
whist.' " Mrs. Gaskell's picture of "Cranford" is
said to have been drawn from a village in Cheshire,
but Bath must have a great deal in common with its
"elegant economies." Do not make the mistake,
however, of supposing that this splendid watering-
place, sometimes spoken of as "the handsomest city in
Britain," is only a city of refuge for people that have
seen better days. Lord Macaulay speaks of it as
"that beautiful city which charms even eyes familiar
with the masterpieces of Bramante and Palladio." If
it is not quite so conspicuous as a fashionable resort
as it was in the days of Beau Nash or of Christopher
Anstey, it has never lost its popularity. Chesterfield
writes in 1764, "The number of people in this place
is infinite," and at the present time the annual influx
of visitors is said to vary from ten to fourteen thousand. Many of its public buildings are fine, and the
abbey church, dating from 1499, is an object of much
curiosity, especially on account of the sculptures on
its western façade. These represent two ladders,
with angels going up and down upon them, — suggested by a dream of the founder of the church, repeating that of Jacob.

On the 14th of July we left Bath for Salisbury.
While passing Westbury, one of our fellow-passengers

exclaimed, "Look out! Look out!" "What is it?" "The horse! the horse!" All our heads turned to the window, and all our eyes fastened on the figure of a white horse, upon a hillside some miles distant. This was not the white horse which Mr. Thomas Hughes has made famous, but one of much less archaic aspect and more questionable history. A little book which we bought tells us all we care to know about it. "It is formed by excoriating the turf over the steep slope of the northern escarpment of Salisbury Plain." It was "remodelled" in 1778, and "restored" in 1873 at a cost of between sixty and seventy pounds. It is said that a smaller and ruder horse stood here from time immemorial, and was made to commemorate a victory of Alfred over the Danes. However that may be, the horse we now see on the hillside is a very modern-looking and well-shaped animal, and is of the following dimensions: length, 170 feet; height from highest part of back, 128 feet; thickness of body, 55 feet; length of head, 50 feet; eye, 6 by 8 feet. It is a very pretty little object as we see it in the distance.

Salisbury Cathedral was my first love among all the wonderful ecclesiastical buildings which I saw during my earlier journey. I looked forward to seeing it again with great anticipations of pleasure, which were more than realized.

Our travelling host had taken a whole house in the Close, — a privileged enclosure, containing the cathedral, the bishop's palace, houses of the clergy, and a limited number of private residences, one of the very best of which was given over entirely into the hands of our party during our visit. The house was about as near the cathedral as Mr. Flower's house, where we stayed at Stratford-on-Avon, was to the Church of the Holy Trinity. It was very completely furnished, and in the room assigned to me as my library I found books in various languages, showing that the residence was that of a scholarly person.

If one had to name the apple of the eye of England, I think he would be likely to say that Salisbury Cathedral was as near as he could come to it, and that the white of the eye was Salisbury Close. The cathedral is surrounded by a high wall, the gates of which, — its eyelids, — are closed every night at a seasonable hour, at which the virtuous inhabitants are expected to be in their safe and sacred quarters. Houses within this hallowed precinct naturally bring a higher rent than those of the unsanctified and unprotected region outside of its walls. It is a realm of peace, glorified by the divine edifice, which lifts the least imaginative soul upward to the heavens its spire seems trying to reach; beautified by rows of noble elms which stretch high aloft, as if in emulation of the spire; beatified by holy memories of the good and great men who have worn their lives out in the service of the church of which it is one of the noblest temples.

For a whole week we lived under the shadow of the spire of the great cathedral. Our house was opposite the north transept, only separated by the road in front of it from the cathedral grounds. Here, as at Stratford, I learned what it was to awake morning after morning and find that I was not dreaming, but there in the truth-telling daylight the object of my admiration, devotion, almost worship, stood before me. I need not here say anything more of the cathedral, except that its perfect exterior is hardly equalled in beauty by its interior, which looks somewhat bare and

cold. It was my impression that there is more to
study than to admire in the interior, but I saw the
cathedral so much oftener on the outside than on the
inside that I may not have done justice to the latter
aspect of the noble building.

Nothing could be more restful than our week at Salisbury. There was enough in the old town besides
the cathedral to interest us, — old buildings, a museum full of curious objects, and the old town itself.
When I was there the first time, I remember that we
picked up a guide-book in which we found a verse that
has remained in my memory ever since. It is an epitaph on a native of Salisbury who died in Venice.

> "Born in the English Venice, thou didst dye
> Dear Friend, in the Italian Salisbury."

This would be hard to understand except for the expla-
nation which the local antiquarians give us of its significance. The Wiltshire Avon flows by or through
the town, which is drained by brooks that run through
its streets. These, which used to be open, are now
covered over, and thus the epitaph becomes somewhat
puzzling, as there is nothing to remind one of Venice
in walking about the town.

While at Salisbury we made several excursions: to
Old Sarum; to Bemerton, where we saw the residence
of holy George Herbert, and visited the little atom of
a church in which he ministered; to Clarendon Park;
to Wilton, the seat of the Earl of Pembroke, a most
interesting place for itself and its recollections; and
lastly to Stonehenge. My second visit to the great
stones after so long an interval was a strange experience. But what is half a century to a place like
Stonehenge? Nothing dwarfs an individual life like
one of these massive, almost unchanging monuments

of an antiquity which refuses to be measured. The "Shepherd of Salisbury Plain" was represented by an old man, who told all he knew and a good deal more about the great stones, and sheared a living, not from sheep, but from visitors, in the shape of shillings and sixpences. I saw nothing that wore unwoven wool on its back in the neighborhood of the monu- ments, but sheep are shown straggling among them in the photographs.

The broken circle of stones, some in their original position, some bending over like old men, some lying prostrate, suggested the thoughts which took form in the following verses. They were read at the annual meeting, in January, of the class which graduated at Harvard College in the year 1829. Eight of the fifty- nine men who graduated sat round the small table. There were several other classmates living, but infirm- ity, distance, and other peremptory reasons kept them from being with us. I have read forty poems at our successive annual meetings. I will introduce this last one by quoting a stanza from the poem I read in 1851: —

As one by one is falling
    Beneath the leaves or snows,
Each memory still recalling
    The broken ring shall close,
Till the night winds softly pass
    O'er the green and growing grass,
Where it waves on the graves
    Of the " Boys of 'Twenty-nine."

THE BROKEN CIRCLE.

I stood on Sarum's treeless plain,
    The waste that careless Nature owns;

Lone tenants of her bleak domain,
    Loomed huge and gray the Druid stones.

Upheaved in many a billowy mound
    The sea-like, naked turf arose,
Where wandering flocks went nibbling round
    The mingled graves of friends and foes.

The Briton, Roman, Saxon, Dane,
    This windy desert roamed in turn;
Unmoved these mighty blocks remain
    Whose story none that lives may learn.

Erect, half buried, slant or prone,
    These awful listeners, blind and dumb,
Hear the strange tongues of tribes unknown,
    As wave on wave they go and come.

"Who are you, giants, whence and why?"
    I stand and ask in blank amaze;
My soul accepts their mute reply :
    "A mystery, as are you that gaze.

"A silent Orpheus wrought the charm
    From riven rocks their spoils to bring ;
A nameless Titan lent his arm
    To range us in our magic ring.

"But Time with still and stealthy stride,
    That climbs and treads and levels all,
That bids the loosening keystone slide,
    And topples down the crumbling wall, —

"Time, that unbuilds the quarried past,
    Leans on these wrecks that press the sod ;
They slant, they stoop, they fall at last,
    And strew the turf their priests have trod.

"No more our altar's wreath of smoke
    Floats up with morning's fragrant dew ;
The fires are dead, the ring is broke,
    Where stood the many stand the few."

— My thoughts had wandered far away,
   Borne off on Memory's outspread wing,
To where in deepening twilight lay
   The wrecks of friendship's broken ring.

Ah me ! of all our goodly train
   How few will find our banquet hall !
Yet why with coward lips complain
   That this must lean and that must fall ?

Cold is the Druid's altar-stone,
   Its vanished flame no more returns ;
But ours no chilling damp has known, —
   Unchanged, unchanging, still it burns.

So let our broken circle stand
   A wreck, a remnant, yet the same,
While one last, loving, faithful hand
   Still lives to feed its altar-flame !

My heart has gone back over the waters to my old friends and my own home. When this vision has faded, I will return to the silence of the lovely Close and the shadow of the great Cathedral.

V.

The remembrance of home, with its early and precious and long-enduring friendships, has intruded itself among my recollections of what I saw and heard, of what I felt and thought, in the distant land I was visiting. I must return to the scene where I found myself when the suggestion of the broken circle ran away with my imagination.

The literature of Stonehenge is extensive, and illustrates the weakness of archæologists almost as well as the "Prætorium" of Scott's "Antiquary." "In

1823," says a local handbook, "H. Browne, of Amesbury, published ' An Illustration of Stonehenge and
Abury,' in which he endeavored to show that both of
these monuments were antediluvian, and that the latter
was formed under the direction of Adam. He ascribes
the present dilapidated condition of Stonehenge to the
operation of the general deluge; for, he adds, ' to suppose it to be the work of any people since the flood is
entirely monstrous.' "

We know well enough how great stones — pillars
and obelisks — are brought into place by means of
our modern appliances. But if the great blocks were
raised by a mob of naked Picts, or any tribe that
knew none of the mechanical powers but the lever,
how did they set them up and lay the cross-stones, the
imposts, upon the uprights? It is pleasant, once in a
while, to think how we should have managed any such
matters as this if left to our natural resources. We
are all interested in the make-shifts of Robinson Crusoe. Now the rudest tribes make cords of some kind,
and the earliest, or almost the earliest, of artificial
structures is an earth-mound. If a hundred, or hundreds, of men could drag the huge stones many leagues,
as they must have done to bring them to their destined
place, they could have drawn each of them up a long
slanting mound ending in a sharp declivity, with a
hole for the foot of the stone at its base. If the stone
were now tipped over, it would slide into its place,
and could be easily raised from its slanting position to
the perpendicular. Then filling in the space between
the mound and two contiguous stones, the impost could
be dragged up to its position. I found a pleasure in
working at this simple mechanical problem, as a change
from the more imaginative thoughts suggested by the
mysterious monuments.

One incident of our excursion to Stonehenge had a significance for me which renders it memorable in my personal experience. As we drove over the barren plain, one of the party suddenly exclaimed, "Look! Look! See the lark rising!" I looked up with the rest. There was the bright blue sky, but not a speck upon it which my eyes could distinguish. Again, one called out, "Hark! Hark! Hear him singing!" I listened, but not a sound reached my ear. Was it strange that I felt a momentary pang? *Those that look out at the windows are darkened, and all the daughters of music are brought low.* Was I never to see or hear the soaring songster at Heaven's gate, — unless, — unless, — if our mild humanized theology promises truly, I may perhaps hereafter listen to him singing far down beneath me? For in whatever world I may find myself, I hope I shall always love our poor little spheroid, so long my home, which some kind angel may point out to me as a gilded globule swimming in the sunlight far away. After walking the streets of pure gold in the New Jerusalem, might not one like a short vacation, to visit the well-remembered green fields and flowery meadows? I had a very sweet emotion of self-pity, which took the sting out of my painful discovery that the orchestra of my pleasing life-entertainment was unstringing its instruments, and the lights were being extinguished, — that the show was almost over. All this I kept to myself, of course, except so far as I whispered it to the unseen presence which we all feel is in sympathy with us, and which, as it seemed to my fancy, was looking into my eyes, and through them into my soul, with the tender, tearful smile of a mother who for the first time gently presses back the longing lips of her as yet unweaned infant.

On our way back from Stonehenge we stopped and took a cup of tea with a friend of our host, Mr. Night-ingale. His house, a bachelor establishment, was very attractive to us by the beauty within and around it. His collection of "china," as Pope and old-fashioned people call all sorts of earthenware, excited the enthu-siasm of our host, whose admiration of some rare pieces in the collection was so great that it would have run into envy in a less generous nature.

It is very delightful to find one's self in one of these English country residences. The house is commonly old, and has a history. It is oftentimes itself a record, like that old farmhouse my friend John Bellows wrote to me about, which chronicled half a dozen reigns by various architectural marks as exactly as if it had been an official register. "The stately homes of England," as we see them at Wilton and Longford Castle, are not more admirable in their splendors than "the blessed homes of England" in their modest beauty. Everywhere one may see here old parsonages by the side of ivy-mantled churches, and the comfortable mansions where generations of country squires have lived in peace, while their sons have gone forth to fight England's battles, and carry her flags of war and com-merce all over the world. We in America can hardly be said to have such a possession as a family home. We encamp, — not under canvas, but in fabrics of wood or more lasting materials, which are pulled down after a brief occupancy by the builders, and possibly their children, or are modernized so that the former dwellers in them would never recognize their old hab-itations.

In my various excursions from Salisbury I was fol-lowed everywhere by the all-pervading presence of the

towering spire. Just what it was in that earlier visit,
when my eyes were undimmed and my sensibilities
unworn, just such I found it now. As one drives
away from the town, the roofs of the houses drop out
of the landscape, the lesser spires disappear one by
one, until the great shaft is left standing alone, —
solitary as the broken statue of Ozymandias in the
desert, as the mast of some mighty ship above the
waves which have rolled over the foundering vessel.
Most persons will, I think, own to a feeling of awe
in looking up at it. Few can look down from a great
height without creepings and crispations, if they do
not get as far as vertigos and that aerial calenture
which prompts them to jump from the pinnacle on
which they are standing. It does not take much imagination to make one experience something of the same
feeling in looking up at a very tall steeple or chimney.
To one whose eyes are used to Park Street and the
Old South steeples as standards of height, a spire
which climbs four hundred feet towards the sky is a
new sensation. Whether I am more "afraid of that
which is high " than I was at my first visit, as I should
be on the authority of Ecclesiastes, I cannot say, but
it was quite enough for me to let my eyes climb the
spire, and I had no desire whatever to stand upon that
"bad eminence," as I am sure that I should have
found it.

I soon noticed a slight deflection from the perpendicular at the upper part of the spire. This has long
been observed. I could not say that I saw the spire
quivering in the wind, as I felt that of Strasburg doing
when I ascended it, — swaying like a blade of grass
when a breath of air passes over it. But it has been,
for at least two hundred years, nearly two feet out of

the perpendicular. No increase in the deviation was found to exist when it was examined early in the present century. It is a wonder that this slight-looking structure can have survived the blasts, and thunder-bolts, and earthquakes, and the weakening effects of time on its stones and timbers for five hundred years. Since the spire of Chichester Cathedral fell in 1861, sheathing itself in its tower like a sword dropping into its scabbard, one can hardly help looking with appre-hension at all these lofty fabrics. I have before referred to the fall of the spire of Tewkesbury Abbey church, three centuries earlier. There has been a good deal of fear for the Salisbury spire, and great precautions have been taken to keep it firm, so that we may hope it will stand for another five hundred years. It ought to be a "joy forever," for it is a thing of beauty, if ever there were one.

I never felt inclined to play the part of the young enthusiast in "Excelsior," as I looked up at the weath-ercock which surmounts the spire. But the man who oils the weathercock-spindle has to get up to it in some way, and that way is by ladders which reach to within thirty feet of the top, where there is a small door, through which he emerges, to crawl up the remaining distance on the outside. "The situation and appear-ance," says one of the guide-books, "must be terrific, yet many persons have voluntarily and daringly clam-bered to the top, even in a state of intoxication." Such, I feel sure, was not the state of my most valued and exemplary clerical friend, who, with a cool head and steady nerves, found himself standing in safety at the top of the spire, with his hand upon the vane, which nothing terrestrial had ever looked down upon in its lofty position, except a bird, a bat, a sky-rocket, or a balloon.

In saying that the exterior of Salisbury Cathedral is more interesting than its interior, I was perhaps unfair to the latter, which only yields to the surpassing claims of the wonderful structure as seen from the outside. One may get a little tired of marble Crusaders, with their crossed legs and broken noses, especially if, as one sometimes finds them, they are covered with the pencilled autographs of cockney scribblers. But there are monuments in this cathedral which excite curiosity, and others which awaken the most striking associations. There is the "Boy Bishop," his marble effigy protected from vandalism by an iron cage. There is the skeleton figure representing Fox (who should have been called Goose), the poor creature who starved himself to death in trying to imitate the fast of forty days in the wilderness. Since this performance has been taken out of the list of miracles, it is not so likely to be repeated by fanatics. I confess to a strong suspicion that this is one of the ambulatory or movable stories, like the "hangman's stone " legend, which I have found in so many different parts of England. Skulls and crossbones, sometimes skeletons or skeleton-like figures, are not uncommon among the sepulchral embellishments of an earlier period. Where one of these figures is found, the forty-day-fast story is likely to grow out of it, as the mistletoe springs from the oak or apple tree.

With far different emotions we look upon the spot where lie buried many of the Herbert family, among the rest,

" Sidney's sister, Pembroke's mother,"

for whom Ben Jonson wrote the celebrated epitaph. I am almost afraid to say it, but I never could admire the line,

"Lies the subject of all verse,"

nor the idea of Time dropping his hour-glass and scythe to throw a dart at the fleshless figure of Death. This last image seems to me about the equivalent in mortuary poetry of Roubiliac's monument to Mrs. Nightingale in mortuary sculpture, — poor conceits both of them, without the suggestion of a tear in the verses or in the marble; but the rhetorical exaggeration does not prevent us from feeling that we are standing by the resting-place of one who was

"learn'd and fair and good"

enough to stir the soul of stalwart Ben Jonson, and the names of Sidney and Herbert make us forget the strange hyperboles.

History meets us everywhere, as we stray among these ancient monuments. Under that effigy lie the great bones of Sir John Cheyne, a mighty man of war, said to have been "overthrown" by Richard the Third at the battle of Bosworth Field. What was left of him was unearthed in 1789 in the demolition of the Beauchamp chapel, and his thigh-bone was found to be four inches longer than that of a man of common stature.

The reader may remember how my recollections started from their hiding-place when I came, in one of our excursions, upon the name of Lechmere, as belonging to the owner of a fine estate by or through which we were driving. I had a similar twinge of reminiscence at meeting with the name of Gorges, which is perpetuated by a stately monument at the end of the north aisle of the cathedral. Sir Thomas Gorges, Knight of Longford Castle, may or may not have been of the same family as the well-remembered

grandiose personage of the New England Pilgrim period. The title this gentleman bore had a far more
magnificent sound than those of his contemporaries,
Governor Carver and Elder Brewster. No title ever
borne among us has filled the mouth quite so full as
that of "Sir Ferdinando Gorges, Lord Palatine of the
Province of Maine," a province with "Gorgeana"
(late the plantation of Agamenticus) as its capital.
Everywhere in England a New Englander is constantly
meeting with names of families and places which
remind him that he comes of a graft from an old tree
on a new stock. I could not keep down the associations called up by the name of Gorges. There is a
certain pleasure in now and then sprinkling our prosaic colonial history with the holy water of a high-
sounding title; not that a "Sir" before a man's name
makes him any better, — for are we not all equal, and
more than equal, to each other? — but it sounds pleasantly. Sir Harry Vane and Sir Harry Frankland
look prettily on the printed page, as the illuminated
capital at the head of a chapter in an old folio pleases
the eye of the reader. Sir Thomas Gorges was the
builder of Longford Castle, now the seat of the Earl
of Radnor, whose family name is Bouverie. Whether
our Sir Ferdinando was of the Longford Castle stock
or not I must leave to my associates of the Massachusetts Historical Society to determine.

We lived very quietly at our temporary home in
Salisbury Close. A pleasant dinner with the Dean, a
stroll through the grounds of the episcopal palace, with
that perpetual feast of the eyes which the cathedral
offered us, made our residence delightful at the time,
and keeps it so in remembrance. Besides the cathedral there were the very lovely cloisters, the noble chap-

ter-house with its central pillar, — this structure has been restored and rejuvenated since my earlier visit, — and there were the peaceful dwellings, where I insist on believing that only virtue and happiness are ever tenants. Even outside the sacred enclosure there is a great deal to enjoy, in the ancient town of Salisbury. One may rest under the Poultry Cross, where twenty or thirty generations have rested before him. One may purchase his china at the well-furnished establishment of the tenant of a spacious apartment of ancient date, — " the Halle of John Halle," a fine private edifice built in the year 1470, restored and beautified in 1834; the emblazonment of the royal arms having been executed by the celebrated architectural artist Pugin. The old houses are numerous, and some of them eminently picturesque.

Salisbury was formerly very unhealthy, on account of the low, swampy nature of its grounds. The Sanitary Reform, dating from about thirty years ago, had a great effect on the condition of the place. Before the drainage the annual mortality was twenty-seven in the thousand; since the drainage twenty in the thousand, which is below that of Boston. In the Close, which is a little Garden of Eden, with no serpent in it that I could hear of, the deaths were only fourteen in a thousand. Happy little enclosure, where thieves cannot break through and steal, where Death himself hesitates to enter, and makes a visit only now and then at long intervals, lest the fortunate inhabitants should think they had already reached the Celestial City!

It must have been a pretty bitter quarrel that drove the tenants of the airy height of Old Sarum to remove to the marshy level of the present site of the cathedral and the town. I wish we could have given more time to the ancient fortress and cathedral town. This is one of the most interesting historic localities of Great Britain. We looked from different points of view at the mounds and trenches which marked it as a strongly fortified position. For many centuries it played an important part in the history of England. At length, however, the jealousies of the laity and the clergy, a squabble like that of "town and gown," but with graver underlying causes, broke up the harmony and practically ended the existence of the place except as a monument of the past. It seems a pity that the headquarters of the Prince of Peace could not have managed to maintain tranquillity within its own borders. But so it was; and the consequence followed that Old Sarum, with all its grand recollections, is but a collection of mounds and hollows, — as much a tomb of its past as Birs Nimroud of that great city, Nineveh. Old Sarum is now best remembered by its long-surviving privilege, as a borough, of sending two members to Parliament. The farcical ceremony of electing two representatives who had no real constituency behind them was put an end to by the Reform Act of 1832.

Wilton, the seat of the Earl of Pembroke, within an easy drive's distance from Salisbury, was the first nobleman's residence I saw in my early visit. Not a great deal of what I then saw had survived in my memory. I recall the general effect of the stately mansion and its grounds. A picture or two of Vandyke's had not quite faded out of my recollection. I could not forget the armor of Anne de Montmorenci, — not another Maid of Orleans, but Constable of France, — said to have been taken in battle by an ancestor of the Herberts. It was one of the first things that made me feel I was in the Old World. Miles Standish's

sword was as far back as New England collections of
armor carried us at that day. The remarkable gallery
of ancient sculptures impressed me at the time, but no
one bust or statue survived as a distinct image. Even
the beautiful Palladian bridge had not pictured itself
on my mental tablet as it should have done, and I
could not have taken my oath that I had seen it. But
the pretty English maidens whom we met on the day
of our visit to Wilton,— daughters or granddaughters
of a famous inventor and engineer, — still lingered as
vague and pleasing visions, so lovely had they seemed
among the daisies and primroses. The primroses and
daisies were as fresh in the spring of 1886 as they
were in the spring of 1833, but I hardly dared to ask
after the blooming maidens of that early period.

One memory predominates over all others, in walking through the halls, or still more in wandering
through the grounds, of Wilton House. Here Sir
Philip Sidney wrote his "Arcadia," and the ever
youthful presence of the man himself rather than the
recollection of his writings takes possession of us.
There are three young men in history whose names
always present themselves to me in a special companionship: Pico della Mirandola, "the Phœnix of the
Age" for his contemporaries; "the Admirable Crichton," accepting as true the accounts which have come
down to us of his wonderful accomplishments; and
Sidney, the Bayard of England, "that glorious star,
that lively pattern of virtue and the lovely joy of all
the learned sort, . . . born into the world to show
unto our age a sample of ancient virtue." The English paragon of excellence was but thirty-two years
old when he was slain at Zutphen, the Italian Phœnix
but thirty-one when he was carried off by a fever, and

the Scotch prodigy of gifts and attainments was only twenty-two when he was assassinated by his worthless pupil. Sir Philip Sidney is better remembered by the draught of water he gave the dying soldier than by all the waters he ever drew from the fountain of the Muses, considerable as are the merits of his prose and verse. But here, where he came to cool his fiery spirit after the bitter insult he had received from the Earl of Leicester; here, where he mused and wrote, and shaped his lofty plans for a glorious future, he lives once more in our imagination, as if his spirit haunted the English Arcadia he loved so dearly.

The name of Herbert, which we have met with in the cathedral, and which belongs to the Earls of Pembroke, presents itself to us once more in a very different and very beautiful aspect. Between Salisbury and Wilton, three miles and a half distant, is the little village of Bemerton, where "holy George Herbert" lived and died, and where he lies buried. Many Americans who know little else of him recall the lines borrowed from him by Irving in the "Sketch-Book" and by Emerson in "Nature." The "Sketch-Book" gives the lines thus: —

> "Sweet day, so pure, so calm, so bright,
> The bridal of the earth and sky."

In other versions the fourth word is *cool* instead of *pure*, and *cool* is, I believe, the correct reading. The day when we visited Bemerton was, according to A——'s diary, "perfect." I was struck with the calm beauty of the scene around us, the fresh greenness of all growing things, and the stillness of the river which mirrored the heavens above it. It must have been this reflection which the poet was thinking of when he spoke of the bridal of the earth and sky.

The river is the Wiltshire Avon; not Shakespeare's Avon, but the southern stream of the same name, which empties into the British Channel.

So much of George Herbert's intellectual and moral character repeat themselves in Emerson that if I believed in metempsychosis I should think that the English saint had reappeared in the American philosopher. Their features have a certain resemblance, but the type, though an exceptional and fine one, is not so very rare. I found a portrait in the National Gallery which was a good specimen of it; the bust of a near friend of his, more intimate with him than almost any other person, is often taken for that of Emerson. I see something of it in the portrait of Sir Philip Sidney, and I doubt not that traces of a similar mental resemblance ran through the whole group, with individual characteristics which were in some respects quite different. I will take a single verse of Herbert's from Emerson's "Nature," — one of the five which he quotes : —

> " Nothing hath got so far
> But man hath caught and kept it as his prey;
> His eyes dismount the highest star:
> He is in little all the sphere.
> Herbs gladly cure our flesh because that they
> Find their acquaintance there."

Emerson himself fully recognizes his obligations to "the beautiful psalmist of the seventeenth century," as he calls George Herbert. There are many passages in his writings which sound as if they were paraphrases from the elder poet. From him it is that Emerson gets a word he is fond of, and of which his imitators are too fond : —

> " Who sweeps a room as for thy laws
> Makes that and the action *fine.*"

The little chapel in which Herbert officiated is perhaps half as long again as the room in which I am writing, but it is four or five feet narrower, — and I do not live in a palace. Here this humble servant of God preached and prayed, and here by his faithful and loving service he so endeared himself to all around him that he has been canonized by an epithet no other saint of the English Church has had bestowed upon him. His life as pictured by Izaak Walton is, to borrow one of his own lines,

" A box where sweets compacted lie; "

and I felt, as I left his little chapel and the parsonage which he rebuilt as a free-will offering, as a pilgrim might feel who had just left the holy places at Jerusalem.

Among the places which I saw in my first visit was Longford Castle, the seat of the Earl of Radnor. I remembered the curious triangular building, constructed with reference to the doctrine of the Trinity, as churches are built in the form of the cross. I remembered how the omnipresent spire of the great cathedral, three miles away, looked down upon the grounds about the building as if it had been their next-door neighbor. I had not forgotten the two celebrated Claudes, Morning and Evening. My eyes were drawn to the first of these two pictures when I was here before; now they turned naturally to the landscape with the setting sun. I have read my St. Ruskin with due reverence, but I have never given up my allegiance to Claude Lorraine. But of all the fine paintings at Longford Castle, no one so much impressed me at my recent visit as the portrait of Erasmus by Hans Holbein. This is one of those

pictures which help to make the Old World worth a
voyage across the Atlantic. Portraits of Erasmus are
not uncommon; every scholar would know him if he
met him in the other world with the look he wore on
earth. All the etchings and their copies give a characteristic presentation of the spiritual precursor of
Luther, who pricked the false image with his rapier
which the sturdy monk slashed with his broadsword.
What a face it is which Hans Holbein has handed
down to us in this wonderful portrait at Longford Castle! How dry it is with scholastic labor, how keen
with shrewd scepticism, how worldly-wise, how conscious of its owner's wide-awake sagacity! Erasmus
and Rabelais, — Nature used up all her arrows for
their quivers, and had to wait a hundred years and
more before she could find shafts enough for the outfit of Voltaire, leaner and keener than Erasmus, and
almost as free in his language as the audacious creator
of Gargantua and Pantagruel.

I have not generally given descriptions of the curious objects which I saw in the great houses and museums which I visited. There is, however, a work of
art at Longford Castle so remarkable that I must
speak of it. I was so much struck by the enormous
amount of skilful ingenuity and exquisite workman-
ship bestowed upon it that I looked up its history,
which I found in the "Beauties of England and
Wales." This is what is there said of the wonderful
steel chair: "It was made by Thomas Rukers at the
city of Augsburgh, in the year 1575, and consists of
more than 130 compartments, all occupied by groups
of figures representing a succession of events in the
annals of the Roman Empire, from the landing of
Æneas to the reign of Rodolphus the Second." It

looks as if a life had gone into the making of it, as a
pair or two of eyes go to the working of the bridal
veil of an empress.

Fifty years ago and more, when I was at Longford
Castle with my two companions, who are no more
with us, we found there a pleasant, motherly old housekeeper, or attendant of some kind, who gave us a
draught of home-made ale and left a cheerful remembrance with us, as, I need hardly say, we did with
her, in a materialized expression of our good-will. It
always rubbed very hard on my feelings to offer money
to any persons who had served me well, as if they
were doing it for their own pleasure. It may have
been the granddaughter of the kindly old matron of
the year 1833 who showed us round, and possibly, if
I had sunk a shaft of inquiry, I might have struck a
well of sentiment. But

"Take, O boatman, thrice thy fee,"

carried into practical life, is certain in its financial
result to the subject of the emotional impulse, but is
less sure to call forth a tender feeling in the recipient.
One will hardly find it worth while to go through the
world weeping over his old recollections, and paying
gold instead of silver and silver instead of copper to
astonished boatmen and bewildered chambermaids.

On Sunday, the 18th of July, we attended morning
service at the cathedral. The congregation was not
proportioned to the size of the great edifice. These
vast places of worship were built for ages when faith
was the rule and questioning the exception. I will
not say that faith has grown cold, but it has cooled
from white heat to cherry red or a still less flaming
color. As to church attendance, I have heard the

saying attributed to a great statesman, that "once a day is Orthodox, but twice a day is Puritan." No doubt many of the same class of people that used to fill the churches stay at home and read about evolution or telepathy, or whatever new gospel they may have got hold of. Still the English seem to me a religious people; they have leisure enough to say grace and give thanks before and after meals, and their institutions tend to keep alive the feelings of reverence which cannot be said to be distinctive of our own people.

In coming out of the cathedral, on the Sunday I just mentioned, a gentleman addressed me as a fellow-countryman. There is something, — I will not stop now to try and define it, — but there is something by which we recognize an American among the English before he speaks and betrays his origin. Our new friend proved to be the president of one of our American colleges; an intelligent and well-instructed gentleman, of course. By the invitation of our host he came in to visit us in the evening, and made himself very welcome by his agreeable conversation.

I took great delight in wandering about the old town of Salisbury. There are no such surprises in our oldest places as one finds in Chester, or Tewkesbury, or Stratford, or Salisbury; and I have no doubt in scores or hundreds of similar places which I have never visited. The best substitute for such rambles as one can take through these mouldy boroughs (or burrows) is to be found in such towns as Salem, Newburyport, Portsmouth. Without imagination, Shakespeare's birthplace is but a queer old house, and Anne Hathaway's home a tumble-down cottage. With it, one can see the witches of Salem Village sailing out of those little square windows, which look as if they were made on purpose for them, or stroll down to Derby's wharf and gaze at "Cleopatra's Barge," precursor of the yachts of the Astors and Goulds and Vanderbilts, as she comes swimming into the harbor in all her gilded glory. But it must make a difference what the imagination has to work upon, and I do not at all wonder that Mr. Ruskin would not wish to live in a land where there are no old ruins of castles and monasteries. Man will not live on bread only; he wants a great deal more, if he can get it, — frosted cake as well as corn-bread; and the New World keeps the imagination on plain and scanty diet, compared to the rich traditional and historic food which furnishes the banquets of the Old World.

What memories that week in Salisbury and the excursions from it have left in my mind's picture gallery! The spire of the great cathedral had been with me as a frequent presence during the last fifty years of my life, and this second visit has deepened every line of the impression, as Old Mortality refreshed the inscriptions on the tombstones of the Covenanters. I find that all these pictures which I have brought home with me to look at, with

> " that inward eye
> Which is the bliss of solitude,"

are becoming clearer and brighter as the excitement of overcrowded days and weeks gradually calms down. I can *be* in those places where I passed days and nights, and became habituated to the sight of the cathedral, or of the Church of the Holy Trinity, at morning, at noon, at evening, whenever I turned my eyes in its direction. I often close my eyelids, and startle my household by saying, "Now I am in Salis-

bury," or "Now I am in Stratford." It is a blessed
thing to be able, in the twilight of years, to illuminate
the soul with such visions. The Charles, which flows
beneath my windows, which I look upon between the
words of the sentence I am now writing, only turning
my head as I sit at my table, — the Charles is hardly
more real to me than Shakespeare's Avon, since I
floated on its still waters, or strayed along its banks
and saw the cows reflected in the smooth expanse,
their legs upward, as if they were walking the skies as
the flies walk the ceiling. Salisbury Cathedral stands
as substantial in my thought as our own King's
Chapel, since I slumbered by its side, and arose in
the morning to find it still there, and not one of those
unsubstantial fabrics built by the architect of dreams.

On Thursday, the 22d of July, we left Salisbury
for Brighton, where we were to be guests at Arnold
House, the residence of our kind host. Here we
passed another delightful week, with everything around
us to contribute to our quiet comfort and happiness.
The most thoughtful of entertainers, a house filled with
choice works of art, fine paintings, and wonderful pot-
tery, pleasant walks and drives, a visitor now and
then, Mr. and Mrs. Goldwin Smith among the number, rest and peace in a magnificent city built for
enjoyment, — what more could we have asked to make
our visit memorable? Many watering-places look forlorn and desolate in the intervals of "the season."
This was not the time of Brighton's influx of visitors,
but the city was far from dull. The houses are very
large, and have the grand air, as if meant for princes;
the shops are well supplied; the salt breeze comes in
fresh and wholesome, and the noble esplanade is lively

with promenaders and Bath chairs, some of them occupied by people evidently ill or presumably lame, some,
I suspect, employed by healthy invalids who are too
lazy to walk. I took one myself, drawn by an old
man, to see how I liked it, and found it very convenient, but I was tempted to ask him to change places
and let me drag him.

With the aid of the guide-book I could describe the
wonders of the pavilion and the various changes which
have come over the great watering-place. The grand
walks, the two piers, the aquarium, and all the great
sights which are shown to strangers deserve full attention from the tourist who writes for other travellers,
but none of these things seem to me so interesting as
what we saw and heard in a little hamlet which has
never, so far as I know, been vulgarized by sight-
seers. We drove in an open carriage, — Mr. and
Mrs. Willett, A——, and myself, — into the country, which soon became bare, sparsely settled, a long
succession of rounded hills and hollows. These are
the South Downs, from which comes the famous mutton known all over England, not unknown at the
table of our Saturday Club and other well-spread
boards. After a drive of ten miles or more we arrived
at a little "settlement," as we Americans would call
it, and drove up to the door of a modest parsonage,
where dwells the shepherd of the South Down flock of
Christian worshippers. I hope that the good clergyman, if he ever happens to see what I am writing, will
pardon me for making mention of his hidden retreat,
which he himself speaks of as "one of the remoter
nooks of the old country." Nothing I saw in England
brought to my mind Goldsmith's picture of "the man
to all the country dear," and his surroundings, like

this visit. The church dates, if I remember right, from the thirteenth century. Some of its stones show marks, as it is thought, of having belonged to a Saxon edifice. The massive leaden font is of a very great antiquity. In the wall of the church is a narrow opening, at which the priest is supposed to have sat and listened to the confession of the sinner on the outside of the building. The dead lie all around the church, under stones bearing the dates of several centuries. One epitaph, which the unlettered Muse must have dictated, is worth recording. After giving the chief slumberer's name the epitaph adds, —

"Here lies on either side, the remains of each of his former wives."

Those of a third have found a resting-place close by, behind him.

It seemed to me that Mr. Bunner's young man in search of Arcady might look for it here with as good a chance of being satisfied as anywhere I can think of. But I suppose that men and women and especially boys, would prove to be a good deal like the rest of the world, if one lived here long enough to learn all about them. One thing I can safely say, — an English man or boy never goes anywhere without his fists. I saw a boy of ten or twelve years, whose pleasant face attracted my attention. I said to the rector, "That is a fine-looking little fellow, and I should think an intelligent and amiable kind of boy." "Yes," he said, "yes; he can strike from the shoulder pretty well, too. I had to stop him the other day, indulging in that exercise." Well, I said to myself, we have not yet reached the heaven on earth which I was fancying might be embosomed in this peaceful looking hollow. Youthful angels can hardly be in the habit of striking from the shoulder. But the well-known phrase, belonging to the pugilist rather than to the priest, brought me back from the ideal world into which my imagination had wandered.

Our week at Brighton was passed in a very quiet but most enjoyable way. It could not be otherwise with such a host and hostess, always arranging everything with reference to our well-being and in accordance with our wishes. I became very fond of the esplanade, such a public walk as I never saw anything to compare with. In these tranquil days, and long, honest nights of sleep, the fatigues of what we had been through were forgotten, the scales showed that we were becoming less ethereal every day, and we were ready for another move.

We bade good-by to our hosts with the most grateful and the warmest feeling towards them, after a month of delightful companionship and the experience of a hospitality almost too generous to accept, but which they were pleased to look upon as if we were doing them a favor.

On the 29th of July we found ourselves once more in London.

VI.

We found our old quarters all ready and awaiting us. Mrs. Mackellar's motherly smile, Sam's civil bow, and the rosy cheeks of many-buttoned Robert made us feel at home as soon as we crossed the threshold.

The dissolution of Parliament had brought "the season" abruptly to an end. London was empty. There were three or four millions of people in it, but the great houses were for the most part left without occupants except their liveried guardians. We kept as quiet as possible, to avoid all engagements. For now we were in London for London itself, to do shopping, to see sights, to be our own master and mistress, and to live as independent a life as we possibly could.

The first thing we did on the day of our arrival was to take a hansom and drive over to Chelsea, to look at the place where Carlyle passed the larger part of his life. The whole region about him must have been greatly changed during his residence there, for the Thames Embankment was constructed long after he removed to Chelsea. We had some little difficulty in finding the place we were in search of. Cheyne (pronounced "Chainie") Walk is a somewhat extended range of buildings. Cheyne Row is a passage which reminded me a little of my old habitat, Montgomery Place, now Bosworth Street. Presently our attention was drawn to a marble medallion portrait on the corner building of an ordinary-looking row of houses. This was the head of Carlyle, and an inscription informed us that he lived for forty-seven years in the house No. 24 of this row of buildings. Since Carlyle's home life has been made public, he has appeared to us in a different aspect from the ideal one which he had before occupied. He did not show to as much advantage under the Boswellizing process as the dogmatist of the last century, dear old Dr. Johnson. But he remains not the less one of the really interesting men of his generation, a man about whom we wish to know all that we have a right to know.

The sight of an old nest over which two or three winters have passed is a rather saddening one. The dingy three-story brick house in which Carlyle lived, one in a block of similar houses, was far from attractive. It was untenanted, neglected; its windows were unwashed, a pane of glass was broken; its threshold appeared untrodden, its whole aspect forlorn and desolate. Yet there it stood before me, all covered with its associations as an ivy-clad tower with its foliage. I wanted to see its interior, but it looked as if it did not expect a tenant and would not welcome a visitor. Was there nothing but this forbidding house-front to make the place alive with some breathing memory? I saw crossing the street a middle-aged woman, — a decent body, who looked as if she might have come from the lower level of some not opulent but respectable household. She might have some recollection of an old man who was once her neighbor. I asked her if she remembered Mr. Carlyle. Indeed she did, she told us. She used to see him often, in front of his house, putting bits of bread on the railing for the birds. He did not like to see anything wasted, she said. The merest scrap of information, but genuine and pleasing; an instantaneous photograph only, but it makes a pretty vignette in the volume of my reminiscences. There are many considerable men in every generation of mankind, but not a great number who are personally interesting, — not a great many of whom we feel that we cannot know too much; whose foibles, even, we care to know about; whose shortcomings we try to excuse; who are not models, but whose special traits make them attractive. Carlyle is one of these few, and no revelations can prevent his interesting us. He was not quite finished in his parental existence. The bricklayer's mortar of his father's calling stuck to his fingers through life, but only as

the soil he turned with his ploughshare clung to the
fingers of Burns.   We do not wish either to have been
other than what he was.   Their breeding brings them
to the average level, carries them more nearly to the
heart, makes them a simpler expression of our common humanity.   As we rolled in the cars by Ecclefechan, I strained my eyes to take in every point of the
landscape, every cottage, every spire, if by any chance
I could find one in that lonely region.   There was not
a bridge nor a bit of masonry of any kind that I did
not eagerly scrutinize, to see if it were solid and honest enough to have been built by Carlyle's father.
Solitary enough the country looked.   I admired Mr.
Emerson's devotion in seeking his friend in his bare
home among what he describes as the "desolate heath-
ery hills" about Craigenputtock, which were, I suppose, much like the region through which we were
passing.

It is one of the regrets of my life that I never saw
or heard Carlyle.   Nature, who seems to be fond of
trios, has given us three dogmatists, all of whom
greatly interested their own generation, and whose
personality, especially in the case of the first and the
last of the trio, still interests us, — Johnson, Coleridge, and Carlyle.   Each was an oracle in his way,
but unfortunately oracles are fallible to their descendants.   The author of "Taxation no Tyranny" had
wholesale opinions, and pretty harsh ones, about us
Americans, and did not soften them in expression:
"Sir, they are a race of convicts, and ought to be
thankful for anything we allow them short of hanging."   We smile complacently when we read this out-
burst, which Mr. Croker calls in question, but which
agrees with his saying in the presence of Miss Seward,

"I am willing to love all mankind *except an American.*"

A generation or two later comes along Coleridge, with his circle of reverential listeners. He says of Johnson that his fame rests principally upon Boswell, and that "his *bow-wow* manner must have had a good deal to do with the effect produced." As to Coleridge himself, his contemporaries hardly know how to set bounds to their exaltation of his genius. Dibdin comes pretty near going into rhetorical hysterics in reporting a conversation of Coleridge's to which he listened: "The auditors seemed to be wrapt in wonder and delight, as one observation more profound, or clothed in more forcible language, than another fell from his tongue. . . . As I retired homeward I thought a SECOND JOHNSON had visited the earth to make wise the sons of men." And De Quincey speaks of him as "the largest and most spacious intellect, the subtlest and most comprehensive, in my judgment, that has yet existed amongst men." One is sometimes tempted to wish that the superlative could be abolished, or its use allowed only to old experts. What are men to do when they get to heaven, after having exhausted their vocabulary of admiration on earth?

Now let us come down to Carlyle, and see what he says of Coleridge. We need not take those conversational utterances which called down the wrath of Mr. Swinburne, and found expression in an epigram which violates all the proprieties of literary language. Look at the full-length portrait in the Life of Sterling. Each oracle denies his predecessor, each magician breaks the wand of the one who went before him. There were Americans enough ready to swear by Car-

lyle until he broke his staff in meddling with our anti-
slavery conflict, and buried it so many fathoms deep
that it could never be fished out again. It' is rather
singular that Johnson and Carlyle should each of them
have shipwrecked his sagacity and shown a terrible
leak in his moral sensibilities on coming in contact
with American rocks and currents, with which neither
had any special occasion to concern himself, and which
both had a great deal better have steered clear of.

But here I stand once more before the home of the
long-suffering, much-laboring, loud-complaining Heraclitus of his time, whose very smile had a grimness
in it more ominous than his scowl. Poor man! Dys-
peptic on a diet of oatmeal porridge; kept wide awake
by crowing cocks; drummed out of his wits by long-
continued piano-pounding; sharp of speech, I fear, to
his high-strung wife, who gave him back as good as
she got! I hope I am mistaken about their every-
day relations, but again I say, poor man! — for all his
complaining must have meant real discomfort, which
a man of genius feels not less, certainly, than a common mortal.

I made a second visit to the place where he lived,
but I saw nothing more than at the first. I wanted
to cross the threshold over which he walked so often, to
see the noise-proof room in which he used to write, to
look at the chimney-place down which the soot came,
to sit where he used to sit and smoke his pipe, and to
conjure up his wraith to look in once more upon his old
deserted dwelling. That vision was denied me.

After visiting Chelsea we drove round through
Regent's Park. I suppose that if we use the superlative in speaking of Hyde Park, Regent's Park will be
the comparative, and Battersea Park the positive,

ranking them in the descending grades of their hie-
rarchy. But this is my conjecture only, and the social
geography of London is a subject which only one who
has become familiarly acquainted with the place should
speak of with any confidence. A stranger coming to
our city might think it made little difference whether
his travelling Boston acquaintance lived in Alpha
Avenue or in Omega Square, but he would have to
learn that it is farther from one of these places to the
other, a great deal farther, than it is from Beacon
Street, Boston, to Fifth Avenue, New York.

An American finds it a little galling to be told that
he must not drive in his *numbered* hansom or four-
wheeler except in certain portions of Hyde Park. If
he is rich enough to keep his own carriage, or if he
will pay the extra price of a vehicle not vulgarized by
being on the numbered list, he may drive anywhere
that his Grace or his Lordship does, and perhaps have
a mean sense of satisfaction at finding himself in the
charmed circle of exclusive "gigmanity." It is a
pleasure to meet none but well-dressed and well-man-
nered people, in well-appointed equipages. In the
high road of our own country, one is liable to fall in
with people and conveyances that it is far from a
pleasure to meet. I was once driving in an open carriage, with members of my family, towards my own
house in the country town where I was then living.
A cart drawn by oxen was in the road in front of us.
Whenever we tried to pass, the men in it turned
obliquely across the road and prevented us, and this
was repeated again and again. I could have wished I
had been driving in Hyde Park, where clowns and
boors, with their carts and oxen, do not find admit-
tance. Exclusiveness has its conveniences.

The next day, as I was strolling through Burlington Arcade, I saw a figure just before me which I recognized as that of my townsman, Mr. Abbott Lawrence. He was accompanied by his son, who had just returned from a trip round the planet. There are three grades of recognition, entirely distinct from each other: the meeting of two persons of different countries who speak the same language, — an American and an Englishman, for instance; the meeting of two Americans from different cities, as of a Bostonian and a New Yorker or a Chicagonian; and the meeting of two from the same city, as of two Bostonians.

The difference of these recognitions may be illustrated by supposing certain travelling philosophical instruments, endowed with intelligence and the power of speech, to come together in their wanderings, — let us say in a restaurant of the Palais Royal. "Very hot," says the talking Fahrenheit (Thermometer) from Boston, and calls for an ice, which he plunges his bulb into and cools down. In comes an intelligent and socially disposed English Barometer. The two travellers greet each other, not exactly as old acquaintances, but each has heard very frequently about the other, and their relatives have been often associated. "We have a good deal in common," says the Barometer. "Of the same blood, as we may say; quicksilver is thicker than water." "Yes," says the little Fahrenheit, "and we are both of the same mercurial temperament." While their columns are dancing up and down with laughter at this somewhat tepid and low-pressure pleasantry, there come in a New York Réaumur and a Centigrade from Chicago. The Fahrenheit, which has got warmed up to *temperate*, rises to *summer heat*, and even a little above it. They enjoy each other's company mightily. To be sure, their scales differ, but have they not the same freezing and the same boiling point? To be sure, each thinks his own scale is the true standard, and at home they might get into a contest about the matter, but here in a strange land they do not think of disputing. Now, while they are talking about America and their own local atmosphere and temperature, there comes in a second Boston Fahrenheit. The two of the same name look at each other for a moment, and rush together so eagerly that their bulbs are endangered. How well they understand each other! Thirty-two degrees marks the freezing point. Two hundred and twelve marks the boiling point. They have the same scale, the same fixed points, the same record: no wonder they prefer each other's company!

I hope that my reader has followed my illustration, and finished it off for himself. Let me give a few practical examples. An American and an Englishman meet in a foreign land. The Englishman has occasion to mention his weight, which he finds has gained in the course of his travels. "How much is it now?" asks the American. "Fourteen stone. How much do you weigh?" "Within four pounds of two hundred." Neither of them takes at once any clear idea of what the other weighs. The American has never thought of his own, or his friends', or anybody's weight in *stones* of fourteen pounds. The Englishman has never thought of any one's weight in *pounds*. They can calculate very easily with a slip of paper and a pencil, but not the less is their language but half intelligible as they speak and listen. The same thing is in a measure true of other matters they talk about. "It is about as large a space as the Common," says the Boston man. "It is as large as St. James's Park," says the Londoner. "As high as the State House," says the Bostonian, or "as tall as Bunker Hill Monument," or "about as big as the Frog Pond," where the Londoner would take St. Paul's, the Nelson Column, the Serpentine, as his standard of comparison. The difference of scale does not stop here; it runs through a great part of the objects of thought and conversation. An average American and an average Englishman are talking together, and one of them speaks of the beauty of a field of corn. They are thinking of two entirely different objects: one of a billowy level of soft waving wheat, or rye, or barley; the other of a rustling forest of tall, jointed stalks, tossing their plumes and showing their silken epaulettes, as if every stem in the ordered ranks were a soldier in full regimentals. An Englishman planted for the first time in the middle of a well-grown field of Indian corn would feel as much lost as the babes in the wood. Conversation between two Londoners, two New Yorkers, two Bostonians, requires no foot-notes, which is a great advantage in their intercourse.

To return from my digression and my illustration. I did not do a great deal of shopping myself while in London, being contented to have it done for me. But in the way of looking in at shop windows I did a very large business. Certain windows attracted me by a variety in unity which surpassed anything I have been accustomed to. Thus one window showed every conceivable convenience that could be shaped in ivory, and nothing else. One shop had such a display of magnificent dressing-cases that I should have thought a whole royal family was setting out on its travels. I see the cost of one of them is two hundred and seventy guineas. Thirteen hundred and fifty dollars seems a good deal to pay for a dressing-case.

On the other hand, some of the first-class tradesmen and workmen make no show whatever. The tailor to whom I had credentials, and who proved highly satis= factory to me, as he had proved to some of my country=men and to Englishmen of high estate, had only one small sign, which was placed in one of his windows, and received his customers in a small room that would have made a closet for one of our stylish merchant tail-ors. The bootmaker to whom I went on good recom-mendation had hardly anything about his premises to remind one of his calling. He came into his studio, took my measure very carefully, and made me a pair of what we call Congress boots, which fitted well when once on my feet, but which it cost more trouble to get into and to get out of than I could express my feelings about without dangerously enlarging my limited vocab-ulary.

Bond Street, Old and New, offered the most invit-ing windows, and I indulged almost to profligacy in the prolonged inspection of their contents. Stretching my walk along New Bond Street till I came to a great intersecting thoroughfare, I found myself in Oxford Street. Here the character of the shop windows changed at once. Utility and convenience took the place of show and splendor. Here I found various articles of use in a household, some of which were new to me. It is very likely that I could have found most of them in our own Boston Cornhill, but one often overlooks things at home which at once arrest his atten-tion when he sees them in a strange place. I saw great numbers of illuminating contrivances, some of which pleased me by their arrangement of reflectors.

Bryant and May's safety matches seemed to be used everywhere. I procured some in Boston with these names on the box, but the label said they were made in Sweden, and they diffused vapors that were enough to produce asphyxia. I greatly admired some of Dr. Dresser's water-cans and other contrivances, modelled more or less after the antique, but I found an abundant assortment of them here in Boston, and I have one I obtained here more original in design and more serviceable in daily use than any I saw in London. I should have regarded Wolverhampton, as we glided through it, with more interest, if I had known at that time that the inventive Dr. Dresser had his headquarters in that busy-looking town.

One thing, at least, I learned from my London experience: better a small city where one knows all it has to offer, than a great city where one has no disinterested friend to direct him to the right places to find what he wants. But of course there are some grand magazines which are known all the world over, and which no one should leave London without entering as a looker-on, if not as a purchaser.

There was one place I determined to visit, and one man I meant to see, before returning. The place was a certain book-store or book-shop, and the person was its proprietor, Mr. Bernard Quaritch. I was getting very much pressed for time, and I allowed ten minutes only for my visit. I never had any dealings with Mr. Quaritch, but one of my near relatives had, and I had often received his catalogues, the scale of prices in which had given me an impression almost of sublimity. I found Mr. Bernard Quaritch at No. 15 Piccadilly, and introduced myself, not as one whose name he must know, but rather as a stranger, of whom he might have heard through my relative. The extensive literature of catalogues is probably little known to most of my readers. I do not pretend to claim a thorough acquaintance with it, but I know the luxury of reading good catalogues, and such are those of Mr. Quaritch. I should like to deal with him; for if he wants a handsome price for what he sells, he knows its value, and does not offer the refuse of old libraries, but, on the other hand, all that is most precious in them is pretty sure to pass through his hands, sooner or later.

"Now, Mr. Quaritch," I said, after introducing myself, "I have ten minutes to pass with you. You must not open a book; if you do I am lost, for I shall have to look at every illuminated capital, from the first leaf to the colophon." Mr. Quaritch did not open a single book, but let me look round his establishment, and answered my questions very courteously. It so happened that while I was there a gentleman came in whom I had previously met, — my namesake, Mr. Holmes, the Queen's librarian at Windsor Castle. My ten minutes passed very rapidly in conversation with these two experts in books, the bibliopole and the bibliothecary. No place that I visited made me feel more thoroughly that I was in London, the great central mart of all that is most precious in the world.

Leave at home all your guineas, ye who enter here, would be a good motto to put over his door, unless you have them in plenty and can spare them, in which case *Take all your guineas with you* would be a better one. For you can here get their equivalent, and more than their equivalent, in the choicest products of the press and the finest work of the illuminator, the illustrator, and the binder. You will be sorely tempted. But do not be surprised when you ask the price of the vol-

ume you may happen to fancy. You are not dealing
with a *bouquiniste* of the Quais, in Paris. You are
not foraging in an old book-shop of New York or Boston. Do not suppose that I undervalue these dealers
in old and rare volumes. Many a much-prized rarity
have I obtained from Drake and Burnham and others
of my townsmen, and from Denham in New York;
and in my student years many a choice volume, sometimes even an Aldus or an Elzevir, have I found
among the trumpery spread out on the parapets of the
quays. But there is a difference between going out
on the Fourth of July with a militia musket to shoot
any catbird or "chipmunk" that turns up in a piece
of woods within a few miles of our own cities, and
shooting partridges in a nobleman's preserves on the
First of September. I confess to having felt a certain
awe on entering the precincts made sacred by their
precious contents. The lord and master of so many
Editiones Principes, the guardian of this great nursery full of *incunabula*, did not seem to me like a simple tradesman. I felt that I was in the presence of
the literary purveyor of royal and imperial libraries,
the man before whom millionaires tremble as they calculate, and billionaires pause and consider. I have
recently received two of Mr. Quaritch's catalogues,
from which I will give my reader an extract or two,
to show him what kind of articles this prince of biblio-
poles deals in.

Perhaps you would like one of those romances which
turned the head of Don Quixote. Here is a volume
which will be sure to please you. It is on one of his
lesser lists, confined principally to Spanish and Portuguese works: —

"Amadis de Gaula . . . folio, gothic letter, FIRST

EDITION, unique . . . red morocco super extra, *doublé* with olive morocco, richly gilt, tooled to an elegant Grolier design, gilt edges . . . in a neat case."

A pretty present for a scholarly friend. A nice old book to carry home for one's own library. Two hundred pounds — one thousand dollars — will make you the happy owner of this volume.

But if you would have also on your shelves the first edition of the "Cronica del famoso cabaluero cid Ruy Diaz Campadero," not "richly gilt," not even bound in leather, but in "cloth boards," you will have to pay two hundred and ten pounds to become its proprietor. After this you will not be frightened by the thought of paying three hundred dollars for a little quarto giving an account of the Virginia Adventurers. You will not shrink from the idea of giving something more than a hundred guineas for a series of Hogarth's plates. But when it comes to Number 1001 in the May catalogue, and you see that if you would possess a first folio Shakespeare, "untouched by the hand of any modern renovator," you must be prepared to pay seven hundred and eighty-five pounds, almost four thousand dollars, for the volume, it would not be surprising if you changed color and your knees shook under you. No doubt some brave man will be found to carry off that prize, in spite of the golden battery which defends it, perhaps to Cincinnati, or Chicago, or San Francisco. But do not be frightened. These Alpine heights of extravagance climb up from the humble valley where shillings and sixpences are all that are required to make you a purchaser.

One beauty of the Old World shops is that if a visitor comes back to the place where he left them fifty years before, he finds them, or has a great chance of finding them, just where they stood at his former visit. In driving down to the old city, to the place of business of the Barings, I found many streets little changed. Temple Bar was gone, and the much-abused griffin stood in its place. There was a shop close to Temple Bar, where, in 1834, I had bought some brushes. I had no difficulty in finding Prout's, and I could not do less than go in and buy some more brushes. I did not ask the young man who served me how the old shopkeeper who attended to my wants on the earlier occasion was at this time. But I thought what a different color the locks these brushes smooth show from those that knew their predecessors in the earlier decade!

I ought to have made a second visit to the Tower, so tenderly spoken of by Artemus Ward as "a sweet boon," so vividly remembered by me as the scene of a personal encounter with one of the animals then kept in the Tower menagerie. But the project added a stone to the floor of the underground thoroughfare which is paved with good intentions.

St. Paul's I must and did visit. The most striking addition since I was there is the massive monument to the Duke of Wellington. The great temple looked rather bare and unsympathetic. Poor Dr. Johnson, sitting in semi-nude exposure, looked to me as unhappy as our own half-naked Washington at the national capital. The Judas of Matthew Arnold's poem would have cast his cloak over those marble shoulders, if he had found himself in St. Paul's, and have earned another respite. We brought away little, I fear, except the grand effect of the dome as we looked up at it. It gives us a greater idea of height than the sky itself, which we have become used to looking upon.

A second visit to the National Gallery was made in company with A——. It was the repetition of an attempt at a draught from the Cup of Tantalus. I was glad of a sight of the Botticellis, of which I had heard so much, and others of the more recently acquired paintings of the great masters; of a sweeping glance at the Turners; of a look at the well-remembered Hogarths and the memorable portraits by Sir Joshua. I carried away a confused mass of impressions, much as the soldiers that sack a city go off with all the precious things they can snatch up, huddled into clothes-bags and pillow-cases. I am reminded, too, of Mr. Galton's composite portraits; a thousand glimpses, as one passes through the long halls lined with paintings, all blending in one not unpleasing general effect, out of which emerges from time to time some single distinct image.

In the same way we passed through the exhibition of paintings at the Royal Academy. I noticed that A—— paid special attention to the portraits of young ladies by John Sargent and by Collier, while I was more particularly struck with the startling portrait of an ancient personage in a full suit of wrinkles, such as Rembrandt used to bring out with wonderful effect. Hunting in couples is curious and instructive; the scent for this or that kind of game is sure to be very different in the two individuals.

I made but two brief visits to the British Museum, and I can easily instruct my reader so that he will have no difficulty, if he will follow my teaching, in learning how not to see it. When he has a spare hour at his disposal, let him drop in at the Museum, and wander among its books and its various collections. He will know as much about it as the fly that buzzes in at one window and out at another. If I were asked whether I brought away anything from my two visits, I should say, Certainly I did. The fly sees some things, not very intelligently, but he cannot help seeing them. The great round reading-room, with its silent students, impressed me very much. I looked at once for the Elgin Marbles, but casts and photographs and engravings had made me familiar with their chief features. I thought I knew something of the sculptures brought from Nineveh, but I was astonished, almost awe-struck, at the sight of those mighty images which mingled with the visions of the Hebrew prophets. I did not marvel more at the skill and labor expended upon them by the Assyrian artists than I did at the enterprise and audacity which had brought them safely from the mounds under which they were buried to the light of day and the heart of a great modern city. I never thought that I should live to see the Birs Nimroud laid open, and the tablets in which the history of Nebuchadnezzar was recorded spread before me. The Empire of the Spade in the world of history was founded at Nineveh by Layard, a great province added to it by Schliemann, and its boundary extended by numerous explorers, some of whom are diligently at work at the present day. I feel very grateful that many of its revelations have been made since I have been a tenant of the travelling residence which holds so many secrets in its recesses.

There is one lesson to be got from a visit of an hour or two to the British Museum, — namely, the fathomless abyss of our own ignorance. One is almost ashamed of his little paltry heartbeats in the presence of the rushing and roaring torrent of Niagara. So if he has published a little book or two, collected a few

fossils, or coins, or vases, he is crushed by the vast-
ness of the treasures in the library and the collections
of this universe of knowledge.

I have shown how not to see the British museum;
I will tell how to see it.

Take lodgings next door to it, — in a garret, if you
cannot afford anything better, — and pass all your
days at the Museum during the whole period of your
natural life. At threescore and ten you will have
some faint conception of the contents, significance, and
value of this great British institution, which is as
nearly as any one spot the *nœud vital* of human civilization, a stab at which by the dagger of anarchy would
fitly begin the reign of chaos.

On the 3d of August, a gentleman, Mr. Wedmore,
who had promised to be my guide to certain interesting localities, called for me, and we took a hansom
for the old city. The first place we visited was the
Temple, a collection of buildings with intricate passages between them, some of the edifices reminding
me of our college dormitories. One, however, was a
most extraordinary exception, — the wonderful Temple
church, or rather the ancient part of it which is left,
the round temple. We had some trouble to get into
it, but at last succeeded in finding a slip of a girl, the
daughter of the janitor, who unlocked the door for us.
It affected my imagination strangely to see this girl
of a dozen years old, or thereabouts, moving round
among the monuments which had kept their place
there for some six or seven hundred years; for the
church was built in the year 1185, and the most recent
of the crusaders' monuments is said to date as far
back as 1241. Their effigies have lain in this vast
city, and passed unharmed through all its convulsions.

The Great Fire must have crackled very loud in their stony ears, and they must have shaken day and night, as the bodies of the victims of the Plague were rattled over the pavements.

Near the Temple church, in a green spot among the buildings, a plain stone laid flat on the turf bears these words: "Here lies Oliver Goldsmith." I believe doubt has been thrown upon the statement that Goldsmith was buried in that place, but, as some poet ought to have written,

> Where doubt is disenchantment
> 'T is wisdom to believe.

We do not "drop a tear" so often as our Della Cruscan predecessors, but the memory of the author of the "Vicar of Wakefield" stirred my feelings more than a whole army of crusaders would have done. A pretty rough set of filibusters they were, no doubt.

The whole group to which Goldsmith belonged came up before me, and as the centre of that group the great Dr. Johnson; not the Johnson of the "Rambler," or of "The Vanity of Human Wishes," or even of "Rasselas," but Boswell's Johnson, dear to all of us, the "Grand Old Man" of his time, whose foibles we care more for than for most great men's virtues. Fleet Street, which he loved so warmly, was close by. Bolt Court, entered from it, where he lived for many of his last years, and where he died, was the next place to visit. I found Fleet Street a good deal like Washington Street as I remember it in former years. When I came to the place pointed out as Bolt Court, I could hardly believe my eyes that so celebrated a place of residence should be entered by so humble a passageway. I was very sorry to find that No. 3, where he lived, was demolished, and a new building erected in its place. In one of the other houses in this court he is said to have labored on his dictionary. Near by was a building of mean aspect, in which Goldsmith is said to have at one time resided. But my kind conductor did not profess to be .well acquainted with the local antiquities of this quarter of London.

If I had a long future before me, I should like above all things to study London with a dark lantern, so to speak, myself in deepest shadow and all I wanted to see in clearest light. Then I should want time, time, time. For it is a sad fact that sight-seeing as commonly done is one of the most wearying things in the world, and takes the life out of any but the sturdiest or the most elastic natures more efficiently than would a reasonable amount of daily exercise on a treadmill. In my younger days I used to find that a visit to the gallery of the Louvre was followed by more fatigue and exhaustion than the same amount of time spent in walking the wards of a hospital.

Another grand sight there was, not to be overlooked, namely, the Colonial Exhibition. The popularity of this immense show was very great, and we found ourselves, A—— and I, in the midst of a vast throng, made up of respectable and comfortable looking people. It was not strange that the multitude flocked to this exhibition. There was a jungle, with its (stuffed) monsters, — tigers, serpents, elephants; there were carvings which may well have cost a life apiece, and stuffs which none but an empress or a millionairess would dare to look at. All the arts of the East were there in their perfection, and some of the artificers were at their work. We had to content ourselves with a mere look at all these wonders. It was a pity; instead of going to these fine shows tired, sleepy, wanting repose more than anything else, we should have come to them fresh, in good condition, and had many days at our disposal. I learned more in a visit to the Japanese exhibition in Boston than I should have learned in half a dozen half-awake strolls through this multitudinous and most imposing collection of all

> "The gorgeous East with richest hand
> Showers on her kings,"

and all the masterpieces of its wonder-working artisans.

One of the last visits we paid before leaving London for a week in Paris was to the South Kensington Museum. Think of the mockery of giving one hour to such a collection of works of art and wonders of all kinds! Why should I consider it worth while to say that we went there at all? All manner of objects succeeded each other in a long series of dissolving views, so to speak, nothing or next to nothing having a chance to leave its individual impress. In the battle for life which took place in my memory, as it always does among the multitude of claimants for a permanent hold, I find that two objects came out survivors of the contest. The first is the noble cast of the column of Trajan, vast in dimensions, crowded with history in its most striking and enduring form; a long array of figures representing in unquestioned realism the military aspect of a Roman army. The second case of survival is thus described in the catalogue: "An altar or shrine of a female saint, recently acquired from Padua, is also ascribed to the same sculptor [Donatello]. This very valuable work of art had for many years been used as a drinking-trough for horses. A hole has been roughly pierced in it." I thought the figure was the most nearly perfect image of heavenly womanhood that I had ever looked upon, and I could have gladly given my whole hour to sitting — I could almost say kneeling — before it in silent contemplation. I found the curator of the Museum, Mr. Soden Smith, shared my feelings with reference to the celestial loveliness of this figure. Which is best, to live in a country where such a work of art is taken for a horse-trough, or in a country where the products from the studio of a self-taught handicraftsman, equal to the shaping of a horse-trough and not much more, are put forward as works of art?

A little time before my visit to England, before I had even thought of it as a possibility, I had the honor of having two books dedicated to me by two English brother physicians One of these two gentlemen was Dr. Walshe, of whom I shall speak hereafter; the other was Dr. J. Milner Fothergill. The name Fothergill was familiar to me from my boyhood. My old townsman, Dr. Benjamin Waterhouse, who died in 1846 at the age of ninety-two, had a great deal to say about his relative Dr. John Fothergill, the famous Quaker physician of the last century, of whom Benjamin Franklin said, "I can hardly conceive that a better man ever existed." Dr. and Mrs. Fothergill sent us some beautiful flowers a little before we left, and when I visited him he gave me a medallion of his celebrated kinsman.

London is a place of mysteries. Looking out of one of the windows at the back of Dr. Fothergill's house, I saw an immense wooden blind, such as we have on our windows in summer, but reaching from the ground as high as the top of the neighboring houses. While admitting the air freely, it shut the property to which it belonged completely from sight. I asked the meaning of this extraordinary structure, and learned that it was put up by a great nobleman, of whose subterranean palace and strange seclusion I had before heard. Common report attributed his unwillingness to be seen to a disfiguring malady with which he was said to be afflicted. The story was that he was visible only to his valet. But a lady of quality, whom I met in this country, told me she had seen him, and observed nothing to justify it. These old countries are full of romances and legends and *diableries* of all sorts, in which truth and lies are so mixed that one does not know what to believe. What happens behind the high walls of the old cities is as much a secret as were the doings inside the prisons of the Inquisition.

Little mistakes sometimes cause us a deal of trouble. This time it was the presence or absence of a single letter which led us to fear that an important package destined to America had miscarried. There were two gentlemen unwittingly involved in the confusion. On inquiring for the package at Messrs. Low, the publishers, Mr. Watts, to whom I thought it had been consigned, was summoned. He knew nothing about it, had never heard of it, was evidently utterly ignorant of us and our affairs. While we were in trouble and uncertainty, our Boston friend, Mr. James R. Osgood, came in. "Oh," said he, "it is Mr. Watt you want, the agent of a Boston firm," and gave us the gentleman's address. I had confounded Mr. Watt's name with Mr. Watts's name. "W'at's in a name?" A great deal sometimes. I wonder if I shall be pardoned for quoting six lines from one of my after-dinner poems of long ago: —

— One vague inflection spoils the whole with doubt,
One trivial letter ruins all, left out ;

A knot can change a felon into clay,
A not will save him, spelt without the k ;
The smallest word has some unguarded spot,
And danger lurks in i without a dot.

I should find it hard to account for myself during
our two short stays in London in the month of August,
separated by the week we passed in Paris. The fer-
ment of continued over-excitement, calmed very much
by our rest in the various places I have mentioned,
had not yet wholly worked itself off. There was some
of that everlasting shopping to be done. There were
photographs to be taken, a call here and there to be
made, a stray visitor now and then, a walk in the
morning to get back the use of the limbs which had
been too little exercised, and a drive every afternoon
to one of the parks, or the Thames Embankment, or
other locality. After all this, an honest night's sleep
served to round out the day, in which little had been
effected besides making a few purchases, writing a
few letters, reading the papers, the Boston "Weekly
Advertiser" among the rest, and making arrangements for our passage homeward.

The sights we saw were looked upon for so short a
time, most of them so very superficially, that I am
almost ashamed to say that I have been in the midst
of them and brought home so little. I remind myself
of my boyish amusement of *skipping stones*, — throwing a flat stone so that it shall only touch the water,
but touch it in half a dozen places before it comes to
rest beneath the smooth surface. The drives we took
showed us a thousand objects which arrested our attention. Every street, every bridge, every building,
every monument, every strange vehicle, every exceptional personage, was a show which stimulated our

curiosity. For we had not as yet changed our Boston eyes for London ones, and very common sights were spectacular and dramatic to us. I remember that one of our New England country boys exclaimed, when he first saw a block of city dwellings, "Darn it all, who ever see anything like that 'are? Sich a lot o' haouser all stuck together!" I must explain that "haousen" used in my early days to be as common an expression in speaking of houses among our country-folk as its phonetic equivalent ever was in Saxony. I felt not unlike that country-boy.

In thinking of how much I missed seeing, I some- times have said to myself, "Oh, if the carpet of the story in the Arabian Nights would only take me up and carry me to London for one week, — just one short week, — setting me down fresh from quiet, wholesome living, in my usual good condition, and bringing me back at the end of it, what a different account I could give of my experiences! But it is just as well as it is. Younger eyes have studied and will study, more instructed travellers have pictured and will picture, the great metropolis from a hundred different points of view. No person can be said to know London. The most that any one can claim is that he knows something of it. I am now just going to leave it for another great capital, but in my con- cluding pages I shall return to Great Britain, and give some of the general impressions left by what I saw and heard in our mother country.

VII.

Straitened as we were for time, it was impossible to return home without a glimpse, at least, of Paris. Two precious years of my early manhood were spent there under the reign of Louis Philippe, king of the French, *le Roi Citoyen.* I felt that I must look once more on the places I knew so well, — once more before shutting myself up in the world of recollections. It is hardly necessary to say that a lady can always find a little shopping, and generally a good deal of it, to do in Paris. So it was not difficult to persuade my daughter that a short visit to that city was the next step to be taken.

We left London on the 5th of August to go *via* Folkestone and Boulogne. The passage across the Channel was a very smooth one, and neither of us suffered any inconvenience. Boulogne as seen from the landing did not show to great advantage. I fell to thinking of Brummel, and what a satisfaction it would have been to treat him to a good dinner, and set him talking about the days of the Regency. Boulogne was all Brummel in my associations, just as Calais was all Sterne. I find everywhere that it is a distinctive personality which makes me want to linger round a spot, more than an important historical event. There is not much worth remembering about Brummel; but his audacity, his starched neckcloth, his assumptions and their success, make him a curious subject for the student of human nature.

Leaving London at twenty minutes before ten in the forenoon, we arrived in Paris at six in the afternoon. I could not say that the region of France through which we passed was peculiarly attractive. I saw no fine trees, no pretty cottages, like those so common in England. There was little which an artist would be tempted to sketch, or a traveller by the railroad would be likely to remember.

The place where we had engaged lodgings was Hôtel d'Orient, in the Rue Daunou. The situation was convenient, very near the Place Vendôme and the Rue de la Paix. But the house was undergoing renovations which made it as unpresentable as a moulting fowl. Scrubbing, painting of blinds, and other perturbing processes did all they could to make it uncomfortable. The courtyard was always sloppy, and the whole condition of things reminded me forcibly of the state of Mr. Briggs's household while the mason was carrying out the complex operations which began with the application of "a little compo." (I hope all my readers remember Mr. Briggs, whose adventures as told by the pencil of John Leech are not unworthy of comparison with those of Mr. Pickwick as related by Dickens.) Barring these unfortunate conditions, the hotel was commendable, and when in order would be a desirable place of temporary residence.

It was the dead season of Paris, and everything had the air of suspended animation. The solitude of the Place Vendôme was something oppressive; I felt, as I trod its lonely sidewalk, as if I were wandering through Tadmor in the Desert. We were indeed as remote, as unfriended, — I will not say as melancholy or as slow, — as Goldsmith by the side of the lazy Scheldt or the wandering Po. Not a soul did either of us know in that great city. Our most intimate relations were with the people of the hotel and with the drivers of the fiacres. These last were a singular look-

ing race of beings. Many of them had a dull red complexion, almost brick color, which must have some
general cause. I questioned whether the red wine
could have something to do with it. They wore glazed
hats, and drove shabby vehicles for the most part;
their horses would not compare with those of the London hansom drivers, and they themselves were not generally inviting in aspect, though we met with no inci-
vility from any of them. One, I remember, was very
voluble, and over-explained everything, so that we
became afraid to ask him a question. They were fellow-creatures with whom one did not naturally enter
into active sympathy, and the principal point of interest about the fiacre and its arrangements was whether
the horse was fondest of trotting or of walking. In
one of our drives we made it a point to call upon our
Minister, Mr. McLane, but he was out of town. We
did not bring a single letter, but set off exactly as if
we were on a picnic.

While A—— and her attendant went about making
their purchases, I devoted myself to the sacred and
pleasing task of reviving old memories. One of the
first places I visited was the house I lived in as a student, which in my English friend's French was desig-
nated as "Noomero sankont sank Roo Monshure ler
Pranse." I had been told that the whole region there-
about had been transformed by the creation of a new
boulevard. I did not find it so. There was the house,
the lower part turned into a shop, but there were the
windows out of which I used to look along the Rue
Vaugirard, — au troisième the first year, au second
the second year. Why should I go mousing about the
place? What would the shopkeeper know about M.
Bertrand, my landlord of half a century ago; or his

first wife, to whose funeral I went; or his second, to whose bridal I was bidden?

I ought next to have gone to the hospital La Pitié, where I passed much of my time during those two years. But the people there would not know me, and my old master's name, Louis, is but a dim legend in the wards where he used to teach his faithful band of almost worshipping students. Besides, I have not been among hospital beds for many a year, and my sensibilities are almost as impressible as they were before daily habit had rendered them comparatively callous.

How strange it is to look down on one's venerated teachers, after climbing with the world's progress half a century above the level where we left them! The stethoscope was almost a novelty in those days. The microscope was never mentioned by any clinical instructor I listened to while a medical student. *Nous avons changé tout cela* is true of every generation in medicine, — changed oftentimes by improvement, sometimes by fashion or the pendulum-swing from one extreme to another.

On my way back from the hospital I used to stop at the beautiful little church St. Etienne du Mont, and that was one of the first places to which I drove after looking at my student-quarters. All was just as of old. The tapers were burning about the tomb of St. Genevieve. Samson, with the jawbone of the ass, still crouched and sweated, or looked as if he did, under the weight of the pulpit. One might question how well the preacher in the pulpit liked the suggestion of the figure beneath it. The sculptured screen and gallery, the exquisite spiral stairways, the carved figures about the organ, the tablets on the walls, — one in particular relating the fall of two young girls from the gallery, and their miraculous protection from injury, — all these images found their counterpart in my memory. I did not remember how very beautiful is the stained glass in the *charniers*, which must not be overlooked by visitors.

It is not far from St. Etienne du Mont to the Pan= theon. I cannot say that there is any odor of sanctity about this great temple, which has been consecrated, if I remember correctly, and, I will not say dese- crated, but secularized from time to time, according to the party which happened to be uppermost. I con- fess that I did not think of it chiefly as a sacred edi- fice, or as the resting-place, more or less secure, of the "*grands hommes*" to whom it is dedicated. I was thinking much more of Foucault's grand experiment, one of the most sublime visible demonstrations of a great physical fact in the records of science. The reader may not happen to remember it, and will like, perhaps, to be reminded of it. Foucault took advan- tage of the height of the dome, nearly three hundred feet, and had a heavy weight suspended by a wire from its loftiest point, forming an immense pendu- lum, — the longest, I suppose, ever constructed. Now a moving body tends to keep its original plane of movement, and so the great pendulum, being set swing- ing north and south, tended to keep on in the same direction. But the earth was moving under it, and as it rolled from west to east the plane running through the north and south poles was every instant changing. Thus the pendulum appeared to change its direction, and its deviation was shown on a graduated arc, or by the marks it left in a little heap of sand which it touched as it swung. This experiment on the great scale has since been repeated on the small scale by the aid of other contrivances.

My thoughts wandered back, naturally enough, to Galileo in the Cathedral at Pisa. It was the swinging of the suspended lamp in that edifice which set his mind working on the laws which govern the action of the pendulum. While he was meditating on this physical problem, the priest may have been holding forth on the dangers of meddling with matters settled by Holy Church, who stood ready to enforce her edicts by the logic of the rack and the fagot. An inference from the above remarks is that what one brings from a church depends very much on what he carries into it.

The next place to visit could be no other than the Café Procope. This famous resort is the most ancient and the most celebrated of all the Parisian cafés. Voltaire, the poet J. B. Rousseau, Marmontel, Sainte Foix, Saurin, were among its frequenters in the eighteenth century. It stands in the Rue des Fossés-Saint Germain, now Rue de l'Ancienne Comédie. Several American students, Bostonians and Philadelphians, myself among the number, used to breakfast at this café every morning. I have no doubt that I met various celebrities there, but I recall only one name which is likely to be known to most or many of my readers. A delicate-looking man, seated at one of the tables, was pointed out to me as Jouffroy. If I had known as much about him as I learned afterwards, I should have looked at him with more interest. He had one of those imaginative natures, tinged by constitutional melancholy and saddened by ill health, which belong to a certain class of poets and sentimental writers, of which Pascal is a good example, and Cowper another. The world must have seemed very cruel to him. I remember that when he was a candidate for the Assembly, one of the popular cries, as reported by the newspapers of the time, was *A bas le poitrinaire!* His malady soon laid him low enough, for he died in 1842, at the age of forty-six. I must have been very much taken up with my medical studies to have neglected my opportunity of seeing the great statesmen, authors, artists, orators, and men of science outside of the medical profession. Poisson, Arago, and Jouffroy are all I can distinctly recall, among the Frenchmen of eminence whom I had all around me.

The Café Procope has been much altered and improved, and bears an inscription telling the date of its establishment, which was in the year 1689. I entered the café, which was nearly or quite empty, the usual breakfast hour being past.

Garçon! Une tasse de café.

If there is a river of *mnēmē* as a counterpart of the river *lēthē*, my cup of coffee must have got its water from that stream of memory. If I could borrow that eloquence of Jouffroy which made his hearers turn pale, I might bring up before my readers a long array of pallid ghosts, whom these walls knew well in their earthly habiliments. Only a single one of those I met here still survives. The rest are mostly well-nigh forgotten by all but a few friends, or remembered chiefly in their children and grandchildren.

"How much?" I said to the garçon in his native tongue, or what I supposed to be that language. "*Cinq sous,*" was his answer. By the laws of sentiment, I ought to have made the ignoble sum five francs, at least. But if I had done so, the waiter would undoubtedly have thought that I had just come from Charenton. Besides, why should I violate the simple habits and traditions of the place, where generation after generation of poor students and threadbare Bohemians had taken their morning coffee and pocketed their two lumps of sugar? It was with a feeling of virile sanity and Roman self-conquest that I paid my five sous, with the small additional fraction which I supposed the waiter to expect, and no more.

So I passed for the last time over the threshold of the Café Procope, where Voltaire had matured his plays and Piron sharpened his epigrams; where Jouffroy had battled with his doubts and fears; where, since their time, — since my days of Parisian life, — the terrible storming youth, afterwards renowned as Léon Michel Gambetta, had startled the quiet guests with his noisy eloquence, till the old *habitués* spilled their coffee, and the red-capped students said to each other, "*Il ira loin, ce gaillard-là!*"

But what to me were these shadowy figures by the side of the group of my early friends and companions, that came up before me in all the freshness of their young manhood? The memory of them recalls my own youthful days, and I need not go to Florida to bathe in the fountain of Ponce de Leon.

I have sometimes thought that I love so well the accidents of this temporary terrestrial residence, its endeared localities, its precious affections, its pleasing variety of occupation, its alternations of excited and gratified curiosity, and whatever else comes nearest to the longings of the natural man, that I might be wickedly homesick in a far-off spiritual realm where such toys are done with. But there is a pretty lesson which I have often meditated, taught, not this time by the lilies of the field, but by the fruits of the garden. When, in the June honeymoon of the seasons, the

strawberry shows itself among the bridal gifts, many
of us exclaim for the hundredth time with Dr. Boteler,
"Doubtless God could have made a better berry, but
doubtless God never did." Nature, who is God's
handmaid, does not attempt a rival berry. But by
and by a little woolly knob, which looked and saw
with wonder the strawberry reddening, and perceived
the fragrance it diffused all around, begins to fill out,
and grow soft and pulpy and sweet; and at last a glow
comes to its cheek, and we say the peach is ripening.
When Nature has done with it, and delivers it to us in
its perfection, we forget all the lesser fruits which have
gone before it. If the flavor of the peach and the fragrance of the rose are not found in some fruit and
flower which grow by the side of the river of life, an
earth-born spirit might be forgiven for missing them.
The strawberry and the pink are very delightful, but
we could be happy without them.

So, too, we may hope that when the fruits of our
brief early season of three or four score years have
given us all they can impart for our happiness; when
"the love of little maids and berries," and all other
earthly prettinesses, shall "soar and sing," as Mr.
Emerson sweetly reminds us that they all must, we
may hope that the abiding felicities of our later life-
season may far more than compensate us for all that
have taken their flight.

I looked forward with the greatest interest to revisiting the Gallery of the Louvre, accompanied by my
long-treasured recollections. I retained a vivid remembrance of many pictures, which had been kept
bright by seeing great numbers of reproductions of
them in photographs and engravings.

The first thing which struck me was that the pictures had been rearranged in such a way that I could
find nothing in the place where I looked for it. But
when I found them, they greeted me, so I fancied,
like old acquaintances. The meek-looking "Belle
Jardinière" was as lamb-like as ever; the pearly
nymph of Correggio invited the stranger's eye as
frankly as of old; Titian's young man with the glove
was the calm, self-contained gentleman I used to admire; the splashy Rubenses, the pallid Guidos, the
sunlit Claudes, the shadowy Poussins, the moonlit Gi-
rardets, Géricault's terrible shipwreck of the Medusa,
the exquisite home pictures of Gerard Douw and Terburg, — all these and many more have always been on
exhibition in my ideal gallery, and I only mention
them as the first that happen to suggest themselves.

The Museum of the Hôtel Cluny is a curious receptacle of antiquities, many of which I looked at with
interest; but they made no lasting impression, and
have gone into the lumber-room of memory, from
which accident may, from time to time, drag out some
few of them.

After the poor unsatisfactory towers of Westminster
Abbey, the two massive, noble, truly majestic towers
of Notre Dame strike the traveller as a crushing con-
trast. It is not hard to see that one of these grand
towers is somewhat larger than the other, but the difference does not interfere with the effect of the imposing front of the cathedral.

I was much pleased to find that I could have entrance to the Sainte Chapelle, which was used, at the
time of my earlier visit, as a storehouse of judicial
archives, of which there was a vast accumulation.
With the exception of my call at the office of the

American Legation, I made but a single visit to any person in Paris. That person was M. Pasteur. I might have carried a letter to him, for my friend Mrs. Priestley is well acquainted with him, but I had not thought of asking for one. So I presented myself at his headquarters, and was admitted into a courtyard, where a multitude of his patients were gathered. They were of various ages and of many different national- ities, every one of them with the vague terror hanging over him or her. Yet the young people seemed to be cheerful enough, and very much like scholars out of school. I sent my card in to M. Pasteur, who was busily engaged in writing, with his clerks or students about him, and presently he came out and greeted me. I told him I was an American physician, who wished to look in his face and take his hand, — nothing more. I looked in his face, which was that of a thoughtful, hard-worked student, a little past the grand climac- teric, — he was born in 1822. I took his hand, which has performed some of the most delicate and daring experiments ever ventured upon, with results of almost incalculable benefit to human industries, and the promise of triumph in the treatment of human disease which prophecy would not have dared to anticipate. I will not say that I have a full belief that hydropho- bia — in some respects the most terrible of all dis- eases — is to be extirpated or rendered tractable by his method of treatment. But of his inventive origi- nality, his unconquerable perseverance, his devotion to the good of mankind, there can be no question. I look upon him as one of the greatest experimenters that ever lived, one of the truest benefactors of his race; and if I made my due obeisance before princes, I felt far more humble in the presence of this great explorer, to whom the God of Nature has entrusted some of her most precious secrets.

There used to be — I can hardly think it still exists — a class of persons who prided themselves on their disbelief in the reality of any such distinct disease as hydrophobia. I never thought it worth while to argue with them, for I have noticed that this disbelief is only a special manifestation of a particular habit of mind. Its advocates will be found, I think, most frequently among " the long - haired men and the short-haired women." Many of them dispute the efficacy of vaccination. Some are disciples of Hahnemann, some have full faith in the mind-cure, some attend the *séances* where flowers (bought from the nearest florist) are materialized, and some invest their money in Mrs. Howe's Bank of Benevolence. Their tendency is to reject the truth which is generally accepted, and to accept the improbable; if the impossible offers itself, they deny the existence of the impossible. Argument with this class of minds is a lever without a fulcrum.

I was glad to leave that company of patients, still uncertain of their fate, — hoping, yet pursued by their terror: peasants bitten by mad wolves in Siberia; women snapped at by their sulking lap-dogs in London; children from over the water who had been turned upon by the irritable Skye terrier; innocent victims torn by ill-conditioned curs at the doors of the friends they were meaning to visit, — all haunted by the same ghastly fear, all starting from sleep in the same nightmare.

If canine rabies is a fearful subject to contemplate, there is a sadder and deeper significance in *rabies humana;* in that awful madness of the human race which is marked by a thirst for blood and a rage for destruction. The remembrance of such a distemper which has attacked mankind, especially mankind of the Parisian sub-species, came over me very strongly when I first revisited the Place Vendôme. I should have supposed that the last object upon which Parisians would, in their wildest frenzy, have laid violent hands would have been the column with the figure of Napoleon at its summit. We all know what happened in 1871. An artist, we should have thought, would be the last person to lead the iconoclasts in such an outrage. But M. Courbet has attained an immortality like that of Erostratus by the part he took in pulling down the column. It was restored in 1874. I do not question that the work of restoration was well done, but my eyes insisted on finding a fault in some of its lines which was probably in their own refracting media. Fifty years before an artist helped to overthrow the monument to the Emperor, a poet had apostrophized him in the bitterest satire since the days of Juvenal: —

> "Encor Napoléon ! encor sa grande image !
>   Ah ! que ce rude et dur guerrier
> Nous a couté de sang et de pleurs et d'outrage
>   Pour quelques rameaux de laurier !
>
> .   .   .   .
>
> "Eh bien ! dans tous ces jours d'abaissement, de peine,
>   Pour tous ces outrages sans nom,
> Je n'ai jamais chargé qu'un être de ma haine, . . .
>   Sois maudit, O Napoléon ! "

After looking at the column of the Place Vendôme and recalling these lines of Barbier, I was ready for a visit to the tomb of Napoleon. The poet's curse had helped me to explain the painter's frenzy against the bronze record of his achievements and the image at its summit. But I forgot them both as I stood under the dome of the Invalides, and looked upon the massive receptacle which holds the dust of the imperial exile. Two things, at least, Napoleon accomplished: he opened the way for ability of all kinds, and he dealt the death-blow to the divine right of kings and all the abuses which clung to that superstition. If I brought nothing else away from my visit to his mausoleum, I left it impressed with what a man can be when fully equipped by nature, and placed in circumstances where his forces can have full play. "How infinite in faculty! . . . in apprehension how like a god!" Such were my reflections; very much, I suppose, like those of the average visitor, and too obviously having nothing to require contradiction or comment.

Paris as seen by the morning sun of three or four and twenty and Paris in the twilight of the superfluous decade cannot be expected to look exactly alike. I well remember my first breakfast at a Parisian café in the spring of 1833. It was in the Place de la Bourse, on a beautiful sunshiny morning. The coffee was nectar, the *flute* was ambrosia, the *brioche* was more than good enough for the Olympians. Such an experience could not repeat itself fifty years later. The first restaurant at which we dined was in the Palais Royal. The place was hot enough to cook an egg. Nothing was very excellent nor very bad; the wine was not so good as they gave us at our hotel in London; the enchanter had not waved his wand over our repast, as he did over my earlier one in the Place de la Bourse, and I had not the slightest desire to pay the garçon thrice his fee on the score of cherished associations.

We dined at our hotel on some days, at different restaurants on others. One day we dined, and dined
well, at the old Café Anglais, famous in my earlier
times for its turbot. Another day we took our dinner
at a very celebrated restaurant on the boulevard. One
sauce which was served us was a gastronomic symphony, the harmonies of which were new to me and
pleasing. But I remember little else of superior excellence. The garçon pocketed the franc I gave him with
the air of having expected a napoleon.

Into the mysteries of a lady's shopping in Paris I
would not venture to inquire. But A—— and I
strolled together through the Palais Royal in the evening, and amused ourselves by staring at the glittering
windows without being severely tempted. Bond Street
had exhausted our susceptibility to the shop-window
seduction, and the napoleons did not burn in the pock-
ets where the sovereigns had had time to cool.

Nothing looked more nearly the same as of old than
the bridges. The Pont Neuf did not seem to me
altered, though we had read in the papers that it was
in ruins or seriously injured in consequence of a great
flood. The statues had been removed from the Pont
Royal, one or two new bridges had been built, but all
was natural enough, and I was tempted to look for the
old woman, at the end of the Pont des Arts, who used
to sell me a bunch of violets, for two or three sous,
— such as would cost me a quarter of a dollar in Boston. I did not see the three objects which a popular
saying alleges are always to be met on the Pont Neuf:
a priest, a soldier, and a white horse.

The weather was hot; we were tired, and did not
care to go to the theatres, if any of them were open.
The pleasantest hours were those of our afternoon

drive in the Champs Elysées and the Bois de Boulogne, — or "the Boulogne Woods," as our American
tailor's wife of the old time called the favorite place
for driving.   In passing the Place de la Concorde,
two objects in especial attracted my attention, — the
obelisk, which was lying, when I left it, in the great
boat which brought it from the Nile, and the statue of
Strasbourg, all covered with wreaths and flags.   How
like children these Parisians do act; crying "A Berlin, à Berlin!" and when Berlin comes to Paris, and
Strasbourg goes back to her old proprietors, instead of
taking it quietly, making all this parade of patriotic
symbols, the display of which belongs to victory rather
than to defeat!

I was surprised to find the trees in the Bois de Boulogne so well grown: I had an idea that they had been
largely sacrificed in the time of the siege.   Among
the objects which deserve special mention are the
shrieking parrots and other birds and the yelping dogs
in the grounds of the Society of Acclimatization, —
out of the range of which the visitor will be glad to
get as soon as possible.   A fountain visited by newly
married couples and their friends, with a restaurant
near by, where the bridal party drink the health of the
newly married pair, was an object of curiosity.   An
unsteadiness of gait was obvious in some of the feast-
ers.   At one point in the middle of the road a mænad
was flinging her arms about and shrieking as if she
were just escaped from a madhouse.   But the drive
in the Bois was what made Paris tolerable.   There
were few fine equipages, and few distinguished-looking
people in the carriages, but there were quiet groups
by the wayside, seeming happy enough; and now and
then a pretty face or a wonderful bonnet gave variety

to the somewhat *bourgeois* character of the procession of fiacres.

I suppose I ought to form no opinion at all about the aspect of Paris, any more than I should of an oyster in a month without an *r* in it. We were neither of us in the best mood for sight-seeing, and Paris was not sitting up for company; in fact, she was "not at home." Remembering all this, I must say that the whole appearance of the city was dull and dreary. London out of season seemed still full of life; Paris out of season looked vacuous and torpid. The recollection of the sorrow, the humiliation, the shame, and the agony she had passed through since I left her picking her way on the arm of the Citizen King, with his old *riflard* over her, rose before me sadly, ominously, as I looked upon the high board fence which surrounded the ruins of the Tuileries. I can understand the impulse which led the red caps to make a wreck of this grand old historical building. "Pull down the nest," they said, "and the birds will not come back." But I shudder when I think what "the red fool-fury of the Seine" has done and is believed capable of doing. I think nothing has so profoundly impressed me as the story of the precautions taken to preserve the Venus of Milo from the brutal hands of the mob. A little more violent access of fury, a little more fiery declamation, a few more bottles of *vin bleu*, and the Gallery of the Louvre, with all its treasures of art, compared with which the crown jewels just sold are but pretty pebbles, the market price of which fairly enough expresses their value, — much more, rather, than their true value, — that noble gallery, with all its masterpieces from the hands of Greek sculptors and Italian painters, would have been changed in a single night into a heap of blackened stones and a pile of smoking cinders.

I love to think that now that the people have, or at least think they have, the power in their own hands, they will outgrow this form of madness, which is almost entitled to the name of a Parisian endemic. Everything looked peaceable and stupid enough during the week I passed in Paris. But among all the fossils which Cuvier found in the Parisian basin, nothing was more monstrous than the *poissardes* of the old Revolution, or the *pétroleuses* of the recent Commune, and I fear that the breed is not extinct. An American comes to like Paris as warmly as he comes to love England, after living in it long enough to become accustomed to its ways, and I, like the rest of my countrymen who remember that France was our friend in the hour of need, who remember all the privileges and enjoyments she has freely offered us, who feel that as a sister republic her destinies are of the deepest interest to us, can have no other wish than for her continued safety, order, and prosperity.

We returned to London on the 13th of August by the same route we had followed in going from London to Paris. Our passage was rough, as compared to the former one, and some of the passengers were seasick. We were both fortunate enough to escape that trial of comfort and self-respect.

I can hardly separate the story of the following week from that of the one before we went to Paris. We did a little more shopping and saw a few more sights. I hope that no reader of mine would suppose that I would leave London without seeing Madame Tussaud's exhibition. Our afternoon drives made us familiar with many objects which I always looked upon with pleasure. There was the obelisk, brought from Egypt at the expense of a distinguished and successful medical practitioner, Sir Erasmus Wilson, the eminent dermatologist and author of a manual of anatomy which for many years was my favorite text-book. There was "The Monument," which characterizes itself by having no prefix to its generic name. I enjoyed looking at and driving round it, and thinking over Pepys's lively account of the Great Fire, and speculating as to where Pudding Lane and Pie Corner stood, and recalling Pope's lines which I used to read at school, wondering what was the meaning of the second one: —

> "Where London's column, pointing to the skies
> Like a tall bully, lifts its head and lies."

The week passed away rapidly enough, and we made ready for our departure. It was no easy matter to get a passage home, but we had at last settled it that we would return in the same vessel in which we had at first engaged our passage to Liverpool, the Catalonia. But we were fortunate enough to have found an active and efficient friend in our townsman, Mr. Montgomery Sears, who procured staterooms for us in a much swifter vessel, to sail on the 21st for New York, the Aurania.

Our last visitor in London was the faithful friend who had been the first to welcome us, Lady Harcourt, in whose kind attentions I felt the warmth of my old friendship with her admired and honored father and her greatly beloved mother. I had recently visited their place of rest in the Kensal Green Cemetery, recalling with tenderest emotions the many years in which I had enjoyed their companionship.

On the 19th of August we left London for Liverpool, and on our arrival took lodgings at the Adelphi Hotel.

The kindness with which I had been welcomed, when I first arrived at Liverpool, had left a deep impression upon my mind. It seemed very ungrateful to leave that noble city, which had met me in some of its most esteemed representatives with a warm grasp of the hand even before my foot had touched English soil, without staying to thank my new friends, who would have it that they were old friends. But I was entirely unfit for enjoying any company when I landed. I took care, therefore, to allow sufficient time in Liverpool, before sailing for home, to meet such friends, old and recent, as cared to make or renew acquaintance with me. In the afternoon of the 20th we held a reception, at which a hundred visitors, more or less, presented themselves, and we had a very sociable hour or two together. The Vice-Consul, Mr. Sewall, in the enforced absence of his principal, Mr. Russell, paid us every attention, and was very agreeable. In the evening I was entertained at a great banquet given by the Philomathean Society. This flourishing institution enrolls among its members a large proportion of the most cultivated and intelligent gentlemen of Liverpool. I enjoyed the meeting very highly, listened to pleasant things which were said about myself, and answered in the unpremeditated words which came to my lips and were cordially received. I could have wished to see more of Liverpool, but I found time only to visit the great exhibition, then open. The one class of objects which captivated my attention was the magnificent series of models of steamboats and other vessels. I did not look upon them with the eye of an expert, but the great number and variety of these beautiful miniature ships and boats excited my admiration.

On the 21st of August we went on board the Aurania. Everything was done to make us comfortable. Many old acquaintances, friends, and family connections were our fellow-passengers. As for myself, I passed through the same trying experiences as those which I have recorded as characterizing my outward passage. Our greatest trouble during the passage was from fog. The frequency of collisions, of late years, tends to make everybody nervous when they hear the fog-whistle shrieking. This sound and the sight of the boats are not good for timid people. Fortunately, no one was particularly excitable, or if so, no one betrayed any special uneasiness.

On the evening of the 27th we had an entertainment, in which Miss Kellogg sang and I read several poems. A very pretty sum was realized for some charity, — I forget what, — and the affair was voted highly successful. The next day, the 28th, we were creeping towards our harbor through one of those dense fogs which are more dangerous than the old rocks of the sirens, or Scylla and Charybdis, or the much-lied-about maelstrom.

On Sunday, the 29th of August, my birthday, we arrived in New York. In these days of birthday-books our chronology is not a matter of secret history, in case we have been much before the public. I found a great cake had been made ready for me, in which the number of my summers was represented by a ring of raisins which made me feel like Methuselah. A beautiful bouquet which had been miraculously preserved for the occasion was for the first time displayed. It came from Dr. Beach, of Boston, *via* London. Such

is the story, and I can only suppose that the sweet little cherub who sits up aloft had taken special charge
of it, or it would have long ago withered.

We slept at the Fifth Avenue Hotel, which we found
fresh, sweet, bright, — it must have been recently
rejuvenated, I thought. The next day we took the
train for New Haven, Springfield, and Boston, and
that night slept in our own beds, thankful to find
ourselves safe at home after our summer excursion,
which had brought us so many experiences delightful
to remember, so many friendships which have made
life better worth living.

In the following section I shall give some of the
general impressions which this excursion has left in
my memory, and a few suggestions derived from them.

VIII.

My reader was fairly forewarned that this narrative
was to be more like a chapter of autobiography than
the record of a tourist. In the language of philosophy,
it is written from a subjective, not an objective, point
of view. It is not exactly a "Sentimental Journey,"
though there are warm passages here and there which
end with notes of admiration. I remind myself now
and then of certain other travellers: of Benjamin of
Tudela, going from the hospitalities of one son of
Abraham to another; of John Buncle, finding the
loveliest of women under every roof that sheltered
him; sometimes, perhaps, of that tipsy rhymester
whose record of his good and bad fortunes at the hands
of landlords and landladies is enlivened by an occasional touch of humor, which makes it palatable to

coarse literary feeders. But in truth these papers have many of the characteristics of private letters written home to friends. They *are* written for friends, rather than for a public which cares nothing about the writer. I knew that there were many such whom it would please to know where the writer went, whom he saw and what he saw, and how he was impressed by persons and things.

If I were planning to make a tour of the United Kingdom, and could command the service of all the wise men I count or have counted among my friends, I would go with such a retinue summoned from the ranks of the living and the dead as no prince ever carried with him. I would ask Mr. Lowell to go with me among scholars, where I could be a listener; Mr. Norton to visit the cathedrals with me; Professor Gray to be my botanical oracle; Professor Agassiz to be always ready to answer questions about the geological strata and their fossils; Dr. Jeffries Wyman to point out and interpret the common objects which present themselves to a sharp-eyed observer; and Mr. Boyd Dawkins to pilot me among the caves and cairns. Then I should want a better pair of eyes and a better pair of ears, and, while I was reorganizing, perhaps a quicker apprehension and a more retentive memory; in short, a new outfit, bodily and mental. But Nature does not care to mend old shoes; she prefers a new pair, and a young person to stand in them.

What a great book one could make, with such aids, and how many would fling it down, and take up anything in preference, provided only that it were short enough; even this slight record, for want of something shorter!

Not only did I feel sure that many friends would

like to read our itinerary, but another motive prompted me to tell the simple story of our travels. I could not receive such kindness, so great evidences of friendly regard, without a strong desire, amounting to a positive necessity, for the expression of my grateful sense of all that had been done for us. Individually, I felt it, of course, as a most pleasing experience. But I believed it to have a more important significance as an illustration of the cordial feeling existing between England and America. I know that many of my countrymen felt the attentions paid to me as if they themselves shared them with me. I have lived through many strata of feeling in America towards England. My parents, full-blooded Americans, were both born subjects of King George III. Both learned in their early years to look upon Britons as the enemies of their country. A good deal of the old hostility lingered through my boyhood, and this was largely intensified by the war of 1812. After nearly half a century this feeling had in great measure subsided, when the War of Secession called forth expressions of sympathy with the slaveholding States which surprised, shocked, and deeply wounded the lovers of liberty and of England in the Northern States. A new generation is outgrowing that alienation. More and more the older and younger nations are getting to be proud and really fond of each other. There is no shorter road to a mother's heart than to speak pleasantly to her child, and caress it, and call it pretty names. No matter whether the child is something remarkable or not, it is *her* child, and that is enough. It may be made too much of, but that is not its mother's fault. If I could believe that every attention paid me was due simply to my being an American, I should feel honored and happy in being one of the humbler media through which the good-will of a great and generous country reached the heart of a far-off people not always in friendly relations with her.

I have named many of the friends who did everything to make our stay in England and Scotland agreeable. The unforeseen shortening of my visit must account for many disappointments to myself, and some, it may be, to others.

First in the list of lost opportunities was that of making my bow to the Queen. I had the honor of receiving a card with the invitation to meet Her Majesty at a garden-party, but we were travelling when it was sent, and it arrived too late.

I was very sorry not to meet Mr. Ruskin, to whom Mr. Norton had given me a note of introduction. At the time when we were hoping to see him it was thought that he was too ill to receive visitors, but he has since written me that he regretted we did not carry out our intention. I lamented my being too late to see once more two gentlemen from whom I should have been sure of a kind welcome, — Lord Houghton and Dean Stanley, both of whom I had met in Boston. Even if I had stayed out the whole time I had intended to remain abroad, I should undoubtedly have failed to see many persons and many places that I must always feel sorry for having missed. But as it is, I will not try to count all that I lost; let me rather be thankful that I met so many friends whom it was a pleasure to know personally, and saw so much that it is a pleasure to remember.

I find that many of the places I most wish to see are those associated with the memory of some individual, generally one of the generations more or less in ad-

vance of my own. One of the first places I should go
to, in a leisurely tour, would be Selborne. Gilbert
White was not a poet, neither was he a great systematic naturalist. But he used his eyes on the world
about him; he found occupation and happiness in his
daily walks, and won as large a measure of immortality within the confines of his little village as he could
have gained in exploring the sources of the Nile. I
should make a solemn pilgrimage to the little town
of Eyam, in Derbyshire, where the Reverend Mr.
Mompesson, the hero of the plague of 1665, and his
wife, its heroine and its victim, lie buried. I should
like to follow the traces of Cowper at Olney and of
Bunyan at Elstow. I found an intense interest in the
Reverend Mr. Alger's account of his visit to the Vale
of Llangollen, where Lady Eleanor Butler and Miss
Ponsonby passed their peaceful days in long, uninter-
rupted friendship. Of course the haunts of Burns,
the home of Scott, the whole region made sacred by
Wordsworth and the group to which he belongs would
be so many shrines to which I should make pilgrimages.

I own, also, to having something of the melodra-
matic taste so notable in Victor Hugo. I admired
the noble façade of Wells cathedral and the grand old
episcopal palace, but I begged the bishop to show me
the place where his predecessor, Bishop Kidder, and
his wife, were killed by the falling chimney in the
"Great Storm." — I wanted to go to Devizes, and see
the monument in the market-place, where Ruth Pierce
was struck dead with a lie in her mouth, — about all
which I had read in early boyhood. I contented myself with a photograph of it which my friend, Mr.
Willett, went to Devizes and bought for me.

There are twenty different Englands, every one of which it would be a delight to visit, and I should hardly know with which of them to begin.

The few remarks I have to make on what I saw and heard have nothing beyond the value of first impressions; but as I have already said, if these are simply given, without pretending to be anything more, they are not worthless. At least they can do little harm, and may sometimes amuse a reader whom they fail to instruct. But we must all beware of hasty conclusions. If a foreigner of limited intelligence were whirled through England on the railways, he would naturally come to the conclusion that the chief product of that country is *mustard*, and that its most celebrated people are Mr. Keen and Mr. Colman, whose great advertising boards, yellow letters on a black ground, and black letters on a yellow ground, stare the traveller in the face at every station.

Of the climate, as I knew it in May and the summer months, I will only say that if I had any illusions about May and June in England, my fireplace would have been ample evidence that I was entirely disenchanted. The Derby day, the 26th of May, was most chilly and uncomfortable; at the garden-party at Kensington Palace, on the 4th of June, it was cold enough to make hot drinks and warm wraps a comfort, if not a necessity. I was thankful to have passed through these two ordeals without ill consequences. Drizzly, or damp, or cold, cloudy days were the rule rather than the exception, while we were in London. We had some few hot days, especially at Stratford, in the early part of July. In London an umbrella is as often carried as a cane; in Paris "*un homme a para-*

pluie " is, or used to be, supposed to carry that useful article because he does not keep and cannot hire a carriage of some sort. He may therefore be safely considered a person, and not a personage.

The soil of England does not seem to be worn out, to judge by the wonderful verdure and the luxuriance of vegetation. It contains a great museum of geological specimens, and a series of historical strata which are among the most instructive of human records. . I do not pretend to much knowledge of geology. The most interesting geological objects in our New England that I can think of are the great boulders and the scratched and smoothed surface of the rocks; the fossil footprints in the valley of the Connecticut; the trilobites found at Quincy. But the readers of Hugh Miller remember what a variety of fossils he found in the stratified rocks of his little island, and the museums are full of just such objects. When it comes to underground historical relics, the poverty of New England as compared with the wealth of Old England is very striking. Stratum after stratum carries the explorer through the relics of successive invaders. After passing through the characteristic traces of different peoples, he comes upon a Roman pavement, and below this the weapons and ornaments of a tribe of ancient Britons. One cannot strike a spade into the earth, in Great Britain, without a fair chance of some surprise in the form of a Saxon coin, or a Celtic implement, or a Roman fibula. Nobody expects any such pleasing surprise in a New England field. One must be content with an Indian arrowhead or two, now and then a pestle and mortar, or a stone pipe. A top dressing of antiquity is all he can look for. The soil is not humanized enough to be interesting; whereas in England so much of it has been trodden by human feet, built on in the form of human habitations, nay, has been itself a part of preceding generations of human beings, that it is in a kind of dumb sympathy with those who tread its turf. Perhaps it is not liter-ally true that

> One half her soil has walked the rest
> In poets, heroes, martyrs, sages ;

but so many of all these lie within it that the whole mother island is a *campo santo* to all who can claim the same blood as that which runs in the veins of her unweaned children.

The flora and fauna of a country, as seen from rail-road trains and carriages, are not likely to be very accurately or exhaustively studied. I spoke of the trees I noticed between Chester and London somewhat slightingly. But I did not form any hasty opinions from what happened to catch my eye. Afterwards, in the oaks and elms of Windsor Park, in the elms of Cambridge and Oxford and Salisbury, in the lindens of Stratford, in the various noble trees, including the cedar of Lebanon, in which Tennyson very justly felt a pride as their owner, I saw enough to make me glad that I had not uttered any rash generalizations on the strength of my first glance. The most interesting com-parison I made was between the New England and the Old England elms. It is not necessary to cross the ocean to do this, as we have both varieties growing side by side in our parks, — on Boston Common, for in-stance. It is wonderful to note how people will lie about big trees. There must be as many as a dozen trees, each of which calls itself the "largest elm in New England." In my younger days, when I never travelled without a measuring-tape in my pocket, it amused me to see how meek one of the great swaggering elms would look when it saw the fatal measure begin to unreel itself. It seemed to me that the leaves actually trembled as the inexorable band encircled the trunk in *the smallest place it could find*, which is the only safe rule. The English elm (*Ulmus campestris*) as we see it in Boston comes out a little earlier perhaps, than our own, but the difference is slight. It holds its leaves long after our elms are bare. It grows upward, with abundant dark foliage, while ours spreads, sometimes a hundred and twenty feet, and often droops like a weeping willow. The English elm looks like a much more robust tree than ours, yet they tell me it is very fragile, and that its limbs are constantly breaking off in high winds, just as happens with our native elms. Ours is not a very long-lived tree; between two and three hundred years is, I think, the longest life that can be hoped for it. Since I have heard of the fragility of the English elm, which is the fatal fault of our own, I have questioned whether it can claim a greater longevity than ours. There is a hint of a typical difference in the American and the Englishman which I have long recognized in the two elms as compared to each other. It may be fanciful, but I have thought that the compactness and robustness about the English elm, which are replaced by the long, tapering limbs and willowy grace and far-spreading reach of our own, might find a certain parallelism in the people, especially the females of the two countries.

I saw no horse-chestnut trees equal to those I remember in Salem, and especially to one in Rockport, which is the largest and finest I have ever seen; no willows like those I pass in my daily drives.

On the other hand, I think I never looked upon a Lombardy poplar equal to one I saw in Cambridge, England. This tree seems to flourish in England much more than with us.

I do not remember any remarkable beeches, though there are some very famous ones, especially the Burn-ham beeches.

No apple-trees I saw in England compare with one next my own door, and there are many others as fine in the neighborhood.

I have spoken of the pleasure I had in seeing by the roadside primroses, cowslips, and daisies. Dande-lions, buttercups, hawkweed looked much as ours do at home. Wild roses also grew at the roadside, — smaller and paler, I thought, than ours.

I cannot make a chapter like the famous one on Ice-land, from my own limited observation: *There are no snakes in England.* I *can* say that I found two small caterpillars on my overcoat, in coming from Lord Tennyson's grounds. If they had stayed on his prem-ises, they might perhaps have developed into "purple emperors," or spread "the tiger moth's deep damasked wings" before the enraptured eyes of the noble poet. These two caterpillars and a few house-flies are all I saw, heard, or felt, by day or night, of the native fauna of England, except a few birds, — rooks, starlings, a blackbird, and the larks of Salisbury Plain just as they rose; for I lost sight of them almost immediately. I neither heard nor saw the nightingales, to my great regret. They had been singing at Oxford a short time before my visit to that place. The only song I heard was that which I have mentioned, the double note of the cuckoo.

England is the paradise of horses. They are bred,

fed, trained, groomed, housed, cared for, in a way to remind one of the Houyhnhnms, and strikingly contrasting with the conditions of life among the wretched classes whose existence is hardly more tolerable than that of those *quasi*-human beings under whose name it pleased the fierce satirist to degrade humanity. The horses that are driven in the hansoms of London are the best I have seen in any public conveyance. I cannot say as much of those in the four-wheelers.

Broad streets, sometimes, as in Bond Street, with narrow sidewalks; *islands* for refuge in the middle of many of them; deep areas; lofty houses; high walls; plants in the windows; frequent open spaces; policemen at near intervals, always polite in my experience, — such are my recollections of the quarter I most frequented.

Are the English taller, stouter, lustier, ruddier, healthier, than our New England people? If I gave my impression, I should say that they are. Among the wealthier class, tall, athletic-looking men and stately, well-developed women are more common, I am compelled to think, than with us. I met in company at different times five gentlemen, each of whom would be conspicuous in any crowd for his stature and proportions. We could match their proportions, however, in the persons of well-known Bostonians. To see how it was with other classes, I walked in the Strand one Sunday, and noted carefully the men and women I met. I was surprised to see how many of both sexes were of low stature. I counted in the course of a few minutes' walk no less than twenty of these little people. I set this experience against the other. Neither is convincing. The anthropologists will settle the question of man in the Old and in the New World before many decades have passed.

In walking the fashionable streets of London cne can hardly fail to be struck with the well-dressed look of gentlemen of all ages. The special point in which the Londoner excels all other citizens I am conversant with is the hat. I have not forgotten Béranger's

> " *Quoique leurs chapeaux soient bien laids*
> **** *** ! moi, j'aime les Anglais ;* "

but in spite of it I believe in the English hat as the best thing of its ugly kind. As for the Englishman's feeling with reference to it, a foreigner might be pardoned for thinking it was his fetich, a North American Indian for looking at it as taking the place of his own medicine-bag. It is a common thing for the Englishman to say his prayers into it, as he sits down in his pew. Can it be that this imparts a religious character to the article? However this may be, the true Londoner's hat is cared for as reverentially as a High-Church altar. Far off its coming shines. I was always impressed by the fact that even with us a well-bred gentleman in reduced circumstances never forgets to keep his beaver well brushed, and I remember that long ago I spoke of the hat as the *ultimum moriens* of what we used to call gentility, — the last thing to perish in the decay of a gentleman's outfit. His hat is as sacred to an Englishman as his beard to a Mussulman.

In looking at the churches and the monuments which I saw in London and elsewhere in England, certain resemblances, comparisons, parallels, contrasts, and suggestions obtruded themselves upon my consciousness. We have one steeple in Boston which to my eyes seems absolutely perfect: that of the Central Church, at the corner of Newbury and Berkeley streets.

Its resemblance to the spire of Salisbury had always struck me. On mentioning this to the late Mr. Richardson, the very distinguished architect, he said to me that he thought it more nearly like that of the Cathedral of Chartres. One of our best living architects agreed with me as to its similarity to that of Salisbury. It does not copy either exactly, but, if it had twice its actual dimensions, would compare well with the best of the two, if one is better than the other. Saint-Martin's-in-the-Fields made me feel as if I were in Boston. Our Arlington Street Church copies it pretty closely, but Mr. Gilman left out the columns. I could not admire the Nelson Column, nor that which lends monumental distinction to the Duke of York. After Trajan's and that of the Place Vendôme, each of which is a permanent and precious historical record, accounting sufficiently for its existence, there is something very unsatisfactory in these nude cylinders. That to the Duke of York might well have the confession of the needy knife grinder as an inscription on its base. I confess in all honesty that I vastly prefer the monument commemorating the fire to either of them. That *has* a story to tell and tells it, — with a lie or two added, according to Pope, but it tells it in language and symbol.

As for the kind of monument such as I see from my library window standing on the summit of Bunker Hill, and have recently seen for the first time at Washington, on a larger scale, I own that I think a built-up obelisk a poor affair as compared with an Egyptian monolith of the same form. It was a triumph of skill to quarry, to shape, to transport, to cover with expressive symbols, to erect, such a stone as that which has been transferred to the Thames Embankment, or that which now stands in Central Park, New York. Each of its four sides is a page of history, written so as to endure through scores of centuries. A built-up obelisk requires very little more than brute labor. A child can shape its model from a carrot or a parsnip, and set it up in miniature with blocks of loaf sugar. It teaches nothing, and the stranger must go to his guide-book to know what it is there for. I was led into many reflections by a sight of the Washington Monument. I found that it was almost the same thing at a mile's distance as the Bunker Hill Monument at half a mile's distance; and unless the eye had some means of measuring the space between itself and the stone shaft, one was about as good as the other. A mound like that of Marathon or that at Waterloo, a cairn, even a shaft of the most durable form and material, are fit memorials of the place where a great battle was fought. They seem less appropriate as monuments to individuals. I doubt the durability of these piecemeal obelisks, and when I think of that vast inverted pendulum vibrating in an earthquake, I am glad that I do not live in its shadow. The Washington Monument is more than a hundred feet higher than Salisbury steeple, but it does not look to me so high as that, because the mind has nothing to climb by. But the forming taste of the country revels in superlatives, and if we could only have the deepest artesian well in the world sunk by the side of the tallest column in all creation, the admiring, not overcritical patriot would be happier than ever was the Athenian when he looked up at the newly erected Parthenon.

I made a few miscellaneous observations which may

be worth recording. One of these was the fact of the
repetition of the types of men and women with which
I was familiar at home. Every now and then I met a
new acquaintance whom I felt that I had seen before.
Presently I identified him with his double on the other
side. I had found long ago that even among Frenchmen I often fell in with persons whose counterparts I
had known in America. I began to feel as if Nature
turned out a batch of human beings for every locality
of any importance, very much as a workman makes a
set of chessmen. If I had lived a little longer in London, I am confident that I should have met myself, as
I did actually meet so many others who were duplicates of those long known to me.

I met Mr. Galton for a few moments, but I had
no long conversation with him. If he should ask me
to say how many faces I can visually recall, I should
have to own that there are very few such. The two
pictures which I have already referred to, those of
Erasmus and of Dr. Johnson, come up more distinctly
before my mind's eye than almost any faces of the living. My mental retina has, I fear, lost much of its
sensitiveness. Long and repeated exposure of an object of any kind, in a strong light, is necessary to fix
its image.

Among the gratifications that awaited me in England and Scotland was that of meeting many before
unseen friends with whom I had been in correspondence. I have spoken of Mr. John Bellows. I should
have been glad to meet Mr. William Smith, the Yorkshire antiquary, who has sent me many of his antiquarian and biographical writings and publications. I do
not think I saw Mr. David Gilmour, of Paisley, whose

"Paisley Folk" and other writings have given me great pleasure. But I did have the satisfaction of meeting Professor Gairdner, of Glasgow, to whose writings my attention was first called by my revered instructor, the late Dr. James Jackson, and with whom I had occasionally corresponded. I ought to have met Dr. Martineau. I should have visited the Reverend Stopford Brooke, who could have told me much that I should have liked to hear of dear friends of mine, of whom he saw a great deal in their hours of trial. The Reverend Mr. Voysey, whose fearless rationalism can hardly give him popularity among the conservative people I saw most of, paid me the compliment of calling, as he had often done of sending me his published papers. Now and then some less known correspondent would reveal himself or herself in bodily presence. Let most authors beware of showing themselves to those who have idealized them, and let readers not be too anxious to see in the flesh those whom they have idealized. When I was a boy, I read Miss Edgeworth's "L'Amie Inconnue." I have learned to appreciate its meaning in later years by abundant experiences, and I have often felt unwilling to substitute my real for my imaginary presence. I will add here that I must have met a considerable number of persons, in the crowd at our reception and elsewhere, whose names I failed to hear, and whom I consequently did not recognize as the authors of books I had read, or of letters I had received. The story of my experience with the lark accounts for a good deal of what seemed like negligence or forgetfulness, and which must be, not pardoned, but sighed over.

I visited several of the well-known clubs, either by special invitation, or accompanied by a member.

The Athenæum was particularly attentive, but I was unable to avail myself of the privileges it laid freely open before me during my stay in London. Other clubs I looked in upon were: the Reform Club, where I had the pleasure of dining at a large party given by the very distinguished Dr. Morell Mackenzie; the Rabelais, of which, as I before related, I have been long a member, and which was one of the first places where I dined; the Saville; the Savage; the St. George's. I saw next to nothing of the proper club-life of London, but it seemed to me that the Athenæum must be a very desirable place of resort to the educated Londoner, and no doubt each of the many institutions of this kind with which London abounds has its special attractions.

My obligations to my brethren of the medical profession are too numerous to be mentioned in detail. Almost the first visit I paid was one to my old friend and fellow-student in Paris, Dr. Walter Hayle Walshe. After more than half a century's separation, two young friends, now old friends, must not expect to find each other just the same as when they parted. Dr. Walshe thought he should have known me; my eyes are not so good as his, and I would not answer for them and for my memory. That he should have dedicated his recent original and ingenious work to me, before I had thought of visiting England, was a most gratifying circumstance. I have mentioned the hospitalities extended to me by various distinguished members of the medical profession, but I have not before referred to the readiness with which, on all occasions, when professional advice was needed, it was always given with more than willingness, rather as if it were a pleasure to give it. I could not have accepted such

favors as I received had I not remembered that I, in
my time, had given my services freely for the benefit of those of my own calling. If I refer to two
names among many, it is for special reasons. Dr.
Wilson Fox, the distinguished and widely known
practitioner, who showed us great kindness, has since
died, and this passing tribute is due to his memory. I
have before spoken of the exceptional favor we owed
to Dr. and Mrs. Priestley. It enabled us to leave
London feeling that we had tried, at least, to show our
grateful sense of all the attentions bestowed upon us.
If there were any whom we overlooked, among the
guests we wished to honor, all such accidental omis-
sions will be pardoned, I feel sure, by those who know
how great and bewildering is the pressure of social life
in London.

I was, no doubt, often more or less confused, in my
perceptions, by the large number of persons whom
I met in society. I found the dinner-parties, as Mr.
Lowell told me I should, very much like the same
entertainments among my home acquaintances. I
have not the gift of silence, and I am not a bad listener, yet I brought away next to nothing from dinner-parties where I had said and heard enough to fill
out a magazine article. After I was introduced to a
lady, the conversation frequently began somewhat in
this way: —

"It is a long time since you have been in this country, I believe?"

"It is a *very* long time: fifty years and more."

"You find great changes in London, of course, 1
suppose?"

"Not so great as you might think. The Tower is
where I left it. The Abbey is much as I remember

it. Northumberland House with its lion is gone, but Charing Cross is in the same old place. My attention is drawn especially to the things which have *not* changed, — those which I remember."

That stream was quickly dried up. Conversation soon found other springs. I never knew the talk to get heated or noisy. Religion and politics rarely came up, and never in any controversial way. The bitter-est politician I met at table was a quadruped, — a lady's dog, — who refused a desirable morsel offered him in the name of Mr. Gladstone, but snapped up another instantly on being told that it came from Queen Victoria. I recall many pleasant and some delightful talks at the dinner-table; one in particular, with the most charming woman in England. I won-der if she remembers how very lovely and agreeable she was? Possibly she may be able to identify her-self.

People — the right kind of people — meet at a dinner-party as two ships meet and pass each other at sea. They exchange a few signals; ask each other's reckoning, where from, where bound; perhaps one supplies the other with a little food or a few dainties; then they part, to see each other no more. But one or both may remember the hour passed together all their days, just as I recollect our brief parley with the brig Economist, of Leith, from Sierra Leone, in mid ocean, in the spring of 1833.

I am very far from despising the science of gastron-omy, but if I wished to institute a comparison between the tables of England and America, I could not do it without eating my way through the four seasons. I will say that I did not think the bread from the bak-ers' shops was so good as our own. It was very generally tough and hard, and even the muffins were not always so tender and delicate as they ought to be. I got impatient one day, and sent out for some biscuits. They brought some very excellent ones, which we much preferred to the tough bread. They proved to be the so-called "seafoam" biscuit from New York. The potatoes never came on the table looking like new fallen snow, as we have them at home. We were surprised to find both mutton and beef overdone, according to our American taste. The French talk about the Briton's "*bifteck saignant*," but we never saw anything cooked so as to be, as we should say, "rare." The tart is national with the English, as the pie is national with us. I never saw on an English table that excellent substitute for both, called the Washington pie, in memory of him whom we honor as first in pies, as well as in war and in the hearts of his countrymen.

The truth is that I gave very little thought to the things set before me, in the excitement of constantly changing agreeable companionship. I understand perfectly the feeling of the good liver in Punch, who suggests to the lady next him that their host has one of the best cooks in London, and that it might therefore be well to defer all conversation until they adjourned to the drawing-room. I preferred the conversation, and adjourned, indefinitely, the careful appreciation of the *menu*. I think if I could devote a year to it, I might be able to make out a graduated scale of articles of food, taking a well-boiled fresh egg as the unit of gastronomic value, but I leave this scientific task to some future observer.

The most remarkable piece of European handiwork I remember was the steel chair at Longford Castle.

The most startling and frightful work of man I ever saw or expect to see was another specimen of work in steel, said to have been taken from one of the infernal chambers of the Spanish Inquisition. It was a complex mechanism, which grasped the body and the head of the heretic or other victim, and by means of many ingeniously arranged screws and levers was capable of pressing, stretching, piercing, rending, crushing, all the most sensitive portions of the human body, one at a time or many at once. The famous Virgin, whose embrace drove a hundred knives into the body of the poor wretch she took in her arms, was an angel of mercy compared to this masterpiece of devilish enginery.

Ingenuity is much better shown in contrivances for making our daily life more comfortable. I was on the lookout for everything that promised to be a convenience. I carried out two things which seemed to be new to the Londoners: the Star Razor, which I have praised so freely, and still find equal to all my commendations; and the mucilage pencil, which is a very handy implement to keep on the writer's desk or table. I found a contrivance for protecting the hand in drawing corks, which all who are their own butlers will appreciate, and luminous match-boxes which really shine brightly in the dark, and that after a year's usage; whereas one professing to shine by night, which I bought in Boston, is only visible by borrowed light. I wanted a very fine-grained hone, and inquired for it at a hardware store, where they kept everything in their line of the best quality. I brought away a very pretty but very small stone, for which I paid a large price. The stone was from Arkansas, and I need not have bought in London what would have been easily obtained at a dozen or more stores in Boston. It was a renewal of my experience with the seafoam biscuit. "Know thyself" and the things about thee, and "Take the good the gods provide thee," if thou wilt only keep thine eyes open, are two safe precepts.

Who is there of English descent among us that does not feel with Cowper,

> "England, with all thy faults, I love thee still"?

Our recently naturalized fellow-citizens, of a different blood and different religion, must not suppose that we are going to forget our inborn love for the mother to whom we owe our being. Protestant England and Protestant America are coming nearer and nearer to each other every year. The interchange of the two peoples is more and more frequent, and there are many reasons why it is likely to continue increasing.

Hawthorne says in a letter to Longfellow, "Why don't you come over, being now a man of leisure and with nothing to keep you in America? If I were in your position, I think I should make my home on this side of the water, — though always with an indefinite and never-to-be-executed intention to go back and die in my native land. America is a good land for young people, but not for those who are past their prime. . . . A man of individuality and refinement can certainly live far more comfortably here — provided he has the means to live at all — than in New England. Be it owned, however, that I sometimes feel a tug at my very heart-strings when I think of my old home and friends." This was written from Liverpool in 1854.

We must not forget that our fathers were exiles from their dearly loved native land, driven by causes which no longer exist. "Freedom to worship God" is found in England as fully as in America, in our day. In placing the Atlantic between themselves and the Old World civilizations they made an enormous sacrifice. It is true that the wonderful advance of our people in all the arts and accomplishments which make life agreeable has transformed the wilderness into a home where men and women can live comfortably, elegantly, happily, if they are of contented disposition; and without that they can be happy nowhere. What better provision can be made for a mortal man than such as our own Boston can afford its wealthy children? A palace on Commonwealth Avenue or on Beacon Street; a country-place at Framingham or Lenox; a seaside residence at Nahant, Beverly Farms, Newport, or Bar Harbor; a pew at Trinity or King's Chapel; a tomb at Mount Auburn or Forest Hills; with the prospect of a memorial stained window after his lamented demise, — is not this a pretty programme to offer a candidate for human existence?

Give him all these advantages, and he will still be longing to cross the water, to get back to that old home of his fathers, so delightful in itself, so infinitely desirable on account of its nearness to Paris, to Geneva, to Rome, to all that is most interesting in Europe. The less wealthy, less cultivated, less fastidious class of Americans are not so much haunted by these longings. But the convenience of living in the Old World is so great, and it is such a trial and such a risk to keep crossing the ocean, that it seems altogether likely that a considerable current of re-migration will gradually develop itself among our people.

Some find the climate of the other side of the Atlantic suits them better than their own. As the New

England characteristics are gradually superseded by those of other races, other forms of belief, and other associations, the time may come when a New Englander will feel more as if he were among his own people in London than in one of our seaboard cities. The vast majority of our people love their country too well and are too proud of it to be willing to expatriate themselves. But going back to our old home, to find ourselves among the relatives from whom we have been separated for a few generations, is not like transferring ourselves to a land where another language is spoken, and where there are no ties of blood and no common religious or political traditions. I, for one, being myself as inveterately rooted an American of the Bostonian variety as ever saw himself mirrored in the Frog Pond, hope that the exchanges of emigrants and re-migrants will be much more evenly balanced by and by than at present. I hope that more Englishmen like James Smithson will help to build up our scientific and literary institutions. I hope that more Americans like George Peabody will call down the blessings of the English people by noble benefactions to the cause of charity. It was with deep feelings of pride and gratitude that I looked upon the bust of Longfellow, holding its place among the monuments of England's greatest and best children. I see with equal pleasure and pride that one of our own large-hearted countrymen has honored the memory of three English poets, Milton, and Herbert, and Cowper, by the gift of two beautiful stained windows, and with still ampler munificence is erecting a stately fountain in the birthplace of Shakespeare. Such acts as these make us feel more and more the truth of the gener-ous sentiment which closes the ode of Washington

Allston, "America to Great Britain:" "We are one!"

I have told our story with the help of my daughter's diary, and often aided by her recollections. Having enjoyed so much, I am desirous that my countrymen and countrywomen should share my good fortune with me. I hesitated at first about printing names in full, but when I remembered that we received nothing but the most overflowing hospitality and the most considerate kindness from all we met, I felt sure that I could not offend by telling my readers who the friends were that made England a second home to us. If any one of them is disturbed by such reference as I have made to him or to her, I most sincerely apologize for the liberty I have taken. I am far more afraid that through sheer forgetfulness I have left unmentioned many to whom I was and still remain under obligations.

If I were asked what I think of people's travelling after the commonly accepted natural term of life is completed, I should say that everything depends on constitution and habit. The old soldier says, in speaking of crossing the Beresina, where the men had to work in the freezing stream constructing the bridges, "Faut du tempérament pour cela!" I often thought of this expression, in the damp and chilly weather which not rarely makes English people wish they were in Italy. I escaped unharmed from the windy gusts at Epsom and the nipping chill of the Kensington garden-party; but if a score of my contemporaries had been there with me, there would not improbably have been a funeral or two within a week. If, however, the super-septuagenarian is used to exposures, if he is an old sportsman or an old officer not retired from active service, he may expect to elude the pneumonia which follows his footsteps whenever he wanders far from his fireside. But to a person of well-advanced years coming from a counting-room, a library, or a studio, the risk is considerable, unless he is of hardy natural constitution; any other will do well to remember, "Faut du tempérament pour cela!"

Suppose there to be a reasonable chance that he will come home alive, what is the use of one's going to Europe after his senses have lost their acuteness, and his mind no longer retains its full measure of sensibilities and vigor? I should say that the visit to Europe under those circumstances was much the same thing as the *petit verre*, — the little glass of Chartreuse, or Maraschino, or Curaçoa, or, if you will, of plain Cognac, at the end of a long banquet. One has gone through many courses, which repose in the safe recesses of his economy. He has swallowed his coffee, and still there is a little corner left with its craving unappeased. Then comes the drop of liqueur, *chasse-café*, which is the last thing the stomach has a right to expect. It warms, it comforts, it exhales its benediction on all that has gone before. So the trip to Europe may not do much in the way of instructing the wearied and overloaded intelligence, but it gives it a fillip which makes it feel young again for a little while.

Let not the too mature traveller think it will change any of his habits. It will interrupt his routine for a while, and then he will settle down into his former self, and be just what he was before. I brought home a pair of shoes I had made in London; they do not fit like those I had before I left, and I rarely wear them. It is just so with the new habits I formed and the old ones I left behind me.

But am I not glad, for my own sake, that I went? Certainly I have every reason to be, and I feel that the visit is likely to be a great source of happiness for my remaining days. But there is a higher source of satisfaction. If the kindness shown me strengthens the slenderest link that binds us in affection to that ancestral country which is, and I trust will always be to her descendants, "dear Mother England," that alone justifies my record of it, and to think it is so is more than reward enough. If, in addition, this account of our summer experiences is a source of pleasure to many friends, and of pain to no one, as I trust will prove to be the fact, I hope I need never regret giving to the public the pages which are meant more especially for readers who have a personal interest in the writer.

GENERAL INDEX

This index covers volumes I—X ; a special index is provided for volume XI at the end of that volume.

DISTRIBUTION OF HOLMES'S

PROSE WRITINGS

VOLS. I–X

VOL.

I. THE AUTOCRAT OF THE BREAKFAST-TABLE.
II. THE PROFESSOR AT THE BREAKFAST-TABLE.
III. THE POET AT THE BREAKFAST-TABLE.
IV. OVER THE TEACUPS.
V. ELSIE VENNER.
VI. THE GUARDIAN ANGEL.
VII. A MORTAL ANTIPATHY.
VIII. PAGES FROM AN OLD VOLUME OF LIFE.
    Bread and the Newspaper.
    My Hunt after "The Captain."
    The Inevitable Trial.
    The Physiology of Walking.
    The Seasons.
    The Human Body and its Management.
    Cinders from the Ashes.
    Mechanism in Thought and Morals.
    The Physiology of Versification.
    Crime and Automatism.
    Jonathan Edwards.
    The Pulpit and the Pew.
IX. MEDICAL ESSAYS.
    Homœopathy and its Kindred Delusions.
    The Contagiousness of Puerperal Fever.
    Currents and Counter Currents in Medical Science.
    Border Lines of Knowledge in Some Provinces of Medical Science.
    Scholastic and Bedside Teaching.
    The Medical Profession in Massachusetts.
    The Young Practitioner.
    Medical Libraries.
    Some of My Early Teachers.
X. OUR HUNDRED DAYS IN EUROPE.

INDEX.

———◆———

A—'s diary in England. *See* Diary.

Abbas, **8**, 357.

Abbott, Lieut., of 20th Mass., **8**, 26, 27, 47.

Abel, the doctor's hired man in *Elsie Venner*. *See* Stebbins, Abel.

Abercrombie, Dr., **9**, 293.

Ability, superior, and long life, **4**, 28; Napoleon opened way for, **10**, 174.

Ablution, missionaries of, **3**, 314.

Abney, Sir Thomas, **5**, 57.

Aborigines, called the provisional races, **2**, 82. *See also* Indians.

About so many, *about* so much, **9**, 432.

Abraham, **5**, 247, 248; burial place of, **3**, 331.

"Absent" persons, unconscious action of, **8**, 281.

Absinthe, prevalence of in Paris, **8**, 340, 341.

Abstinence, total, better than brutalities, **2**, 33.

Abuse, liability to, **1**, 81; flattery of, **2**, 202.

Academic gown, splendor of, **10**, 87.

Academic villages, change very slowly, **8**, 253.

Accent, connected with the movement of the pulse, **8**, 319, 320.

Accident, the great chemist and toxicologist, **9**, 289; at Boston theatre, **10**, 31.

Accidents of life confounded with life itself, **3**, 296.

Accomplishments, the two, common to mankind, **8**, 121.

Accountability. *See* Responsibility, **5**, 248.

Accuracy, medical, not to be looked for in the unprofessional public, **9**, 70, 71.

Achievement, laborious, a victory over inertia, **9**, 396.

Achilles, little better than a Choctaw brave, **4**, 74.

Acquisitions, we never outgrow the possibility of new, **9**, 375.

Act, an, to make the poor richer by making the rich poorer, **3**, 3.

Action, reflex. *See* Unconscious mental action.

Actius, **5**, 222.

Active powers, decay of, welcomed by some, **4**, 39.

Actors change less than other people, **3**, 329.

Acts, good and bad, may not be forgotten, **2**, 233.

Acupuncture, instrument for, **3**, 121, 122, 289.

Adam and Eve, creation of, **3**, 83.

Adam, Stonehenge said to have been formed under direction of, **10**, 114.

Adamites, sect of, **8**, 351.

Adams, Charles Francis, on the attitude of Great Britain during the civil war, **8**, 97.

Adams, George, the astronomer, **8**, 84.

Adams, Hannah, "first tenant of Mount Auburn," **8**, 167.

Adams, John, envoy to England, **8**, 98.

Adams, J. Q., endorses the Winthrop eye-water, **9**, 335.

Adams, Samuel, at Commencement, **2**, 41; as governor, 42; his accents of liberty, **8**, 84; quoted, 115.

Addison's disease, **3**, 67.

Addison's dying sentiment, **2**, 292.

Adjectives, used in *triads*, **1**, 85.

Admirable Crichton, The, **10**, 124.

Advertisement, imaginary, of implements of torture, **2**, 207; trap to obtain, for new book, **3**, 302.

Advice, to a poetical aspirant, **4**, 42; to young men and women with literary aspirations, **3**, 158.

Aerial swimming, only triumph of human locomotion yet to be accomplished, **1**, 169.

Æstivation, **1**, 263.

Aëtius, **9**, 410.

Affections, need of the soul for, **2**, 249; sprinkled or poured out, **4**, 218; women decant their, from old bottles into new, **6**, 296.

Affinities, elective, **3**, 129, 130; not to be settled by the almanac, **4**, 263.

Affinity, in love, **1**, 220; manifestations of, 182, 291.

African freedman. *See* Terence.

African kraal, scolding duets of women in, **8**, 291.

After dinner poems and speeches, compared to pulling up flowers by the roots, **1**, 222.

After the Curfew, **4**, 69.

Afternoon tea, in England, **10**, 26; at Mr. Haweis's, 41; at Devonshire House, 42; at Archdeacon Farrar's, 62.

Agassiz, **1**, 7 n.; **7**, 13; **8**, 223; **9**, 406; **10**, 183.

Age, softening effects of, **1**, 81; Balzac's statement as to when men are most dangerous to hearts of women, 149; none in souls, **6**, 177; a factor in the production of moral obliquities, **8**, 338, 339.

Agnew, Sir Andrew, **10**, 5.

Agreeable, the wish to be, is essence of gentle breeding, **2**, 133; art of being, **6**, 289.

Agrippa, Cornelius, **4**, 163.

Ails and grievances, talking of, **2**, 139.

Ainsworth, Dr., **9**, 210.

Air, of Old World used up, **2**, 249; New England's air better than Old England's ale, 250; our first and last food, **8**, 198, 199; necessity for plenty of, and purity of, 213. *See also* Ventilation.

Air-pump, painful experiment with, **1**, 304.

Akenside, his classification of the poets, **8**, 295.

Albany, interest in arrival of first boat in the spring at, **8**, 137.

Albert Edward, Prince of Wales, **10**, 34, 35, 36.

Albert Victor, prince, **10**, 34, 43.

Albiness, **2**, 80.

Albinus, **6**, 141; **9**, 220, 412, 423.

Albret, Marshal d', **7**, 89.

Album, author never refuses to write in, **10**, 55; Princess of Wales's, 55, 56.

Album Verses, **1**, 15.

Alchemy, old books of, **3**, 27; **4**, 160; superstitions of, **9**, 214.

Alcoholic stimulants, **4**, 184; **8**, 220–224.

Alcibiades, a dandy, **1**, 258.

Alderbank, town in *The Guardian Angel*, residence of Clement Lindsay, **6**, 96.

Alderson, Dr., his practice of Perkinism, **9**, 36, 78.

Aldiborontiphoscophornio, **2**, 19.

Aldus edition, **9**, 409; **10**, 148.

Alembert, d', on authors, **9**, 413.

Alembic, in Henchman's shop, **2**, 231.

Alexander the Great, **4**, 74; coins of, **3**, 111; **5**, 222; at the Cydnus, **8**, 228; shrewd trick of his physician, 233; and Homer, **9**, 396.

Alger, Rev. Mr., **10**, 186.

Algonquin and Atalanta, boat-race between, in *A Mortal Antipathy*, **7**, 46–52.

Alibert, Baron, **9**, 437.

Alien elements, medicine consisting of, injurious, **9**, 201, 204, 254, 263.

Aliment. *See* Food.

Alison, Dr., on contagion, **9**, 119, 166.

Allchin, Dr., **10**, 58.

Allegiance to what is highest in one's own nature, **3**, 270.

Allegoria senectutis, **1**, 151.

"Allein's Alarm," **2**, 277.

Allen, the three brothers, of Northampton, **8**, 406.

Allen, Mrs., her hair-restorer, **2**, 79, 311.

Allen, J. M., president of Jefferson College, **9**, 299.

Allen, Ethan, **2**, 46; **4**, 186.

Allibone, S. A., his "Dictionary of Authors," **9**, 403.

Allopathists, and other *pathists*, **8**, 234–236.

Allopathy, **9**, 289.

Allotropism, **5**, 470; **9**, 215.

Alloxan, **9**, 284.

Allston, Washington, **7**, 3; ode of, **10**, 206.

Almanacs, dealing with medicine, **8**, 186.

Alnwick castle, the Percy lion at, **1**, 281; **10**, 6.

Alopecia, **4**, 125.

Alphabet of organization of the human body, **9**, 228.

Altomaris, **5**, 222.

Amadis of Gaul, **10**, 148, 149.

Amantis Dignotio, **7**, 233.

"Amatoors," **3**, 250.

Amazons, **7**, 40.

Ambassador, Austrian, to England, **10**, 51; Turkish, 37.

Ambition, defeated, **6**, 394.

America, lack of permanent homes in, **3**, 11; owes its political freedom to Protestantism, **5**, 253.

American civil war, memorials to young men of favored social position who served in, **1**, 261; opening of, in 1861, **6**, 375; the enthusiasm in Oxbow village, *The Guardian Angel*, 385; to many youth who enlisted it seemed only organized barbarism, 411; simplifying our mode of being, **8**, 3; different from earlier wars, 6, 7; destroys petty social distinctions, 8; lessons of, 8–14; unprepared mental condition of the North at beginning of, 79; moral nature of the issue, 80; inevitableness of, 82, 83, 92; causes of, 85; purpose of, 94; attitude of Great Britain toward the North, 97; attitude of France and Italy during, 99, 100; best that it was not too easily ended, 101; impossibility of honorable peace until the South was conquered, 103, 104; probable results if the South were victorious, 106–108; fears that the government might become a tyranny, 108, 110; possible sacrifices and hardships to be endured in order to finish, 111–113; general glance at discussion of principles involved, 114–119; Carlyle's meddling with, **10**, 140; England's sympathy with the South shocked the North, 184. *See also* Copperheads.

American, the, is the Englishman reinforced, **1**, 238.

American, every, owns all America, **2**, 86

American, ideal life of an, **7**, 31.
American girl, character in *Over the Teacups*. *See* Annexes, the two.
American idea of freedom is congenial, **2**, 81.
American Indians. *See* Indians, American.
American literature, certain tendencies in, **4**, 110.
" American Magazine," **7**, 4.
American Revolution, war passion of the, **8**, 7; effect of, in spiritual matters, 411.
American Tract Society, **6**, 226.
American, young, his opportunities, **2**, 283; dangerously stimulated by his conditions of life, **6**, 221.
Americanization of religion, **2**, 207.
Americans, the great assimilating people, **1**, 19; are like cuckoos, **3**, 10; the talking dynasty hard upon, 265; their love of the superlative, **4**, 104; their appetite for titles of distinction, 222, 231; extravagant tendencies of the medical mind among, **9**, 192, 193; illustration of the ascending scale of vitality among, 199; inferior to the French in prescribing for disease, 204; at first sight of English scenes, **10**, 52; recognized before they speak, 130; Johnson's harsh opinion of, 138; their taste for superlatives, 195.
" Amie Inconnue, L'," Miss Edgeworth's, **10**, 197.
Amines of parasitical literature, **1**, 67.
Amory, Charles, **9**, 425.
Amour-propre, universal, **1**, 51.
Amsterdam galiots, **8**, 58, 59.
Amusements on the planet Saturn, **4**, 65.
Amussat, **9**, 90, 91.
Anacreon, had a quicker respiration than Homer, **3**, 319.
Anæsthetics, of Nature, **5**, 191; **9**, 365; why not end incurable suffering with, **8**, 66; rapidly appropriated by physicians, 235; humanity has a right to use, to secure euthanasia, 238; in childbirth, 238.
Analogies, power of seeing, **1**, 83; in nature, 84.
Ananias, supposed critic of lecture, **2**, 120.
Anatomist's Hymn, The, **1**, 175.
Anatomy, simple statement with reference to, **8**, 190-197; human, an almost exhausted science, **9**, 220; general, the geology of the body, 222; regional, 223; Japan anticipated Europe in a rude regional anatomy, 224; pathological, 231; slight change in our knowledge of, 422, 423.
Ancestors, may have a secondary, yet self-conscious life in the personality of descendants, **6**, 22; their traits in embryo, 26 *et seq.;* reappearance of, in Myrtle's vision in *The Guardian Angel*, 91.
Anchor Tavern, **7**, 36, 251.

Anchorite, **5**, 416.
" Ancient Mariner," quoted, **7**, 91; **8**, 202.
Andover, Mass., large elm at, **1**, 287; seminary clock at, 287; descriptions and reminiscences of, **8**, 245-259.
Andover discussion, **4**, 251.
Andral, **9**, 60, 79, 429, 430.
André, Major, exhumation of, **10**, 96.
Ane, L', de Buridan, **8**, 374.
Angel, the recording, destroys old record-books, **4**, 48; an angel with the influenza, 99.
" Angel of Bethesda," C. Mather's, résumé of, **9**, 359-362.
Angelina's verses, how to treat them, **3**, 153.
Angels might learn from human beings, **3**, 248.
Anger, is insanity, **8**, 335.
Angès, vulgar error for Agnes, **2**, 95.
Angier, Joseph, poem in memory of, **3**, 115.
Anglican church, would gladly be rid of the Athanasian creed, **8**, 420.
Anglo-American anthropology, projected work of the Professor in *Elsie Venner*, **5**, 8.
Anglo-Saxon chronicle quoted, **10**, 66.
Anglo-Saxons die out in America, **1**, 238.
Animal chemistry. *See* Chemistry.
Animal functions tend to assume periodical type of movement, **1**, 155.
Animal magnetism, **5**, 221; **9**, 37.
Animals, eccentrically formed, **2**, 236; learned quadrupeds, **8**, 91; government mules, 32, 33; in winter, 179; chemistry of, 187-190; domestic, must be " salted," 216; revival of apparently obsolete impressions in, 300.
Animus tuus oculus, a freshman's Latin, **3**, 302.
Anise-seed, oil of, **9**, 65.
Ankle, wonderful effects of breaking a bone in, **3**, 97.
Ann-street children, **5**, 324.
Anne, queen of England, **9**, 3.
Annexes, The two, characters in *Over the Teacups*, **4**, 52; their interest in Delilah, the maid, 224; they go with the young Doctor to an " exhibition," 265; their surprise, 271.
Anniversaries, dreaded by the Poet, **1**, 222; dinners at, rules for those who attend, **5**, 122, 123; natural, **8**, 154; fondness of Americans for, 361.
Anodyne, Nature's, **4**, 30.
Anonymous scribblers, **2**, 118.
Another's, one of Gifted Hopkins's poems in *The Guardian Angel*, **6**, 224.
Anstey, Christopher, **10**, 107.
Answer, a *reply* not equivalent to an, **9**, 81.
Answers, unwritten, to correspondents, **4**, 310, 311.
Ant, red, **2**, 245.
Antagonism, laws of, **3**, 130.

Anthropology, legendary, Protestantism must give up, **2**, x ; theology is little more than traditional, **8**, 324 ; is in its infancy, 357 ; replacing scholastic divinity, **9**, 417. *See also* Man.

Antietam, wounded at, **8**, 29, 30 ; battle-field of, 40–42 ; letter picked up at, 42 ; cornfield at, 169.

Antimonial cup, **9**, 341.

Antimony, **9**, 289, 333, 335, 348, 366.

Antipathies, **5**, 207, 443 ; various kinds of, **7**, 63, 64, 143 ; record of, 87–93 ; to sight of blood, 236 ; to cats, 242, 243, 245.

"Antiquary," Scott's, **10**, 113.

Antiquities of Egypt, **4**, 100.

Antiquity, of many modern customs, **3**, 322 ; charm of, not conferred by lapse of fifty years, **7**, 2.

Anxiety at sea, unavoidable, **10**, 15.

Apex family in *The Guardian Angel*, **6**, 289, 312.

Aphorism by the Professor, **2**, 57.

Aphorisms, several specimens of, **6**, 404–406 ; fondness for writing in the form of, natural to strong thinkers, **8**, 384.

Apollinean Institute, a young ladies' school in *Elsie Venner*, **5**, 47 ; called the Broken-Victuals Instltoot by Colonel Sprowle, 132 ; flattering tributes to, in annual reports of committee, 164–167.

Apology, egotism wrong side out, **2**, 139 ; hateful to the world of readers, **4**, 293 ; for human nature, **3**, 20.

Apoplexy, case of, on hearing of Napoleon's return from Elba, **8**, 3 ; sometimes helped by a vegetable diet, 217, 218 ; the archbishop's flavor of, in the memory, 296.

Appetite, false, in many intelligences, **9**, 245.

Apple-trees, anecdote of, **1**, 160 ; **10**, 191.

Apples, smell of, disagreeable to some persons, **7**, 88, 89.

Appleton, Thomas Gold, his mot, "Good Americans when they die go to Paris," **1**, 125 ; his mot about green and mock turtle, **4**, 275 ; **10**, 74.

Approximations, vague, to be avoided in medicine, **9**, 431, 432.

"April Days" of T. W. Higginson, **8**, 139.

Apron strings of American mother made of India rubber, **2**, 285.

"Arabian Nights," prescription of physician in, **6**, 181 ; carpet of, wished for, **10**, 160.

Arago, **3**, 138 ; **10**, 167.

Aram, Eugene, quoted, **8**, 334.

Arblay, Madame d', **10**, 89.

"Arcadia," Sidney's, **10**, 124.

Arcady, South Downs might answer for, **10**, 134.

Arch, beauty and endurance of the, **4**, 211, 212.

Archangel, an, can smile, **4**, 60.

Archbishop, agitation in presence of, **10**, 54.

Archer, the jockey, **10**, 36, 40.

Archimedes, grave of, **2**, 247.

Architecture, an imperfect copy of some divine rule, **2**, 241 ; Greek, common motive in, **8**, 84.

Arcus senilis, **1**, 95.

Area of consciousness, **4**, 11.

Argonauta, **1**, 97.

Arguments, which spoil conversation, **1**, 10 ; common, employed in defence of every doctrine, **9**, 30 *et seq.* ; with certain minds, a lever without a fulcrum, **10**, 172.

Argyll, Duke of, **10**, 51.

Aristocracy, forming in America, **1**, 259 ; money its corner-stone, 260 ; its weak point its lack of thorough manhood, 260 ; pluck should be the backbone of, 261 ; hard-handed, **4**, 218 ; hostile to the North in Civil war, **8**, 97, 98 ; characteristics of, **5**, 1. *See also* Brahmin caste.

Aristotle, **1**, 259 ; **5**, 222 ; **9**, 177.

Ark, Christianity compared to an, **2**, 218.

Arlington Street Church, **10**, 194.

Arm, beautiful cast of, **2**, 48 ; fine arm of cripple, 100, 259 ; sketch of fine, 236 ; strength momentarily centred in, 237.

Arminian heresy, **5**, 44.

Armstrong, Dr., essay by, on puerperal fever, **9**, 135, 136.

Arnold, Dr., of Heidelberg, **9**, 86.

Arnold, Sir Edwin, **4**, 298.

Arnold, Matthew, **10**, 71.

Arnold, Dr. Thomas, his definition of a priest, **8**, 403.

Arnold House, **10**, 132.

Arrowhead Village, scene of *A Mortal Antipathy*, **7**, 35, 36 ; changes in, 297 *et seq.*

Arrowheads, Indian, **2**, 245.

Arrowsmith, **9**, 222.

"Ars Poetica" modernized, **4**, 89.

Arsenic, experiments with, **9**, 61 ; eating of, 255.

Art, the contributions of realism to, **4**, 107 ; distinction between imaginative art and science, 108, 110 ; question between "art" and "nature" in the medical profession, **9**, 181 ; definition of the terms of, 196.

Artemis, the many breasted, of Ephesus, **8**, 77.

Arthur's Seat, Edinburgh, **10**, 83, 85, 47.

Articulated sound, fascination of, **3**, 46, 47.

"Artillery election," not to be counted with 'lection days, **8**, 146 ; **10**, 33.

Artisans, means of, for defending besieged city, **9**, 435.

Artistic nature, frankness of, **2**, 221 ; **6**, 220.

Artists, apt to call in stimulation for their intellects, **1**, 187, 191 ; method of securing portrait, **2**, 191 ; need freedom from disturbance, **3**, 100; their idiosyncrasies, 102.

Asclepiades, **9**, 65.

Ascutney mountain, **5**, 143.

Ases, the, and the *Ifs*, **4**, 121, 122.

Ashburnham, Lord, possessor of the ring of Thothmes III., **3**, 111.

Ashmole, Dr., **9**, 354.

Asia, prophets of, **8**, 206.

Asiatic modes of thought, **8**, 309.

"Asides" of the Autocrat, **1**, 201.

Aspect of things changes entirely in a single generation, **3**, 328.

Assafœtida for hysterics, **6**, 171.

Assessors, Heaven's, **1**, 92.

Assimilable elements, a medicine consisting of, unwholesome food, **9**, 201, 204, 263.

Assimilation of ourselves to external object of interest, **2**, 156; further illustration of, 190.

Assize, the last grand, **4**, 313.

Association of ideas, **1**, 78; "laws of," **8**, 267; mystery of unconscious mental action exemplified in, 285, 286.

Associations, early, **5**, 157.

Asthma, **9**, 413; **10**, 10-12; cure for, 11.

Astrology, **9**, 33; in Boston, 367.

Astronomer weighing Uranus or Neptune, **1**, 276.

Astruc, criticism of the Pentateuch by, **8**, 417; **9**, 298, 366.

Asylum, The. *See* McLean Asylum, **1**, 247.

At the Pantomime, **4**, 198.

At the Turn of the Road, **4**, 288.

Atavism in religious beliefs, **8**, 422.

Athanasian creed, **4**, 258; **5**, 412; an incubus on the Anglican Church, **8**, 420.

Athenæum Club, **10**, 198.

Athenæum picture gallery, **7**, 2.

Athletes, liability of, to consumption, **8**, 230.

Athletics, languishing condition of, **1**, 171.

Athos, Mount, monks of, **3**, 106.

"Atlantic Monthly," first appearance of *The Autocrat* in, **1**, iii.; pun on, 55; *The Professor* came out in, **2**, ix.; *Elsie Venner* published in, **5**, vii.; the author invited to become a contributor, **7**, 9; founded at Z. Porter's inn, **8**, 171.

Atmosphere, moral, effects upon character, **2**, 242; theological, its change in thirty years, **4**, 306; a slow poison, **8**, 373.

Atmospheric reformers, women are born, **8**, 215.

Atmospheric rings, a woman's, **4**, 286.

Atragene Americana, **5**, 101.

Atrophy of heart, women subject to, **2**, 249.

Attention long fixed on a single object, strange effects of, **3**, 107.

Atterbury, **9**, 11.

Attitude, religious, of old age, **4**, 45.

Attraction, laws of, **3**, 130; two principles of, **4**, 283.

Aubrey, quoted on Harvey, **9**, 292, 293.

Audacity in young girls, **2**, 222.

Audiences, intellectual average not high, **1**, 140; "remarkably intelligent" ones much the same in all places, 141; kindness often shown by, to lecturer, 142.

August, **8**, 156, 157.

Augustan age, common motive and force in, **8**, 84.

"Auld Lang Syne," **6**, 200.

"Aunt Sally," **10**, 32.

Aunt Tabitha, **3**, 87.

Aurania, the, steamship, **10**, 179, 181; entertainment on board, 181.

Aurelianus, Cœlius, **9**, 65.

Aureola (Halo), meaning of, **7**, 244.

Auscultation, first work on, in America, **9**, 355.

Austrian ambassador, **10**, 51.

Authors, importance of jockeying to, **1**, 37; vanity of, 49; ashamed of being funny, 50; letters sent to, 69 *et seq.*; they get tired of finding fault when they begin to grow old, 81; repeat in conversation what they have said in their books, **3**, 206; compliments to authors, 207; fate of presentation copies of their books, 301; they should read friendly and unfriendly criticism, 303; personality of, impossibility of concealing it, **4**, 20; their pleasure in renewing relations with the public, 22; blunders of, 156; difficulty of admitting new authors as intimates after a certain period of life, 157; idiosyncrasies of, 297; authors and their characters, 299, 300; character of some, quoted by Hahnemann, **9**, 63; a new generation of, **10**, 38; lonely feeling in the midst of a new generation of, 39.

Authorship, rewards of, **3**, 160; penalties of, **4**, 23; unsuccessful, pathos of, **6**, 291; lead-poisoning of, **9**, 423.

Auto-da-fe, the last, **2**, 208.

Autobiographical character of *Our Hundred Days in Europe*, **10**, 182.

Autocrat, works at carpenter's bench, **1**, 179; **2**, 17, 18, 21, 22; **4**, 304.

Autograph-albums, **1**, 6; **5**, 394.

Autographs, the author's, always genuine, **10**, 25.

Automatism: automatic principles in body, mind, and morals, wide range of, **1**, 85; automatic action of the mind, 134; creative action of mind is automatic, 191; automatic action in morals, **5**, 227, 228; "automatic actions of the secondary kind" *may* be voluntary, **8**, 278, 281; and crime, 322-360; a glance at, 329. *See also* Heredity; Responsibility; Unconscious Mental Action; Will.

Autumn, **5**, 420; **8**, 161-173; leaves, cause of change in color, 165.

Averages, their awful uniformity, **1**, 140; close law of, **2**, 166; **3**, 130; human, steadiness of, 221 *et seq.*; **5**, 272; and law — two dominant words of our time, **9**, 180.

Aversions, personal, indulgence in, **3**, 333.

Avicenna, **5**, 222.

Avis, character in *Over the Teacups*. *See* Delilah.

Avon, the, **10**, 92, 99, 126.

Axe and block, ghastly literature of, **8**, 266, 267.

Babbage's calculating machine, **1**, 9.

Babel, new tower of (Eiffel tower), **4**, 104.

Babies, old, **1**, 154; **5**, 322; badness of, **5**, 257.

Babinet, M., his prophecy of the destruction of the earth, **8**, 425, 426.

Baby's fingers, **3**, 51.

Baccius, Andreas, **5**, 222.

Bachelder, Rev. Stephen, **4**, 37.

Bachelors, have late in life a grand-paternal instinct, **6**, 47.

Back Bay, Boston, **1**, 164.

Backbones, cartilaginous, **4**, 121.

Backgammon, life is like to most men, **6**, 238; good throws at, 361.

Bacon, Miss Delia, insane attempt of, **10**, 95.

Bacon, Lord, **9**, 6, 7, 179; on action of the heart after death, 201; on man and nature, 292; on our opinion of God, 400.

Bacon, Roger, his study at Oxford, **10**, 81.

Bacon's "Essays" at fifty guineas a sheet, **4**, 8.

Badlam, Miss Cynthia, second cousin to Miss Silence Withers in *The Guardian Angel*, **6**, 9; her fears for Myrtle's career, 10; Nurse Byloe scrutinizes her closely, 12; her warnings to Myrtle as to evil ways, 79; watches Rev. Mr. Stoker and Myrtle, 166; calls on Mrs. Hopkins, 167; her mysterious interest in the twins, 169 *et seq.*; plots against Myrtle's interests, 332 *et seq.*; Master Gridley calls on her, 345 *et seq.*; surrenders a paper, 352 *et seq.*; her death, 423; her bequest applied to the benefit of the twins, 426.

Baglivi, **7**, 180 *et seq.*

Baillarger, on cause of right-handedness, **3**, 268.

Baillie, Dr., **9**, 81.

Baillière, publisher of homœopathic books in Paris, **9**, 89.

Baked beans unknown in Philadelphia, **8**, 70.

Balaklava, Captain Nolan at, **2**, 251; charge of the six hundred at, **9**, 297.

Ballad-mongering, **4**, 85.

Ballad poetry, accommodated to the rhythm of breathing, **8**, 319.

Ballet dancing, **3**, 95, 96 : instructive in anatomy of the leg, **8**, 191.

Balloon, toy, **2**, 108.

Balloon-voyagers, **2**, 228.

Baltimore, called the gastronomic metropolis of the Union, **2**, 84; sixth Mass. regiment in, **8**, 7, 13; newsboys of, 48.

Balzac, **7**, 234, 235; his statement as to age when men are most dangerous to hearts of woman, **1**, 149; his "Peau de Chagrin," **4**, 72; **9**, 373.

Bambino, **3**, 308.

Bancroft, George, **4**, 27, 292; his comment on Calvin, **3**, 184; on Jonathan Edwards, **8**, 361, 362, 399; son of a clergyman, 411.

Bangor, Maine, named after hymn of that name, **6**, 87.

Bank of Benevolence, Mrs. Howe's, **10**, 172.

Banner and Oracle. *See* State Banner and Delphian Oracle.

Banshee, **6**, 80.

Barbarisms in medicine, **2**, 105; in law, 106; in religion, 106.

Barbeyrac, Charles, **9**, 281, 343.

Barbier's satirical lines on Napoleon's tomb, **10**, 173.

Barclay, Mr., **10**, 83, 85.

Bard, The, horse, **10**, 36, 82.

Barnes, Phinehas, **8**, 249.

Barnum, P. T., **2**, 165; **3**, 127; **10**, 91.

Barrators, common among doctors as well as lawyers, **9**, 392.

Barron, Dr., on puerperal fever, **9**, 122.

Barry, Martin, **9**, 250.

Bartholinus, Thomas, **9**, 341.

Bartlett, Elisha, **9**, 292, 374, 384.

Bartlett, Sidney, **4**, 27.

Bartolozzi's peppery burin, **2**, 29.

Barzillai, his condition at eighty, **4**, 26, 33.

Base ball, distinctively American, **1**, 36 n.; importance of, **10**, 93.

Basil's Cave, Andover, **8**, 257.

Baskerville edition, of Virgil, **2**, 61; of Addison, **5**, 198.

Basket, huge, of the Manuscript reader, **6**, 303.

Basle, Dance of Death at, **2**, 266.

Bath, Eng., **10**, 105-107; Grand Pump-Room Hotel, 105; old Roman baths, 106; shops in, for slender purses, 106; spoken of by Macaulay, 107; number of visitors, 107; abbey church sculptures, 107.

Bath, convenience of the, one great advantage of city life, **8**, 228.

Battle of the Standard for liberty to each soul, **2**, 78.

Battlefields, all alike, **8**, 13; Antietam, 29; centripetal and centrifugal force of, 29; relics of, repulsive, 42.

Battles, the great vivisectors, **9**, 289.

Baudelocque, on puerperal fever, **9**, 106, 123, 165.

Baxter, Richard, on conversion, **6**, 162.

Beach, Dr., **10**, 181.

Beacon, at Great Malvern, ascent of, **10**, 102.

Beacon Street, door-plate in August, an eye rayless as, **1**, 65 ; latitude of, **8**, 138.

Bean, the Rev. Didymus, mentioned in *Elsie Venner*, **5**, 44, 61.

Bear Hill, in *The Guardian Angel*, **6**, 19.

Bearding the world, **5**, 10.

Beaumont, Dr., his experiments on Alexis St. Martin, **8**, 218.

Beauties, running the gauntlet of years, **1**, 160 ; vulgar, their virtuous indignation at being looked at, 194.

Beauty, Divinity taking outlines and color, **1**, 113 ; human, **2**, 283 ; of New England girl, **5**, 71 ; the perfect sort attained only by repose, 124 ; a luxury monopolized by rich, 124, 125 ; carries repulsion as well as attraction with it, 125, 126 ; a terrible fact, **7**, 246.

Becquerel, **5**, 305.

Bed bug, called a " flat-pattern live timekeeper," **1**, 112.

Bed-time, false modesty in regard to, **1**, 208.

Bee, architecture of, **2**, 241 ; parasites of, **3**, 76 ; peculiar tastes of, **8**, 158.

Beecher, E., theory of the moral world, **8**, 328.

Beeches, **10**, 191.

Beehive, giant, planing-mill compared to, **3**, 325.

Beesly of Everton, **8**, 303.

Beggarly, Mrs., **9**, 341.

Being, great end of, **2**, 1, 4.

Belgium, a bowling alley for kings' cannon-balls, **8**, 23.

Belief : cherished beliefs like ancient drinking-glasses, **1**, 15 ; those in which we are trained, indelible, **3**, 327 ; those of rigid theologians soften in their later years, **4**, 39 ; constitution has much to do with, **5**, 317 ; divorced from character, **8**, 308 ; not to be confounded with evidence, **9**, 108 ; old, still alive, 367.

Belknap, Jeremy, honored historian, **8**, 409.

Bell, the inventor, moving in parallel path with other inventors, **8**, 84.

Bell, Sir Charles, **9**, 293.

Bell, John, as a medical writer, **9**, 225.

Bell-glass, fatal experiment of society in placing young woman under, **1**, 305.

Bellamy, Dr., prophecy of, about the year 1866, **8**, 407.

Belle Poule, La, **6**, 270.

Belles, ball-room, their coquetries, **6**, 260.

Bellingham, Spencer Perceval's assassin, **5**, 226.

Bellows, John, the antiquarian, **1**, 33 n. ; **10**, 40, 116, 196.

Belmont spring water, **10**, 12.

Bemerton, England, **10**, 110, 125 ; George Herbert's church at, 127.

Bend Or, a Derby winner, **10**, 22, 33.

Benedict, Joel, quoted on prophecy of Dr. Bellamy, **8**, 407.

Benevolence, its practice by impostors, **9**, 35, 87.

Benicia Boy, **1**, 173.

Benjamin Franklin, the landlady's son in *The Autocrat* and *The Professor*, **1**, 12 ; called B. F. or Frank, 57 ; his French exercise, 58 ; another French exercise, 136 ; his addition to the bridecake, 311 ; other mention, 53, 87, 116, 135, 246 ; **2**, 4, 21, etc. *See also* Doctor B. Franklin.

Benjamin of Tudela, **10**, 182.

Bennett, John Hughes, **9**, 295, 297.

Benson, Edward W., Archbishop of Canterbury, **10**, 73.

Benson, Mrs., at Lambeth Palace, **10**, 73.

Bentham's logic against ghosts, **2**, 189.

Berengarius, the anatomist, **6**, 141 ; **9**, 411.

Béranger's lines on England quoted, **10**, 193.

Beresina, the, old soldier's saying about, **10**, 206.

Berkeley, Bishop, his treatise on tarwater, **8**, 418 ; **9**, 12.

Berkshire County, Massachusetts, **1**, 235, 245, 265.

Berkshire Mountains, **2**, 245.

Berlin, University of, **9**, 406.

Berne, jump of Weinzäpfli's horse at, **1**, 281.

Bertrand, Dr., on the convict prisons of France, **8**, 345.

Berwick on Tweed, **10**, 6.

Best, one can't be all the time trying to do one's, **1**, 278.

Best man in a fight, **5**, 26.

Bethesda, pool of, stirred by an author, **4**, 10.

Beverly, Massachusetts, oak at, **10**, 48.

Beverly Farms, large oak at, **1**, 288 n.

Bezoar, East Indian, **9**, 340, 341.

Bible, a seeming defence of right to have three wives derived from, **2**, 5 ; skepticism afraid of new translations, 7 ; resorted to from different motives, 122 ; many people get their Scripture from Vinegar edition, **5**, 326.

Bichat, **4**, 123 ; **8**, 320 ; **9**, 179, 222, 226, 228.

Bicycle, **1**, iv., 168 n.

Bidloo, **9**, 411.

Bifteck saignant, **10**, 201.

Bigamists, love-letters of, rich in poetical extracts, **4**, 92.

Bigel, Dr., **9**, 99.

Bigelow, George Tyler, **2**, 49 ; **4**, 29.

Bigelow, Henry J., **9**, 439.

Bigelow, Jacob, **9**, 351, 433, 435 ; " Modern inquiries," **8**, 144, 145, 183 ; on poisoning from eating partridges, 219, 220 ; formula of, to obtain a long, healthy life, 234.

Biglow, W., Dr. Holmes's schoolmaster, 8, 240.
Bigot, the mind of, compared to the pupil of the eye, 1, 144.
Billiard-ball, the Model of all the Virtues compared to, 2, 71.
Billiards, 9, 376.
Billings, John S., catalogue of, 9, 406, 407.
Billionaire's easy method of planning for large party, 5, 86.
Biography, cost of being its subject, 3, 163 et seq.
Birds which have no fear, 2, 96; sketch of solitary, 238; voices of, 5, 185; eggs of, 266; advent of, in spring, 8, 142, 144; of winter, 179.
  Blackbird, 10, 191.
  Canary, 1, 85; 2, 94; 6, 59.
  Crow, 1, 29.
  Cuckoo, 10, 50, 191.
  Heron, 2, 236.
  King-bird, 1, 29.
  Lark, 10, 191.
  Nightingale, 10, 191.
  Purple finch, 2, 94.
  Rook, 10, 191.
  Sparrow, English, 3, 314.
  Starling, 10, 191.
Birs Nimroud, 10, 123, 152.
Birth, a second natural, 2, 243.
Birthday, The Dictator's, 4, 290 et seq.
Birthday books, author never refuses to write in, 10, 55.
Birthday cake for author, 10, 181.
Birthmark, 5, 278.
Birth-year of author, and of Gladstone, Tennyson, Darwin, the same, 10, 44.
Biscuit, called "crackers" in Boston, 2, 169; seafoam, 10, 201.
Bishop, Bridget, 9, 358.
Bishop, English, not ashamed that his son was a doctor, 8, 410.
Black drop, Nature's, 4, 30, 39.
Black Hawk, anecdote of, 7, 6.
Black powder, mystical remedy, 9, 280, 330.
Blackberry, 2, 187; an imitative fruit, 8, 157.
Blackstone, 3, 314; believed the moon to affect the insane, 8, 212.
Blair's chronology, 3, 83.
Blake, Mr., his "Jesse Rural," 1, 90.
Blanket-shawl, 1, 19.
Blenheim, 10, 6.
Blessed are those who have said our good things for us, 4, 10.
Blessed Virgin, torturing-implement, 2, 208; 10, 202.
Blessing, propriety of asking one, at Col. Sprowle's party in Elsie Venner, 5, 106, 107.
Blind, mental action of the congenitally, 8, 269, 270.
Blind spot of the eye, 4, 166.
Blindness, said to be caused by sleeping in moonlight, 8, 212.
Blitz, Signor, 1, 38.

Blondes, two kinds of, 1, 183; "positive" variety of, 2, 54, 222; the "negative" variety, 222; spiritual transparency of, 229; the boiled parsnip sort, 6, 259.
Blood, enormous number of swimming glands in, 2, 59; necessary to courage, and to successful love, 7, 235; fainting at sight of, 89, 236; corpuscles of, 8, 192; 9, 238; wanted by whatever organ is at work, 230; change in that which goes to the brain after severe mental labor, 263; itself an organ, 266.
Blood-letting, 9, 295, 325, 331, 428, 432, 433.
"Blooded" horse not same as "blood" horse, 1, 37.
Bloody Mary, was hysterical, 6, 171.
Bloomer costume, 2, 155.
Blossoms of the Soul, title of Gifted Hopkins's manuscript poems, 6, 301; its fate at the hands of the Manuscript reader, 306 et seq.
Blue vitriol, 9, 10.
Blundell, Dr., on puerperal fever, 9, 139, 140, 166.
Blunders, clerical, in speech, pardonable, 1, 111.
Blushing, 5, 358, 359; meaningless, 1, 193.
Boarders, peculiar, 2, 168.
Boarding-house, the, in The Professor, arrangements of boarders in, 2, 21; fare in, 168; its limitations as to quantity, 169.
Boarding-house fever, 3, 64.
Boarding-houses, unprotected girls in, 2, 223; their usual inmates, 3, 244; trials of keeping, 341.
Boarding-schools have same general features, 5, 171.
Boat race between the Algonquin and the Atalanta, in A Mortal Antipathy, 7, 46-52.
Boating, the Professor's pleasure in, 1, 164; shape of his boat, 168; nearest approach to flying, 168; greatest labor for muscles in, 169; boats on steamship, fearful possibilities suggested by, 10, 16, 181.
Bodleian Library, 10, 81.
Body, human, only looked on as a temporal possession, 2, 19; structure of, has suggested many modern contrivances, 3, 322; management of, 8, 186-238; twelve chemical elements of, 189; geology of, 191; cells of, 192, 193; fibres and membranes of, 193, 194; decay and renewal of, 198-200, 266; exhalations of, 200; a soil capable of being improved, 216; the cook makes, the apothecary cobbles the, 217; respiration and pulse time-keepers of, 315; alphabet of its organization, 9, 229.
Boerhaave, 5, 19; 9, 375.
Boileau, Abbé, story of Pascal told by, 7, 90.

Bois de Boulogne, **10**, 176.
Bolt Court, London, Johnson's house in, **10**, 154.
Bombazine, a soubriquet for the Poor Relation, which see.
Bon mots of the Seven wise men of Boston, **1**, 124 *et seq.*
Bonaparte, Prince Lucien, **9**, 418.
Bond Street, London, **10**, 145.
Bones, of nature, **8**, 74 ; substance of, 196.
Bonnet, M., his experiments with cinchona, **9**, 61.
Bonneville de Marsangy, account of the Colonie pénitentiare of Mettray, **8**, 354 ; on the case of Dumollard and capital punishment, 356.
Bonninghausen, Okie's, **9**, 414.
Boo, word agreed upon for universal ejaculation, **1**, viii.
Book, a dead. *See* " Thoughts on the Universe."
Book advertisement, trap to obtain, **3**, 302.
Book-agent, **9**, 422.
Book-hunter, delights of the, **9**, 410, 411.
Book-hunger, **4**, 150.
Book infirmary, should be attached to every library, **3**, 25 ; the Master's, 213.
Book-miser, **9**, 409.
Book of Life, God opens it to doctors, **5**, 325.
Book of the three maiden sisters, **2**, 230.
Book-shop, Quaritch's, **10**, 146–149.
Book-tasting, **4**, 151 ; women in, 157.
Bookworms, extravagance of, **4**, 115 ; picture of a bookworm, 150.
Books, of a man of family, **1**, 22 ; subtle influence of, 23 ; candid hate for, 62 ; society draws the virtue of best reading, 62 ; easy feeling in their presence, 132 ; sight of, sometimes hateful, 134 ; a woman's and a man's use of, 275 ; their greeting, **2**, 29 ; old books, 210 ; fate of presentation copies of, **3**, 301 ; like leaky boats on a sea of wisdom, 302 ; rare, **4**, 116 ; **10**, 148 ; lists of books, **4**, 149 ; books in our libraries which we know by sight only, 159 ; dusting, **6**, 370 ; intimate relations between, and their owners, **7**, 78 ; medical, 177 ; different sorts of, **8**, 352 ; evolution of, **9**, 400 ; a scholar should not be in a hurry to part with his, 408 ; prices of, 149.
Boot, cast-iron, **2**, 207.
Bootmaker, English, **10**, 145.
Border land of legitimate instincts and affections, **6**, 151.
Border lines of knowledge in some provinces of medical science, **9**, 209–272.
Border states, perilous condition of in American civil war, **8**, 96.
Border warfare between England and Scotland, **8**, 107, 108.

Bores, all men are, except when we want them, **1**, 6 ; the same everywhere, 279 ; may be good talkers, **3**, 301 ; a peculiarity of, **4**, 83 ; specialists may become, 156.
Boscovich, on our knowledge of matter, **8**, 264.
Bossuet, **8**, 366.
Bostock, Dr., his opinion of French medical treatment, **9**, 205 ; his " Physiology," 225.
Boston, indebtedness of Edwards to, for his descriptions of Hell, **8**, 385, 386.
Boston, Seven wise men of, their sayings, **1**, 124 ; like other places of its size, 126 ; drains a large water-shed of intellect, 127 ; boating around, 164 ; walks in, 165 ; picturesque spots in, 272, 273 ; the Little Gentleman's pride in, **2**, 3 ; has opened turnpikes to free thought and speech, 3 ; early patriots in, 15 ; great macadamizing place, 16 ; has much of England about it, 45 ; the battle of the three-hilled against the seven-hilled city, 78 ; sunsets in, 82 ; thinking centre of the planet, 83 ; wealth and influence fairly divided, 84 ; evil results of sneering at, 281 ; heart of the world under it, 301 ; its disfiguring monuments, **4**, 104, 105 ; Brattle Street Church, **8**, 6, 14 ; beautiful suburbs of, 75 ; fair bosom of, 76 ; latitude of, 138 ; Frog pond on the Common, 138, 146 ; trees on the Common, 139 ; Granary burial-ground, 163 ; old burial-grounds, 166 ; West Boston bridge, 178, 181 ; percentage of phthisis in, 206 ; mortality in, from consumption, **9**, 294 ; epidemics of small-pox in, **9**, 345, 346 ; brightness of, remarked by Dickens, **10**, 23 ; State House dome, 38 ; blessed centre of New England life, 66 ; provisions for its wealthy children, 204.
Athenæum, **7**, 2.
Back Bay, **1**, 169.
Chambers Street, **1**, 272.
Charles Street, **1**, 273.
Christ Church, **2**, 307.
Common, **1**, 277 ; **2**, 42, 316 ; **3**, 313, 315 ; duel on, **1**, 239.
Copp's Hill burying-ground, **2**, 3, 306, 316.
Cornhill, **10**, 145.
Faneuil Hall, **2**, 3.
Essex Street, **1**, 272.
Franklin Place, **1**, 272.
Frog pond, **2**, 3 ; **3**, 314.
Granary burying ground, **1**, 239.
Graveyards, **3**, 329.
Hancock House, **2**, 42.
King's Chapel, **10**, 132.
Montgomery Place, **10**, 136.
Myrtle street, **1**, 165, 272.
North End, **2**, 3.
Paddock elms, **1**, 239.
Park Street Church, **2**, 11.

Public Garden, **1**, 273.
Quincy Market, **2**, 196.
State House, **1**, 125; **2**, 55, 217; **4**, 308.
Streets, **3**, 324.
West Boston bridge, **2**, 2.
Boston Athenæum, medical collection in, **9**, 398.
Boston Daily Advertiser, quoted, **9**, 418.
Boston girl and New York girl, their conversation, **6**, 269.
Boston Natural History Society, **4**, 16.
Boston Public Library, medical collection in, **9**, 398.
" Boston Recorder," **7**, 4.
Boston Theatre, accident at, **10**, 31.
Boswell, **1**, 280 ; **10**, 139, 154.
Boteler, Dr., quoted on strawberries, **8**, 153 ; **10**, 169.
Botticelli, **10**, 151.
Bouillaud, **9**, 428, 437.
Boulogne, **10**, 161.
Boundary mark between certain classes, the napkin-ring, **7**, 298.
Bouveries, Earls of Radnor, **10**, 121.
Bowditch, Dr. H. I., **9**, 296, 397.
Bowie-knife, **1**, 19.
Bowing both ways at once, **10**, 89.
Box, its fragrance, **5**, 437.
Box, small tin, presented to author, **10**, 13 ; its useful contents, 16.
Boxing, **1**, 171 ; behavior of a gentleman in a contest, 172 ; possible good effects of on clergy, 172.
Boy, a healthy, finds nothing in common with child of weakened vitality, **2**, 194 ; finds his materials of thought in very simple sources, **8**, 251.
" Boy Bishop," **10**, 119.
" Boy of Windermere," Wordsworth's, **2**, 160 : **8**, 18.
Boyer, Baron, **9**, 427.
Boyle, Robert, **3**, 216 ; **9**, 187, 251, 354.
Boylston, Zabdiel, first to inoculate for small-pox, **9**, 347, 418.
" Boys, The," the Professor dines with, **1**, 121.
Boys, The, **2**, 49.
Bracelet, antique, **6**, 186, 218, 241, 261, 277, 312.
Brackets used by the Autocrat, attention called to, **1**, 201.
Bradford, Ruth, wife of Selah Withers, in *The Guardian Angel*, accused of witchcraft, **6**, 24, 93.
Bradley, Dean, tea with, **10**, 30.
Bradshaw, Mr. William Murray, an ambitious but unscrupulous young man in *The Guardian Angel*, taken into partnership with Jacob Penhallow, **6**, 5 ; description of, 44 *et seq.* ; his plan of life laid out, 46 ; seen to abstract document from the Withers family papers, 57 *et seq.* ; begins to show an interest in Myrtle's affairs, 64 ; calls in Dr. Hurlbut professionally, 138 ; meets Clement Lindsay, 234 *et seq.* ; introduces him to Myrtle, 244 ; de-
cides to offer himself to Myrtle, 313 *et seq.* ; calls upon Myrtle just as she has accepted Clement Lindsay, 390 *et seq.* ; tells his love to Myrtle, 397 *et seq.* ; in rage at her rejection of him, he destroys what he supposes to be a paper entitling her to a large fortune, 401 ; enlists as officer in the Civil war, 401 ; Myrtle finds him mortally wounded, 418 *et seq.*
Braham, anecdote of his forgetting a song, **2**, 24.
Brahmin caste of New England, not a conventional aristocracy, **5**, 3 ; social type in colleges, 3, 4 ; productive of hereditary scholarship, 5 ; never has the saddle-leather skin, 286 ; count as men, **8**, 9.
Braid, Mr., on hypnotism, **5**, 205.
Brain, possibly a double organ, **1**, 74 ; upper and lower stories of, 179 ; like clock, 185 ; stimulation of, 187 ; some which contain the ovarian eggs of future civilization, 195 ; possibility of running dry, **2**, 22 ; close resemblance of different, 167 ; Byron's small brain, 200 ; soul in core of, according to Descartes, 247 ; a wick of the lamp of life, 260 ; like a tinder-box, **4**, 14 ; action through space, 15 ; squinting, 96, 99, 111, 114, 115, 162, 166, 204, 281, 282 ; **6**, 205 ; **8**, 175 ; wanting in bilateral symmetry, 282, 283 ; crook in the, **5**, 247 ; a three-story, **6**, 117 ; how related to the heart, **7**, 235 ; cells of, **8**, 192 ; best time for work of, 193 ; necessary to thought, 263 ; change in blood that goes to, after severe mental labor, 263 ; a double organ, 264, 267 ; *may* be inscribed with material records of thought, 264 ; must be fed, 265, 293 ; relative strength of the two halves of, 268 ; vast amount of blood sent to, 292 ; said to be lifted by every stroke of the pulse, 320 ; a good, not enough without a stout heart, **9**, 429. *See also* Automatism ; Memory ; Mind ; Thought ; Unconscious mental action.
Brain-force, laws of, **4**, 16.
Brain-tappers, **4**, 12, 179.
Brainard, mourning over himself, **8**, 397, 398.
Brainey, Professor, his phrenological analysis of faculties, **2**, 201.
Branded shoulder of French servant, **1**, 106.
Brant House, Harrisburg, **8**, 64.
Braowne, Arvilly, in *Elsie Venner*, **5**, 28.
Brattle Street Church, cannon ball in, **8**, 6, 14.
Bravery, Revolutionary, believed to have died out, **8**, 10 ; of the working people overlaid, not smothered, 10.
Brazer, Dr. James, **9**, 303.
Bread, and the newspaper, **8**, 1–15 ; from English bakers' shops, not so good as American, **10**, 200.

Breadroot, the great industrial product of the planet Saturn, **4**, 63.

Bread-tree, as described in " Our Sumatra correspondence," **1**, 119.

Breakfast, least convenient time for writing, **10**, 25 ; at St. John's College, Cambridge, 78 ; good one at York, 82 ; at Parisian Café, 1833, 174.

Breakfast-Table Series, viz. : vol. **1**, *The Autocrat;* vol. **2**, *The Professor ;* vol. **3**, *The Poet;* epilogue to, **3**, 349.

Breaking down, in young men and women, **9**, 297.

Beathing, difficult in heart disease, **2**, 257.

Breeding shows itself in one's religion, **1**, 312 ; gentle, lies in the wish to be agreeable, **2**, 133 ; takes everything coolly, 142.

Breschet, **9**, 90, 91.

Brewster, Jonathan, **9**, 355.

Bridget in *The Autocrat*, moved by sentiment, **1**, 100 ; her wedding-present to the Schoolmistress, **1**, 313 ; insists that Little Gentleman was a Catholic, **2**, 309.

Bridgeport, Connecticut, **8**, 75.

Bridges of Paris, **10**, 175.

Briggs, Mr., adventures of, compared with Mr. Pickwick's, **10**, 162.

Briggs, Abner, the bully of school in Pigwacket, in *Elsie Venner*, **5**, 24 ; vanquishes Master Weeks, 25 ; is thrashed by Bernard Langdon, 37–39.

Briggs, Richard, **4**, 163.

Briggs, Mr. and Mrs., in *Elsie Venner*, **5**, 92.

Bright, John, a friend to the North in Civil war, **8**, 99 ; **10**, 86, 88.

Bright people sometimes tiresome, **1**, 6.

Bright thought, salability of, **1**, 27.

Bright's disease, patient knows what it means, **9**, 389.

Brighton, England, **9**, 296 ; **10**, 132–135.

Brinvilliers, Marchioness of, **2**, 305.

" British and Foreign Medical review," **9**, 403.

British aristocracy, hostile to the North in civil war, **8**, 97.

British captain, struck by cannon ball, story of, **5**, 391.

British dogmatists, dynasty of, **9**, 302.

British Museum, catalogue of, **9**, 405 ; how not to see it, **10**, 151 ; Elgin Marbles, 152 ; sculptures from Nineveh, 152 ; lesson learned from a visit to, 152 ; how to see it, 153.

Britons once looked on as enemies, **10**, 184.

Britons' stockades, **2**, 245.

Broad church, **2**, 296 ; must have creed in the heart and not in head, 298 ; one finds what it means in war times, **8**, 11.

Brodie, Sir Benjamin, **9**, 161, 298.

Broken Circle, The, **10**, 111.

Broken-Victuals Instytoot, **5**, 132.

Bronze skin, **3**, 67.

Brook, mountain, **5**, 45, 46.

Brooke, Rev. Stopford, **10**, 197.

Brooks, John, **9**, 345.

Broomstick Train, The, **4**, 226, 312.

Broussais, **9**, 186, 188, 205, 349, 429, 430.

Brown, Professor Alexander Crum, **10**, 83.

Brown, Dr. John, **9**, 286, 293 ; **10**, 83 ; his sister, 83.

Brown-Séquard, **9**, 243, 293.

Brown stone front, **6**, 274.

Browne, Miss Clara, in *The Guardian Angel*, **6**, 273.

Browne, H., of Amesbury, his opinion on Stonehenge, **10**, 114.

Browne, Simon, the man without a soul, dedication of his Answer to Tindal's " Christianity as old as the Creation," **3**, 215.

Browne, Sir Thomas, a sentiment of his, **1**, 93 ; quoted, 153.

Brownell, Henry Howard, **4**, 153 ; quoted, **9**, 385.

Browning, Oscar, **10**, 78.

Browning, R., **4**, 41 ; his " Grammarian's Funeral," 133, 175 ; **10**, 28, 37, 40, 68, 86, 89 ; a vital element of London Society, 56.

Brownson, O. A., **5**, 324 ; teachings of, **8**, 419, 420.

Bruce's Address, alteration of, **1**, 47.

Brummel, Beau, **10**, 161.

Bruno, Giordano, **4**, 163.

Brunonian stimulating treatment, **9**, 258, 261.

Bryant, **2**, 109 ; **4**, 41, 247, 248 ; **7**, 5 ; use of facts of observation by, **8**, 134.

Bryant and May's safety-matches, **10**, 146.

Bryce, Professor James, **10**, 54.

" Bub," abbreviation of Beelzebub, **3**, 7.

Bucephalus Capensis, **5**, 223.

Buck, Jefferson, in *Elsie Venner*, **5**, 97.

Buckminster, J. S., son of a clergyman, **8**, 411.

Buckwheat, " fragrant," **8**, 157.

" Budget, A, of Paradoxes," by Augustus De Morgan, **4**, 161.

Buenos Ayres, " the City of wholesome breezes," **5**, 154.

Buffaloes, **2**, 236.

Bugbee, Miss Rose, in *The Guardian Angel*, **6**, 272, 287.

Bullet going through glass without glancing, **5**, 330.

Bumble-bee, **9**, 416.

Bumps. *See* Phrenology.

Bumpus and Crane, Messrs., their Physiological Emporium of phrenology, **2**, 196.

Bun, 'lection, **2**, 42 ; **8**, 146 ; offered before dinner as a test of age, 57.

Buncle, John. *See* John Buncle, **10**, 182.

Bunker Hill, battle of, **10**, 75 ; ignorance concerning, **10**, 92 ; monument, rocking of, **1**, 286 ; monument, **3**, 95,

148, 149, 166; **10**, 194; man of the monument, **3**, 151, 166.

Bunyan, John, quotation from, **3**, 276; anticipates Galton and the Professor, 303; "Pilgrim's Progress," **6**, 76; quoted, **8**, 48, 388; his Christian a victim of melancholia, **8**, 416; **10**, 186.

Burdach, **9**, 219.

Burial grounds, change their outward aspect less than other places, **3**, 329; old, in Boston, Watertown, Cambridge, and Dorchester, **8**, 166; in Andover, 256, 257; in Boston, vandalism in, **1**, 239, 240.

Burke-and-Hare business, **8**, 44; **10**, 65.

Burnett, Waldo, **9**, 299.

Burning chamber, a party is Society's, **5**, 94.

Burning cross seen at night, **6**, 91, 95.

Burns, R., proposed alteration of line in his "Scots wha hae," **1**, 47; centenary, **2**, 26; his friendship must have been a terrible thing, 241; quoted, **4**, 253; method of composing verses, **8**, 286, 287; Dr. Holmes's verses on, 314; influence of, on Scotch theology, 431; haunts of, **10**, 186.

Burns, treatment of, **9**, 68.

Burnt toad, practice of giving as a remedy, **9**, 262, 280, 331.

Burroughs, George, **2**, 262.

Burroughs, J., on the coming of the dandelion, **8**, 143; enthusiastic descriptions of, 183.

Burton's "Anatomy," quoted, **8**, 334.

Bush, Paul, **9**, 320.

Bushnell, H., theory of the moral world, **8**, 328.

Bust of Liberty, in *The Guardian Angel*, **6**, 245; 251 *et seq.*

Butcher, The, the Manuscript Reader so called, in *The Guardian Angel*, **6**, 304 *et seq.*

Butler, Lady Eleanor, **10**, 186.

Butler, W. A., **8**, 351.

Buttercups, **2**, 231.

Butterfly, image of the beatified spirit, **1**, 113.

Butters, Rev. Mr., in *Elsie Venner*, **5**, 166.

Button wood, **1**, 153.

Butts, Dr., a prominent character in *A Mortal Antipathy:* his characteristics, **7**, 82 *et seq.;* studies the history of antipathies, 83, 87, 88; reads paper before the Pansophian Society, 166 *et seq.;* calls on Miss Tower, 186; Maurice Kirkwood becomes his patient, 202 *et seq.;* his reflections upon Kirkwood's story, 240 *et seq.;* his letter to Mrs. Kirkwood, 296; his letter to Mrs. Butts, 301.

Byles, Mather, facetiæ of, **8**, 409.

Byloe, Nurse, in *The Guardian Angel*, **6**, 7; defends Myrtle's character, 11, 15; her art of handling the young, 28; sent for to take care of Myrtle, 28;

grows watchful of influence of Dr. Hurlbut over Myrtle, 139.

Byron, Lord, **4**, 49, 86; his line about "striking the electric chain," **1**, 78; "Edinburgh Review's" attempt to put down Master George Gordon, 296; his small brain, **2**, 200; his deformity, 278; quoted, **10**, 17, 74.

Cabalistic sentence, **4**, 164.

Cabalistic teachers, belief of, **9**, 33.

Cabinet desk, discovery of a secret drawer in, **2**, 91.

Cabinet, mysterious, in *The Professor*, contents of, **2**, 304.

Cabinet, of the United States, theft and perjury in, **8**, 86.

Cabot, Mr., on birds, **8**, 179, 183.

Cacoethes scribendi, **4**, 93.

Cache, children instinctively make a, **1**, 204.

Caddice-worm, **3**, 211.

Cadenus, captivating Stella and Vanessa, **2**, 89.

Cæsars, **6**, 222.

Café Anglais, Paris, **10**, 175.

Café Procope, Paris, **10**, 166–168.

Caffè Pedrocchi, Padua, a mausoleum called a place of entertainment, **8**, 64.

Cake, varieties of, **5**, 109; birthday, for author, **10**, 181.

Calais, **10**, 7; associated with Sterne, 161.

Calamities grow old rapidly in proportion to their magnitude, **1**, 31; recollection of, returns freshly after first sleep, 32; act like a stain, **8**, 4; impressions of great, 4.

Calculating, Babbage's machine for, **1**, 8; least human of qualities, 9.

Caleb, the son of Jephunneh, **4**, 25, 34.

"Caleb Williams," **6**, 275.

Calef, Robert, burning of his book on witchcraft, **2**, 8; **8**, 414; quoted on the clergy, **8**, 413, 414.

Calhoun, J. C., **4**, 45; **8**, 83.

Call him not old, whose visionary brain, **1**, 174.

Callouses, **2**, 259.

Calmet's Dictionary, **6**, 371.

Calomel, **2**, 112; **9**, 275.

Calton Hill, Edinburgh, **10**, 83.

Caltrops, **1**, 295.

Calumet, owned by Autocrat, **1**, 102.

Calvin, in a state of religious barbarism, **2**, 106; criticised by Bancroft, **3**, 184; preface to his Institutes, **9**, 310.

Calvinism, **6**, 17; **8**, 380.

Cam River, **10**, 71, 77.

Cambridge, England, visit to, **10**, 71–73; rooms in Trinity, 71; relationship with, 72; second visit, 74–79; degree of Doctor of Letters, 75; demonstrative students, 76; cordial reception at, 76; extract from Latin speech, 76; leaves delightful impression, 77; the gathering of boats, 77; the river, 77;

library of Trinity College, 77; King's College chapel, 77; dinner at Vice-Chancellor's, 78; hospitalities, 78; breakfast at St. John's College, 78; verses from "Lines of Greeting" to author by Mr. Heitland, 79.

Cambridge, Massachusetts, flats of, **1**, 170; in the author's boyhood, **7**, 25, 26; arsenal guarded by students, **8**, 12; East, chimneys of, 77; Commencement at, 158–161; old burial ground at, 166; appearance of, and of Cambridgeport in 1820, 240; daughter of Cambridge in England, **10**, 72.

Cambridgeport, appearance of in 1820, **8**, 240; Port school, 240–243.

Camden, William, **10**, 98, 103.

Camel, **2**, 236.

Campbell, Dr., cases of puerperal fever, **9**, 157 et seq.

Campbell, Thomas, misquotation of, **1**, 71; his "Gertrude of Wyoming," **8**, 49.

Camperdown, Lady, **10**, 41.

Campo Santo, **7**, 28.

Canal, spinal, **9**, 243.

Canal boats, mighty passion to be captain of one, **8**, 21.

Canary birds, **1**, 86; **6**, 59.

Candidates, trial of, for pulpit, **5**, 473, 474.

Candles in railroad cars, **8**, 52.

Candlestick, seven-branched, **3**, 332.

Candor liable to degenerate into weakness, **9**, 2.

Canker worm, **8**, 151; its omega-like shape, 152.

Cannibalism, **3**, 150; literary, **4**, 23.

Cannon, story of British captain struck by cannon-ball, **5**, 391; firing, to raise bodies of the drowned, **6**, 15.

Canoe, white, in A Mortal Antipathy, **7**, 53.

Canoe Meadow, in Berkshire mountains, **2**, 245; **5**, 266; **10**, 77.

Cant or slang, worse than punning, **1**, 256.

Cantabridge, three maiden sisters at, **2**, 230; arrowheads from there, 245; mysterious young stranger in, **7**, 60.

Canterbury, Archbishop of (E. W. Benson), **10**, 73.

Canute, King, **3**, 187, 267.

Cap, spinster's, of the lasciate ogni speranza pattern, **6**, 346.

Capacity, most of us overrate our, **4**, 312.

Cape Ann, the magnolia on, **2**, 244.

Capital punishment. See Punishment.

Capitalist, in The Poet, his economics, **3**, 40; treated by Dr. B. Franklin, 253; his unexpected generosity, 346.

Capsheaf girls, in The Guardian Angel, **6**, 289.

Capsheaf, Miss Victoria, **6**, 312.

Capsulæ suprarenales, **3**, 68.

Captive, who preserved his reason by means of a pin, **6**, 74.

Caput mortuum, **3**, 281.

Caravan hastening over desert, dying compared to, **2**, 276.

Carbon as fuel in human economy, **1**, 155.

Carbonate of lime as prepared by Hahnemann for medicine, **9**, 44.

Cardanus, **5**, 222.

Cardinal flower, **8**, 156.

Caricatures in "Punch," **10**, 42.

Carlyle, Thomas, **3**, 265; **7**, 17, 88, 177; his "Characteristics," **1**, 55; on Boswell, 280; his picture of an editor, **4**, 10; smoking with his mother, 33; clotted English of, **9**, 302; **10**, 136–138; his house at Chelsea, 136, 137, 140; on Coleridge in "Life of Sterling," 139; his meddling with our anti-slavery conflict, 130; his wife, 140.

"Carmen," Marie Roze in, **10**, 73.

Carpenter, Miss, belief of, in regard to criminals, **8**, 345.

Carpenter's bench, Autocrat's, **1**, 180.

Carpet in "Arabian Nights," wished for, **10**, 160.

Carriages, of friends, **10**, 28; waiting for, after a party, 45, 46.

Carstairs, William, tortured, **8**, 395.

Cartilage, **9**, 229; fibro-cartilage, 230.

Casaubon, preface of, **9**, 310.

Cashmere shawl, old, **1**, 312.

Casper, Dr., his statistics of phthisis, **8**, 206.

Cassia, the Doctor's mare, in Elsie Venner, **5**, 137, 138.

Caste, Brahmin, in New England. See Brahmin caste.

"Castle of Otranto," **6**, 275.

Castles, Ruskin's aversion to a country without, **3**, 11.

Casuistical divinity, **6**, 162.

Cats: superannuated cat, her enviable lot, **4**, 34; antipathy for, **5**, 443; **7**, 64, 242.

Catalepsy, **2**, 237.

Catalogues, literature of, **10**, 146; Quaritch's, 148, 149.

Catamount, **6**, 19, 125.

Caterpillar, alluded to by Miss Rossetti, **8**, 153; racing with a canker-worm, 153; on Tennyson's estate, **10**, 191.

Cathedrals, dream of one, **5**, 408–410; flowers of stone from aerolites as seeds, **8**, 84; glorify a town, **9**, 399. Chester, **10**, 19, 20. Salisbury, **10**, 108, 109, 118, 119, 121. Wells, **10**, 186.

Cato, chief speaker in "De Senectute," **1**, 156, 158; learned Greek when old, 159; thought of learning to play the fiddle, 163.

Cattle-sense of those content to be led in spiritual matters, **5**, 254.

Catullus, his story of the cockney Roman, **3**, 324.

Cause, a great, makes great souls, **6**, 415.

Cavendish, Lady Edward, **10**, 42.

Cavern, sunless, under road, **2**, 179.

Cedar Lake, in *A Mortal Antipathy*, **7**, 36.

Cedar of Lebanon, **10**, 189.

Celebrations, American and English, **4**, 272 *et seq.*

Celebrities of to-day all look alike, **3**, 103.

Celebrity, a literary, experiences of, **7**, 139, 140.

Celibacy, **4**, 68 ; **5**, 325 ; **7**, 245.

Cells, of the human body, **8**, 192, 193 ; **9**, 228, 233 ; necessity of supplying proper materials for, 252.

Cemeteries. *See* Burial grounds.

Centenarians, well-known, **4**, 26.

Central church, Boston, spire of, **10**, 193, 194.

Central Park, **8**, 74 ; to be compared, not with Boston Common, but with suburban scenery of Boston, 75 ; Central Park *ex*centric, 75.

Centrifugal principle of separation of a family, **5**, 152.

Cephalonia, the, **10**, 13.

Cerebral action, spasmodic, not altogether an evil, **1**, 189.

Cerebral induction, **4**, 15.

Cerebral strabismus. *See* Squinting brain.

Cerebration, passive, **3**, 316.

Cerebricity, **4**, 15, 166.

Certificates of recommendation like ostrich eggs, **5**, 17.

" César Birotteau," **7**, 234, 235.

Chadwick, James R., **9**, 398.

Chair, fantastic, **6**, 182, 184.

Challenge offered to homœopathic physician in Paris in 1835, **9**, 62.

Chamber, the Little Gentleman's, the Professor's entrance into, **2**, 255 ; solution of the mysteries in, 307–309.

Chambered Nautilus, The, **1**, 97 ; verse of, copied for Princess of Wales, **10**, 56.

Chambers, the oarsman, died of consumption, **8**, 230.

Chambers, John, bishop, **9**, 320.

Chambers Street, Boston, **1**, 272.

Chameleons, human beings are all, **8**, 199.

Chamouni, **1**, 267.

Chambre Ardente, **5**, 94.

Champion of aggressive liberty, it is said, ought to reach the same gallows as the arch-traitor, **8**, 89.

Champion of the Heavy Weights, **1**, 56.

Champlain, Lake, malaria about, **8**, 207 ; **9**, 324.

Champs Élysées, **10**, 176.

Chancery, court of, **2**, 106.

Changes in methods of medical treatment, **9**, 175, 258 *et seq.*

Channel, English, passage of, **10**, 161, 178.

Channing, **2**, 16 ; his Baltimore discourse, 117.

Chaos, precedes artistic creation, **6**, 221.

Chapin, W. D., **9**, 406.

Chaplain, the, **8**, 28–43.

Character, negative virtues lead to emaciation of, **1**, 262 ; must have a weak spot or two before we can love it, **2**, 72 ; study of, as by triangulation, 90 ; genius should marry, 287 ; its force in life, 288 ; affected by soil, **3**, 21 ; sudden development of, 306 ; shaped by surrounding conditions, **4**, 40 ; influenced by diet, 185 ; the mother's, more important to most children than the father's creed, 247.

" Characteristics," Carlyle's, **1**, 55.

Characters, development of, by writers, **4**, 5 ; confusion of, in the reader's mind, 53.

Charitable institutions, establishment of, **9**, 350.

Charity of the old for the failings of others, **4**, 46.

Charles I., his death warrant, **10**, 52, 53 ; opening of his coffin, 96.

Charles II., of England, **9**, 4.

Charles Martel, **8**, 107.

Charles River, boating on, **1**, 164 ; has a voice full of meaning, **2**, 246 ; either Hiddekel or Euphrates, **8**, 153 ; not more real than the Avon, **10**, 132.

Charles Street, Boston, **1**, 273.

Charlestown Navy Yard, **1**, 206 ; lofty chimneys of, **8**, 76.

" Charley," friend of " the Captain," **8**, 51, 70.

Charming by serpents, **5**, 190, 191, 205 *et seq*. *See also* Rattlesnakes.

Chartier, Alain, kiss given, **2**, 268.

Chasse-café, **10**, 207.

Chatterton, **2**, 241.

Chatwood's safes, **9**, 288.

Chaucer, compared to a pear, **1**, 83 ; quoted, **8**, 302 n., 376 ; **9**, 376.

Chauncy, Charles, both doctor and minister, **8**, 406 ; **9**, 329 ; sons of, both doctors and ministers, **9**, 329.

Check book, Autocrat's experience with, **2**, 22.

Cheerfulness, desirable in a doctor, **2**, 143 ; in a clergyman, 144 ; its part in the attainment of long life, **4**, 182.

Cheeses, old, cathedrals resemble, **10**, 20.

Chelsea, England, **4**, 278 ; Carlyle's house at, **10**, 136, 137, 140.

Chelsea beach, gathering of animals on, **2**, 164.

Chelydra serpentina, **6**, 125.

Chemical school of medicine, good done by, **9**, 319.

Chemist's shop, library compared to, **2**, 25.

Chemistry, animal, **8**, 187–190 ; of eggs, 187–189 ; its contributions to our knowledge, **9**, 212 ; debt of medicine to, 274 ; there was none 250 years ago, 281 ; apt to spoil on one's hands, 372. *See also* Allotropism.

Cheshire cheese, **10**, 20.

Chess, played by masters of the game, **1**,

64 ; players of, evenly matched, **2,** 167 ; life a game of, **4,** 66 ; **6,** 238.

Chester, **10,** 18, 19 ; daisies at, 19 ; cathedral, 19, 20.

Chester and Lancaster counties, the England of Pennsylvania, **8,** 51.

Chesterfield, Lord, quoted as to Bath, **10,** 107.

Chevreul, Michel Eugène, **4,** 27.

Cheyne, Sir John, his bones, **10,** 120.

Cheyne Walk and Row at Chelsea, **10,** 136.

Chichester cathedral, spire of, **10,** 118.

Chickweed, one of the first spring flowers, **8,** 139.

Child in French hospital, sweet voice of, **1,** 216.

Childhood, impressions of, **2,** 186–189 ; preservation of the sensibilities of, **6,** 209 ; brings its inspiration from God, **8,** 92.

Children, as reared, superstitious and spiritual cowards, **1,** 204 ; instinctive reserve, 204 ; superstitious observances of, 205 ; unfulfilled promises made by, 207 ; first act of wrong, 209 ; their disgust for heaven, **2,** 185 ; indifference to earthly things, 193 ; such are like windfalls, 194 ; disgust excited in healthy childhood by instances of early spiritual development, 194, 195 ; directness of logic, 209 ; aged features in some, 239 ; modified by the soil of the region in which they are born, **3,** 20, 21 ; their likeness to animals, 82 ; some who form friendships with ophidians, **5,** 220, 224, 397 ; easy to criticise other people's method of dealing with, 271 ; at first purely selfish, 321 ; hard to hold them accountable for inherited tendencies, 322, 323 ; of Ann-Street and Five-Points, 324 ; a personal equation in their tempers, 421 ; theory that all their motives and instincts are radically wrong, **6,** 30 ; may be whipped into obedience, not into virtue, **8,** 306 ; cruelty of, 307, 308 n. ; killed by drinking hot water from spouts of tea-kettles, 327 ; congenitally criminal, 337, 338 ; Jonathan Edwards on the nature of, 393 ; of clergymen, 411 ; creed of clergymen's, 421 ; their tendencies early betrayed, **9,** 245 ; complexion of English, **10,** 22 ; wealthy, provision for, in Boston, 204.

China ware, Mr. Nightingale's collection of, **10,** 116.

"China," the hymn, a cry of despair, **6,** 80.

Chinese, not in a condition to listen to modern civilization, **8,** 325, 326 ; carvers, 388 ; punishment of, **10,** 89.

Chipmunk, **10,** 148.

Chiron, M. D., **5,** 139.

Chloroform, effect on the Professor, **1,** 295 ; a few whiffs of, secure a visit to the world of death with perhaps no return ticket, **8,** 265.

Choice, exercise of, includes the moral universe, **8,** 301.

Cholera, **9,** 72, 352.

Chomel, **9,** 431.

Christ, **1,** 287 ; his fondness for talking at meat, **2,** 32 ; loved healthy as well as sickly children, 195 ; life full of sentiment, 313 ; Jewish estimate of, **8,** 47 ; his sepulchre not in Palestine, 117.

Christ church, Boston, **2,** 307.

"Christabel," Coleridge's, quoted, **2,** 208 ; **5,** 220, 225.

Christian, prince, **10,** 35, 89.

Christian, princess, **10,** 89.

Christian equality alone can prevent social divisions, **2,** 134.

Christian heathenism, **4,** 250.

Christian optimism, **8,** 430.

Christian pessimists, **8,** 425, 431 ; favorite tunes of, **6,** 80 ; natural antagonists of, 431, 432.

Christian sects, should be polite to each other, **4,** 196.

Christians, widely different in the North and South, **8,** 105.

Christianity, compared to an ark, **2,** 218 ; slow work launching it, 219 ; full of sentiment, 302.

Christopher, Saint, of Paris, **1,** 88.

"Chronological History of New England," by Thomas Prince, **3,** 121.

Chryso-aristocracy, American, weak point in, **1,** 260.

Church, Benjamin, **9,** 345.

Church, of Saint Polycarp, **2,** 211 ; of the Galileans, its simple worship, 213 ; impossibility of a universal, 296 ; compared to a garden, 296.

Church door, human skin nailed to, **1,** 108.

Church-going, its humanizing effect, **3,** 193.

Churchill the poet, quoted, **5,** 224.

Cicero's "De Senectute," **1,** 150 ; a leisurely performance, 156 ; imaginary report of it delivered as a lyceum lecture, 157.

Cid, Chronicle of, rare edition of, **10,** 149.

Cider, useful for dyspepsia, **8,** 224.

Cigars, **1,** 102 ; **2,** 137.

Ciliary muscle, **9,** 249.

Cinchona, experiments of M. Double and M. Bonnet with, **9,** 61 ; claims to the credit of introducing, 443.

Ciphering hand-organ, calculating machine called, **1,** 9.

Circe, a, who turns her victims into lambs, **4,** 217, 238.

Circle about intellect, **1,** 266.

Circumstances, conviction of having been in precisely the same before, **8,** 299.

Citadel of belief, the fewer its outworks the better, **3,** 319.

Cities, esteem in which each is held by its inhabitants, **1,** 126 ; charms of smaller ones, 128; leaking of nature into, 273; American, comparisons of, **2**, 84-87; gain to health from life in, **3**, 278; provincialism of, **4**, 277; excitements of, **5**, 160, 161; places to mature beauty of all kinds, 303, 304; advantages of large, for seeing much disease in a little time, **9**, 373.

Citizen, a good enough term for anybody, **4**, 222; simple preventive against injustice to, **8**, 110; difference between a good and bad, 110.

City of wholesome breezes (Buenos Ayres), **5**, 154.

Civil war of 1861. *See* American civil war.

Civility a Christian virtue, **4**, 195 *et seq.*

Civilization, future, the ovarian eggs of, carried by half a dozen men, **1**, 195; as influenced by clergy, **2**, 8; in danger of senile dementia, 11; confronting of two civilizations, 36; necessities of modern, 283; power of, over natural forces, **3**, 271; a foundling hospital, **4**, 54; crowds out superstitions, 254, 255; state of medicine an index of, **9**, 313; old, deeply buried, **10**, 106.

Clairvoyance, **5**, 394; **7**, 177; **8**, 18, 270.

Clams, effect of, on the Pilgrims, **9**, 315; thanks offered over a dish of, 321, 322.

Clarendon Park, **10**, 110.

Clark, Dr. John, **9**, 195, 326, 327, 343.

Clark, William, his epitaph, **2**, 306.

Clarke, Dr. Edward H., **7**, 15-17.

Clarke, James Freeman, **2**, 49; **4**, 28, 29, 30, 34, 68, 196.

Clarke, Dr. Joseph, on puerperal fever, **9**, 156; and the Dublin hospital, 294, 364.

Clarke, Pitt, typical example of the union of doctor and clergyman, **8**, 406.

Clarke, Samuel, on free will, **8**, 378.

Class of 1829, Harvard College, **4**, 28; **10**, 111.

Class-teaching, only way of, **9**, 299.

Classes, spiritual standard of different, **2**, 121.

Classics and modern literature, **4**, 158.

Claude Lorraine, **10**, 127, 170.

Clay, Henry, silver tones of, **8**, 83.

Cleaveland, Prof., meteorological record of, **8**, 175, 183.

Cleopatra, **4**, 284.

Clergymen, rarely hear sermons, **1**, 29; many of their patients not only fools and cowards, but also liars, 86; their part in civilization, **2**, 8; respect expressed for, 104; should be cheerful, 144; varieties of, **3**, 16, 17; characteristics of, 125; Perkinism endorsed by many, **9**, 25, 26. *See also* Ministers, Priests.

Clerks in "stores," **5**, 174.

Cleveland, Father, **4**, 26.

Clever people do not hate each other,**1**, 3.

Clift, Mr. William, **10**, 4, 7.

Clifton, England, **9**, 296.

Climacteric, the grand, **4**, 30, 38.

Climate, influences of, produce new patterns of humanity, **1**, 171; to be cut according to your constitution, 265; effect on hospitality, 302; American, predisposes to morbid religious excitement, **6**, 155; of New England, trying, **8**, 206, 207; problem of, in medicine, **9**, 296; of Massachusetts, 320-322; of England, **10**, 187, 204, 206.

Clinical teaching, **9**, 273-311.

Clock, compared with the brain, **1**, 185; at Andover Seminary, 287; the Terrible, Number Five's story of, **4**, 169; an old-fashioned, **6**, 34.

Clodius, **5**, 266.

Clopton, Sir Hugh, **10**, 94.

Closet, in old house, **1**, 78; contents of old, **6**, 77.

Clothing, well enough understood by men, **8**, 226, 227.

Clowns, melancholy people, **2**, 312.

Club-foot, **2**, 9.

Clubs, benefits of, **1**, 63; of London, **10**, 198.

Coale, Dr., **9**, 416.

Coarse people, **3**, 275; in the professions, **2**, 263.

Coat, constructed on a priori grounds, **1**, 67; a scholar's, **6**, 113.

Cobbe, Frances Power, **10**, 41, 56.

Cobra, **5**, 223.

Cocaine, **4**, 251.

Cock, man who looked like a, **5**, 222.

Cockney, Roman, **3**, 324.

Coffee, its depressing effects, **1**, 246, 248; exhilaration of the morning cup of, **4**, 6; effects of, in excess, **8**, 224.

Coffin, Admiral Sir Isaac, **2**, 52.

Coffin, Long Tom, **5**, 139.

Coincidences, **1**, 73, 75; **2**, 56; curious instance of, **4**, 13, 18, 19, 304; between manners and speech of antiquity and those of our own time, **3**, 323; periods of, continual, **8**, 17, 18; illustrating alleged plagiarisms, 45, 287, 288; of match-box of Drs. Holmes and Thompson, 45; of Dr. Holmes's name, 45; in medical practice, **9**, 75; between great political and intellectual periods and the appearance of great medical reformers, 177.

Coins, **3**, 111; **7**, 154 *et seq.*

Coke, Sir Edward, limit of amount of sleep, **8**, 231.

Cold-blooded creatures, **1**, 130.

Cold feet, a good sign when writing, **1**, 7.

Cold in summer, persons in easy circumstances suffer from, **1**, 265.

Cold seeds, the four great, **9**, 280.

Cold snap, **8**, 177, 178.

Coleridge, Lord and Lady, **10**, 89.

Coleridge, advised literary men to have a profession, **1**, 179; **8**, 231; "Christabel" quoted, **2**, 208; **5**, 220, 225; quoted on Newgate Calendar, **3**, 263, 265; "Genevieve" quoted, **6**, 316, 389; **7**, 233, 246; "Ancient Mariner" quoted, **7**, 91; **8**, 202; "Æolian Harp" quoted, **8**, 287; "Remorse" quoted, **8**, 355; silver speech of, **9**, 302; what he says of Johnson, **10**, 139; his conversation as reported by Dibdin, **10**, 139; De Quincey's admiration of, 139; Carlyle's portrait of, 139.

Colet, Louise, **7**, 137, 138.

Coliseum, **1**, 280.

College boys. *See* Boys, The.

College tricks, **2**, 58; college libraries fated to burn up, 62; college dormitory, strange breach in walls of, 187; college theatricals, **4**, 17; two social types in American colleges, **5**, 314.

Collier, the artist, **10**, 151.

Collins, Mr., the English Paganini, **10**, 5.

Colman farm in Deerfield, large elm on, **1**, 288.

Colonial exhibition, **10**, 155.

Color, effect of, on health, **8**, 210, 211.

Color-blindness, moral, **8**, 380.

Colored regiment. *See* Negro regiment.

Combe, George, **9**, 245.

Combination Room, Cambridge, England, **10**, 78.

Combinations, chemical, law of, **9**, 215.

Come! fill a fresh bumper, — for why should we go! **1**, 48.

Comedians, melancholy people, **2**, 212.

Comets, **1**, 24; **8**, 357.

Comfort, essential to enjoyments, **1**, 265; provisions for, on board ship, **10**, 13, 14.

Comic papers, **8**, 286.

Commencement, **8**, 158-161; and other celebrations, **4**, 272 *et seq*.

Commodores of the last generation, **5**, 8.

Common, Boston, **1**, 277; **2**, 42, 316; duel on, **1**, 239; as a place for studying the heavens, **3**, 313; tradition regarding one of its paths, 315.

Common-place people sometimes have a deep inner life, **3**, 204, 205.

Common-place, the wish to be remarkable is, **1**, 290.

Common sense, **1**, 14; **5**, 396; watchfulness of, **2**, 89; and science, **3**, 120.

Commons boarders at Harvard College, a trick of, **2**, 58.

Communications received by the Autocrat, **1**, 289.

Communications, military, of far more importance in America than in Europe, **8**, 23.

Communion, admission of unconverted persons to, **8**, 392.

Companionship in worship, **4**, 258.

Company on board ship, **10**, 14.

Comparative theology as necessary as comparative anatomy, **3**, 149.

Comparison, the Autocrat relinquishes claim on a clever one, **1**, 145; of merits in American cities, **2**, 86.

Compensation, an instance of, in the sensibility accompanying early decay, **2**, 195; system of, in the distribution of talents and instincts, **8**, 313.

Complementary aspect of objects in poetry and art, **1**, 181.

Complexions, fresh, **2**, 45; of English children, **10**, 22.

Compliments, some advice in regard to paying them, **3**, 208.

Compositions, girls', **5**, 70.

Compromisers trying to curve the straight lines of eternal law, **8**, 81.

Compton, Lady William, **10**, 97, 98.

Compton Wynyate, an interesting English mansion, **10**, 97, 98.

Conceit, is to character as salt to ocean, **1**, 9; as natural as centre to a circle, 10; the audacious sort always imposing, 10; makes people cheerful, 10.

Concert at Lady Rothschild's, **10**, 46.

Condescension, graciousness mistaken, **3**, 55.

Condie, Dr., on puerperal fever, **9**, 124, 143.

Confederate prisoners. *See* Prisoners, Confederate.

Confederate states, cold calculation of, **8**, 94; allies of, in the North, 96; condition of, in 1863, 101; "unanimity" of, 102; Unionists in, 103; fanaticism for slavery in, sincere, 105; highest culture in, 106; Southerners the Saracens of the 19th century, 106.

Confessional not unknown in Protestantism, **6**, 160.

Confessor, sphere of, **9**, 364.

Confidence, the way to obtain, to *deserve*, **9**, 383.

Congenital inheritances. *See* Inherited tendencies.

Congenital sinfulness, **5**, 256.

Congestion of the portal system, **9**, 389.

Congregational singing, **2**, 215; imperfections of, 216.

Congregationalists, history of, in New England, **8**, 404; national council of, in 1865, 408.

Congress boots made for author in London, **10**, 145.

Connecticut Medical Society, **9**, 20.

Connecticut valley, **1**, 244.

Conscience, its approval or disapproval, **2**, 209; paralysis of, **3**, 268; a sick, **5**, 169; may be unscrupulous, 170; not to be reasoned with, 317; a tender, supported by the trembling knees of a weak intelligence, **8**, 81; impossible to prevent the uprising of, against a great wrong, 93.

Conscious life the aim and end of creation, **3**, 105.

Consciousness, one latch-key of, fits many doors, **4**, 10; area of, 11; modulated or musical, **8**, 271, 272.

Consciousness, Dual. *See* Dual consciousness.

Conservation of force, **9**, 217.

Conservative, a bad sort portrayed, **2**, 15.

Consistent people apt to contradict themselves, **2**, 34.

Consolations of religion, **2**, 292 ; of old age, **4**, 46.

Conspirators painted of dark hue, **2**, 229.

Constitution, early collapse of in American female, **1**, 43 ; should decide one in choosing summer residence, 265 ; meaning of, **8**, 203–206.

Constitution, frigate, proposed demolition of, made the subject of an early poem by the author, **7**, 8.

Constitution of the United States, the North fighting for, **8**, 116.

Consumption, called " White plague of the North," **5**, 140 ; tendency of nuns toward, **8**, 2 ; relative mortality from, in various cities, 206 ; seems to be arrested by a vegetable diet, 218 ; liability of athletes to, 230 ; Giles Firmin's treatment of, **9**, 283 ; mortality from, in Boston, 294 ; Sydenham's treatment of, 344 ; Massachusetts doctors on, 352.

Contagion, in sickness, **2**, 119 ; carried by physicians, **9**, 195. *See also* Puerperal fever.

Contemplation, necessary conditions of, **3**, 106.

Contentment, **1**, 268.

Continuations almost always sag a little, **4**, 307.

Contracts, written in blood, **2**, 189.

Contradiction, may turn a good talker into an insufferable bore, **3**, 301 ; perpetual, a pelting hail-storm, **4**, 281.

Contraria contrariis, in medicine, **9**, 318.

Controversy, equalizes fools and wise men, **1**, 114.

Conundrums indulged in at Boardinghouse, **1**, 251.

Conversation, a serious matter, **1**, 5, 6 ; prevailing faults of, 10 ; spoiled by certain kinds of argument, 10 ; a code of finalities necessary to, 11 ; compared to Italian game of mora, 15 ; shapes thoughts, 27 ; *Blair*-ing of, 40 ; should not be too literal, 52 ; one of the fine arts, 52 ; compared to chessplaying, 64 ; depends on taking things for granted, 64 ; ruts and grooves of, 65 ; instance of the veneered sort, 143 ; with a stranger, **2**, 30 ; mechanical talk of pretty women, 30 ; women can keep their minds detached from their talk, 31 ; skirmishing at beginning of, 35 ; easiness in, 139 ; commonplace character of ordinary, **3**, 246 ; in mixed company should be suggestive rather than exhaustive, **4**, 6 ; " symphony concert " of, 52 ; at London dinners, **10**, 199, 200. *See also* Talking.

Conversationalist, discomfort of being thought one, **3**, 44.

Conversazione and fête in the parish of St. James Marylebone, **4**, 274 *et seq*.

Conversion, unconsciousness of, in some cases, **6**, 162 ; its paroxysmal character, 194.

Convert to an old faith, is shaky in parts, **5**, 418 ; cannot enter into its working conditions, 456.

Convicts, pine for tobacco more than for freedom, **8**, 225 ; prisons for, in France, 345.

Conway, the actor, **4**, 284.

Conybeare, Mrs., daughter of Mr. Herkomer, **10**, 80.

Cooke, Elisha, **9**, 345.

Cookeson, William, of All-Souls College, his autograph, **1**, 87.

" Cool as a cucumber," a Galenism, **9**, 318.

Cooper, Miss, " Rural hours " of, **8**, 134 ; on skunk-cabbage, 139 ; on buckwheat, 157 ; on autumn leaves, 165 ; interesting walks of, 183.

Cooper, the actor, **3**, 329.

Cooper, Sir Astley, **9**, 202.

Cooper, J. Fenimore, **7**, 5.

Cooper, Rev. Dr. Samuel, **7**, 21 ; **8**, 406, 408 ; **9**, 205.

Cooper's crazy wife, The, of Dorchester, **9**, 357.

Copland's Medical Dictionary, **9**, 104, 111, 171.

Copley, paintings of, **1**, 20 n. ; **2**, 183 ; **7**, 3, 21 ; portrait of the merchant-uncle, and great-grandmother, 21 ; dressing-gown affected in his pictures, 186.

Copp's Hill burying ground, **2**, 3, 306, 316.

" Copperheads," loathsomeness of, **8**, 109, 110.

Corain, Captain, and his sinking ship, **3**, 171.

Coral-reef island, if inhabited by one man, pretty woman would appear upon, **2**, 51.

Corey, Giles, **10**, 45.

Corinna Institute, in *A Mortal Antipathy*, **7**, 36.

Corn, English and American definition of, **10**, 144. *See also* Indian corn.

Cornelia, mother of the Gracchi, **2**, 288.

" Corner Bookstore," **4**, 150.

Cornhill, Boston, **10**, 145.

" Corpus Juris Civilis," Elzevir edition of 1664, **6**, 59.

Correggio, **10**, 170.

Correspondence, The Dictator's, **4**, 136 *et seq*., 306, 309 *et seq*.

Correspondents, curious letters received by authors from, **1**, 69 n.

Corrosive sublimate, **9**, 275.

Corvisart on frequency of heart diseases in French revolution, **8**, 2.

Cosmetic (Mrs. Allen's), **2**, 79.

Costume of young girl, **6**, 370.

Cotton, John, quoted on Gov. Winthrop, **9**, 330 ; theocracy of, 355.

Coughs, ingratitude of, **2,** 132.

Counsellor, character in *Over the Tea-cups,* **4,** 51 ; relates his legal experience with love letters, 91 ; " stirs up " the Young Doctor, 123 ; wishes to live until he is eighty, 190, 192 ; asks Number Five's advice, 240.

Counterparts, of people in different cities, **1,** 138 ; precise, not necessary for marriage, **2,** 287.

Counting on time, excites nervousness, **2,** 255.

Country, eye for, possessed by military men, **3,** 105.

Country boys, apt to betray their early ways of life, **2,** 44 ; in college, **5,** 3, 4 ; make the best horsemen outside of cities, 149.

Country doctors, **5,** 20, 21 ; **9,** 173, 352, 353, 374.

Country life, some dangers of, **3,** 278.

Country people, with nothing to do, fall into bad habits, **5,** 82.

Coupon bonds, **4,** 72, 73.

Courage dependent upon blood, **7,** 235.

Courbet, **10,** 173.

Courier maid, an androgynous personage, **10,** 12.

Courses of reading, **4,** 149.

Courtesies, needful to the old, **6,** 18.

Courtier, time of day with the, to his sovereign, **9,** 407.

Courting, make-believe, **4,** 136 ; of women, often a surprise to their relatives, **5,** 270.

Cousin, on Hartley, **8,** 378.

Cow, will eat fish, **8,** 217.

Cowbells, recalled the tinkling of wine-glass, **1,** 78.

Cowardice, may call for lenient judgment, **5,** 253 ; how related to centre of inhibition, **7,** 235.

Cowley, his " Chronicle," **6,** 214 ; quoted on the English walnut, **8,** 264, 265.

Cowper, **1,** 184 ; poem on his mother's portrait, 281 ; lines on the " Royal George," 281 ; quoted, **2,** 183 ; his mental neuralgia, **3,** 101 ; his despair when dying, **4,** 251 ; quoted, 253 ; **5,** 203 ; **7,** 177 ; silence of, **8,** 84 ; Taine on, 397 ; **10,** 166, 186, 203.

Crabs, Miss, teacher in Apollinean Institute, in *Elsie Venner,* **5,** 166, 428.

" Cracker," word used in Boston for biscuit, **2,** 169.

Cradock, Matthew, on the antimonial cup, **9,** 341.

Craigenputtock, Emerson at, **10,** 138.

Crane, Mrs., and her daughters, in *Elsie Venner,* their arrival at the Sprowles' party, **5,** 91.

Crane, Ada Azuba, in *Elsie Venner,* **5,** 91.

Crane, Mahala, in *Elsie Venner,* **5,** 91 ; enjoys herself at party in an old green de-laine dress, 95.

Cranks, **4,** 161.

" Cranford," Mrs. Gaskell's, **10,** 107.

Crazy people, most of them found where the battle of intelligence is fought, **2,** 218.

Cream, maxims regarding, **5,** 301, 302.

Creamer, Mrs. Blanche, in *Elsie Venner,* **5,** 291 ; a tumble-to-pieces, Greuzeish looking blonde, 301 ; her revenge on the widow Rowens, 310–312.

Creation, Usher's precise date of, **2,** 113, 210 ; conscious life its aim and end, **3,** 105 ; artistic, preceded by chaos, **6,** 221.

Creative action of mind is automatic, **1,** 191.

Creative power demands freedom from disturbance, **3,** 100.

Creatures, an Eden of humped and crooked, **2,** 236.

Creed, the Autocrat's, consisting of two first words of the Paternoster, **1,** 89 ; a child's, **2,** 210 ; all have much in common, 216 ; of the heart, 298 ; the father's, of less importance to most children than the mother's character, **4,** 247 ; growing out of a narrow, 247 ; the Athanasian, 258 ; of supposed medical society, **2,** 111, 112 ; usually inherited, **8,** 420 ; the Athanasian, an incubus in the Anglican Church, 420 ; ill-bred to throw his father's in a man's face, 422 ; ought to expect changes in, 425 ; many demand revision, 433.

Crême de noyau, **5,** 55.

Crichton, The Admirable, **10,** 124.

Crickets, evening, memory of, **1,** 212.

Crime, which is not sin, **5,** 220 ; only one step below indifference to consequences, **7,** 267 ; harvest of, 'the fruits of sin, **8,** 86 ; and automatism, 322–360 ; must be studied calmly, 325 ; the most frightful, may be without any moral character whatever, 336 ; inherited insanity a predisposing cause of, 338 ; age a cause of, 339 ; sex and intoxication causes of, 339, 340 ; strange instances of, hand in hand with devotion, 340 ; usually runs in the blood, 343 ; guilt of, depends wholly on the question of self-determination, 347 ; preventive treatment of, 347–349 ; in punishing, we do not punish sin, 360.

Criminal, position of instinct, law and theology with reference to the, **8,** 322–325 ; absence of emotion in the, 332 ; is devoid of ordinary moral instincts, 333, 334 ; his religious professions of small account, 340 ; treatment of the, 344–348 ; undisturbed condition of, in cities, 348, 349 ; Irish system of treatment of, 353, 354 ; rights of the, 359, 360.

Criminal practices in sexual relations, **9,** 295.

Crinoline, of Otaheite, **1,** 19.

Crippled souls, **1,** 219.

Criticism, too much should not be made

of flaws and overstatements, **1**, 51 ; softening influence of hospitality on critical spirit, 115 ; patience under, **2**, vi. ; based on personal feeling, **3**, 85 ; needlessness of much of it, 152 ; that which falls upon the critics themselves, 153 ; private criticism, 153 *et seq.*

Critics, the chips left after authors were manufactured, **2**, 25 ; their painful duty of reminding author of the decline of power, 26 ; the gratification afforded them by an old author, **4**, 22 ; their food, 23.

Crockett, incendiary, **8**, 352.

Crooked Footpath, **2**, 102.

Croserio, Dr., **9**, 90, 93.

Cross, a burning, seen at night, **6**, 91, 95.

Crotalus durissus. *See* Rattlesnakes.

Crow pursued by king-bird, **1**, 29.

Crowninshield, Francis Boardman, **2**, 49.

Crows' nests, **2**, 222 ; **5**, 266.

Crucifix, ivory, **2**, 304.

Crusaders' monuments, **10**, 119, 153, 154.

Cruveilhier, **9**, 437.

Crystalline lens, change in form of, **9**, 249.

Crystallization, forms of, **9**, 214.

Cuckoos, resemblance of Americans to, **3**, 10 ; heard at Windsor, **10**, 50 ; of the poets, Wordsworth's lines on, 52 ; double note of, 191.

Cullen, **9**, 262, 379.

Culpeper, Nicholas, **9**, 342, 414.

Cumming, Dr., **9**, 302.

Cumulative effect of certain remedies, **9**, 264.

Cunningham, Dr. George, **10**, 79.

Cupid, statuette of, taken for "statoo of deceased infant," **1**, 109.

Cure, real meaning of the word, **4**, 189 ; **9**, 308.

Cures, wonderful, statements concerning, of little value, **9**, 70.

Curie, Dr., **9**, 81, 92, 93.

Curiosity, invariable in mature females, **2**, 252 ; resembles fear, 255 ; indirect ways of gratifying, **6**, 59.

Currents of thought, stratification of the, **4**, 166 ; and counter-currents in medical science, **9**, 173–208.

Curtin, Camp, visit to, **8**, 57, 58.

Currie, Dr. William, **9**, 384.

Curtis, Benjamin Robbins, 1809–1874, **2**, 50 ; **4**, 28.

Curtis, George William, **7**, 10.

Curve, of health, **4**, 187 ; of life, **7**, 84.

Cushing, Caleb, **5**, 150.

Cushing, William, his index to the "North American Review," **9**, 402, 403.

Cushion, feather, of the kind which feels like a nest of young kittens, **6**, 8.

Custard, **5**, 110.

Customs, modern, antiquity of many, **3**, 322.

Cutis ænea, **3**, 67.

Cutler, Manasseh, manifold accomplishments of, **8**, 409.

Cutler's Phi Beta Kappa poem, **8**, 8.

Cutterr, Alminy, in *Elsie Venner*, **5**, 28 ; warns Mr. Langdon the schoolmaster, 34.

Cuvier, **3**, 240 ; **5**, 318 ; **8**, 358 ; **9**, 120 ; **10**, 178.

Cuyler, Dr., chief army hospital inspector, **8**, 62.

Cycles, thought moves in, **1**, 73.

Cyclopædia, man who was well read up in first volume of one, **1**, 143.

Cymon and Iphigenia, **4**, 285.

Cynics, **4**, 148.

Cyrus, pride of, in trees he had planted, **1**, 159.

Dæmons, **3**, 127.

Dagger, three-bladed, **5**, 216.

Daguerre, moving in parallel path with other inventors, **8**, 84.

Daguerreotype gives features one particular look, **2**, 191.

Dahomey, king of, his female bodyguard, **7**, 40.

Dairy, products of the, antipathy of a famous family in New England to, **7**, 88.

Daisies, **2**, 234 ; **10**, 19, 124, 191.

Dalhonde, L., **9**, 347.

Dalhousie, Lady, **10**, 37.

Daltonism, mental, **8**, 312 ; frequent existence of, 337.

Damnation, infant. *See* Infant damnation.

Dana, R. H., Sr., **7**, 5.

Dana, R. H., Jr., as a school-boy, **8**, 241.

"Dance of Death" at Basle, **2**, 266.

Dancing, **3**, 97 ; discussed by Colonel Sprowle and Deacon Soper, in *Elsie Venner*, **5**, 95, 96 ; one of Elsie Venner's wild dances, 147, 357.

Dandelion, **2**, 231.

Dandies, their uses, **1**, 257 ; have pluck, 258 ; distinguished ones, 259.

Danforth, Dr., **9**, 309.

Danger, slight sense of, an agreeable stimulus, **5**, 55 ; a good counter irritant, 276.

Dante, on the neutral angels, **8**, 118 ; theology of, 368 ; his "Paradiso" quoted, 374.

Danvers, Whittier's favorite tree at, **10**, 69.

D'Arblay, Madame, **10**, 89.

Darden, Miles, the fat man, **8**, 229.

Dark, its effect upon tadpoles, **2**, 242.

Darley, F. O. C., illustrations by, **8**, 125–128.

Darley, Helen, over-worked teacher in Apollinean Institute, in *Elsie Venner*, **5**, 49, 68, 123 ; her attractiveness, 125 ; Silas Peckham's undervaluation of, 128 ; tortured by neuralgic conscience, 169 *et seq.* ; Langdon's sympathy for, 229, 230 ; her appearance at widow Rowen's tea-party, 305 ; Dudley Venner finds her interesting, 308 *et seq.*; talks with Langdon about presentiments, 361 *et seq.*; goes to take care of Elsie, 431; Dudley Venner tells his love, 467; Peckham's attempt to squeeze down her salary, 474–479; married to Dudley Venner, 483, 484.

Darshour, pyramid of, **9**, 230.

Darwin, Dr., **2**, 82.

Darwin, Charles, **10**, 44.

Darwinism, **3**, 82, 83, 305; **5**, 94; **10**, 2.

Davenport, John, quoted, **9**, 334.

David, tomb of, **3**, 332; **4**, 26, 33; **5**, 257; his Psalms hold the flavor of remembered frailties, **6**, 121, 123.

"David Elginbrod," Macdonald's, quoted, **8**, 167.

Davidson, Lucretia and Margaret, **1**, 184; effect upon one of them of the singing of Moore's melodies, **3**, 313.

Davis, George Thomas, **2**, 49; **4**, 29.

Davy, Sir Humphry, experience of, with nitrous oxide gas, **8**, 284.

Dawkins, W. Boyd, **10**, 183.

Day, of rich experience to author in England, **10**, 51.

"Day Dream," Tennyson's, quoted, **8**, 287.

"Day of Doom," Wigglesworth's, **8**, 304 n.

"De Senectute." *See* Cicero.

Deacon's Masterpiece, The, **1**, 252.

Dead book. *See* "Thoughts on the Universe."

Dead, The, interest in their destiny, **2**, 107; may have a secondary, yet self-conscious life within the personality of living descendant, **6**, 22, 94.

Deadheads apt to have lively appetites, **3**, 281.

Dead man's hand, swelling cured by, **2**, 246; as a cure for wens, **9**, 360.

Dead-Man's Hollow, in *Elsie Venner*, **5**, 101, 141, 465.

Deaf-mute child, **2**, 229.

Deafness in right ear of sporting men, **10**, 58.

Dean, Emma, Squire Dean's daughter, in *Elsie Venner*, **5**, 51.

Dean, Dr. John, **9**, 241, 242.

Death, compared to a black steamtug, **1**, 94; first experience of, 209, 210; of Latin tutor, **2**, 65; idea of rest inseparable from, **2**, 276; making ready for, 291–293; presence of, 304; perhaps a prolonged unconsciousness, **5**, 390–392; caused by fright, **7**, 91; definition of, **8**, 201; growth and muscular action after, 201, 202; euthanasia a right of civilized humanity, 237.

Death-bed literature, **2**, 291; death-bed pictures, **5**, 296.

Death-warrant of Charles the First, **10**, 52, 53.

Deborah, less agreeable than Queen Esther, **2**, 136.

Decade, every one a defence of the next, **4**, 36.

Decay of active powers welcomed by some, **4**, 39.

December, a warm day in, **8**, 135.

Decillionth dilution of a scientific proof, **9**, 392.

Declaration of Independence, meaning of, **2**, 295.

Decussation of the pyramids, **9**, 243.

Deductive reasoning, suspicious in medicine, **9**, 276.

Deer-stealer's fate, **1**, 282–284.

Deerfield, elm on Colman farm at, **1**, 288.

Defeat may be a gain, **8**, 118, 119.

Deformity, idealization of, **2**, 236; life-long suffering from, 263, 265, 301.

Degeneracy, of American youth, **1**, 170; in families, **8**, 204, 205; tendency to, 205, 206; theory of, as applied to American life, **9**, 199.

De Gray, Lady (Gladys Herbert), **10**, 46.

Degree at Cambridge, **10**, 76; at Edinburgh, 84; at Oxford, 87, 88.

Dejazet, M'lle, the actress, **3**, 329.

Delacoste's, Madam, fashionable school for young ladies, in *The Guardian Angel*, **6**, 265; account of, 268 *et seq.*

De Lacy, Miss Euphrosyne, in *The Guardian Angel*, **6**, 270.

Delilah, the hand-maiden, character in *Over the Teacups*, **4**, 61; forgets her place, 143; a mystery about her, 199; how she got her name, 200; her song, 202; her attractiveness, 224; the Young Doctor's admiration for her, 225, 241; at the "exhibition," 268; her engagement to the Young Doctor becomes known, 270.

Delphi, and a Pythoness in every human breast, **8**, 286.

Delusions, medical, **9**, 1 *et seq.*

Dementia senilis, **5**, 473.

Demetz, M., on the "Maison paternelle," **8**, 354.

Demonstrator, a good, **9**, 425, 426.

De Morgan, Augustus, **4**, 161 *et seq.*; 203; "Budget of Paradoxes" of, **9**, 415.

Denner, **9**, 220.

Dentists, **2**, 112; new horrors associated with chair of, **4**, 17.

Depolarization, of religious thought, **2**, 6; of sacred books, 117.

De Quincey, his "Opium-Eater" quoted, **2**, 238; his admiration of Coleridge, **10**, 139.

Derby day, **10**, 6, 31; emptiness of London on, **1**, 35; Commencement day compared to start at, 95; of year 1834, 32, 33; Gladstone's impression of, 31; Doré's exclamation at, 31; the horses, 33; the race, 35, 36; recollections, 40; weather, 39, 187.

Dermestes lardarius, **3**, 93.

De Sauty, **2**, 26.

Descartes, his location of the soul, **2**, 247; "Principes" quoted, **8**, 294; his idea of lower animals and man, 329 ; on motion, **9,** 217 ; library of, 400.

Deserter, recognized by sudden order given him by officer, **1,** 107.

Desor, Mr., pamphlet of on dryness of atmosphere, **8,** 207.

Despair, discipline of, **4,** 151.

Despine, Prosper, notice of "Psychologie naturelle " of, **8,** 331–360 ; quoted on the sleep of criminals, 334 ; his examination of murderer, 341, 342 ; examples of moral color-blindness to be found in his "Psychologie naturelle," 380.

Deterioration, physical. *See* Degeneracy.

Determination. *See* Will.

Deus ex machina, **8,** 302.

Development, sudden, in some characters, **3,** 306.

Devil, lent to the lawyers by theology, **8,** 324 ; Jonathan Edwards's opinion 371.

"Devil's footsteps " in pastures, **2,** 187.

Devil's Sonata, Tartini's, **2,** 308 ; **8,** 283.

Devizes, woman struck dead at, with a lie in her mouth, **1,** 281 ; **10,** 186.

Devonshire House, **10,** 42.

Devotion, hand in hand with crime, **8,** 340.

Devotions, good management in closing the day with, **8,** 231.

Devout disposition and weak constitution, correlation between, **3,** 303.

Dewberry, **2,** 187.

Dewees, Dr., opposed to the doctrine of the contagiousness of puerperal fever, **9,** 106, 123, 131, 146.

Dexter, Lord Timothy, **4,** 231 *et seq. ;* **5,** 14.

Diagnosis, the Professor's, of the Little Gentleman, **2,** 258.

Diamond burned by Number Five, **4,** 144, 146.

Diaphragm, moral effects of disease above and below, **2,** 293 ; laughter, epilepsy of the, **8,** 19.

Diary, pathetic minuteness of a, **2,** 232 ; of the author's daughter, while in England, **10,** 9 ; extracts from, 47, 51, 57, 78, 89.

Dibdin, conversation of Coleridge as reported by, **10,** 139.

Dickens, his "Pickwick Papers," **6,** 275 ; author's estimate of, **8,** 313, 314 ; remarked brightness of Boston, **10,** 23.

Dictator, The, character in *Over the Teacups,* **4,** 24 ; his discourse on the " Peau de Chagrin," 72 *et seq. ;* interprets Number Seven's abridged history of the world, 117 ; his feeling in regard to English blood, 176 ; gives advice as to the attainment of long life, 181 ; he turns preacher, 244.

Dictionaries, English, " Webster's Unabridged," **2,** 40 ; rivalry of various, 44 ; French and English, by John Bellows, **10,** 40.

"Didadascalos, Our dear," Lowell so referred to, **1,** 23.

Dido, **2,** 61.

"Dies Iræ," key-note cf, **8,** 307 ; quoted, 311.

Diet, its influence on character, **4,** 185 ; all-importance of, **9,** 297.

Digby, Sir Everard, story of his head speaking after decapitation, **8,** 265.

Digby, Sir Kenelm, quoted, **5,** 223 ; on consumption in London, **8,** 206 ; his cure for fever and ague, **9,** 354, 381; his Sympathetic powder, **8,** 279 ; **10,** 58.

Digby, Sir Kenelm, a descendant, **10,** 57.

Digestibility, relative, of various substances, **8,** 218–220.

Digestive system, legislates largely for our habits, **8,** 315 ; **9,** 237.

Dighton Rock, inscription on, **1,** 246.

Digitalis, **9,** 264.

Dilutions, doctrine of, in homœopathy, **9,** 42, 52 *et seq.*

Dimensions, three, ideas handled as if they had, **1,** 85.

Dinely, Fathergone, **9,** 317.

Dinely, William, lost in a snow-storm, **9,** 317.

Dinners, wine a specific against dull, **2,** 32 ; at Lady Harcourt's, **10,** 24 ; the full-blown flower of social life, 27 ; at American minister's, 37, 50 ; Sir William Harcourt's, 43 ; Archdeacon Farrar's, 57 ; Literary Club, 62 ; at Mr. Lowell's, 66, 67 ; Sir Henry Thompson's, 68 ; political matters not talked of at, 75, 200 ; at Vice-Chancellor Jowett's, 78, 89 ; with Dean of Salisbury, 121 ; in Paris, 174 ; dinner parties like those at home, 199 ; conversation at, 200.

Diorama, seen by Autocrat, of Mont Blanc, with two figures in foreground, **1,** 267.

Diphtheria, **9,** 348.

Diploma, effect of time on size of, **9,** 373.

Disappointments, reliefs from, **6,** 249.

Discipline of despair, **4,** 151.

Discobolus, **2,** 283.

Discussion, fear of, **2,** 109 ; gain in freedom of, **3,** 185 ; discussions, religious, worth and dangers of, 187 *et seq. ;* of great questions, necessary in a republic, **8,** 80 ; right of free, 89.

Disease, long illness, the real vampirism, **1,** 202 ; dismantling process of, **2,** 130 ; **8,** 249 ; a manifestation of the vital processes, **3,** 305 ; advantages of a mortal, **4,** 183 ; as to curing, 189 ; moral views of, changing, **5,** 323 ; a result of depressing moral influences, **8,** 2, 3 ; egotism in, 28 ; querulousness in, 82 ; influence of light in, 209 ; of color in, 211 ; of the moon in, 212 ; prevailing over a wide region, attributed to epidemic influence, **9,** 113 ; prevailing in a single locality to local cause, 113 ; natural course of, ignorance concerning, **9**, 76 ; remedies for, more eagerly sought than causes of, 195 ; a penalty, 197, 198 ; sometimes a congenital incapacity for life, 200 ; French superior to English and Americans in prescribing for, 204 ; poison-cure, doctrine of, **9**, 256, 257, 262, 266 ; change in the character of diseases, 260 ; rhythms of, 273 ; interpretation and treatment of, throw much light on superstitions, 314 ; it is Flagellum Dei pro peccatis mundi, 359 ; sensitiveness and fastidiousness of, 386 ; a large proportion get well of themselves, 434.

Dislocation of the lower jaw common among the inhabitants of Saturn, **4**, 65.

Disorganizing conceptions, **8**, 383, 384.

Disraeli, **4**, 194 ; **8**, 275.

Dissection, dangers encountered in, in post-mortem examination of patients who have died of puerperal fever, **9**, 160, 161, 162 ; popular prejudice against, 416, 417.

Distinctions, social, **2**, 134 ; **3**, 57.

Distribution, of manhood, **8**, 10, 11 ; of talents and instincts, **8**, 313.

Disturbance, nervous, **7**, 83, 215 ; periods of, minds bewildered in, **8**, 78.

Diversities, as social beings, depend largely on physical conditions, **8**, 315.

Divine image, each age shapes the one it worships, **4**, 40.

Divine right of kings, Napoleon gave death blow to, **10**, 174.

Divinity student, in *The Autocrat* and *The Professor*, usually addressed by the Autocrat on more abstruse topics, **1**, 1 ; admires power of seeing analogies, 83 ; asks Autocrat for his creed, 88 ; reads over the Schoolmistress's shoulder, 135 ; his interest in School-mistress's sister, 218 ; asks about love at first sight, 220 ; his wedding-present to the Autocrat, 311 ; prays with the Little Gentleman while dying, **2**, 302 ; finally engaged to marry the sister of the Schoolmistress, 309.

Dixwell, John, one of the regicide judges, **10**, 53 ; his descendants in America, 53.

Doctor, the Young, character in *Over the Teacups. See* Young Doctor.

Doctor B. Franklin, in *The Poet*, his education, **3**, 38 ; he is consulted by the Poet, 64 ; his office, 65 ; the examination, 66 ; treats the Capitalist, 253.

"Dr. Oliver," an inherited prescription, **9**, 336.

Doctor's Paradise, streets with only one side to them, **5**, 19.

Doctor's wife, duty of, **7**, 93.

Doctors, old doctor's list of books suggested for relief of persons with broken kneepans, **1**, 157 ; childish fear of a, **2**, 69 ; should always inspire hope, 143 ; old, preferred to young, **3**, 118 ; young doctors start with much professional but little practical knowledge, 123 ; doctors in this country have less culture than lawyers and ministers, 126 ; doctors in earlier days, 305 ; family, **4**, 124 ; old Egyptian, 128 ; successful, **5**, 19 ; country doctor, 20, 21 ; **9**, 173, 352, 353, 374 ; appears at a distance as a wheel-animal, **5**, 139 ; his sulky, 139, 140 ; believe and trust in God more than other people, **5**, 315 ; not atheists, 319, 320 ; lenient with human nature, 322, 323 ; the best-natured people, 325 ; God opens Book of Life to, 325 ; where an able young one ought to settle, 482, 483 ; nature studied by, from above downwards, **7**, 81 ; choice of, **8**, 232, 233 ; so-called "schools" of, 234-238 ; have given the clergy more trouble than other laymen, 414 ; called atheists, 414 ; piety and charity of, 415 ; intimate relations which should exist between ministers and, 415, 416 ; many know more about theology than medicine, 417 ; motives imputed to, for opposing medical delusions, **9**, 19, 35 ; their ability not to be tested by the degree of mortality among their patients, 73 ; their readiness to accept new doctrines, 98 ; country, 173, 352, 353, 373 ; their greatest duties, 184 ; errors to which they are subject, 185 ; scholastic and bedside teaching of, 273-311 ; business of, 274 ; who do not practise, 297 ; a disadvantage to young, to have any accomplishment outside of profession, 298, 384 ; physicians, 312-370 ; relations of those of Massachusetts with those of the Old World, 312 ; union of callings among early Massachusetts, 317 ; great names among Massachusetts, 317 ; were often clergymen, 319, 320, 329, 330 ; part taken by, in sanitary movements, 352 ; share of, in the Salem witchcraft delusion, 357, 358 ; sphere of, 364 ; faith of, 365, 366 ; young, know the rules, old, the exceptions, 377 ; old, knows patient's family, 377 ; character requisite for successful, 383 ; genius not requisite in, 384 ; personal habits of, 386 ; professional odor of old-fashioned, 387 ; punctuality a requisite in, 387 ; should have weather-gauge of patient, 387 ; face of, should be impenetrable, 388 ; phrases of shrewd, for their patients, 389 ; firmness indispensable to, 389 ; principles on which to choose, 390, 391 ; welcome any remedy proved to be useful, 391 ; relations of, with each other, 392, 393 ; a part of their business they are apt to forget, 433, 434.

Doctors of divinity, many people qualified to be, **1**, 29.

Doctrinal finalities, no air-tight reservoir, **2**, ix.

Doddridge's "Life of Colonel Gardiner," **6**, 95.

Dog-days, **8**, 155.

Dogmas, little heard of in war times, **8**, 11.

Dogmatists, the three, Johnson, Coleridge, Carlyle, **3**, 262 *et seq.* ; **9**, 302 ; **10**, 138.

Dollar, as an armorial bearing, **6**, 268.

Domesday book, **10**, 65, 66.

"Don Quixote," **6**, 275 ; recommended by Sydenham to medical students, **7**, 162, 167, 168 ; **9**, 293, 354.

Donatello, shrine ascribed to, **10**, 156.

Donkey preferred to the horse in a forest landscape, by Gilpin, **10**, 61.

Dorcas, death of, **2**, 233.

Dorchester, pudding-stone at, **2**, 256 ; old burial ground at, **2**, 263 ; **8**, 166.

Doré, Gustave, characterizes the Derby as brutal, **10**, 31, 36.

Double, M., his experiments upon cinchona, **9**, 61.

Double consciousness. *See* Dual consciousness.

Double star, **3**, 73, 139, 317, 346.

Doubt, spiritual, **3**, 148 ; age of, 194.

Doughnut, genteel form of, **6**, 231.

Douglass, Dr. William, simple remedies of, **9**, 320 ; quoted, 346 ; on inoculation, 347 ; on remedies, 348.

Douw, Gerard, **10**, 170.

Dowdyism, an expression of imperfect vitality, **2**, 136.

Dowler, Dr., on muscular action after death, **8**, 201, 202.

Dragon, fire compared to, **2**, 158.

Drainage, effect of, upon bills of mortality, **9**, 259.

Drake, J. Rodman, **7**, 5.

Dramatic element in Frenchmen, **8**, 350, 354.

Dramatis personæ, usefulness of, **4**, 53.

Draper, Professor, his theory as to the photographic nature of vision, **9**, 249.

Drawing, early childish efforts of Iris, in *The Professor*, **2**, 69 ; Number Seven's plan for teaching, **4**, 82.

Drawing-book of Iris, **2**, 173, 184 ; disclosures of its contents, 228.

Drayton's "Poly-Olbion," **4**, 133.

Dream, Number Five's, **4**, 56.

Dream-chemistry, **4**, 67.

Dreams, like broken mosaics, **4**, 68 ; dreams idealize and render fascinating, 286 ; personality often doubled in, **8**, 282, 283.

Dress-suit, full, only a gentleman endurable in, **5**, 103.

Dresser, Dr., his inventions, **10**, 144.

Drinking glasses, which spill contents if set down, **1**, 15.

Drinking habit is oftenest a punishment, **1**, 190.

Drinking-trough, shrine of saint used as, **10**, 156, 157.

Drinks, **8**, 220–225.

Droll, authors dislike to be called, **1**, 49.

Dromedary, **2**, 236.

Drowned, firing artillery to raise the, **8**, 9.

Drowning, panorama of past lives seen in, **8**, 299.

Drudgery of writing, **3**, 299.

Drugs, bad things, **2**, 12 ; now and then save life, **8**, 233 ; effect of, upon healthy persons as studied by Hahnemann, **9**, 58, 66 ; we have *un*learned the habit of constant use of, **9**, 435.

Drunkenness, non-alcoholic, **6**, 158. *See also* Intemperance ; Intoxication.

Drury Lane Theatre, **10**, 41, 73, 74.

Dry belly-ache, **9**, 282.

Dry crying. **2**, 76.

Dryden, quoted, **10**, 4.

Dual consciousness, **4**, 154, 165 ; **3**, 81, 206, 207, 227, 243 ; **5**, 356 ; **8**, 280, 282, 283. *See also* Plural personality.

Dublin hospital, **9**, 294, 364.

Dudley, Honorable Thomas, Esquire, builder of Dudley Mansion, in *Elsie Venner*, **5**, 142.

Dudley House, in London, **10**, 59.

Dudley, Lady, **10**, 59.

Dudley Mansion, residence of the Venners, in *Elsie Venner*, **5**, 141–145 ; its treasures, 197, 198 ; in moonlight, 334.

Duel of Benjamin Woodbridge, **1**, 239.

Duelling, French quotation concerning, **4**, 151.

Duff, Mrs., the actress, **2**, 329.

Dugès, opinion of, as to the contagiousness of puerperal fever, **9**, 106, 165.

Dull faces fatal to lecturer, **1**, 141.

Dull people, **2**, 290 ; solacing effect of, **1**, 6, 61 ; **8**, 268 ; sometimes make safest doctors, **9**, 300.

Dulness of life, on the planet Saturn, **4**, 65 ; in any ideal state of society, 67.

Du Maurier, **10**, 67.

Dumollard, murderer, **8**, 44, 341 ; Bonville de Marsangy on the case of, 356.

Dunhams, the, in *Elsie Venner*, **5**, 102.

Duplicates met in London, **10**, 196.

Dupuytren, **8**, 209 ; **9**, 427.

Dusting books, **6**, 370 ; a woman's way of, **1**, 275.

Dutch method of weighing furs with the Indians, **8**, 62.

Duty, the hardest, bravely performed, becomes a pleasure, **5**, 438 ; of accepting good fortune when it defrauds no one, **3**, 293.

Duval, Claude, **1**, 294.

Dwight, Josiah, humorous anecdotes of, **8**, 410.

Dwight, Timothy, **7**, 5 ; his "Greenfield Hill," quoted, **8**, 137.

Dwight, Wilder, **8**, 17, 24, 25.

Dyer, Mary, **9**, 356.

Dying, compared to moving, **2**, 276 ; much sagacity shown in patient's estimate of his condition, 277 ; testimony of the dying, to be received with caution, **2**, 292 ; torturing the dying, for evidence in favor of certain belief, 293 ; business of, better understood by Roman Catholics than by Protestants, **4**, 250 ; **5**, 450. *See also* Death.

Dynamization, Hahnemann's theory of, **9**, 419.

Dynasty, the talking, **3**, 263, 265 ; **9**, 302 ; **10**, 138.

Dyspepsia, mental, **4**, 148 ; and hypochondriasis, their influence, as shown by Carlyle and Cowper, **7**, 177, 178 ; helped by cider, **8**, 224.

"E pur si muove," **8**, 377.

Ear-rings, **2**, 99.

Early piety, instance of, **2**, 67.

Ears, stopping and unstopping, **5**, 97.

Earth, sweet smell of fresh, **2**, 265.

Earthquake, to launch the Great Eastern, **1**, 72 ; superstitions about, **9**, 355.

East Indian lady, **10**, 56 ; her children's salaam to the Princess Louise, 57.

East wind, **8**, 151, 206 ; **10**, 39.

Eating, readiness for, at any hour, a test of youth, **2**, 57.

Eaton Hall, seat of the Duke of Westminster, **10**, 20 ; its stables, 21.

Eau médicinale, **8**, 237.

Eberty, G. F. F., his "Stars and the Earth" referred to, **1**, 265.

Eblis, Hall of, **1**, 247.

"Ecce Homo," publication of, **8**, 407, 408.

Eccentrically formed animals, **2**, 236.

"Eccentrics," mostly of the male sex, **4**, 281.

"Ecclesiastical History of England," Dr. Harpsfield's, **9**, 4.

Ecclefechan, **10**, 138.

Eclecticism, spirit of, **9**, 2 ; literature of, 415.

Eclipse, the racer, portrait of, **10**, 40.

Economist, the brig, brief parley with, **10**, 200.

Economy, epidemic, **8**, 1 ; everything sacrificed to, 208.

Ectopia cordis, **2**, 259.

Edelweiss, **5**, 185.

Eden, an, of humped and crooked creatures, **2**, 236.

Edgeworth, Miss, children educated on her "Frank," etc., **8**, 172 ; her "L'Amie Inconnue," **10**, 197.

Edinburgh, fascination of, **10**, 6, 7, 83 ; degree of LL. D. at, 84 ; speech at, 84 ; former rambles in, 85 ; Salisbury crags, 85.

"Edinburgh Review," its attempt to put down Byron, **1**, 296.

Editors, appeals to their benevolence, **1**, 293 ; most of them get callous, 294 ; as pictured by Carlyle, **4**, 10.

Education, most of our people have had a professional, **1**, 28 ; begins through the senses, 117 ; towards the beautiful is mainly through women, **5**, 172 ;

often only a wearing conflict of alien lives, **6**, 29 ; theological, should include pathology and toxicology, **3**, 304 ; **8**, 417 ; through the pretentious intellect to the humble accuracy of instinct, **9**, 376.

Edwards, Jerusha, **8**, 365.

Edwards, Jonathan, the elder, laymen's commentary on the preaching of, **2**, 114 ; his creed might have softened with age, **4**, 40 ; and children, 249 ; on hatred of God for mankind, 252 ; his call was to study-work, **6**, 18 ; essay on, **8**, 361–401 ; one of the two Americans of his time with a European reputation as a scholar, 362 ; parallel between, and Pascal, 363–366 ; personal appearance of, 363 ; not witty, but could be satirical, 364 ; greatly influenced by women, 365 ; born with Scriptural texts latent in his thinking marrow, 367 ; his mother, 367 ; faith of, 367, 368 ; his "Work of redemption," "God's chief end in creation," "Nature of true virtue," 373 ; on "Freedom of the Will," 374–382 ; condensed statement of, quoted, 375 ; quoted on "Original Sin," 382 ; indebtedness of, to T. Boston, 385–387, 395 ; "Treatise on the religious affections," 387, 388 ; exegetical treatises, 388, 389 ; life of, short and melancholy, 389 ; belonged in Scotland, not to New England, 394 ; an unpublished manuscript of, said to be in existence, 396, 426–430 ; an habitual sufferer, 396 ; influence of, on religious opinion, 424–426.

Effluence, correlative of influence, **7**, 244.

Egg-pop, on holidays in Boston, **2**, 3.

Eggs, ovarian, of future civilization, **1**, 195 ; the Creator's private studio, **3**, 106 ; chemistry of, **8**, 187–189.

Egotism, in disease, **8**, 28 ; essence of, 147.

Egotist, the great original American, **4**, 232.

Egypt, obelisks of, **3**, 149 ; antiquities of, **4**, 100 ; doctors of, 128 ; **9**, 412 ; as a health resort, 296.

Ehrenbreitstein of the Chesapeake, **8**, 95.

Ehud, **2**, 119.

Eidolon, no more harm in, than in Imago, **8**, 404.

Eiffel tower, **4**, 104.

Eighth Massachusetts regiment, the, **8**, 10.

Elbridge, coachman to the Venners in *Elsie Venner*, **5**, 383–386.

Elder, boiling oil of, for gunshot wounds, **9**, 270.

Eleazar, Indian youth, **9**, 329.

Election bun, **2**, 42 ; **8**, 146.

Election day, **8**, 146.

Election sermon, **6**, 387.

Elective character of social position, **2**, 135.

Elective affinities. *See* Affinities, elective.

Electric light, burning but unconsumed, 1, iv.

Electricity, brain-cell power corresponding to, 4, 15 ; 9, 246 ; force stripped stark naked, 215.

Elements, the, may pervert the moral nature, 5, 435 ; chemical, of eggs, 8, 189 ; of the human body, 189.

Elgin Marbles, 10, 152.

Elijah, by brook Cherith, 6, 74.

Eliot, Ephraim, 9, 348.

Eliot, Jared, his Plato, 8, 409.

Eliot, John, quoted, 9, 277, 278, 328 ; under Mr. Greenland's mercurial ministrations, 339, 340.

Elginbrodde, Martin, epitaph of, 8, 167.

Elizabethan authors, common force in, 8, 84.

Ellicott, C. J., Bishop of Gloucester and Bristol, 10, 41, 54.

Ellsler, Fanny, 3, 95.

Ellsworth, Colonel, 8, 13.

Elm, American, 1, 231 ; the Johnston elm, 233 ; at Springfield, 234 ; at Hatfield, Sheffield, West Springfield, 235 ; at Pittsfield, Newburyport, Cohasset, 236 ; compared with English elm, 237 ; Paddock elms, 239 ; at Andover, Norwich, 287 ; at Deerfield, 288 ; 3, 19 ; great elm on Boston Common, 313 ; 10, 81 ; American and English, useful lesson of, 4, 38 ; has a soul, 5, 56 ; at Longfellow's house, 10, 69 ; at Lowell's, 69 ; of New England, 81 ; one in grounds of Magdalen College, 81, 82 ; at Springfield, 81 ; comparison of those of Old and New England, 189, 190 ; American not long-lived, 190 ; hint of a typical difference in the American and Englishman, 190.

Elpit, a boy christened Lord Pitt, called, 2, 95.

Elsie Venner, illustrates author's theory of the will, 2, 35 n. *See also* Venner, Elsie (the character).

Elstow, 10, 186.

Elzevirs, 1, 87 ; 6, 59 ; 9, 409 ; 10, 148.

Embryo, development of, 9, 250.

Emeritus, professor, a title to be accepted but not longed for, 6, 265.

Emerson, G. B., his " Report upon the trees and shrubs of Massachusetts," 1, 234.

Emerson, R. W., 1, 2 n. ; 7, 5, 7 ; remembered the time made by Flora Temple, 36 n. ; sceptical of the existence of a certain man, 245 n. ; recognized approach of age, 4, 38 ; on pie, 186 ; on Christian intolerance, 195 ; held to literary traditions, 233 ; tribute of author to, 7, 17, 18 ; his " Titmouse," quoted, 8, 179 ; son of a clergyman, 411 ; urges author to go to Europe, 10, 10 ; calls William and the Normans " twenty thousand thieves," 66 ; his obligation to George Herbert, 126 ; at Craigenputtock, 138 ; quoted, 169.

Emmons, N., 9, 292.

Emotions, excited by sight-seeing, not those usually to be expected, 1, 279, 280 ; have periods of incubation, 5, 420 ; we live on our, 8, 1 ; heart-disease caused by, 2, 3 ; clairvoyance of faculties in intense, 18 ; we have only a partial control of, 330. *See also* Disturbance ; Excitement ; Feelings.

Empiricism, 9, 275, 432.

Encouragement to young writers, 3, 159.

Encyclopædic information, instance of, 1, 143.

Encysted griefs, 5, 249.

Endicott, Gov., Dr. Fuller's visit to, 9, 325 ; sends bezoar to Gov. Winthrop, 340.

Enforced economies, 3, 296.

Engagements, matrimonial, 2, 286.

England, is one great menagerie, 1, 303 ; monarchs of, their touch supposed to cure scrofula, 9, 3, 354, 413 ; fifty years ago (1834), 10, 1 ; first impressions of, 22 ; climate in May and June, 39, 56, 187 ; looting of, by William's "twenty thousand thieves," 66 ; sympathy of, with slave-holding in the American Civil war, 184 ; twenty different Englands, 187 ; soil of, 188 ; fossils, 188 ; relics of different peoples, 188 ; a *Campo Santo*, 189 ; desirable as a home for Americans, 203–205.

England of Pennsylvania, 8, 51.

English, the, their blood apt to tell well on the stock upon which it is engrafted. 4, 176 ; called by Napoleon a nation of shopkeepers, 8, 10 ; inferior to French in prescribing for disease, 9, 204 ; country houses of, 10, 177 ; fists, 134 ; compared with New Englanders, 192 ; their feeling for the hat, 193 ; Béranger's lines on, quoted, 193.

English girl, character in *Over the Teacups*. *See* Annexes, the two.

English ladies, dear old, 10, 26–28 ; 106.

" English Lands, Letters, and Kings," Donald G. Mitchell's, 4, 133.

English language, must be correctly used by public men, 1, 111.

English sparrow, 3, 314.

English universities, 9, 277.

English vitality, descending scale of, 9, 199.

English walnut, fair model of the human brain, 8, 264, 265.

English workmen compared with Continental, 9, 288, 289.

Englishman, lives and dies under protest, 2, 81.

Enlistment, age of, among Romans, 1, 151.

Entertainments on first visit to England, 10, 6.

Enthusiasm, the source of all great thoughts and deeds, 6, 221.

Environment, in restrictions of human will, 1, 86; of intellect, 266.

Epicures, old people have a right to be, 4, 184.

Epidemic economy, 8, 1.

Epidemic of thinking, 3, 269.

Epigaea repens, first spring flower, 8, 139.

Epigram, nothing harder than to forgive the sting of an, 4, 306.

Epilepsy, nitrate of silver for, 2, 105; 8, 190; 9, 441; of the diaphragm, 8, 19; vegetable diet good for, 217; artificial production of, in animals, 9, 243; hoof of a horse prescribed for, 262.

Epilogue to the Breakfast-table series, 3, 349.

Epitaphs, who writes? 8, 166; quoted, 166, 167; at Andover, 257; one by Ben Jonson, 10, 119; one at South Downs, 134.

Epithets, follow isothermal lines, 1, 114.

Epsom, Derby day at, 10, 6, 31-37; special train for, 34; grand stand, 35; luncheon, 37; windy gusts at, 39, 206.

Equality, 1, 20; and *the* quality, 2, 133; only an ideal Christian equality can prevent social divisions, 134; political and social, of the inhabitants of Saturn, 4, 62, 63.

Equation, eye for, 3, 105.

Equilibrium, human beings cannot long rest in state of, 2, 275.

Equinoctial storm in *Elsie Venner*, 5, 459 *et seq.*

Erasmus, his " Colloquies," 1, 87; his " Naufragium," 88; portrait of, by Holbein, 10, 127, 128, 196.

Erasistratus, 9, 177.

Error, removed from the mind gradually, 9, 108.

Errors, to which physicians are liable, 9, 185, 186, 198.

Erysipelas, connection of, with puerperal fever, 9, 147, 149, 154, 155, 163, 164, 169, 170.

Esquimaux, morning call on, 1, 302.

Esquirol, 9, 78, 79.

Essex County, 2, 244.

Essex Street, Boston, 1, 272.

Esther before Ahasuerus, 1, 308; 2, 136; 6, 123.

Eternal punishment, 4, 244 *et seq.*; 8, 383 *et seq. See also* Infant damnation.

Eternity, remembering one's self in, 1, 201.

Ether, a few whiffs of, a ticket to the world of death and return, 8, 265; Dr. Holmes's experience with a dose of, 283, 284; of the physicists, 373; discovery of, 9, 349, 350. *See also* Anæsthetics.

Euphrasia, prescribed for disease of the eye, 9, 360.

Europe, aristocracy of, hostile to the North in Civil war, 8, 98; first visit to, 10, 3-6; risk of the trip in advanced years, 206; benefits of visit to, 207.

Eustachius, 9, 412.

Evans, John, on the antimonial cup, 9, 341.

Eve, moral responsibility of, 5, xii.; as embodying creative idea of woman, 6, 193.

Eveleth, the Rev. Ambrose, in *The Guardian Angel*, 6, 5, 194.

Eveleth, Cyprian, in *The Guardian Angel*, 6, 13; starts in search of Myrtle, 20, 64; his friendliness for Myrtle, 197 *et seq.*; interrogated by Gifted Hopkins as to his poetic qualities, 206 *et seq.*; marries Bathsheba Stoker, 428.

Eveleth, Olive, in *The Guardian Angel*, 6, 36; Myrtle's letter to her at her flight, 62; her religious character, 193, 194; married to Dr. Hurlbut, 419.

" Evenings at Home," 4, 206, 207.

Everett, Edward, quotation from the " Æneid," 4, 9; quoted on melons, 8, 161; son of a clergyman, 411.

Everlasting, the herb, emotions evoked by its smell, 1, 76; 2, 187.

Evidence, not to be confounded with belief, 9, 108.

Evil, dreadful business of being a prophet of, 3, 252; moral, not an entity but a condition, 8, 307; responsibility of, 328.

Evil eye, 5, 212, 219, 223, 224; 7, 65, 67.

Evil words, man's vocabulary terribly retentive of, 4, 109.

Evolution, process of, reversed, 4, 125; doctrine of, 255; moral, in children, 8, 307, 308 n.; iconoclastic doctrines of, 328.

" Ex pede Herculem," the remark of a dull person, 1, 110.

Examinations, worth of, 9, 372.

Excitement, effect of, on nervous system, 8, 12. *See also* Disturbance; Emotions.

Exclusiveness, Puritan, 4, 194; has its conveniences, 10, 141.

Execution of Holloway and Haggerty, 2, 188; 10, 44.

Exercise, pleasure of, 1, 167; not easy to lay down rules for, 8, 228-230.

Exhalations of the human body, 8, 200.

" Exhibition " at a young ladies' school, 4, 263 *et seq.*

Exhibiting one's self, authors have the right of, 1, 303.

Existence, previous state of, 1, 73, 74; every stage of, has its trials and consolations, 4, 37; infinite, the one miracle, 9, 219.

Experience, a fowl which cackles oftener than it lays eggs, 1, 271; not always the basis of medical prescriptions, 9, 175; meaning of, 375.

Experts, our pride in the superiority of, 3, 243; meaning of the word, 9, 375.

Explanations, bad between lovers, 6, 230.

Explosion, ratio of violence of, **8**, 102.

Exposure, relative ability of the sexes to endure, **8**, 214, 215; Prof. Harris quoted on woman's endurance of, 227; required to make images permanent, **10**, 104, 196.

Expressions which fix a man's position, **1**, 106; mere expressions indicative of lack of breeding, 109.

Extermination, divine impulse of, **5**, 168.

External conditions valued too highly, **3**, 296.

Extravagance of bookworms, **4**, 115.

Eyam, Devonshire, **10**, 186.

Eye, for an equation, **3**, 105; for country possessed by military men, 105; blind spot of the, **4**, 166; adjustment of, to different distances, **9**, 249; evil. See also Evil eye.

Eyebrows, line between the, **3**, 52.

Eyelids of ophidians immovable, **5**, 209.

Eyes of a cripple, **2**, 88; varieties of, **5**, 179; of rattlesnake, 209.

"Eyes and No Eyes," **4**, 206, 207.

Eyesight, failing, unusual remedy for, **1**, 173.

Eye-water, heirloom in the Winthrop family, **9**, 335.

Faber, Peter John, **3**, 27.

Faces, negative, in audience, **1**, 141; that of doctor and diplomatist should be impenetrable, 388; some women's a revelation of a great secret, **2**, 178; influence of a girl's face, 181; we have different ones for different persons, 191; analysis of, in ancestral elements, 193; face or figure, which the more attractive, 204; sketched on borders of drawing-book, 238.

Facsimile of each of us to be found somewhere, **3**, 36.

Facts, not allowed at the table by the Autocrat, **1**, 5; are bullies, 55; men of, 142; remote, collision of, **2**, 56; as mental food, **3**, 174; reluctance to accept those which throw doubt upon cherished beliefs, 185; the patrimony of cheats, **9**, 29; surest way of acquiring, 287, 372.

Faculties, clairvoyance of, **8**, 18, 270.

Fagan, Kitty, house-servant at the Poplars in *The Guardian Angel*, **6**, 8; rescues Myrtle from garret, 32; welcomes Myrtle back to the Poplars, 119; confides to Master Gridley about Bradshaw's designs, 328 *et seq.*; listens to conversation between Bradshaw and Cynthia Badlam, 331.

Fainting, **7**, 234; at sight of blood, 89, 236; at sight of any object of a red color, 89, 92.

Fair, English, properly conducted fight at, **2**, 52.

"Fair Maid of Perth," chieftain in, **5**, 253.

Fairweather, Reverend Chauncy, the minister of the liberal church in *Elsie Venner*, **5**, 63–65; begins to grow dissatisfied with his own belief, and to turn longingly towards Catholicism, 250–254; called on by Rev. Dr. Honeywood, 254–259; forgets selfishly to consider Elsie's request for prayers, 401–411; consults Dr. Kittredge professionally, who prescribes spiritually, 401–407; his dream, 408–410; in his own pulpit, 413 *et seq.*; calls upon the dying Elsie, 449–451; becomes a Roman Catholic, 473.

Fairmount, Pa., **8**, 71.

"Fairy Queen," Spenser's, **6**, 203.

Faith, means self-trust, **2**, x.; is self-reliance, 93; stronger in women than in men, **3**, 186; the strength and weakness of women, **5**, 391; is the man in tempestuous times, **8**, 79; true, and true philosophy ought to be one, 312; seen to end in child-murder, 394; the kind which breeds heroes better than an unbelief that leaves nothing worth being a hero for, 404; different methods of instilling required by different persons, 419; restless ones under every form of, 420, 421.

Fall of man, doctrine of the, **4**, 252; belief in, fading away, **8**, 398; at the bottom of religious difficulties, 401.

Fallopius, **9**, 279, 412, 423.

False quantity, fatal mis-step for public men, **1**, 110.

False sentiment, **3**, 136.

Falsehoods, old, squirming when they are turned over, **1**, 113.

Falstaff quoted, **10**, 26.

Fame, struggle for, usually ends in notoriety, **1**, 290; desire for, **3**, 160, 163; the penalty of, 161, 162; short cut to, **4**, 86.

Familiarity in speaking of public characters, **4**, 236.

Families, vicissitudes of old, **5**, 11, 12; centrifugal principle of, 152; deterioration of certain, **8**, 204, 205.

Family, man of, **1**, 20.

Family doctors. *See* Doctors.

Family portraits, those necessary to a man of family, **1**, 21.

Family silver, **5**, 198.

Fancies, beliefs frighten less than, **2**, 162.

Fandango, Moorish, danced by Elsie Venner, **5**, 147.

Fantasia, **3**, 61.

Faraday, **8**, 312; **9**, 215, 217.

Farmer's Almanac, **6**, 85; **8**, 163.

Farming, defect of, in New England, **9**, 277.

Farr, on contagiousness of puerperal fever, **9**, 104, 111; on contagiousness of small-pox, 133.

Farrar, Archdeacon, **10**, 53, 57; guide at Westminster Abbey, 59, 61; sermon, 73.

Farringford, visit to Tennyson at, **10**, 68.

Fascination, of spoken sounds, **3**, 46, 47; arts of, used by ministers, **6**, 158. *See also* Charming; Evil Eye; Rattlesnakes.

Fashion, intensely alive, **2**, 136, 150; an attempt to realize art in living forms, 151; foolish talk about, 152. *See also* Society.

Fashionable life, misery of semi-provincial, **6**, 256.

Fashionable people, vocabulary of some very, **8**, 274. *See also* Society.

"Fast train and ' slow ' neighbor," the author's motto in railroad travel, **8**, 19.

Fasting for forty days, stories of, **10**, 119.

Fat, microscopic examination of, **8**, 192.

"Fat " in printing, **6**, 290.

Fat man, **2**, 132.

Fate of books given by authors to their friends, **3**, 301.

Father, creed of, less important for most children than the mother's character, **4**, 247.

Fauna of England, **10**, 191.

Fay, Frank B., of Chelsea, **8**, 38.

Fear, resemblance of nervousness to, **2**, 255; power of, **3**, 127; fear, superstitious, not easily banished, 328; as a restraint in religion, **4**, 258; the gate of, easily opened by love, **7**, 246.

Features, immovable, characteristic of humorists, **6**, 227.

February, a warm day in, **8**, 135; 14th of, 135.

Fechter, his belief as to genius of Rachel, **7**, 243.

Feeble-minded children, rhyming as an amusement for, **4**, 80.

Feeders for the mind, **3**, 80.

Feeding-establishments, odious, **5**, 171.

Feeling, that we have been in same circumstances before, **1**, 73; explanations of it, 74, 75; between England and America, **10**, 184, 203.

Feelings, each person has front-door and side-door to, **1**, 128; keys to, 129. *See also* Emotions.

Feline character of sea, **1**, 264.

Felton, President of Philadelphia, Wilmington & Baltimore R. R., **8**, 72.

Females. *See* Women.

Femineity, does not like muliebrity, **5**, 126.

Ferns, **5**, 141; **6**, 88; maiden hair, **5**, 46.

Fernelius, **9**, 279, 375.

Ferry-boats, Chelsea, **2**, 289.

Fever, sick man nourished by, **8**, 1; diet in, **9**, 268; Sydenham's treatment of, 344. *See also* Malaria.

— puerperal, the contagiousness of, **9**, 103–172; belief that it is sometimes carried from patient to patient by medical assistance, 112, 131; the alleged laws of contagion deduced in other diseases not to be cited in this, 113; not a common disease, 113; all forms of, not equally contagious, 132; contagion of, not always followed by the disease, 133; may be produced and modified by many causes besides contagion, 133; series of cases of, in Massachusetts, 146 *et seq.* ; its connection with erysipelas, 147, 149, 154, 155, 163, 164, 170; precautions to be taken by practitioners in cases of, 168, 169; additional authorities on both sides of the question, 165, 166, 169 *et seq.*

— typhoid, **7**, 203 *et seq.* ; 261 *et seq.*

Fiacres, drivers of, **10**, 162, 163.

Fibres, of the body, **8**, 193; involuntary muscular, 195 ; must be exercised, 202.

Fichte, story of, **9**, 406.

Fiction, physiological basis of, **5**, vii., **ix.**

"Field, The," quoted, **10**, 31, 33.

Field of thought, **8**, 269.

Fields, James T., **1**, 21 n.

Fielitz, Dr., **9**, 83.

Fifth Avenue Hotel, **10**, 182.

Fifty years make everything old-fashioned without charm of antiquity, **7**, 2.

Fight, between a Marylander and a butcher, **2**, 51 ; well-conducted fight at English fair, 52; all of us have a little speck of, 152; between John and the Koh-i-noor, 279.

Fighting-boy of school, his paleness before contest, **2**, 268.

"Fighting Gladiator," **2**, 236.

Figure or face, which the more attractive, **2**, 204.

"Fils de Saint Louis, monte au ciel," **8**, 404.

Fincelius, **5**, 222.

Finch, purple, in cage, **2**, 94.

"Fingering Slaves," Wordsworth's, **9**, 366.

Finnegass, Henry, Esq., in *The Professor*, **2**, 313.

Fire, compared to a dragon, **2**, 158.

Firebugs, political, **3**, 3.

"Fire-hang-bird's Nest," Myrtle Hazard's room in *The Guardian Angel*, **6**, 22, 431.

Fire-places, open, comfort of, **8**, 182; healthfulness of, 208.

Firmin, Giles, **9**, 278–283, 328.

Firmness, an indispensable quality in a doctor, **9**, 389.

First old age, an infant's life has character of, **2**, 66.

First scholars, **7**, 174.

Fisher, landscapes by, in Athenæum Picture Gallery, **7**, 3.

Fisher, Dr., of Beverly, **9**, 307.

Fisher, Prof., on original sin, **8**, 383; on the need of candor in dealing with religious inquiries, 400.

Fishes, in sunless cavern, **2**, 179 ; transparency of small kinds, 229; one which stopped the leak in Captain Corain's ship, **3**, 171; in Mammoth Cave, **9**, 373.

Fishing, through the ice, **8,** 180, 181 ; an emotional employment, 181, 182.
Fists, rotary motion of, **2,** 18 ; English, **10,** 134.
Five-Points children, **5,** 324.
Flagroot, **8,** 140.
Flat-Head Indian pappooses, **5,** 392.
Flattery, more agreeable when acted than when spoken, **2,** 136 ; woman's subtle method of, 137 ; of abuse, 202.
Flaubert, **4,** 106 *et seq.*
Flavor, nothing knows its own, **1,** 55.
Flaying of Danish pirates, **1,** 107.
Fleet, companions in life compared to a, **1,** 94.
Fleet Street, **10,** 154.
Fleury, Louis, his experiments in homœopathy, **9,** 61, 81.
Flies, house, **3,** 244 *et seq.*
Flint, Professor Austin, **9,** 122.
Flirting, **4,** 136.
Floating-island, **5,** 110.
Floor, effect of scraping, with chair, **1,** 50.
Florence, **2,** 85.
Florida, as a resort for consumptives, **9,** 296.
Flournoy, J. J., his dissertation on the marrying of three wives, **2,** 5.
Flower, Charles E., **10,** 91, 94.
Flower, Mrs. Cyril, **10,** 37, 56.
Flower, Edgar, **10,** 94.
Flower, Professor W. H., **10,** 67.
Flower-de-luce, **6,** 81 ; **8,** 148, 149.
Flowers, poets' fondness for, **1,** 228 ; in church, **2,** 214 ; sketches of, in drawing book, 234 ; in old garden, 248 ; old-fashioned, **5,** 60 ; the earliest spring, **8,** 139–143 ; wild, **10,** 191.
— and plants, namely : —
  Ailanthus, **8,** 155.
  Alder, **8,** 140.
  Anemone, **8,** 142.
  Aster, **8,** 161.
  Atragene Americana, **5,** 101.
  Azalea, **8,** 154.
  Bdellium, **5,** 142.
  Blackberry, **2,** 187.
  Bloodroot, **8,** 142, 143.
  Box, **5,** 142, 437.
  Buckwheat, **8,** 159.
  Buttercup, **2,** 231 ; **8,** 142.
  Cardinal flower, **8,** 156.
  Chickweed, **8,** 139, 143.
  Columbine, **8,** 142.
  Cowslip, **8,** 143.
  Crocus, **8,** 145.
  Daffodil, **4,** 207 ; **8,** 143.
  Daisies, **2,** 234 ; **10,** 19.
  Damask rose, **1,** 227, 229.
  Dandelion, **2,** 231 ; **8,** 143.
  Epigæa repens, **8,** 139, 154.
  Everlasting, **1,** 73.
  Fern, **5,** 46, 141 ; **6,** 88.
  Flower-de-luce, **6,** 81 ; **8,** 148, 149.
  Golden-rod, **8,** 161.
  Hepatica, **8,** 139, 142.
  Hollyhock, **8,** 148, 155.
  Honeysuckle, **2,** 248 ; **8,** 154.
  Houstonia, **8,** 143.
  Hyacinth, **8,** 148, 149 ; **10,** 18 ; blue, **1,** 228, 229.
  Larkspur, **8,** 148.
  Laurel, **6,** 88.
  Lilac, **1,** 228, 229 ; **5,** 143 ; **8,** 145, 146.
  Lily, **8,** 63.
  Lily of the valley, **4,** 226.
  Lupin, **8,** 148.
  Maidenhair fern, **1,** 46.
  Marguerite, **4,** 209.
  Marigold, **8,** 162.
  Marsh marigold, **8,** 142.
  Mignonette, **2,** 182.
  Morning glories, **4,** 293 ; **6,** 73 ; **8,** 162.
  Peony, **8,** 148.
  Phlox, **8,** 142.
  Pond-lily, **8,** 143, 153.
  Primrose, **10,** 18.
  Rose, **8,** 146, 148, 149, 150, 153.
  Saxifrage, **8,** 142, 143.
  Shad-flower, **8,** 142.
  Skunk-cabbage, **8,** 139, 141.
  Succory, **8,** 154.
  Sunflower, **8,** 150.
  Tulip, **8,** 148.
  Valerian, **1,** 70.
  Violet, **8,** 142, 143, 144.
  Wheat, **4,** 209.
  Witch-hazel, **8,** 140.
  Yellow lilies, **6,** 88.
  Zinnia, **8,** 162.
Floyer, Sir John, **9,** 413.
Fluid as typifying the mobility of restricted will, **2,** 34.
Fly-paper, **8,** 5.
Flying, boating near approach to, **1,** 168.
Flying Childers, **10,** 40.
Flynt, Henry, **5,** 27.
Fog at sea, **10,** 181.
Fog whistle, **10,** 181.
Foliage, grotesque shapes of, **5,** 266.
Folly often teaches wisdom, **2,** 13.
Fontanelle, women influence men as it were by pressure on, **1,** 222.
Food, and longevity, **4,** 184 ; our first and last, is air, **8,** 199 ; elements to be supplied in, 203 ; amount and nature of, 215–220 ; digestibility of various substances of, 218–220 ; definition of, **9,** 197 ; definition of aliment, 255 ; presumption in favor of, 265 ; its part in medical curative treatment, 267 ; English and American compared, **10,** 200, 201. *See also,* Air ; Nitrogen ; Pigs' feet ; Pork ; Tripe ; Vegetarians ; Veal ; Venison.
Foot, function of, in walking, **8,** 123.
Forbes, Sir John, **9,** 182.
Forbes, John M., called Lord of the Manor at Naushon, **1,** 39 n.
Force, intellectual products not in the category of physical, **8,** 293 ; what changes the form of, 294 ; conservation of, **9,** 217 ; nature of, 218, 235.
Forces of nature, development of, **4,** 31 ; warfare of man with, 54.

Foreign correspondence in newspapers, 1, 117.
Foreign language, peculiar delight in reading a, 8, 350.
Foreknowledge, divine, 8, 302.
"Forest Scenery," by William Gilpin, 4, 27, 213.
Forests, built up mainly from air-currents, 2, 67.
Forestus, 9, 65.
Forget, we must *get* before we can, 9, 300.
Forgotten, pleasure of being, 3, 161.
Fork, trick of impaling meat with, at a Commons-table, 2, 58.
Formulæ, as a substitute for character, 9, 367.
Forrester, Miss Letty, in *Elsie Venner*, 5, 234 *et seq.* ; her prettiness, 302, 303 ; feels subtle influence of Elsie, 309 *et seq.* ; engaged to Bernard Langdon, 485–487.
Fort Hill, sliced down, 8, 160.
Forty days' fasting, stories of, 10, 119.
Foster, Birket, his pictures of English landscape, 10, 22.
Foster, John, of Brighton, 3, 14.
Fothergill, Dr. John, Franklin's encomium of, 10, 157.
Fothergill, Dr. J. Milner, 10, 157.
Foucault's grand experiment, 10, 165.
Foundlings, planetary, 4, 40, 54, 55.
Fountain, genius compared to, 2, 288.
Fourscore, the Mont Blanc of, 4, 27.
Fourteen-syllable verse, 8, 317.
Fourth of July, author's oration on, Boston, 1863, 8, 79 ; the day remembered by the author in England, 10, 94.
Fowls, fondness of, for sunlight, 8, 210.
Fox, the fasting man, 10, 119.
Fox, Rev. Jabez, of Woburn, 3, 13.
Fox, Dr. Wilson, 10, 199.
Fox-fire, 6, 95.
Foxglove, 2, 261.
Fra Angelico, two faces by, 2, 178.
Frailties of the rich, 3, 296.
Framingham, Mass., 8, 76.
France, attitude of, toward the North in Civil war, 8, 100 ; 10, 178 ; the France of Louis Philippe, 10, 1 ; from Boulogne to Paris, unattractive, 161.
Francis, Dr., 9, 141.
Franklin, Benjamin, quoted, 1, 124; not ashamed to be born in Boston, 2, 15 ; ballad by, mentioned, 306 ; his look, 3, 6; as referred to, by Dr. Johnson, 265 ; one of the two Americans who established a European reputation as a philosopher, 8, 362; his encomium of Dr. John Fothergill, 10, 157.
Franklin, " Sir Ben," 8, 64.
Franklin, Benjamin, the Landlady's son in *The Autocrat*. *See* Benjamin Franklin.
Franklin, Dr. B., the Landlady's son in *The Poet*. *See* Doctor B. Franklin.
Franklin, Governor, William, 9, 23.

Franklin-place, Boston, front yards in, 1, 272.
Frankland, Sir Harry, 10, 121.
Freaks of nature. *See* Monstrosities.
Frederick, Maryland, in 1862, 8, 25, 26 ; natural beauty of, 47.
Freedom, in America and England, 2, 81; religious and political must be maintained, 125; freedom from disturbance demanded by creative power, 3, 100 ; freedom of discussion in scientific questions, 182; gain in, 185; of thought, Boston's influence for, 2, 3 ; as related to the convictions of others, 3, 307; in politics always generates a new type of religious character, 8, 310 ; of speech, 9, 206.
— of the will. *See* Will.
Freeman, the " American giant," 8, 230.
Freeman, Rev. James, 4, 196.
Freemasonry, 2, 298.
Freethinker, a term of reproach in England, 2, 81.
French, the, their dramatic way of putting things, 8, 350, 354 ; we learn wonderful things of ourselves in their books, 351 ; their ingenuity in twisting English, 352 ; superior to English and Americans in prescribing for disease, 9, 204; criticisms on their surgical practice, 205.
French and English Dictionary, Bellows's, 10, 40.
French institute, obduracy of, 9, 49.
French language, study of, 1, 57 ; the Landlady's son's exercise in, 58, 136 ; as taught in Apollinean institute in *Elsie Venner*, 5, 49.
Frenchman, the eccentric, 3, 225.
Frère Jacques, 9, 366.
Friendship, does not authorize disagreeable things to intimates, 1, 51 ; friends shown up by story-writers, 61 ; a person learns his own progress in noticing that of others, 93 ; a calm, clear mind the best basis for, 131 ; intellectual companionship not necessary to, 131; unexpected, the result of sympathetic disposition, 3, 154; no time for, among naturalists, 249.
Fright, death caused by, 7, 91.
Frog pond, 2, 3, 281 ; 3, 314 ; 8, 138, 146.
Frogs, 6, 88 ; adapted by nature for the purposes of the physiologist, 8, 195 ; nervous system of, 196.
Front and side doors to feelings, 1, 128.
Frost, the first, 8, 162.
Froude, as to Bloody Mary's hysterics, 6, 171.
Frozen limbs, treatment of, 9, 67.
Fruit, intellectual green, the United States a market for, 1, 261 ; " mourning " fruit, 307 ; early loss of, compensated, 10, 169.
Fuel, carbon for, in human economy, 1, 155.
Fuller, Dr., of England, a Perkinist, 9, 19.

Fuller, Margaret, her eyes, **5**, 101 ; as a school-girl, **8**, 241-243.

Fuller, Dr. Samuel, **9**, 325.

Fuller's " Holy War," **2**, 235 ; its title-page, **4**, 117.

Fulton, Robert, moving in parallel path with other inventors, **8**, 84.

Funny, authors and actors ashamed of being, **1**, 50.

Furrows, three, on forehead, the result of three dogmas, **6**, 124.

Future life, solemnity commonly thought essential to idea of, **1**, 92.

Future of human race, vision of, **6**, 406.

Future punishment. *See* Punishment, future.

Gaffarel, **5**, 223.

Gaffield, Mr., experiments of, on the effect of sunlight on glass, **8**, 210.

Gager, Wm., **9**, 325.

Gahs, the Boarding-house lighted with, **2**, 317.

Gainsborough, **10**, 47 ; his Blue Boy, 54.

Gairdner, Professor, **10**, 197.

Galen, **5**, 315 ; **9**, 178, 251 ; story of, **7**, 232, 252 ; psalm of praise of, **8**, 415 ; medical system of, **9**, 318 ; Molière, satirized system of, 319 ; Galenists were herb-doctors, 319.

Galileo, **9**, 94 ; in Cathedral of Pisa, **10**, 166.

Galiots, Amsterdam, **8**, 58, 59.

Gall, Dr., on modern therapeutics, **8**, 307.

Galton, Francis, **3**, 303 ; **8**, 397 ; **10**, 151, 196.

Galvani, noticed the twitching of frog's legs, **8**, 378.

Galvanic signals, velocity of, **8**, 272.

Galvanism, origin of, **7**, 242.

Gambetta, his fiery youth, **10**, 168.

Gambling, fostered by horse-racing, **1**, 34 ; not republican, 34.

Gambrel-roofed house, **2**, 188, 230 ; **7**, 22 ; the Poet's recollections of, **3**, 10 *et seq. ;* its unpretentiousness, 12 ; its tenants, 13, 18 ; its clerical visitors, 14 ; its trees, 19 ; its garden, 20 *et seq. ;* its outlook, 22 ; its cellar, 23 ; its garret, 24 ; the old books of the garret, 26 ; its historic associations, 28 ; its later use, 28 ; its romances, 29 ; its improvements, 30 ; **4**, 100 ; description of, **7**, 23, 29, 30, 31 ; destruction of, 23.

Garden, the hired-man's, in *Elsie Venner*, **5**, 137 ; a terraced, 142 ; old-fashioned, **8**, 147-150.

Garden parties, formidable, **10**, 56 ; one at Kensington Palace, 56, 57, 187, 206 ; at Stratford-on-Avon, 98, 99.

Gardiner, Colonel, miraculous appearance seen by, **6**, 95.

Gargoyle, **5**, 410.

Garibaldi, **8**, 100.

Garret, old, awfulness of, **6**, 31.

Garrick, **5**, 224.

Garrison, W. L., **8**, 83.

Garter of J. Howell, **9**, 9.

Gaskell, Mrs., her " Cranford," **10**, 107.

Gasparin, Count, a friend to the North in Civil war, **8**, 99.

Gaspings for Immortality, **4**, 88.

Gastric juice, **9**, 237.

Gavarret, **9**, 431.

Gay, Dr. George H., **8**, 17.

Gay, John, **10**, 59.

Geddings, Dr., **9**, 416.

Geese, for swans, **1**, 273 ; flying south, **8**, 169.

Gellius, Aulus, quoted, **9**, 287.

Genevieve, St., sarcophagus of, **1**, 280 ; **8**, 64 ; **10**, 164.

" Genevieve," Coleridge's, **6**, 316, 317, 389 ; **7**, 233, 246.

Genius, a weak flavor of, not agreeable to common people, **1**, 3 ; geniuses may admire each other, 3 ; types of, 7 ; its advent a surprise, 54 ; tendency of, to stimulation, 187 ; must be demonstrated, 290, 291 ; end of, when its special affinities are worked out, **2**, 25 ; a union of strength and sensibility, 223 ; compared with talent, 240 ; should marry character, 287 ; wife of, compared to tug invisibly drawing tall ship, 289 ; truthfulness is essence of, 290 ; hereditary, **4**, 90 ; the strange, divine, dread gift of, **6**, 100 ; the last triumph of the gift of, 319 ; in clusters, rarely a single star, **8**, 84 ; not necessary in a physician, **9**, 384.

Genius for religion, **3**, 128.

Gentility, humanity comes before, **2**, 145 ; pretensions to, 153 ; heroism is, **8**, 8.

Gentleman : few gentlemen are ruined by drinking, **1**, 190 ; the face of a, 193 ; a congenital incapacity for being a, 219 ; misuse of word, **2**, 144 ; what constitutes a, 204 ; alone endurable in full dress, **5**, 103 ; indifference of a, to gossip of inferiors, 277 ; signs of a, **7**, 54, 55, 76.

Gentry, mansion-house sort of, in *Elsie Venner*, **5**, 102.

Geology, **5**, 318 ; of the human body, **8**, 191 ; objects of, **10**, 188.

George III., **10**, 184.

George IV., **10**, 96.

Gerard, Herball of, **9**, 280.

Gerhard, Dr., on contagion, **9**, 119.

Géricault's " Wreck of the Medusa," **10**, 16, 170.

German women, sweet voices of, **1**, 215.

Germany, welcomed the practice of Paracelsus, **9**, 319.

" Gertrude of Wyoming," **8**, 49.

Ghosts, Bentham's logic against, **2**, 189 ; false, 257 ; no opportunities for, in modern houses, **3**, 23 ; of boyhood, met on revisiting old haunts, 254-259 ; Mme. de Staël's feelings with regard to, 429 ; lacking at English country-house, **10**, 98.

Giant, Irish, **10**, 67, 68.
Gibbon's story of the monks of Mount Athos, **3**, 106.
Gibraltar of the Gulf, **8**, 95.
Gideon, test of, **4**, 122.
Gift-enterprises, Nature fond of, **1**, 55.
Gigmanity, **10**, 141.
Gil Blas, and the Archbishop, **1**, 51; quotation from Introduction to "Gil Blas," 199.
Gilbert, the French poet, quoted, **1**, 185.
Gilman, Arthur, the architect, **1**, 21 n.; **10**, 194.
Gilmour, Mr. David, **10**, 196.
Gilpin, Rev. William, a set of his works, **1**, 231; his orange-juice landscapes, 232; story from his "Forest Scenery," **4**, 27; his study of trees, 213; thought the donkey more picturesque than a horse in a landscape, 273; **10**, 61.
Gingko tree, **1**, 277.
Girardet, **10**, 170.
Girls, fall of two girls from a gallery in a church, **1**, 280; **10**, 165; a beautiful girl is a terrible fact, **2**, 176; influence of a girl's face, 181; strange audacity often blended with delicacy in young girls, 222; unprotected girls in board-ing-houses, 223; depths of their na-ture, 228; revelations of soul of a girl through her poems and drawings, 229-240; souls of young, **6**, 73; attractive costume of, 370; beauty of, in New England, **7**, 50; education of, 172 *et seq.*; hysteria of, 194, 221, 322; grass makes, **8**, 51. *See also* Women.
Giving up on account of age, not to be thought of, **1**, 162.
Gladiators, unwinking, **5**, 209, 332.
Gladstone, **4**, 34, 136, 292; said to think himself too old to cross the ocean, **10**, 9; at Epsom races, 31; his military aspect at Lady Rosebery's, 44; his speech on the Irish question, 63, 64.
Gladstone, Mrs., **10**, 43.
Glands, vascular, **9**, 238.
Glasgow, **8**, 387; **10**, 7.
Glass, change of color in, by sunlight, **8**, 210.
Glass-blower anticipated by Nature, **9**, 233.
Glendower, Owen, **9**, 382.
Gloucester, England, **10**, 41.
Gloucester and Bristol, bishop of, **10**, 54.
Gloucester, Mass., men of, and the devils, **9**, 355.
Glove-maker's sign, Autocrat's childish fear of, **1**, 205.
God, human life as compared to, **2**, 10; opens the Book of life to doctors, **5**, 325; the God of Edwards not a trinity but a quaternity, **8**, 368; often pic-tured as Moloch, 414; of the physi-cian, **9**, 365.
Gods of the heathen, servants of to-day, **3**, 271.

Goethe, pictured thought of, **8**, 282.
Gold, the charm and power of, **3**, 255 *et seq.*; the "innocent sin-breeder," **6**, 218.
Gold piece hung about the neck of scrof-ulous persons, **9**, 3.
Goldback, a greenback of no value with-out a, **9**, 404.
Golden blonde, the, at school, **8**, 241.
Golden book of Venice, **2**, 86.
Goldenrod, Mrs. Midas, in *The Poet*, her visits to The Lady, **3**, 55; her likes and dislikes, 294.
Golden rule in matters of religion, **4**, 197.
"Golden Treasury," **10**, 52.
Goldsmith, **7**, 177; **10**, 35, 133, 154, 155, 162; his "Madam Blaize" borrowed from the French, **2**, 231; his old sol-dier, **8**, 10.
Gondolas, Venetian, uniformly black, **5**, 103.
Gooch, Dr., on puerperal fever, **9**, 137, 138.
Good-breeding easily adjusts itself, **5**, 304, 305.
Good-bye, the Dictator's, **4**, 314.
Good manners, worth of, **3**, 58.
Good Samaritan, **3**, 306.
Good time going, A, **1**, 223.
Goodwood cup, **1**, 34.
Gooseberry fool, young talent compared to, **1**, 261.
Gordon, Dr., of Aberdeen, Scotland, **9**, 103, 134, 135, 166, 221.
Gorgeana, capital of Province of Maine, **10**, 121.
Gorges, Sir Thomas, **10**, 120, 121; asso-ciations with his name, 121.
Gorton, Samuel, **9**, 334.
Goschen, Mr., **10**, 51.
Gospel, of Saint Petroleum, **3**, 40; of dread tidings, **8**, 384, 432.
Gosse, Mr. Edmund, **10**, 53; at Cam-bridge, England, 71.
Gosse, P. W., argues for the existence of the sea serpent, **8**, 168; his belief with respect to fossil skeleton, 168, 311.
Gossip of inferiors, indifference of gen-tlemen to, **5**, 277.
Gould, Dr., report of, on Transatlantic longitude, **8**, 272; **9**, 443.
Gould, Miss Hannah F., **7**, 8.
Gower, Lord Ronald, **10**, 53.
Gown, academic, splendor of, **10**, 87.
Graaf, de, **9**, 412.
Gracchi, the, **2**, 288.
Grace before meat in England, **10**, 78, 130.
Grace of God not private property, **3**, 327; grace opposed to nature in the scholastic theology, **3**, 304.
Graciousness mistaken for condescen-sion, **3**, 55.
Graduates, college. *See* "Boys, The."
Graduates from the Academy of love, **4**, 243.

Grafted trees, **3**, 165.

Grammar, higher law in, **1**, 40.

"Grammar of assent," Newman's, **1**, 14.

Granary Burying-ground, **1**, 239, 240 ; elms of, torn up, **8**, 163.

Grand Assize, the last, **4**, 312.

Grand climacteric, **4**, 30, 38.

Grand manner, **3**, 334.

Grand-paternal instinct in bachelors, **6**, 47.

Grand Pump-Room Hotel, at Bath, **10**, 105.

Granville, Lady, **10**, 28.

Granville, Lord, **10**, 31.

Grape, wild, **9**, 321.

Grass makes girls, **8**, 51.

Gratiolet, on the development of the brain, **8**, 268.

Grauvogel, **9**, 414.

Gravel, clean, an anodyne, **2**, 265 ; gravel walks, rents in nature's green garment, **8**, 149.

Graves, Dr., of Dublin, **9**, 298.

Gravestones, transplanting of, **1**, 239.

Graveyards. *See* Burial grounds ; Granary.

Gray, Asa, **9**, 439 ; **10**, 183.

Gray's "Elegy," **7**, 167.

Grayden, James, the driver, **8**, 28–43.

Great Britain, attitude of, toward the U. S. in the Civil war, **8**, 97 ; commentary on British institutions, 98, 99 ; border warfare of England and Scotland, 107, 108 ; bears an income-tax of 10 per cent. in the Napoleonic wars, 111.

Great Eastern, cost of the, **1**, 72.

Great fire in London, **10**, 154, 179.

Great Malvern, **10**, 101, 102 ; ascent of the Beacon, 102.

Great men, not commonly great scholars, **1**, 132 ; all schools have some who are destined to be, **8**, 250.

Great names, authority of, in religious opinions, **8**, 423–426.

Great organ in Boston Music Hall, **3**, 95.

Great secret, a, intimations of, in many persons, **2**, 177 ; it is nov the secret of love, 180.

Great Teacher, the, **2**, 32.

"Greek Anthology," **6**, 203.

Greek young men, beauty of, **2**, 283.

Green, Mrs., in *Elsie Venner*, **5**, 114, 115.

Green fruit, intellectual, United States a great market for, **1**, 261.

Greene, J. S. C., **9**, 425.

Greene, Nathaniel, **8**, 10.

"Greenfield Hill" of Timothy Dwight, **8**, 137.

Greenland, Mr., **9**, 340.

Gregory the Great, his pun on Saxon children, **10**, 23.

Gregory, Dr., on contagion, **9**, 118.

Gridley, Byles, M. A., a retired school-master and college professor in *The Guardian Angel*, **6**, 2 ; his study, 39, 108, 141 ; his character, 138 *et seq.*;

his wisdom, 40, 41 ; the father of a dead book, 42, 43 ; his capacity for seeing out of the back of his head, 55 ; finds Myrtle, 112 *et seq.* ; warns young Dr. Hurlbut about Myrtle, 140 *et seq.*; warns Myrtle from the Rev. Mr. Stoker, 175 *et seq.* ; helps Myrtle to go to the city to school, 263 *et seq.* ; invites Gifted Hopkins to go with him to publisher, 293 *et seq.* ; his appearance at Mrs. Ketchum's party, 317 *et seq.* ; compels Cynthia Badlam to surrender a paper, 352 *et seq.* ; comforts Susan Posey as to her lost love for Clement Lindsay, 372 *et seq.* ; is asked to take charge of the Withers property for Myrtle, 414 ; comes to live at The Poplars, 423 ; Myrtle calls him her Guardian Angel, 431. *See also* "Thoughts on the Universe."

Grief, having been love once, may be love again, **5**, 470 ; griefs which are never put into words, 194, 195, 249.

Grierson, Col., **8**, 102.

Griesselich, Dr., **9**, 83.

Grisi, **10**, 5.

Groom, Yorkshire : his fight with sophomore, **2**, 53.

Grosvenor House, pictures at, **10**, 54.

Grotius, Hugo, quoted, **8**, 115.

Ground-bait, literary, **1**, 38.

Groups, facts most easily acquired in, **9**, 287.

Growth, process of, in human body, **8**, 198.

Grysant, physician and pope, **9**, 320.

Guano, **9**, 372.

Guarnerius violin, **2**, 308.

Guelph spine and neck, **10**, 89.

Guérin, Maître, quoted on sleep of assassin, **8**, 334.

Guest, undesired, **5**, 156.

Guibourt, **9**, 79.

Guides, queer notions of, **8**, 63, 64.

Guido Reni, **10**, 170.

Guillotine, abolition of, advocated, **8**, 265.

Guilt, heritable, doctrine of, **3**, 268. *See also* Automatism ; Heredity ; Imbeciles, moral ; Original sin ; Responsibility ; Sin.

Guinea-worm, its burrowing compared to intemperance, **1**, 188.

Gulf-stream, **2**, 14.

Gull, Sir William, **10**, 27.

Gulliver, **2**, 247.

Gun-shot wounds, as treated by Paré, **9**, 270 ; treated with water, 270.

Gunn, Richard, toys of, **8**, 160.

Gwyllyn, David Ap, **3**, 325.

Gymnotus, **3**, 45.

Gynophobia, account of a case of, **7**, 230 *et seq.*

Gypsies, averse to civilization, **5**, 317.

Habits, a mask of age, **1**, 155 ; an approximation of animal system to the organic, 155 ; formation of, ought to be special characteristic of age, 156 ; force of, **4,** 27 ; the crutch of old age, 37 ; take place of self-determination, **5,** 252 ; of doctors, **9,** 386.

Hackett, Horatio B., as a school-boy at Andover, **8,** 248.

Hadfield, would-be murderer of George III., **5,** 226.

Hadrian, Emperor, **4,** 45.

Hagen, Prof. H. A., **9,** 439.

Hahnemann, Samuel, **9,** 41 *et seq. ;* character of some of the authors quoted by, 63 ; misquotations of, 65 ; vender of secret remedies, 98 ; his inability to weigh the value of testimony, 185 ; his theory of "dynamization," 419 ; bust of, **10,** 101 ; disciples of, 172.

Hailes, Joseph, "the spider," the muscles of, **8,** 229 ; died of consumption, 230.

Hair, variety of, **2,** 80.

Hair-cutting, associated with cutting grass and rum, **8,** 154.

Hair-spring of watch, meddling with, **2,** 43.

Hale, Edward Everett, **4,** 9.

Hale, Sir Matthew, sanctioned conviction for witchcraft, **8,** 423.

Half-knowledge, **9,** 407.

Half-time allowed to college students, **5,** 16.

Halford, Sir Henry, **3,** 102 ; **10,** 96.

Hall, Bishop, on the election of a wife, **3,** 304 ; **6,** 195.

Hall, Marshall, **5,** 227.

Hall, Robert, on Jonathan Edwards, **8,** 362 ; read and re-read the " Freedom of the Will," 374.

Hall-mark of silver, **1,** 308.

Hall of Eblis, in " Vathek," insane asylum compared to, **1,** 247.

Halle, John, the Halle of, **10,** 122.

Halleck, Fitz-Greene, **4,** 41 ; **7,** 5.

Haller, as quoted by Dr. Laycock, on record on the brain, **8,** 299 ; quoted on Abbas, 357, 358 ; on *vis insita* of the muscular fibre, **9,** 240 ; at a disadvantage by being a poet, 298 ; would have admired Dr. Billings's catalogue, 406.

Halley, and the law of gravitation, **8,** 84.

Hallucinations, caused by religious stimulants, **8,** 416.

Halo, meaning of, **7,** 244.

Hamilton, Lady Claude, **10,** 47.

Hamilton, *Sir* Wm. R., his period of incubation in discovery of quaternions, **8,** 281, 282.

"Hamlet," quoted, **8,** 275 ; **9,** 376.

Hammond, Dr. William A., favored importation of light wines, **8,** 223 ; on the use of tea and coffee, 225 ; quoted on the relations of brain and mind, 262, 263.

Hammond, Governor, **8,** 105.

Hancock, Goodman, **9,** 337.

Hancock house, Boston, **2,** 42.

Hand, wooden, a glove-maker's sign,

Autocrat's fear of, **1,** 205 ; influence of a cold, damp, **2,** 71 ; of dead man cures swellings, 246 ; **9,** 360.

Handwriting of persons with squinting brain, **4,** 204.

Hanging, not the best use to which the criminal can be put, **8,** 345.

Hanging-point, the only fixed standard of punishments, **8,** 324.

Hangman's stone, various legends of, in England, **1,** 282 *et seq. ;* **10,** 6, 119.

Hannibal, **3,** 300.

Happy Valley, in " Rasselas," **6,** 77.

Harcourt, Lady, **10,** 24, 28, 42, 179.

Harcourt, Sir William, **10,** 43 ; rooms at Cambridge, 71.

Harford, Canon, sermon of, in Westminster Abbey, **10,** 29.

Harlan, Dr., rejected the notion that the moon caused insanity, **8,** 212.

Harpsfield, Dr., **9,** 4.

Harris, Dr., of New York, on inherited crime, **8,** 343.

Harris, Thaddeus Mason, D. D., **3,** 15.

Harris, Prof. William T., quoted on the habit of women of opening car windows, **8,** 214; quoted on woman's methods of clothing, 227 ; on closing the day with devotions, 231.

Harrisburg, Pennsylvania, description of, **8,** 63 ; Brant House at, 64.

Harry, a handsome Marylander in *The Professor,* **2,** 51 ; his fight with butcher on muster-day, 52.

Hartford, **1,** 244 ; **8,** 76.

Hartington, Lord, **10,** 42.

Hartley, David, on reflex actions, **8,** 277, 278, 378 ; **9,** 248.

Hartmann, Dr., of Leipsic, **9,** 83.

Hartshorn, spirits of, uses of, **6,** 344.

Harvard College, Memorial Hall, **1,** 20 n. ; burning of Calef's book in yard, **2,** 8 ; **8,** 414 ; Samuel Adams at Commencement, 41 ; trick at Commons-table, 58 ; mysterious mark in wall of dormitory, 187 ; Harvard hall, **3,** 10; Massachusetts hall, 10 ; Holden, 10 ; Class of 1829, **4,** 28 ; **10,** 111 ; Commencement as it was, 272 ; growth of, **7,** 27 ; students guard the Cambridge arsenal, **8,** 12 ; Commencement, 158–161 ; ugliness of " University building," 246 ; founding of the Medical school, **9,** 349 ; two medical libraries of, 398 ; growth of medical faculty, 421 ; the author, professor at, for thirty-five years, **10,** 7, 79.

"Harvard Lyceum," quoted, **8,** 166.

Harvey, William, **3,** 106 ; **9,** 94, 97, 179, 222, 292, 412.

Hastings, Henry, his robust longevity, **4,** 27.

Hastings, battle of, **10,** 65.

Hat, the vulnerable point of the outer man, **1,** 177 ; anecdote of a Leghorn straw, 177 ; shabby gentility betrayed by, 178 ; the ultimum moriens of respectability, 178 ; on wrong side foremost, 242; on one side, a sign of exuberant vitality in a mature man, **8**, 62; English feeling for the, **10**, 193.

Hatfield, large elm at, **1**, 235.

Hathaway, Anne, cottage of, **10**, 97, 130.

Hatred, **1**, 219.

Haughton, Prof., quotation of, from "Medicine in Modern Times," **8**, 262.

Haunted house, fear of, **2**, 162.

Havelocks, **8**, 116.

Haven, Bishop Gilbert, quoted, **8**, 413.

Haverhill, Mass., visited, **8**, 252.

Haweis, Rev. H. R., **4**, 273 et seq.; **10**, 11, 28, 41, 54.

Hawthorn, in Windsor Park, **10**, 49.

Hawthorne, **1**, 2 n.; "The Marble Faun," **5**, x.; "The Scarlet Letter," **7**, 7; **8**, 18; day of his burial, 145; squashes described by, 149; illuminated the memory of Dr. Swinnerton, **9**, 358; letter to Longfellow, **10**, 203.

Haygarth, Dr., **9**, 21; story told by, concerning Perkinism, 27; his success in its practice, 36, 78; early advocate of vaccination, 96.

Haying time, smell of rum in, **8**, 154.

Hayley, first part of this century suffering from the song of, **8**, 84.

Hays, Catharine, burnt at Tyburn, **1**, 33 n.

Hayward, George, **9**, 353.

Hazard, R. G., on freedom of the will, **8**, 302, 378.

Hazard, Captain Charles, father of Myrtle in The Guardian Angel, **6**, 26.

Hazard, Myrtle, heroine of The Guardian Angel, advertisement for, **6**, 6; shut in garret to break her will, 31; finds her uncle Malachi hanging dead, 34; depressing influences upon her, 78; steals from The Poplars by night, 85 et seq.; vision seen by her of her dead ancestors, 91-95; rescued from drowning by Clement Lindsay, 104; returns home with Master Gridley, 118; becomes hysterical, 131 et seq.; comes under spiritual fascinations of Rev. Mr. Stoker, 159 et seq.; Master Gridley warns her, 175 et seq.; her revery, 180 et seq.; her religious character, 195; her three admirers, 212 et seq.; meets Clement Lindsay for second time, 244; he idealizes her in a bust of Liberty, 252 et seq.; early experiences at the city school, 268 et seq.; her strange part in the tableaux, 278 et seq.; at Mrs. Ketchum's party, 311 et seq.; meets Clement Lindsay there, 324; return to Oxbow Village, 325; Clement Lindsay calls upon her, 382; accepts Lindsay's affection, 388 et seq.; William Murray Bradshaw offers his love and is rejected, 396 et seq.; receives the news that the Withers property is settled in her favor, 412 et seq.; married to Clement,

and then accompanies him to the front in Civil war, 417 et seq.

Head, Sir Francis, speaks of showers parting on the Cordilleras, **8**, 46.

Head, erectile, men of genius have, **1**, 7; double walls of, unfavorable to phrenology, **2**, 199; grows as the intellect expands, **8**, 289.

Headache, acquires dignity if called cephalalgia, **3**, 127; reflex, **4**, 129; varieties of, **5**, 69; caused by bad air, **8**, 213.

Healing art, its professional hardness, **2**, 263. See also Medicine.

Health, how to preserve, **4**, 186; curve of, 187.

Health resorts, **9**, 296.

Hearing, nerve of, **4**, 98; **8**, 271.

Heart, should not grow cold with age, **1**, 174; inscriptions on, 246; wild, hidden under decorum, **2**, 94, 158; full of combustibles, 159; our hearts held to our homes by innumerable fibres, 247; women subject to atrophy of, 249; displacement of, 259; a wick of lamp of life, 260; creed of, 298; how influenced by the emotions, **7**, 232; mechanism of its action, 234; its relation to the brain, 235; power of Col. Townsend to suspend its action, 237; action of, after death, **8**, 201; palpitation of, caused by tea, 224; action of, involuntary, 329.

— disease of, **2**, 251; difficult breathing in, 257; caused by emotion, **8**, 2; by over-exertion, 230.

Heart-hunger, **4**, 217.

Heart-starvation, **4**, 309.

Heat, artificial, necessary to human beings raised under glass, **8**, 208; animal, production of, **9**, 239.

Heathen, goodness of, **2**, 121.

Heathenism, Christian, **4**, 250.

Heaven, assessors of, **1**, 92; to reach port of, we must sail and not drift, 93; voices of, 217; inward disgust for, in children, **2**, 185; an experiment, **4**, 35; its way of putting questions to mortals, **8**, 15; books of, kept by double entry, 305.

Heberden, William, **9**, 311.

Hecquet, Dr., **9**, 299.

Hedges, **10**, 22.

"Hedging," the only safe rule in prophesying, **8**, 12.

Heitland, Mr., his poem of greeting to Dr. Holmes, at St. John's college, Cambridge, **10**, 79.

Hell, of the church is the Tartarus of the heathen world, **4**, 254; as conceived by Edwards, **8**, 384, 399.

Helmholtz, **9**, 217.

Helminthia, one of the twins in The Guardian Angel, **6**, 53.

Helmont, Van, **9**, 279.

Hemlock, **1**, 264, 286; **5**, 47, 187.

Henchman's apothecary shop, **2**, 231.

Henniker, Lord, **9**, 23.

Henry, Matthew, quoted on the effect of troubles, **8,** 306 n.

Henry, Patrick, accents of liberty of, **8,** 84.

Hepatica triloba, one of the first spring flowers, **8,** 139.

Heraclitus, Carlyle compared to, **10,** 140.

Herb-doctors are Galenists, **9,** 319.

" Herball," of Gerard, **9,** 280.

Herbert, George, **3,** 110 ; residence of, **10,** 110, 125–127 ; Emerson's obligations to, 126 ; his little chapel, 127.

Herbert, Gladys (Lady Lonsdale and Lady de Grey), **10,** 46.

Herbert family, **10,** 119.

Herbs : the smell of everlasting, **1,** 76 ; bundles of, in old closet, 78 ; employed by Gov. Winthrop, **9,** 332 ; Sir W. Temple's list of helpful, 361.

Hercules, **2,** 89.

Hereditary genius, **4,** 90.

Hereditary instincts. *See* Inherited tendencies.

Hereditary scholarship of Brahmin caste of New England, **5,** 5.

Heredity, some qualities not easily accounted for by, **2,** 68 ; its development, **3,** 166 ; hard to hold child accountable for inherited bad qualities, **5,** 322, 323 ; moral character of, 304 ; now discussed, rather than predestination, 327 ; certainty of, 344 ; we recognize, 380. *See also* Automatism ; Guilt ; Responsibility ; Sin ; Will.

Heresy, master of ceremonies of burning for, easy to find in any city, **1,** 33 ; a word fallen into disuse, **2,** 118 ; does not sound so dangerous coming from pretty lips, **6,** 163.

Heretics, **2,** 208 ; **5,** 320.

Hering, Dr., **5,** 225 ; **9,** 71.

Heritable guilt, doctrine of, **3,** 268.

Herkomer, Hubert, **10,** 80.

Hero, every one is the, of his baptism, wedding, and funeral, **9,** 420.

Heroic treatment of disease, **9,** 257.

Heroic verse, in relation to rhythm of respiration, **8,** 317.

Heroic will, the, **2,** 205.

Heroism of fashionable people, **2,** 140 ; is gentility, **8,** 8.

Herons, **2,** 236.

Herophilus, **9,** 177.

Herring's, " Plenipotentiary," **5,** 296 ; **10,** 6, 33, 40.

Herring's safes, **9,** 288.

Herschel, his discovery of Georgium Sidus, **3,** 218 ; his telescope, 219 ; **10,** 6 ; apology of, **8,** 269.

Herschell, Lady, **10,** 86.

Herschell, Lord Chancellor, **10,** 37, 86.

Hester Prynne, Hawthorne's, **8,** 18.

Hey's saw, **9,** 326.

Hezekiah's advice, **2,** 23.

Hicks-Beach, Sir Michael, **10,** 63.

Hidden soul, the. *See* Unconscious mental action.

Hiera picra, **6,** 296.

Higginson, Francis, saying of, **2,** 250 ; on Massachusetts climate, **9,** 322, 323 ; death of his children, 323.

Higginson, Mary, the first of the Pilgrims to die at sea, **9,** 323.

Higginson, T. W., author of " Saints and their Bodies," **1,** 163 ; his " April Days," **8,** 139, 143, 183.

High Church service, responses in, **3,** 128.

Highlands, the, of Scotland, **10,** 7.

Hildanus, Fabricius, **9,** 6, 375.

Hildreth, Richard, son of a clergyman, **8,** 411.

Hill, Ann, her remarkable cure, **9,** 36.

Hill, Pres. Thomas, experiences in wood and meadow, **8,** 140–142.

Hillard, G. S., quoted, **8,** 249.

Himrod's asthma cure, **10,** 11.

Hingham boxes, **2,** 299.

Hippocrates, the Oath of, **6,** 141, 142 ; **9,** 311, 383, 394 ; first aphorism of, **7,** 172 ; on the doctrine of medicine, **8,** 233 ; an " Old School " physician, 236 ; his effect on medical knowledge, **9,** 177 ; stated case on side of Nature, 181 ; his " Aphorisms," 410.

Hippodamoio, genitive of an honorable epithet, **10,** 21.

Hippolytus and Phædra, picture of, in the Luxembourg Gallery, **7,** 4.

Hiram, name written on old piece of paper, **2,** 93 ; uncouthness of name, 95.

Hired-man, the New-England, **5,** 134–138.

" Histoire naturelle des bêtes ruminans et rongeurs, bipèdes et autres," **1,** 59.

Histology, **9,** 353, 422.

" Historie of the Holy Warre," Fuller's, its title-page, **4,** 117.

History, abridged, of two worlds, Number Seven's, **4,** 117.

History, why it repeats itself, **8,** 379.

Hoar, Leonard, both doctor and minister, **9,** 329.

Hobbes, simile of, on freedom of the will, **8,** 377.

Hogarth, **10,** 149, 151.

Hodge, Dr. Hugh L., on the non-contagiousness of puerperal fever, **9,** 103, 109, 110, 116, 124, 127, 171.

Hodges, Dr., **9,** 210.

Holbein, portrait by, of Erasmus, **10,** 127, 128.

Holden Chapel. *See* Harvard College.

Holding the tongue, significance of, in women, **3,** 300.

Holland, Lady, **10,** 41, 57.

Holland, Sir Henry, **10,** 10.

Hollow beneath a road, **2,** 179.

Holloway and Haggerty, execution of, **2,** 188 ; **10,** 44.

Hollyhock, **8,** 155.

Holme castle, **10,** 103 ; meaning of " holme," 103.

Holmes, Mr., Queen's Librarian at Windsor Castle, **10**, 48, 147.

Holmes, Rear Admiral Charles, **10**, 4.

Holmes, Oliver Wendell, steel portrait, **1** (frontispiece); anecdote of two meetings with Mrs. Sigourney, 8 n.; his mother carried out of Boston during the siege, **8**, 6, 26; alleged plagiarism, of, 45; Phi Beta Kappa poet at Brown, 52, 53; coincidence in name, 54; one string of ancestors of Batavian origin, 58; his father pastor of a church in Midway, Ga., 60; Phi Beta Kappa poet at Yale, 73; Fourth of July orator at Boston, 1863, 78–120; the garden, at Cambridge, 147–150; quotes himself, 156; reminiscences of school-days, 239–259; meets ghost of boyhood at Andover, 254–259; delivers Phi Beta Kappa oration at Harvard, 1870, 260–314; experience of, with a dose of ether, 283, 284; quotes from his poem on Burns, 314; delivers valedictory address at Bellevue hospital, 1871, **9**, 370; quotes from his lecture on the medical profession in Massachusetts, 381; reminiscences of his study in Europe and work as professor, 420–440; studied law for a year, 423; first visit to Europe, from 1833 to 1835, **10**, 3; rapid sketch of trip, 3–8; second trip in 1886, 9; liable to asthma at sea, 10; arrival at Liverpool, 18; at Chester, 19, 20; at London, 23–37, 40–68; at the Epsom races, 31–37; admits to a feeling of loneliness in the newer generations of authors, 38, 39; visit to Windsor, 47–50; reception by Dr. Holmes and party in London, 54, 55; visit to Westminster Abbey, 59–62; to House of Commons, 63–65; visit to Tennyson, 68–71; to Cambridge, 71–73; second visit, 74–79; received degree of Doctor Litt., 75, 76; first visit to Oxford, 79–82; to Edinburgh, 83–85; receives degree of LL. D. at Edinburgh, 84; second visit to Oxford, 86–90; decree of D. C. L. at Oxford, 87, 88; Stratford-on-Avon, 90–101; professor at Harvard College for thirty-five years, 99; Great Malvern, 101–105; a week at Bath, 105–107; Salisbury, 108–132; Stonehenge, 110–115; has read forty poems at meetings of his class, 111; to Brighton, 132–135; to Carlyle's house in Chelsea, 136–140; again in London, 141–160; visit to Quaritch's book-shop, 146–149; to British Museum, 151–153; to Paris, 161–178; visit to house in which he lived as student, 163; farewell reception at Liverpool, 180; arrival home, 182.

Holmes, Oliver Wendell, Jr., the Captain in *My Hunt after the Captain*, **8**, i., 16–77.

Holmes house in Cambridge. *See* Gambrel-roofed house.

Holy-stoning the quarter-deck, **8**, 109.

Holyoake, Ann, an ancestor of the Withers in *The Guardian Angel*, burnt by Papists, her portrait, **2**, 23, 417; her influence over the family, 23; vision of, 93.

Holyoke, Dr., **2**, 8; **4**, 26, 184; **8**, 134, 183; **9**, 283, 284, 306, 348.

Holyrood Palace, **10**, 83.

Home, poets want a, **2**, 246; associations with, 247; lack of permanent homes in America, **3**, 11; remembrances of, **10**, 113; homes of England, 116; few such in America, 116; safe arrival at, 182.

Homer, **3**, 47; **4**, 74, 75; quoted on woman's logomachy, **8**, 292; had a slower respiration than Anacreon, 319; birthplace, **9**, 287.

Homer, Jonathan, his external resemblance to Voltaire, **3**, 15.

Home-sickness, **8**, 245.

Homesick in Heaven, **3**, 32.

Homesickness, possible hereafter, **10**, 168.

Homo caudatus, **4**, 155.

Homo unius libri, **4**, 140.

Homœopathic pills and prescriptions, **4**, 187.

"Homœopathic Times," quoted, **9**, 419.

"Homœopathische Rundschau," quoted, **9**, 415.

Homœopathy, **2**, 12; Miss Vincent's opinion about, in *A Mortal Antipathy*, **7**, 284; **9**, 39 *et seq.*; its hostile attitude to the medical profession, 39; its doctrines as stated by Hahnemann, 42 *et seq.*; present condition of belief, 48; want of relation between these doctrines, 51; examination of their proofs, 58 *et seq.*; homœopathic treatises and journals, 74; two public trials of, 78 *et seq.*; homœopathic literature, 84; its present condition, 85 *et seq.*; its probable disappearance, 98; considered as a reaction, 181, 206; the basis of some of its medicines, 187; early form of, **9**, 279; long encysted, 301; parody of mediæval theology, 391; fantastic, 414; fading out, 415, 418, 419; pseudological insanity, 419; a theory of universal poisoning, 442; traces of, still survive in Europe, **10**, 101.

Homoousians and Homoiousians, **8**, 11.

Hone, fine-grained, **10**, 202.

Honey, impossibility of completely emptying jug of, **1**, 17.

Honeysuckle, **2**, 248.

Honeywood, Reverend Doctor, in *Elsie Venner*, of strict theology, but of broad nature, **5**, 61, 62; thinks over his sermon on depravity, 233 *et seq.*; his enlightened sermon preached after talk with Old Sophy, 247; discusses theology and other matters with Dr. Kittredge, 313–328; consoles Elsie while dying, 452 *et seq.*

Hood, investment of candidate for degree at Edinburgh with, **10**, 84.

Hooke, Dr., and law of gravitation, **8**, 84; on number of ideas the mind is capable of entertaining, 274.

Hooper, Bishop, burning of, **1**, 33 n.

Hoosac Tunnel, **1**, 25 n.

Hope, Dr., on heart disease, **8**, 230.

Hope, a terrible thing to take away, **9**, 389.

Hopkins, Ammi, deceased husband of Mrs. Hopkins in *The Guardian Angel*, **6**, 2; some of his sayings, 170.

Hopkins, Mrs., mother of Gifted Hopkins in *The Guardian Angel*, **6**, 2; visits the Rev. Mr. Stoker's study with Susan Posey, 152; speaks her mind, 167; makes her son and Master Gridley ready for their visit to city, 295; consents to change of names for the twins, 426.

Hopkins, Gifted, the village poet of Oxbow in *The Guardian Angel*, **6**, 20; an account of the growth of his poetical genius, 200; experiences remarkable emotion at sight of Myrtle, 201; Master Gridley's practical advice, 203; recites his verses to Clement Lindsay, 228; discovers that he loves Susan Posey, 240; consults Master Gridley as to publishing his poems, 290; their visit to the publisher, 298 *et seq.*; his appearance at Mrs. Ketchum's party, 318 *et seq.*; tells Susan Posey of his love and resolves to devote his poetic genius to his country in the Civil war, 386; baptism of their baby Byron Tennyson Brownlng Hopkins, 421.

Hopkins, Mark, baccalaureate sermon of, **8**, 45, 46.

Hopkins, Samuel, **2**, 16.

Hopkins, Wealthy Amadora, deceased daughter of Mrs. Hopkins, in *The Guardian Angel*, **6**, 52.

Horace, **3**, 323; quoted, **6**, 58, 203; **8**, 118, 311, 335; his "Ars Poetica," **4**, 89.

Horatiis, M. de, **9**, 79.

Horner, Dr., **9**, 121.

Horse-chestnut trees, **1**, 272; one at Rockport, 289 n.; **10**, 190.

Horse-chestnuts for rheumatism, **9**, 368, 381, 382.

Horse-mackerel, taken for sea-serpent, **2**, 257.

Horse-subduer, and hero synonymous, **5**, 150; an honorable epithet, **10**, 21.

Horse-trading, **5**, 287.

Horsemen, the best outside of cities are country-boys, **5**, 149.

Horses, love of the Autocrat for, **1**, 34; trotting, not racing, is a republican institution, 34; race-horses encourage gambling, 37; "thoroughbred" should not be called "blooded," 37: costly fodder of saddle-horses, 166: friskiness of, on cool morning, **2**, 14; two sent to Massachusetts by Admiral Coffin, 53; close average of fast time in trotters, 166; list of official records, 166 n.; Norman breed, 236; switch-tailed kind, **5**, 286; pictures of famous, 296; look of biting horse, **6**, 160; shrewdness of men who live with, **8**, 63; health of, 227; anecdotes of revival of apparently obsolete impressions in, 300; those at Eaton Hall, **10**, 21, 22; at Epsom, 33, 36; pictures of, 6, 33, 40; figure of white horse on hillside at Westbury, England, 108; public horses of Paris not comparable to those of London, 163; of London, 192; England the paradise of, 191, 192. *See also* Rarey.

— famous, viz. : —
Bard, The, **10**, 36, 82.
Bay Middleton, **10**, 33.
Bend Or, **10**, 22, 33.
Boston, **5**, 296.
Crucifix, **10**, 33.
Dexter, **1**, 36 n.; **2**, 166 n.
Don John, **10**, 33.
Eclipse, **1**, 34; **10**, 40.
Ethan Allen, **2**, 166.
Flora Temple, **1**, 36 n.; **2**, 166.
Flying Childers, **10**, 40.
Goldsmith Maid, **2**, 166 n.
Iroquois, **10**, 40.
Lady Suffolk, **1**, 36 n.; **2**, 166; **5**, 296.
Little John, **1**, 34.
Maud S., **1**, 36 n.; **2**, 166 n.
Ormonde, **10**, 33, 36, 40.
Peacemaker, **1**, 34.
Plenipotentiary, **1**, 34; **10**, 6, 33, 40.
Prospect, **1**, 34.
Queen of Trumps, **10**, 33.
Revenge, **1**, 34.

Hospital department of a library, **4**, 301.

Hospitals, unjust grounds of judgment concerning, **9**, 73; great, the true centres of medical education, **9**, 374; of Paris, 427–438.

Hospitality, at Naushon, **1**, 40; is a matter of latitude, 302.

Hot day, phenomena of, **1**, 302.

Hot-water bag, indispensable at sea, **10**, 14.

Hotel, arrival at, **6**, 67.

Hotel clerk, **8**, 20, 53, 65; **10**, 21.

Hotel Cluny, Museum of, **10**, 170.

Hôtel de l'Univers et des États-Unis, **1**, 126.

Hôtel des Invalides, **9**, 427; **10**, 174.

Hôtel Dieu, **9**, 427, 431.

Hotels : Brady House, Harrisburg, **8**, 53; Brant House, Harrisburg, 64; Continental, Phila., 21, 71; Eutaw, Baltimore, 23, 24, 48; Fifth Avenue, N. Y., 73; Herr House, Jones House, Harrisburg, 52, 62; U. S. Hotel : at Frederick, 26, at Harrisburg, 55; Porter's Inn, Cambridge, 171; Davenport's Tavern, Cambridge, 244; Mansion House, Andover, 254.

Hottentots, **5**, 323; peculiar hair of, **2**, 80.

Houbraken, print by, **2**, 29.

Houghton, Lord, **10**, 44, 59, 185.

Hour-glass, **4**, 100.

Housatonic River, **1**, 244 ; **10**, 77.

House on fire, **2**, 158.

House, gambrel-roofed. *See* Gambrel-roofed house.

House of Commons, **10**, 63–65.

House-cleaning, **9**, 411.

House-flies, **3**, 244 *et seq.*

Houses : one at Cambridgeport, built by Irishman, with his own hands, **1**, 19 ; those with second story projecting, 127 ; dying out of, 241 ; **7**, 22 ; shape themselves to our natures, 242 ; when they become homes. 242 ; noisiness of an old house, **6**, 333 ; old, in New England, **10**, 19 ; wooden, a better kind of wigwam, 20 ; old, at Tewksbury, England, 103. *See also* Gambrel-roofed house.

Houyhnhnms, as man-tamers, **1**, 227 ; **10**, 192.

Howard, the philanthropist, temper of, **8**, 35.

Howe, Dr. S. G., **9**, 352 ; on the mental action of the congenitally blind, **8**, 269, 270.

Howe, Mrs., her Bank of Benevolence, **10**, 172.

Howell, J., **9**, 9.

Huc's anecdote of Chinese gentlemen, **2**, 30.

Huckleberries, **1**, 230, 308 ; **8**, 157.

Hudson River, opening of, for travel in the spring, **8**, 137, 138 ; closing of, the official seal of winter, 178.

Hufeland, **9**, 375.

Hugh of Evesham, **9**, 320.

Hughes, Thomas, **10**, 108.

Hugo, Victor, **10**, 186.

Huldy and Zekle, **10**, 49.

Hulks of enslaved intelligences, **5**, 252, 253.

Hull, Massachusetts, how a line of Pope is quoted there, **1**, 128.

Huma bird, anecdote of, **1**, 8.

Human averages, tolerable steadiness of, **3**, 221 *et seq.*

Human beings, to tell whether one is young or old, **2**, 57 ; raised under glass, **3**, 278.

Human body. *See* Body, human.

Human life. *See* Lives, human.

Human nature, apologies for, **3**, 20 ; perversion of its tendencies, **5**, 236.

Human race, future of, **6**, 406.

Humane society in heaven, **4**, 257.

Humanity, America has a different one from Europe, **2**, 122 ; comes before gentility, 145 ; tenderness for, 217 ; revival of, **3**, 305 ; virtues of, 306 ; of more importance than any belief, 327 ; normal state of, **8**, 206 ; rights and dignity of, 309 ; tested by theology in a scholastic vacuum, 324 ; laws of, 379. *See also* Man.

Humanizing effect of church-going, **3**, 193.

Humility, taken for granted as existing in every sane being, **8**, 310. *See also* Self-abasement.

Humor, lack of, in philanthropists, **8**, 34 ; in New England ministers, 409, 410.

Humorists, remarkable for their immovable features, **6**, 227.

Hunger, book, **4**, 150.

Hunt, Mr. Holman, **10**, 40.

Hunt, Dr. William, of Philadelphia, **8**, 23.

Hunter, John, **9**, 116, 293, 414.

Hunting in couples, instructive, **10**, 151.

Hurlbut, Dr. Fordyce, in *The Guardian Angel*, **6**, 5 ; affords relief to Myrtle's hysterics, 133 ; his growing power over her character, 135 *et seq.* ; is warned by Master Gridley as to this influence, 140 *et seq.* ; married to Olive Eveleth, 419.

Hurlbut, Dr. James, intemperance of, **9**, 386.

Hurlbut, Dr. Lemuel, the medical patriarch of Oxbow Village in *The Guardian Angel*, **6**, 5, 16 ; makes a professional visit on Myrtle, 127 ; his death, 419.

Hurry, vulgar to be in a, **2**, 139.

Husbands, and wives, grow to look alike, **2**, 156 ; the sort of men women take for, 157 ; husband of a woman of genius must be a true, not a great man, 290.

Hutchinson, Mr., on proportion of inspirations and heart-beats, **8**, 316.

Hutchinson, Ann, **3**, 224 ; **9**, 356.

Huxley, his definition of thought, **8**, 262 ; on volitions, 303 ; quoted on popular ignorance of hygienic laws, **9**, 379.

Hyacinth, **1**, 228, 229 ; **10**, 18.

Hyacinth Cottage, residence of Widow Rowens, in *Elsie Venner*, **5**, 295.

Hyde Park, England, **10**, 140, 141.

Hydrocyanic acid, **9**, 264.

Hydrophobia, **10**, 171, 172.

Hydrostatic paradox of controversy, **1**, 114.

Hydrosudopathy, **9**, 99.

Hygiene, **8**, 186–238 ; necessity of favorable hygienic conditions in disease, **9**, 203.

Hygienic map, **9**, 296.

Hygrodeik, **6**, 157.

Hymn, depressing, **6**, 80–82 ; a more inspiriting one, 87.

Hymn of Trust, **2**, 282.

Hyperbola, **2**, 237.

Hypnotism, **5**, 205.

Hypochondriasis, **5**, 170 ; **8**, 397 ; and dyspepsia, **7**, 177.

Hypocrisy of kind-hearted people, **4**, 310.

Hyrtl, on right-handedness, **8**, 268.

Hysteria and hysterics, **5**, 69, 71, 194, 221, 322 ; **6**, 129, 131 *et seq.* ; valerian in, **1**, 70 ; shows reciprocal convertibility of laughter and tears, 90 ; women apt to be hysterical when there is a young minister round, **6,** 171 ; of the intelligence, 286 ; moral perversions of, 339 ; the physic-practising clergyman's idea of, **9,** 358.

Hysteric ball, **2,** 96.

I Like you and I Love you, **4,** 144.
" I love you," **2,** 180 ; **5,** 472.
I 'm the fellah that tole one day, **1,** 296.
I-My-Self-and-co, **4,** 166.
Ice cream, looked upon with awe, in rural places, **5,** 113 *et seq.*
Iceberg, slight effect of sun on, **2,** 288.
Iced water and ice-cream, English notions about, **10,** 28.
Ichaboe, a nursery of female loveliness, **8,** 52.
Iconoclasm, only way to get at truth♣ **2,** 117.
Ideal state of society, life dull in, **4,** 67.
Ideas. worthy of repetition, **1,** 7 ; rapid maturity of, 31 ; handled as if they had three dimensions, 85 ; difficulty of transmission does not imply lack of, **2,** 25 ; interpenetration of, better than mere courtesy, 36 ; transplanted, **3,** 146 ; association of, by their accidental cohesion rather than by their vital affinities, 289 ; spores of, **8,** 46 ; association of, 267 ; easy to calculate the number of possible, in a lifetime, 274 ; remembered ones smuggle themselves in as original, 287 ; novel ones must meet the weight of vested opinions, 325 ; we have only a partial control of, 330.
Identity and resemblance, distinction between in Homœopathy, **9,** 69.
Idiocy, congenital, no disqualification for writing poetry, **4,** 78.
Idiosyncrasies, of artists, **3,** 102 ; of writers and speakers, **4,** 297.
Idiot, the prize, **4,** 112.
Idiotic area in the brain, **4,** 12, 156, 166.
Idolaters, we are all more or less, **8,** 308, 404.
Idolatry, all but immortal, **9,** 367.
Idols of the market, must be treated as stocks and stones by the anthropologist, **8,** 325.
Ifs, the, and the *Ases,* **4,** 121, 122.
Ignorance, men and women who hate to admit, **4,** 156 ; often cured by pain, **8,** 306 ; presumption of, 312 ; science the topography of, **9,** 211 ; ignorance and knowledge, points of contact between, in medicine, 212, 237 ; a solemn and sacred fact, 382 ; reaction of the public's, on itself and medicine, 416 ; what the ignorant ignorantly decide to be, 417.
Ignorance of what people do not want to know, chair to teach, **8,** 258.
Ik Marvel, **4,** 133.
Ill health gives a common character to all faces, **8,** 249.
Illative sense, **8,** 312.

Illness. *See* Disease.
Imagination, poetic, of two kinds, **1,** 184 ; man in bondage to his, **8,** 404 ; less to work on in the New World, **10,** 131.
Imaginative art and science, distinction between, **4,** 108, 110.
Imbeciles, moral, **5,** 227, 228 ; simply obey the impulse of their desires, **8,** 333 ; as innocently acting out their inherited tendencies as a rattlesnake, 336 ; suffer under the gravest of inherited calamities, 337, 344 ; predisposing causes of, 338 ; Drs. Ribot and Lucas on, 358.
Imponderables move the world, **1,** 136.
Impressions, that same thing has happened before, **1,** 73, 74 ; enormous number of, **2,** 58 ; of childhood, 186–189 ; periods of vivid, and of continual coincidences, **8,** 17, 18 ; effect of a strong one upon the mind, **9,** 37, first one never to be repeated, **10,** 23, 187.
Impromptu poems, **1,** 17.
Improvisators, we are all more or less, **8,** 289.
" In Memoriam," Tennyson's, **6,** 223 ; quoted, **8,** 432.
Inborn idiosyncrasies. *See* Heredity.
Incapacity, congenital, for life, **9,** 200.
Incendiaries, two, hanged in Boston in 1836, **8,** 351, 352.
Incendiarism, a specialty of young persons, **8,** 339.
Incunabula, **9,** 400.
Independence and Union, two hard words to spell, **2,** 41.
Independence, American literary, **4,** 233 *et seq.*
Index society, **9,** 405.
Indexes, **9,** 402–405.
India, conflict of races in, **1,** 66.
India-rubber, **3,** 322.
Indian corn, beauty of, **8,** 168 ; **10,** 144.
Indian Ridge, Andover, beauty of, **8,** 258.
Indian summer, **6,** 164 ; **8,** 165, 166.
Indians, American, caltrops set for, **1,** 295 ; only a provisional race, **2,** 83 ; no individuality in their history, 245 ; called " Screeching Indian Divells " by our forefathers, **5,** 43 ; afraid of rattlesnakes, 45 ; congenitally averse to civilization, 317, 318 ; their limitations, 323 ; pappooses, 392 ; place of their powwows, 89 ; not in a condition to listen to modern civilization, **8,** 326 ; dug up the bones of their ancestors when they moved, 361 ; pestilence among, **9,** 314, 315 ; at Hatfield, 338.
Indifference to consequences, next step above inclination to crime, **7,** 267.
Individual personality of each one may not be the sole tenant of his corporeal frame, **6,** 22.
Individuality, good breeding does not overestimate, **2,** 140 ; none in history

of Indians, 245 ; is to be maintained, **5**, 254.

Induced current of thought, **8**, 292.

Induction, false, from genuine facts of observation, **9**, 186 ; electrical, 216.

Inequality, the one thing dreaded by the inhabitants of Saturn, **4**, 63 ; of races, the corner-stone of the new-born (Southern) dispensation, **8**, 87.

Infallible book, an, dangerous to intellectual virility, **8**, 388.

Infant damnation, Romanists and others fear, **8**, 304 n. ; Edwards and Wigglesworth on, 372 ; Edwards quoted on, 393.

Infants, sinfulness of, **9**, 360.

Infidels, not plenty, **5**, 320.

Infinite and finite, **6**, 404.

Infirmary, for invalid books, **3**, 25 ; the master's, 213.

Infirmity, is sometimes a help to holy living and to poetry, **1**, 184 ; liable to leave injurious effects on the race, **2**, 20.

Influence, correlative of effluence, **7**, 244.

Ingleby, Mr., on puerperal fever, **9**, 159, 160, 164.

Inheritance of the world belongs to the phlegmatic people, **3**, 41.

Inherited beliefs stronger with many than the evidence of the senses, **8**, 311 ; persistence of, 422. *See also* Beliefs.

Inherited instincts. *See* Heredity.

Inherited tendencies. *See* Heredity.

Inherited prescriptions, **9**, 335, 336.

Inhibition, centre of, **7**, 235, 236, 246 ; cowardice and unsuccessful love, how related to, 235.

Injection, minute, in the study of anatomy, **9**, 227.

Injustice, to the citizen, simple preventive against, **8**, 110.

Innovations, not natural to the old, **10**, 3.

Inoculation, introduced in America by C. Mather and Z. Boylston, **8**, 418 ; for small-pox, **9**, 345-347, 362, 363.

Insane, recollections of the, at McLean Asylum, **1**, 247 ; bad men should be treated as, **5**, 228 ; the worst cases are those diseases of the moral sense not considered as insane, 400.

Insanity, the logic of an accurate mind overtasked, **1**, 42 ; great amount of, wherever the battle of intelligence is fought, **2**, 218 ; not always an unalloyed evil, **6**, 73 ; caused by sudden mental shock, **7**, 91 ; Miss Vincent's notions about, in *A Mortal Antipathy*, 161 *et seq.* ; influence of the moon on, **8**, 212 ; the state of mind at the moment of awaking from sleep or from an anæsthetic is, 284 ; many criminals come from families tainted by, 338 ; most atrocious crimes committed in a state of moral mania, 347 ; literature of, **351**; not a sufficient reason against

discipline, 356 ; called *possession*, 357. *See also* Imbeciles, moral.

Insect life disturbed by turning a stone, **1**, 112.

Instantaneous photographs, **8**, 124.

Instinct, more divine than reason, **2**, 241 ; position of, with reference to the criminal, **8**, 322, 323, 336, 337 ; still moves as it did in Cain, 357 ; humble accuracy of, **9**, 37 ; our knowledge concerning, still in its infancy, 247.

Instincts, mystery of the permitted crushing out of, **1**, 304 ; theory that all childish, are wrong, **6**, 30 ; have a basis beyond the reach of will, **8**, 261 ; the great spring of human action, 332.

Insurance offices, how they might make money, **4**, 184.

Intellect, average, of five hundred persons not very high, **1**, 140 ; circles drawn about, 266 ; in a woman should travel to lips through the heart, **2**, 147 ; no fusion of, likely, 297 ; varieties of, **3**, 43 ; our knowledge concerning the, still in its infancy, **9**, 247 ; in training, 376 ; pretentious claims of, 376. *See also* Brain ; Mind.

Intellectual bankruptcy, cant or slang the blank checks of, **1**, 256.

Intellectual invalids, **3**, 17.

Intellectual irritation produced by rubbing against other people's prejudices, **3**, 6.

Intellectual life of race gains nothing from unquestioning minds, **3**, 270.

Intellectual man, his composition, **1**, 62.

Intellectual myopes, **8**, 268.

Intellectual opium-eating, **3**, 99.

Intellectual over-feeding, **4**, 148.

Intellectual productions not in the category of force as defined by physicists, **8**, 293.

Intelligence, general diffusion of, **3**, 302.

Intemperance, should be met with proper weapons, **1**, 188 ; the habit is oftenest a punishment, 190 ; more common to poets and artists, because body and mind have previously flagged, 191 ; lassitude, languor, and vacuity of mind precede, 192 ; in a doctor partakes of homicide, **9**, 386. *See also* Intoxication.

Intercommunication, perpetual, effects of, **8**, 7.

Interests, incompatibility of, a sufficient warrant for social separation, **7**, 299.

Intermittent, poetical, **1**, 248.

Intermittent fever. *See* Malaria.

Interpenetration of ideas, better than mere courtesy, on, **2**, 36.

Interrupted literary work, supposed case of, **3**, 8.

Interviewing one's self, **3**, 1.

Intoning prayers, by anti-papal clergymen, **5**, 314.

Intoxication : one may become intoxicated with music, poetry, or love, **1**, 189 ; some forms of alcoholic exaltation apparently a benefit, 189; as a recreation among the inhabitants of Saturn, **4**, 65; offers to the weak brain a Brahma's heaven, **8**, 222; effect of, on memory, 296, 297; cause of crime, 339, 340.

Invalid vampires, **4**, 183.

Invalides, Hôtel des, **9**, 429; **10**, 174; dome of, **4**, 308.

Invalidism, certain persons born to, **8**, 204; the normal state of many organizations, **9**, 200.

Invalids, intellectual, **3**, 17; occupation of, **6**, 75.

Inventions, recent, anticipated in the human body, **3**, 322.

Inventive power the divinest of faculties, **1**, 238.

Investigations, psychological, **4**, 16.

Invincible ignorance, Catholic doctrine of, **5**, 456.

Invitâ Minervâ, **4**, 314.

Invitations to author, in England, **10**, 24, 58; issued by him in London, 55.

Involuntary actions. *See* Automatism; Unconscious mental action.

Io, **5**, 169.

Ipecacuanha, **9** 361, 387.

Iphigenia and Cymon, **4**, 285.

"Ira furor brevis est," **8**, 335.

Isomerism, **9**, 216.

Isomorphism, **9**, 216.

Ireson, Floyd, **3**, 323.

Iris, **1**, 71.

Iris, character in *The Professor*, daughter of the Latin tutor, a description of, **2**, 54; her story told by the Professor, 60–73; John's summary of her character, 169; her drawing-book, 173; the Marylander tells his love to her, 315.

Iris, her Book, **2**, 226.

Irish giant, the, **10**, 67, 68.

Irish servant, good manners of, **2**, 143.

Irish system of prison reform, **8**, 353, 354.

Irishman's house at Cambridgeport built by himself, **1**, 19.

Irishmen, regiment of gallant, **8**, 11.

Iroquois, winner of Derby, **10**, 40.

Irving, Edward, **3**, 183.

Irving, Henry, at Lyceum, **10**, 30.

Irving, Washington, **4**, 278; **7**, 5; quotation from, regarding New York streets, **3**, 324; his emotions on seeing Mr. Roscoe, **10**, 52.

Island, The. *See* Naushon.

Isopodic societies, **4**, 64.

Isosceles, one of the twins in *The Guardian Angel*, **6**, 53.

Issues of to-day, discussion of, proscribed within easy remembrance, **8**, 326.

Italy, **2**, 245; her attitude toward the North in Civil war, **8**, 100.

Itch, **9**, 45, 49, 57, 82.

Itch-insect, **9**, 289.

Ithuriel, **1**, 189.

Itinerary, motive for, **10**, 184.

"Ivanhoe," **6**, 247: regarded as a sinful work by Deacon Rumrill in *The Guardian Angel*, 376.

Jackson, Andrew, predicts the revolution caused by slavery, **8**, 85; a hater of secession, 96; oath of, 115.

Jackson, Dr. James, **9**, 303–311, 351, 438, 441; **10**, 197; carried two watches, 308, 387.

Jackson, James, Jr., **9**, 425.

Jackson, John B. S., **9**, 351.

Jackson, Dr. Samuel, **9**, 145, 146, 164.

Jacob's ladder of poetic fame, **6**, 204.

Jacquemier, a disbeliever in the contagiousness of puerperal fever, **9**, 123.

Jacques, Frère, **9**, 366.

Jahr's Manual, **9**, 48.

James I., King of England, **7**, 236; **9**, 9; his fear of a naked sword, **5**, 222.

James, Henry, **10**, 66.

James, William, **4**, 166.

Janin, Jules, **4**, 42.

Janson. *See* Jenson.

January thaw, **8**, 178.

Japanese, the, wrap small-pox patients in scarlet, **8**, 210; anticipated Europe in a rude regional anatomy, **9**, 224.

Japanese exhibition in Boston, **10**, 156.

Japanese figures with points for acupuncture, **3**, 121, 122.

Jaques, Colonel, the cattle-breeder, **5**, 324.

Jarvis, Charles, **9**, 345.

Jarvot, murderer, **8**, 340.

Jaundice, as a token of affection, **1**, 133.

Javelli, Leon, **8**, 228.

Jaw, lower, dislocation of, common among the inhabitants of Saturn, **4**, 65.

Jeddo, moat at, **2**, 11.

Jefferson, Thomas, **4**, 233; foresaw the danger of slavery, **8**, 85.

Jeffries, Dr. John, **9**, 349; on poisoning from eating partridges, **8**, 219.

Jenkins, Henry, **4**, 26.

Jenkins, Mr. Livingston, in *The Guardian Angel*, **6**, 276; praises Myrtle, 284.

Jenks, Dr., on Scott's indebtedness to Matthew Henry, **8**, 385.

Jenner, **9**, 94, 96, 97, 116.

Jenson, Nicholas, **6**, 370.

Jerky minds, **1**, 6.

Jerusalem governs Massachusetts, **8**, 310.

Jerusalem chamber, **10**, 30.

Jettatura. *See* Evil eye.

Jewelry, a mother's, **2**, 99.

Jewett, C. C., **9**, 416.

Jews, fable of their sweating gold, **2**, 163; prejudice against, **4**, 193 *et seq.*; their estimate of the Christ, **8**, 47; their horror of the New Testament, 47.

Jews-harp, **6**, 208.

Jockeying in literature, **1**, 37.

Joe, a handsome Marylander, in *The Professor*, **2**, 51.

Joerg, Professor, **9**, 64.
John, St., Gospel of, quoted, **9**, 381.
John and Thomas, their dialogue as six persons, **1**, 53.
John de Ketam. *See* Ketham.
John of Gaddesden, attends the son of Edward II. in small-pox, **8**, 210.
John, the young fellow called, in *The Autocrat* and *The Professor*, his illogical appropriation of peaches, **1**, 54; his tremendous conviction about smoking, 73; surmise as to age of a pie in boarding-house, 79; circulates puns and conundrums, 251; eats mourning fruit in memory of Schoolmistress, 307; presents wedding flowers, 312; invites the Professor to his room, **2**, 165; his fight with the Koh-i-noor, 279; his wife and baby, 316.
"John Buncle," **10**, 182.
Johnny, That Boy's friend, in *The Poet*, his first appearance, **3**, 281; his family history, 283.
Johns, the three, personalities to be considered in one individual, **1**, 53.
Johnson, Edward, on the health of the Pilgrims, **9**, 322.
Johnson, Samuel: his use of adjectives, **1**, 85; disappointed because one of his pamphlets was unattacked, 114; put beginning of life's decline at thirty-five, 151; a superstitious weakness of, 205; and the poor young woman, 280; his estimate of scientists, **3**, 263; what he might say on receiving a cable-gram, 264; his reference to Franklin, 265; his indebtedness to Morhof, **4**, 160; carried to Queen Anne, 205; **9**, 3; date of his birth and death, **7**, 20; bond of relationship between him and the author, 21, 22; quoted on reading, **8**, 270; dream of contest of wit of, 282; on the doctrine of necessity, 302; on free will, 377; and the orange-peel, **9**, 308; quoted, **10**, 80; definition of word "hood," 84; his harsh opinions about Americans, 138; Coleridge on his bow-wow manner, 139; statue in St. Paul's, 150; places in London identified with, 154; Boswell's "Life" dear to all, 154; portrait, 196.
Johnston elm in Rhode Island, **1**, 233.
Joke-blindness, **3**, 247.
Jokes, old, in travelling, **1**, 278.
Jones, E. Burne, **10**, 67.
Jones, Herbert, of Monmouth, **5**, 224.
Jonson, Ben, epitaph by, **10**, 59, 119, 120.
Jordan, Sarah, afterwards wife of Colonel Sprowle, in *Elsie Venner*, **5**, 82.
Jordan, Tekel, in *Elsie Venner*, **5**, 82.
"Jordan," the hymn, **6**, 87.
Jouffroy, **10**, 166 *et seq.*
Jourdain, M., **4**, 77, 78; **8**, 122, 425.
Jowett, Dean, **10**, 86, 89, 90.
Judæa seems to have a yearning for New England, **8**, 310.
Judas, Leonardo's picture of, **2**, 229.

Judgment, standard of, **1**, 14.
Judgments, hasty, regarding facts not within every-day experience, **7**, 33.
Judicial intellects, achromatic, **8**, 268.
Jukes family, **8**, 343.
July, Fourth of, **10**, 94.
June, beauties of morning in, **1**, 170; of 1859, **6**, 84; beauty of night in, 88; a shawl on her shoulders and a cold in her head, **8**, 150; Seventeenth of, why memorable, **10**, 75.
Justice, a rare virtue, **2**, 149; respect of good man for, 150; human conception of, **3**, 270; has a technical meaning when applied to the Supreme Being, **8**, 304; and law, 324; the fourth person in Jonathan Edwards's quaternity, 368, 395.
Juvenile poems, **1**, 18.

Kaimes, Lord, attacked by Edwards, **8**, 381.
Kane, Dr., use of coffee and tea in his expedition, **8**, 225.
Kant, his idea of time and space, **1**, 266; on the will, **8**, 377, 378; satirized by Julius Müller, 377.
Karoli, Count, the Austrian ambassador to England, **10**, 51.
Karr, Alphonse, **7**, 137.
Katydid, **8**, 158.
Keats, **1**, 184; **6**, 203; his "Lamia," **2**, 163; **5**, x., 213, 220, 225; his "Endymion," **3**, 306; his "Grecian Urn," **4**, 302.
Keble's "Christian Year," **1**, 311.
Keeley's motor, **10**, 28.
Keller, Helen, **4**, 140 *et seq.*
Kellogg, Clara Louise, **10**, 181.
Kellogg, Elijah, **3**, 15.
Kennebec River, opening of, in the spring, **8**, 138.
Kensal Green cemetery, **10**, 179.
Kensington Palace, **10**, 56, 187.
Keren-Happuch, **6**, 263.
Ketam. *See* Ketham.
Ketchum, Mrs. Clymer, in *The Guardian Angel*, **6**, 36, 268; calls on Myrtle, 284; her party, 309 *et seq.*
Ketham, Johannes de, **6**, 141; **9**, 411, 433.
Keys to the feelings, **1**, 129.
Kidder, Bishop, and his wife killed by falling chimney, **10**, 186.
Kimball, Dr., of Lowell, **9**, 266.
Kindness, pitying, is a bitter sweet, **4**, 191.
King, Dr., on puerperal fever, **9**, 140.
King's Chapel, Boston, **10**, 132.
King's College Chapel, Cambridge, **10**, 77.
King's evil, **4**, 205. *See* Scrofula.
Kirby's "Wonderful Museum," **4**, 17.
Kirkwood, Maurice, the leading character in *A Mortal Antipathy*, his solitary way of living, **7**, 54 *et seq.*; rescues a student from drowning, 69; is invited to attend the meetings of the

Pansophian Society, 73, 118; his control over horses, 74, 117, 142; his books, 79, 80; paper supposed to be written for the Pansophian Society by, 96 *et seq.*; is interviewed, 154; is attended by Dr. Butts in a severe illness, 202; story of his life, 207 *et seq.*; is rescued by Euthymia Tower from death by fire, 270; she visits him daily during his convalescence, 277 *et seq.*; becomes her accepted lover, 282 *et seq.*

Kiss, a stolen one meditated, 2, 267; memorable ones, 268; Iris, in *The Professor*, kisses the Little Gentleman when he is dying, 302; called the twenty-seventh letter of the alphabet, the love labial, the limping consonant, which it takes two to speak plain, 5, 390.

Kittredge, Dr., the old physician in *Elsie Venner*, his knowledge of women, 5, 98; his advice concerning Elsie, 193 *et seq.*; his library in his head, 210; talks with Langdon about Elsie, 211 *et seq.*; discusses theology and other matters with Rev. Dr. Honeywood, 313–328; his talk with old Sophy, 347–354; drives Richard, after his assault on Langdon, beyond the limits of the State, 377, 378; prescribes spiritually to Rev. Mr. Fairweather, 401–407; his theory of Elsie's life, 445.

Knee, 8, 123.

Kneeland, Dr., 9, 210; on the contagiousness of puerperal fever, 9, 122, 170.

"Knickerbocker's history," Irving's, quotation from, regarding New York streets, 3, 324.

Knife, as an instrument for conveyance of food, 2, 142.

Knights, called "prize-fighters with iron pots on their heads," 2, 135; of Labor, too unfortunate, 4, 219 *et seq.*

Knocking a man down, difficulty of carrying out the threat, 2, 279.

Knot-grass, 2, 235.

Knopp, Nicholas, 9, 328.

Knowledge, cannot be confined by professions, 2, 15; its specialization, 3, 265; its advance, 267; pursuit of, difficult, 307; some, on every subject, impossible, 4, 149; ways of gaining knowledge, 152; condensation of, 157; the best part of our, 9, 211; and ignorance, points of contact between, in medicine, 212, 237; systematic, involves much that is not practical, 9, 284–291, 372; what is not wanted dies out, 373.

Knox, Robert, groaning in 1850 over the battle of Hastings, 8, 357; his "Races of Men," 9, 198; 10, 65; asked author to breakfast, 10, 6.

Koh-i-noor, a vulgar character in *The Professor*, who wears a large diamond (?) pin, 2, 4; his fight with John, 279; leaves the boarding house in disgrace, 311.

Kölliker, 9, 240.

Kopp, Dr., 9, 86.

Kuyper, Jan, 2, 29.

"L. B.," 2, 9, 20. *See also* Leah.

La Berge, de, 9, 441.

Labor, subdivision of, a triumph of civilization, 6, 311.

Laboring classes, a suggestion for, 3, 299.

Laboulaye, a friend to the North in Civil war, 8, 99.

La Bruyère, a character of, who threw his wine into the backgammon-board and swallowed the dice, 8, 281.

Lacenaire, criminal, 8, 341.

Lachapelle, Madame, 4, 131.

Ladies, on the streets, leave their virtuous-indignation countenance at home, 1, 195; of "the quality" preferred, 2, 136; misuse of word, 144; young ladies have taken place of young women in domestic service in New England, 5, 135; grand old, of London society, 10, 26–28; old English, 106.

Lady, The, in *The Poet*, her history, 3, 54; her friendship for Scheherezade, 85; her letter to the Poet, 187 *et seq.*; her acquaintance with the Register of Deeds, 196; her growing interest in him, 289; this intimacy explained, 289; her good fortune, 292.

Lady-boarder, with autograph-book, 1, 6.

Lady Suffolk, mare, 5, 296.

Lady's portrait with sword-thrusts through it, 2, 188.

Laennec, 2, 249; on consumptive tendency of nuns, 8, 2.

Lake, a, as a refuge and place of rest, 7, 100, 251.

Lallemand, on alcohol, 8, 221.

Lamb, Charles, 7, 33; 8, 149.

Lamb tavern, 3, 344.

Lambeth, 10, 73.

"Lamia," Keats's, 2, 163; 5, x., 2, 3, 220, 225.

La Monnoye's "Monsieur de la Palisse," 2, 231.

Lancaster county, Pennsylvania, fertility of, 8, 51.

Lancet, change in opinion concerning its use, 9, 259, 260.

Land, first sight of, a relief, 10, 17.

Landlady, in *The Autocrat*, the story of her life, 1, 53, 73; the pathos of her story, 80; weeps, 107; her surprise at the Autocrat's love for Schoolmistress, 304; makes bride-cake, 311; in *The Professor*, 2, 21; critical remarks on Iris, 97, 98; anxiety at the appetites of her boarders, 169; on marrying for money, 204, 205; tries to quiet the Little Gentleman's tongue, 206; as seen through a window, 318; in *The*

Poet, personal appearance, **3**, 37 ; her family, 38 ; her fitness for matrimony, 38, 39 ; fame of her house brought superior people, 48 ; her mistake regarding complementary colors, 140 ; character of her conversation, 252 ; probable characteristics of her deceased husband, 253 ; her reminiscences, 283 ; tells the story of the Lady's good fortune, 290 *et seq.*

Landlady's daughter, in *The Autocrat*, pen-portrait of, **1**, 16 ; says " Yes ? " 18 ; plays the accordion, 57, 307 ; in *The Professor*, is thought to favor the company of the Koh-i-noor, but after his thrashing by John she discards him, **2**, 311 ; is to marry a young undertaker, 312.

Landon, Letitia, **1**, 306.

Landscape, stillness of, in Indian summer, **6**, 164 ; revolving, from railroad train, **8**, 20 ; of England and New England, **10**, 22.

Lang, Andrew, **10**, 67.

Langdon, Bernard C., the young schoolmaster in *Elsie Venner*, one of the " hereditary scholars " of the Brahmin class of New England, **5**, 7; schoolmaster at Pigwacket, 27 ; vanquishes Abner Briggs, 37–39 ; first appearance at the Apollinean Institute, 49 ; at Colonel Sprowle's party, 103 *et seq.* ; plans to protect and help Miss Darley in her work, 169 ; his effect upon the girls in the Institute, 174–176 ; goes up on the mountain, 185 *et seq.* ; Elsie saves him from rattlesnake, 190, 191 ; determines to solve mystery of Elsie, 204 ; procures some rattlesnakes, 206 *et seq.* ; talks with Dr. Kittredge about Elsie, 211 *et seq.* ; is armed by doctor against Richard Venner, 217 ; feels a sense of impending danger, 365–368 ; lassoed by Richard, 369, 370 ; his feelings with reference to Elsie, 396–399 ; Elsie asks him to love her, 422, 423 ; visits her just before her death, 446–448 ; wins the love of Letty Forrester, 486–487.

Langdon, the Reverend Jedediah, grandfather of Bernard, in *Elsie Venner*, **5**, 11.

Langdon, Samuel, **3**, 28.

Langdon, Wentworth, Esq., father of Bernard, in *Elsie Venner*, **5**, 11 ; typical of " slackwater gentry," 11, 13.

Language, plasticity of spoken, **1**, 28 ; the blood of the soul, **2**, 41 ; grows out of life, 43 ; compared to a watch with hair spring, 43 ; its ineffectiveness at times, 181 ; management of, in poetry, **3**, 98 ; its inadequacy for expression of spiritual ideas, 183 ; inexactness of, 217 ; difference in use of English, with Americans and English, **10**, 143, 144.

Languor, beliefs and fancies take advantage of us in hours of, **8**, 282.

Lansdowne House, **10**, 29.

Larch, **5**, 141.

Lark, emotions on neither seeing nor hearing, **10**, 115 ; on Salisbury Plain, 191.

Larned, Miss, story of Josiah Dwight quoted from, **8**, 410 ; story of Zephaniah Swift quoted, 411, 412.

Larrey, Baron, **9**, 427.

Larvæ, spiritual, Roman Catholics considered as, **2**, 242.

Lasso, used by Richard, in *Elsie Venner*, **5**, 265, 332 *et seq.*, 351.

Last Blossom, The, **1**, 161.

Last Leaf, The, mentioned, **10**, 38..

Latch-key of consciousness, **4**, 10.

Latent caloric of character, **2**, 288.

Latent consciousness. *See* Unconscious mental action.

Latham, Dr., **9**, 286.

Latin, familiar language of prescriptions, **9**, 394 ; speech in, at Cambridge, England, quoted, **10**, 76.

Latin tutor, mentioned in *The Autocrat*, who wrote eclogues on a hot summer in town, **1**, 262 ; the father of Iris, in *The Professor*, his selection of her name, **2**, 60–62 ; his wife, 63 ; death, 65.

Latreille, Pierre André, **3**, 240.

Latter-day Warnings, **1**, 24.

Laudanum, overdose of, **2**, 105.

Laudator temporis acti, **4**, 31.

Laughter turns the machinery of sensibility, **1**, 90.

Laugh, a grand, elemental, **2**, 17 ; the mob-law of the features, 72 ; of a girl, 138 ; the epilepsy of the diaphragm, **8**, 19.

Launching of the ark of Christianity, **2**, 219.

Law, barbarisms of, **2**, 106 ; a coarse tool, not a mathematical instrument, **8**, 323 ; attitude of, toward the criminal, 323, 324, 336, 337 ; comes to us from a set of marauders, 357.

Law and average — two dominant words of our time, **9**, 180.

Lawrence, Abbott, met in London, **10**, 142.

Laws governing mind and body, **1**, 71.

Lawyers, unsympathetic, **3**, 124 ; half learn a thing quicker than members of any other profession, **6**, 138.

Lay-sermon, gives the parallax of thought and feeling, **2**, 7 ; punishment of mechanic for preaching one, 115.

Layard, **9**, 404 ; **10**, 28, 152.

Laycock, Dr., on the possible number of ideas in a life-time, **8**, 274 ; anecdote of cavalry horses quoted from, 300.

Layers of habitual thought, **4**, 11.

Layman, the, rights of, out of the pew, **8**, 413 ; right of, to call attention of the clergy to errors, 422.

Lead, the only metal found on the planet Saturn, **4**, 62.

Lead-poisoning, of authorship, **9**, 423.

Leah, the witch ancestor of the Little Gentleman in *The Professor*, **2**, 261 ; her portrait, 262. *See also* L. B.

"Lear " quoted, **10**, 14.

Learned quadrupeds, **8**, 91.

Learning, surest and easiest way of, **9**, 287, 372.

Leaves, autumn, cause of change in color of, **8**, 165.

Leaving a room, difficulty of, **1**, 17.

Lebanon, cedar of, **10**, 189.

Lebrun, Charles, figures of, **10**, 42.

Lechmere, Sir Edmund, **10**, 105.

Lechmere, Judge Richard, royalist, his house at Cambridge, **10**, 105.

Lechmere's Point, now East Cambridge, **10**, 105.

Lecky, on beliefs and fancies in hours of languor, **8**, 282.

Lecture-room literature, **9**, 194.

Lecturers, grooves in their mind, **1**, 65 ; get homesick, 142 ; attacks upon, 303.

Lectures, trials of delivering, **1**, 43 ; frequently delivered ones the best, 139 ; ought to be of common interest, 140 ; imaginary report of one, in time of Cicero, 157 ; lecturing by literary people, 303 ; exhaustion of ideas by a scholar when lecture is half delivered, **2**, 24 ; supposed effect of adverse criticism of, by Ananias and Shimei, 120 ; value of in medicine, compared with bedside teaching, **9**, 273.

Lee, Dr., on the Homœopathic hospital at Leipzig, **9**, 85, 86 ; on puerperal fever, 104, 140.

Leech, widow, in *Elsie Venner*, **5**, 107, 114, 298.

Leete, Graciana, **9**, 334.

Leete, William, **9**, 334, 339.

Leeuwenhoek, **9**, 226.

Left-handed people, the right half of the brain the strongest in, **8**, 268.

Left-handedness, moral, **3**, 222.

Leghorn-straw hat, anecdote of, **1**, 177.

Legs in walking, **1**, 72.

Leibnitz, observation of, **1**, 1 ; on unconscious mental action, **8**, 276, 278 ; on his " l'âne de Buridan," 374, 375 ; simile of, of magnetic needle and the will, 377 ; on motion, **9**, 217.

Lemaire, Charles, murderer, **8**, 341, 342.

L'Enclos, Ninon de, **1**, 189 ; **4**, 284.

Leo-Wolf, Dr., **9**, 86.

Leonardo's picture of Judas, **2**, 229.

Leptandra Virginica, **9**, 341, 342.

Le Sage, introduction to " Gil Blas," quoted, **1**, 199.

Letter, to aspiring young man, **1**, 289 ; to the Professor, expressing fear as to his opinions, **2**, 104 ; case of lady who used only one page in writing a, 204 ; one picked up at Antietam, **8**, 42.

Letters, sent to authors, **1**, 69 ; Red republic of, **3**, 10. *See also* Love-letters.

Lettsom, Dr., **9**, 96.

Levelling process, **3**, 4, 5.

Leverrier, **8**, 84.

Leviathan. *See* Great Eastern.

Lewis, Dr. Winslow, **9**, 425, 426.

Leyden jar, **5**, 118.

Liability of misjudging our fellows, **3**, 255.

" Liberal " denominations, **8**, 421.

" Liberator, The," **8**, 85.

Liberty, battle for spiritual, **2**, 78 ; often a burden on a weak man, **5**, 252 ; bust of, in *The Guardian Angel*, **6**, 245, 251 ; the true mother of the Union, **8**, 80 ; champion of aggressive, should, it is said, reach the same gallows as the arch-traitor, 89 ; worth paying for as well as fighting for, 111 ; Sam. Adams's words on, 115.

Liberty to dislike us accorded a certain number of people, **3**, 333.

Librarian, the old, in *A Mortal Antipathy*, **7**, 57, 78, 79, 131.

Librarian, qualities of a good, **9**, 416.

Libraries, a sort of mental chemist's shop, **2**, 25 ; college, fated to burn up, 62 ; book infirmary should be attached to, **3**, 25 ; use of, in many fine houses, 209 ; how they should grow, 211 *et seq.* ; the Dictator's, **4**, 159 ; its hospital department, 301 ; are temples, **9**, 396 ; nests that hatch scholars, 399 ; the standing armies of civilization, 406 ; of scholars, 409 ; of the Old World gradually coming to the New, 410 ; must exercise the largest hospitality, 411 ; every book in, wanted by somebody some time, 413.

Licetus, Fortunius, his " De Monstris." **5**, 232 ; **9**, 280.

Lichens, eat the names off gravestones, **8**, 46.

Lie, like a sphere, easy to roll, **1**, 116 ; for first real lie woman should be tenderly chloroformed, 270 ; monument to woman struck dead for telling a, 281.

Liebig, justifies the use of tea and coffee, **8**, 224 ; his theory of the production of animal heat, **9**, 239.

Life, a tremendous thing, **1**, 59 ; has more of humanity than books, 134 ; may be analyzed into fifteen periods, 153 ; varied experience in, 275 ; human, measured by life of tree, 286 ; a great bundle of little things, **2**, 1 ; getting into the pith and core of, 10 ; the truest lives cut with many facets, 33 ; only the edge of the ocean of existence, 107 ; obstacles in, 179 ; as a mighty sculptor, 193 ; in New England may be lean and impoverished, 244 ; better adjusted to wants of men, 249 ; three wicks to lamp of, 260 ; opportunities in America for large, noble life, 284 ; the dying not in condition to judge fairly of, 293 ; conscious, the aim and end of creation, **3**, 105 ; fullness of, to the poet, 107 ; chances of, better in cities than in towns, 279; its accidents confounded with life itself, 296; the naturalness of clinging to it, **4**, 35; some people get more than they want, 35; the struggle for, 55; a game of chess, not of solitaire or checkers, 65; dullness of, on the planet Saturn, 65; a *petit verre*, 292; second or fractional, of the dead in the living, **6**, 94, 219; life is like backgammon to most men, 238; an ideal one, for an American, **7**, 31; curve of, 84; noble only when held cheap by the side of honor, **8**, 77; general facts of physical, 197, 207; definition of, 201; prologue, five acts, and possible after-piece of, 313; nothing that a man will not do or suffer to save his, **9**, 378, 379.

Light, necessary to health, **8**, 209.

Likes and dislikes, metaphysics of, **3**, 71; ground of, 333 *et seq.*

Lilac, **1**, 228, 229; **8**, 144, 145.

Lilies, yellow, **6**, 88.

Limbs, human, weight of, **8**, 123, 124.

Lime, carbonate of, as prepared by Hahnemann for medicine, **9**, 44.

Limitations, human, **5**, 321.

Lincoln, Abraham: his letter of June 12th, 1883, **8**, 109; speech of, at Gettysburg, **9**, 396.

Lindens, **10**, 189.

Lindsay, Charles Hazard, infant son of Clement and Myrtle Hazard Lindsay, in *The Guardian Angel*, **6**, 429.

Lindsay, Clement, in *The Guardian Angel*, receives letter from Susan Posey, **6**, 96; realizes that he has grown away from his early love, 101; rescues Myrtle from drowning, 104 *et seq.*; Master Gridley approves of him, 117; the story of his mistaken love, 219; his artistic nature, 220; his visit to Susan Posey, 225 *et seq.*; meets Myrtle for second time at party, 244; resolves to fight down his love for Myrtle by hard work, 249; meets Myrtle for third time at Mrs. Ketchum's, 324; gives Susan Posey back her freedom, 374; tells Myrtle of his love, 388 *et seq.* ; enlists in Civil war, 410; married to Myrtle, 417; makes a bust of Master Gridley, 431.

Line between the eyebrows, **3**, 52.

Lines to a Pretty Little Maid of Mamma's, **4**, 154.

Links of Forth, **10**, 6.

Linwood, Miss, her needlework, **2**, 183.

Lion, leaden, at Alnwick, **1**, 281; **10**, 6.

Liqueur, glass of, after dinner, **10**, 207.

Lisfranc, Dr., **9**, 325, 427, 428.

Listener, a good, **2**, 17.

Liston, thought himself a tragic actor, **1**, 91; as Paul Pry, **10**, 5.

Lists of books, **4**, 149.

Literary adviser, confidential, much expected of him, **3**, 158.

Literary cannibals, **4**, 23.

Literary celebrity, **7**, 139, 140.

Literary Club, London, **10**, 62.

Literary correspondence, **4**, 137 *et seq.*

Literary aspirants, difficulties of dealing with, **3**, 155 *et seq.*

Literary independence, American, **4**, 233 *et seq.*

Literary people, dangerous for them to indulge sense of the ridiculous, **1**, 91; Coleridge advised them to have a profession, 179; **8**, 231; mechanical employment a relief to, **1**, 180; amiable relations between, **2**, 75.

Literary pickpockets, **1**, 51.

Literary police, **3**, 152.

Literary roughs with brass knuckles, **3**, 275, 346.

Literary teapot, **1**, 62.

Literature, "jockeying" in, **1**, 37; respect for conventional reputations in, 38; unripe state of American, 261; the contributions of realism to, **4**, 105; tendencies in American, 110; modern literature and the classics, 158; homœopathic, **9**, 84; of the lecture room, 194; a small matter to the struggling world, **10**, 93.

Little Boston, a nickname of the Little Gentleman, which see.

Little Gentleman, a cripple, in *The Professor*, who actively defends Boston and Boston ways, **2**, 3, 4, 15, 16; mysterious noises in his room, 161; attempt of Professor to visit his room, 186; his dying hours, 301–306; his burial-place, 306, 307.

"Little King Pippin," **2**, 231.

Live folks only dead folks warmed over, **6**, 129.

Liver, riding good for, **1**, 166; and gizzard of chicken never mistaken, 309; its sugar-making faculty, **9**, 238.

Liverpool, **10**, 18, 23, 180.

Lives. *See* Life.

Living, convenience of, in Old World, **10**, 204.

Living Temple, The, **1**, 175.

Livingston, Edward, quoted, **8**, 345.

Llangollen, Vale of, **10**, 186.

Lloyd, Dr., **9**, 438.

Local influences, how greatly they affect the human organization, **3**, 277.

Localism, dwarfing to mind, **2**, 87.

Lochiel rocked in cradle when old, **1**, 82.

Locke, John, as physician, **9**, 343, 344, 366.

Locke, William, letter of, in Massachusetts Archives, **9**, 338, 339.

Locker, Frederick, **10**, 62, 68.

Locomotive pedal, **1**, 168 n.

Log, heaving the, compared to noting one's progress by friendships, **1**, 94.

Logic, use of, **1**, 14; of a restored patient, **9**, 380, 381.

Loisne, M., parting of the streams on the Alps elaborated by, **8**, 46.

Lombardy poplar, **3**, 19; **10**, 191.

London, a nation of itself, **4,** 278 ; stopping place of author in, during his second visit to England, **10,** 24 ; round of social engagements in, 24, 25, 56 ; grand old ladies of London society, 26–28 ; professional friends met in, 27 ; receptions attended, 28, 29, 37, 43, 54 ; official receptions, 43, 44 ; dinners, 37, 43, 50, 57, 62, 66, 68 ; parks, 140, 141 ; social geography, 141 ; shops, 144, 145, 149 ; Quaritch's bookshop, 146–149 ; time needed to study it, 155 ; a place of mysteries, 157 ; a day's activity in, 159 ; multitude of objects of interest, 159 ; no one person knows it, 160 ; return to, 178 ; author's last visitor in, 179 ; weather in, 187 ; small stature of people, 192 ; the gentlemen well dressed, 193 ; clubs, 198.

"London Morning Post" quoted, **10,** 33.

Londoness, octogenarian, **10,** 26.

Lonely feeling in midst of new generation of authors, **10,** 39.

Long, John St. John, **9,** 94, 414.

Long path, on Boston Common, **1,** 277 ; of life, 277, 304, 313.

Long Tom Coffin, **5,** 139.

Longevity, examples of : Moses, Caleb, Henry Jenkins, Thomas Parr, Dr. Holyoke, Father Cleveland, Colonel Perkins, Lord Lyndhurst, Josiah Quincy, Sidney Bartlett, Von Ranke, Chevreul, Henry Hastings, Benjamin Peirce, James Freeman Clarke, B. R. Curtis, George T. Bigelow, George T. Davis, **4,** 25–29 ; Gladstone, 33 ; Metastasio, Bryant, Longfellow, Halleck, Whittier, Tennyson, Browning, 41 ; Madame Saqui, 42 ; Theophrastus, 190 ; Mrs. Thrale, 284 ; Bancroft, 292 ; prescription for, 183 ; as affected by food, alcohol, and tobacco, 184.

Longfellow, 1, 2 n. ; **4,** 40, 41 ; **7,** 5 ; his "Evangeline," **8,** 69 ; elms at his house, **10,** 69 ; his house, 105 ; bust in Westminster Abbey, 60, 205.

Longford Castle, **10,** 116, 121, 127 ; wonderful steel chair at, 128.

Longings which are like a skulking procession of bloodless murders, **6,** 151.

Lonsdale, Lady, **10,** 46.

Looking-glasses, none on the planet Saturn, **4,** 64.

Lord Lovel's grave, **2,** 267.

Lord of the Manor at Naushon (J. M. Forbes), **1,** 39 n.

Lorne, Marquis of, **10,** 51.

Lorraine, Claude, **10,** 127, 170.

Lorraine, Mrs. Felix, **6,** 55.

Lothair, Disraeli's, quoted, **8,** 275.

Louis XIV., anecdote of, **3,** 185 ; **4,** 168.

Louis Napoleon, **9,** 215.

Louis Philippe, **4,** 223 ; **10,** 1, 161, 177.

Louis, Dr. Pierre C. A., **9,** 220, 431–433 ; his name a dim legend in Paris, **10,** 164.

Louise, Princess, **10,** 34, 51 ; garden-party by, 56.

Louvre, Gallery of the, **10,** 155, 169, 170 ; its danger from mob, 177.

Love, should be rich and rosy, **1,** 43 ; a calm, clear mind the best basis for, 131 ; intellectual companionship not necessary to, 131 ; first experience of, 210 ; all men love all women, 220 ; **5,** 104 ; at first sight, **1,** 221 ; capacity for, is a congenital endowment, 270 ; solubility of, in speech of men and women, 271 ; finally in store for all, 305 ; the universal experience, **2,** 93 ; women's choice in, 159 ; at certain age all excitements run to, in women, 160 ; is the one secret most women have to tell, 180 ; indications of, 285 ; not essential that all pairs should be "born for each other," 286 ; the flower of young love, **4,** 147 ; or loves ? 301 ; art of, may be read in Encyclopædia under title Fortification, **5,** 181 ; a second consciousness, 274 ; study of, like that of meteorology, 282 ; beneficent effect of a second love, 283, 284 ; women know its meaning, 469 ; and religion, paths at fork of the road which every maiden travels, **6,** 163 ; first love to the young an unprecedented phenomenon, 220 ; works strange transformations in young women, 387 ; the real world is within to those who love, 411 ; the master key that opens the gates of fear, **7,** 246 ; unsuccessful, how dependent upon the centre of inhibition, 235.

Love-cure believed in by women, **3,** 272.

Love-labial, a kiss the, **5,** 390.

Love-letters, remarkable sameness in, **4,** 91 ; those of bigamists and polygamists rich in poetical extracts, 92 ; those of women, 92.

Lovering, Professor, **8,** 183.

Lovers, as talkers, **3,** 95 ; their vocabulary, **4,** 91 ; explanations bad between, **6,** 230.

Loving cup presented to the author, **4,** 42.

Lowe, Mr., quoted on English universities, **9,** 277.

Lowell, James Russell, **1,** 23 n. ; **7,** 5, 9 ; **10,** 66, 67, 86, 183, 199 ; son of a clergyman, **8,** 411 ; elms at his home, **10,** 69.

Lowell, John, on blooming of fruit trees, **8,** 145.

Lower jaw, dislocation of, common among the inhabitants of Saturn, **4,** 65.

Loyalty of English, not understood by Americans, **2,** 36.

Lucas, Dr., on moral imbeciles, **8,** 358.

Lucerne, Bridge at, **2,** 266.

Lucretia, **2,** 60.

Lucretius, wicked pleasure spoken of by, **8,** 178.

Ludicrous, the, a divine idea, **1,** 92.

Lunatics, "dreadful depravity of," **8**, 311. *See also* Insanity.

Luncheon, a convenient affair, **10**, 25; those attended by author during his visit to England : at Mrs. Bloomfield Moore's, 28; at Lord Rosebery's, 29; at the Derby, 36; at Mrs. Pfeiffer's, 40; at Lady Camperdown's, 41; with Mr. Peel, the Speaker of the House of Commons, 53; at Bishop of Gloucester and Bristol's, 54; at Mrs. Cyril Flower's, 56; at Newstead Abbey, 57; at Cambridge, 75, 89.

Lungs, one wick of the lamp of life, **2**, 260.

Lunites, **4**, 59, 60.

Lusus naturæ, **8**, 358.

Luther, preaches the same gospel as Zwingli, **8**, 84; his way of repeating Pater Noster, 115; compared with Vesalius, **9**, 178.

Luxembourg gallery, **7**, 4.

Luxor, obelisk of, **10**, 1, 176.

Lycanthropy, **5**, 222.

Lyceum Theatre, London, **10**, 30.

Lying is unprofitable, **1**, 117.

Lynch-law, the result of instinct, **8**, 322, 323; Latin motto for, 323.

Lyndhurst, Lord, **4**, 27.

Lyric conception hits like a bullet, **1**, 98.

M. S. M. A. = Member of the Society of Mutual Admiration, **1**, 5.

Ma'am Allen, nickname for the Koh-i-noor in *The Professor*, **2**, 79.

Macadam, Mrs., **10**, 7.

Macalister, Professor and Mrs. Alexander, **10**, 74, 78.

Macalister, Dr. Donald, **10**, 74, 78.

Macaulay, on simultaneous intellectual movement, **8**, 85; mouthable lines of, **10**, 71; quoted about Bath, 107.

Macaulay-flowers of literature, **1**, 13.

MacCormac, Dr., **9**, 297.

Macdonald, G., epitaph in "David Elginbrod," **8**, 167.

Macedonia's madman, **4**, 74.

Machpelah, Cave of, **3**, 331.

Mackay, Charles, dinner to, on his departure from America, **1**, 222.

Mackellar, Mrs., **10**, 135.

Mackenzie, Dr. Morell, **10**, 198.

Mackintosh, Sir James, **5**, 228; recognized the ability of Jonathan Edwards, **8**, 362; on Bishop Berkeley, **9**, 11.

McLane, Robert M., minister to France, **10**, 163.

McLean Asylum, **1**, 247.

Maconochie, Captain, inventor of the Irish system of treatment of criminals, **8**, 353; does not condemn punishment as such, 356.

McShane, Father, priest, in *Elsie Venner*, **5**, 251, 252, 259.

"Madame Blaize," **2**, 231.

'Madame Bovary," **4**, 106.

Madder, artificial, **9**, 421.

Madeira wine, **2**, 123; **5**, 111.

Maelzel : his automaton Turk, **2**, 16; **4**, 38; wooden children of, **8**, 122.

Magdalen College, Oxford, **10**, 81; great elm at, 82.

Magendie, **9**, 437.

Magistrates, likely to grow cruel, **8**, 346.

Magnetism, in iron, **8**, 294, 295.

Magnetism, animal, **6**, 133 *et seq.*

Magnolia on Cape Ann, **2**, 244.

Mahogany, old, **5**, 144.

Mahomet, Bible of, **8**, 88.

Maiden-hair fern, **5**, 46.

Maidens, pretty English, **10**, 124.

Maine, produces a large proportion of our natural nobility, **3**, 276; amount of snow in, in winter, **8**, 136.

Maison d'Or, La, **4**, 172.

Maison paternelle, **8**, 354.

Majority, vote of, in spiritual matters, **5**, 253, 407; rule of, **9**, 207.

Malaria, in New England, **8**, 207; **9**, 324; Sir K. Digby's cure for, 354, 381.

Malcolm, Capt. Daniel, his grave on Copp's Hill, **2**, 3, 306.

Malebranche, **9**, 11.

Mall, the telescope in the, **4**, 305.

Malpighi, **9**, 412.

Malpractice, **9**, 417.

Malvern, abbey church of, **10**, 104.

Mal-vitalization, **9**, 295.

Mal-volition, to rate gravity of, by its consequences, is sensational materialism, **8**, 305, 306; liabilities incurred by a, to be measured on a finite scale, 306; scale of equivalents between, and physical suffering, 306, 307.

Mammoth Cave, blind fishes in, **9**, 373.

Man, as man, so thought of in America, **2**, 36; a symbol worshipper by nature, 117; study of, **3**, 183, 184, 268; it needs a new terminology, 307; natural man, 234; martyrdom of, **4**, 54; his warfare with natural forces, 54; a wheel with two spokes, **8**, 129; raised under glass, 206, 208; primitive condition of, 212; as looked at by Edwards, 369, 370; born with conservative or aggressive tendencies, 419; a sporting as well as a praying animal, **10**, 6. *See also* Humanity.

Man of family, preference for, **1**, 20.

Man of letters, in *The Poet*, **3**, 52; his air of superiority, 151; leaves the boarding house, 202.

Man of the Monument (Bunker Hill), **3**, 151, 166.

Man without a soul. *See* Browne, Simon.

"Man-taming extraordinary" (from Houyhnhnm Gazette), **1**, 227.

Mandans, Indians, extirpated by small-pox, **9**, 315.

Mangetus, **9**, 412.

Manhood, of American aristocracy, not

sufficiently manifest, **1**, 260; occidental, based on self-respect, **3**, 270; oriental, based on self-abasement, 270; **8**, 309; distribution of, **8**, 10, 11; time to assert itself, 112.

Manière de prince, **10**, 35.

Manifestations, spirit, **6**, 24.

Mankind, two divisions of, **4**, 120 *et seq.*

Manly art of self-defence. *See* Boxing.

Manners, a few points of, taken up, **2**, 139; among the highly bred, 140; vulgar, 142; of royalty, **10**, 35.

Mansion-house, in *Elsie Venner*, **5**, 57; gentry, 102.

Mantis religiosa, **3**, 239.

Manufacture of poetry, **4**, 84 *et seq.*

Manuscript reader. *See* Butcher, The.

Manuscript is to type what fresh dandelions are to boiled, as to bulk, **6**, 291.

Map, outline of, on wall, **1**, 243; sanitary, needed of every State in the Union, **3**, 280; hygienic, usefulness of, **9**, 296.

Maple, **5**, 46.

Marathon, mound at, **10**, 195.

"Marble Faun," Hawthorne's, did not suggest *Elsie Venner*, **5**, x.

Marblehead, people of, like the Phæacians, **3**, 323.

Marbles, holes for playing, made by choir boys in Westminster Abbey, **10**, 61; game of, 93.

Marcet, Professor, on the influence of the moon on weather, **8**, 212.

March, six weeks' sleighing in, **8**, 136.

Marcus Aurelius, a dandy, **1**, 259.

Mare Rubrum, **1**, 122.

Margaret of Scotland, her kissing Alain Chartier, **2**, 268.

Marigold, smell of, **1**, 76.

Marjolin, **9**, 90, 437.

Mark Twain, **10**, 103.

Marmontel, **10**, 166.

Marriage, difficulties in the way of, for a young man, **2**, 170; for money, Landlady's opinion of, 204; chances for happiness in, **4**, 176; is jumping overboard, **6**, 287.

Marriage service, vulgar alteration in, **2**, 145.

Married maid-of-all-work, a wife called a, **1**, 43.

Marseilles, the Autocrat once quarantined at, **1**, 180.

Marsh, Dr., of Wethersfield, wig of, **8**, 407.

Martha's faith, that of languid thinkers, **8**, 83.

Martin, Dr., **9**, 188.

Martin, Hannah, school girl, in *Elsie Venner*, **5**, 76.

Martineau, Dr., **10**, 197.

Martyrdom of man, **4**, 54.

Mary, Bloody, was hysterical, **6**, 171.

Mary, Queen of Scots, cabinet of, **4**, 16.

Maryland, scenery and people of, **8**, 31, 32.

Marylander, the, in *The Professor*, gradually becomes the lover of Iris; his looks, **2**, 45; tells his love, 315.

Marylanders, two manly specimens of, **2**, 51.

Mascagni, **9**, 411, 423.

Mascarene, Elizabeth, an ancestor of the Venners, in *Elsie Venner*, **5**, 145, 182.

Mask, a, of no advantage to a writer, **4**, 20.

Mason, George, on the effects of slavery, **8**, 85.

Mason, Dr. John M., **4**, 196.

Massachusetts, Protest of Province of, **8**, 85; would like to colonize Jerusalem, 310; medical profession in, **9**, 312–369; climate of, 320–322.

Massachusetts General Hospital, **9**, 398.

Massachusetts Hall. *See* Harvard College.

Massachusetts Medical Benevolent Society, **9**, 174.

Massachusetts Medical Society, Poem written for, by author, **1**, 225; as a representative of the medical profession, **8**, 234; addressed by author, **9**, 206–208; founding of, 349; members of, 398.

Massasoit, nursed by Edward Winslow, **9**, 189.

Massey, Edmund, preached against inoculation, **9**, 347.

Master, The, in *The Poet*, his prejudices, **3**, 6; his originality, 41; his experiments, 174 *et seq.*; his library, 210 *et seq.*; his book infirmary, 213; his book, 221; his ambition, 262; his physiological observations, 277; his reasons for having written books, 319 *et seq.*; begins to tell the story of his life, and to disclose the central fact in the Order of Things, 337 *et seq.*; is interrupted by the Landlady, 339.

Master and servant, **7**, 249, 286.

Master George Gordon. *See* Byron.

Mastigophori, the whip-holders, **3**, 274.

Masury, Mr., quoted on art of housepainting, **8**, 211.

Match-boxes, coincidence connected with, **8**, 45; luminous, **10**, 202.

Matches, **10**, 146.

Matchless Mitchel. *See* Mitchel.

Materia medica, results if it were destroyed, as now used, **9**, 203, 444. *See also* Drugs; Medicines.

Materialist: his conception of the brain, **8**, 262; has worked strange confusion in the moral world, 301.

Maternal instinct, **1**, 304.

Maternity, woman borrows half her tenderness from, **8**, 91; bed of anguish of, smoothed by anæsthetics, 238.

Mathematical ability lacking in many strong minds, **3**, 104.

Mathematics tends to breed despotic way of thinking, **1**, 9, 56.

Mather, Cotton, his "Magnalia" quoted,

1, 67, 299 ; quoted, **2,** 115 ; **3,** 14, 327 ; on the splenetic maladies in New England, **6,** 156 ; and the demons of Gloucester, **8,** 371 ; on a person who was burned to death, 386 ; helped to introduce inoculation for small-pox, 418 ; agency of, in the witchcraft delusion, 423 ; on the Indians, **9,** 314 ; medical work left in manuscript by, 320 ; on the content of the Pilgrims, 321, 322 ; on sons of C. Chauncy, 329 ; on Leptandra Virginica, 341 ; used Spigelius's Anatomy, 343 ; and inoculation for small-pox, 346, 347, 362, 363 ; letter of, on witch-marks, 347 ; résumé of his medical writings, 359–363 ; on original sin, 360 ; slave of, 362, 363.

Mather, Increase, orders Calef's book to be burnt, **2,** 8 ; **8,** 414 ; on comets, **3,** 224 ; agency of, in the witchcraft delusion, **8,** 423.

Mather, Katharine, **9,** 342.

Mathers, grave of the, **2,** 306.

Mathews, Charles, the elder, **10,** 5.

Matrimonial mésalliances, **1,** 215 ; **5,** 18 ; **6,** 249.

Matter, Mind and, **8,** 262–264 ; called frozen force, 264.

"Maud," Tennyson's, difficulty of reading aloud, **8,** 318.

Maupassant, **4,** 251.

Mausoleum, a rich man builds a, and calls it a place of entertainment, **8,** 64.

May, in England, **10,** 37, 39.

May-day, as shrill as a step-mother, **8,** 144.

Mayerne, Dr., **9,** 10.

Me-Number-One and Me-Number-Two, **4,** 154.

Mean man, a, **5,** 427.

"Measure for Measure," quoted, **7,** 232.

Meat-pie, inland term for mince pie, **5,** 97.

Meccas, various, of medical students, **9,** 438, 439.

Mechanical employment, a relief to literary men, **1,** 180.

Mechanical talk of women, **1,** 30.

Mechanism, in thought and morals, **8,** 260–314 ; that part of mental and bodily life independent of volition, 261. *See also* Automatism.

Mecklenburg resolutions, **8,** 85.

Medford rum, **7,** 275, 276.

Mediator, a comfort to humanity, **8,** 403.

Medical accuracy not to be looked for in the unprofessional public, **9,** 70, 71.

Medical Christianity, **9,** 383.

Medical delusions, **9,** 1 *et seq.*

Medical journals, **9,** 193.

Medical libraries, **9,** 396–419.

Medical literature, much in, unfit for public reading, **7,** 177 ; quoted by early physicians, **9,** 342, 343 ; little, in Massachusetts in 18th century, 350 ; low ebb of English, in 17th century, 354 ; living and dead, 400.

Medical mind, American, tendencies of the, **9,** 192, 193.

Medical profession, author's wish to meet, in London, **10,** 55.

Medical school, business of, **9,** 276.

Medical society, creed of a, supposed, **2,** 111.

Medical specialists, **4,** 125 *et seq.*

Medical students, some suggestions to, **9,** 107 *et seq.*

Medical superstitions, **9,** 380.

Medical terms, definition of some, **9,** 196.

Medicated novels, **3,** 26 ; *Elsie Venner* called one, **5,** ix. ; **8,** 358.

Medicine, errors of, **2,** 11–13 ; barbarisms in, 105 ; ministers' opinion about, 110 ; effect upon the sympathies, 263 ; and theology, **7,** 81; the honest truth about, **8,** 233–238; study of, perhaps tends to produce disbelief, 414 ; changes in the practice of, **9,** 175, 256, 258, 266 ; influenced by the conditions of society, 177 ; scholastic and bedside teaching of, 273–311 ; debt of, to chemistry, 274 ; appropriates everything of the slightest use to disease, 289 ; in Massachusetts, 312–370 ; state of, an index of civilization, 313 ; great names in the Massachusetts profession of, 317 ; two principal schools of, in the New World, 318, 319 ; relation between, and theology, 319, 320, 358, 364–367 ; specialties in, 352 ; marrow of, 363 ; materializing influences of the practice of, 366 ; great hospitals, true centres of instruction in, 374 ; the community is hopelessly ignorant in regard to, 379 ; the most difficult of sciences, 384 ; reforms in, 435 ; positive and negative facts in, 435, 436. *See also* Disease; Fevers; Galen; Hippocrates ; Homœopathy ; Patients ; Perkinism ; Sympathetic powders ; Weapon ointment.

Medicines, mode of preparation of, as described by Hahnemann, **9,** 42 ; demand for, by the public, 186 ; as tricks to make money, 191 ; those which hurt a well man, likely to hurt a sick one, 201. *See also* Drugs ; Materia medica.

Mediocrity, genius an insult to, **2,** 241 ; often given to a thought by publicity, **3,** 344 ; its pleasure in having its superiors brought within range, **4,** 22 ; much verse stamped with, 313 ; magnificent constituency of, **5,** 272.

Medlar-tree, **10,** 79.

"Medusa, Wreck of the," Géricault's **10,** 16, 170.

Meerschaum, its process of coloring, **1,** 101 ; as a relief from trouble, **6,** 249.

Meetinghouse-Hill at Dorchester, **2,** 256.

Meeting-houses, New England, **5,** 61, 62.

Meetings, mysterious, **2,** 56.

Meigs, Dr. Charles D., on the childbed fevers, **9**, 103, 109, 110, 115, 118, 119, 121-125, 127, 144, 171.

Melancholia, Taine quoted on, **8**, 397 ; caused by religious stimulants, 416.

Melanchthon, his gentleness, **6**, 19.

Melusina, Elsie Venner compared with, **5**, x.

Melville, Major, subject of the author's *The Last Leaf*, **7**, 8.

Member of the Haouse, character in *The Poet*, **3**, 1 ; his native place, 7.

Membrane, nictitating, developed by theological students, **7**, 81.

Memorials of places, appropriateness of, **10**, 195.

Memory, appealed to quickly through smell, **1**, 75 ; curiosities of, **3**, 219 ; pleasures of, 328 ; pleasures of, to the old, **4**, 46 ; retentive of evil images, 109 ; duration of associated impressions on the, **8**, 275, 276 ; Pepys on a person of wonderful, 276 ; problem of, connected with the mechanical relation between thought and structure, 296 ; is it a material record, 297 ; effect of age, disease, a blow, or intoxication on, 296, 297 ; material record of, illustrated by microscopic photography, 298, 299 ; much more recorded by, than we take cognizance of, 299 ; revival of obsolete impressions, 300 ; record of, often perishes before the organ, 301 ; gains by rhythmical association, **9**, 288 ; pleasing task of reviving, **10**, 163, 168.

Men, self-made, **1**, 19 ; grow sweeter in disposition as they mature, 81 ; like pears, 82 ; all men love all women, 220 : **5**, 104 ; life adjusted to wants of, **2**, 249 ; those who have eye for horseflesh also have one for women, **5**, 287 ; those who are far from modest often blush easily, 359.

Men of science. *See* Science.

Menagerie, England is one great, **1**, 303.

Mental action. *See* Mind.

Mental ballast, **3**, 321.

Mental cud is sometimes lost, **8**, 267.

Mental dynamometer, **8**, 276.

Mental dyspepsia, **4**, 148.

Mental experience differs little in different people, **4**, 10.

Mental obliquity. *See* Squinting brain.

Mental soprano, barytone, and basso, **2**, 37.

Mental squint. *See* Squinting brain.

Mental suffering, danger a counter-irritant for, **5**, 276.

Menzel, **9**, 2.

Mephistopheles, **5**, 176.

Mercury, use and abuse of, **9**, 255 ; in medicine, 348 ; C. Mather on, 361.

Mercy, has a technical meaning when applied to the Supreme Being, **8**, 304.

Mermaids, **2**, 257.

Merrimack River, **8**, 251, 252.

Merriman, Dr., case of puerperal fever occurring in the practice of, **9**, 160, 161.

Merritt, Mrs., **10**, 31.

Mésalliances, matrimonial, **1**, 215; **5**, 18 ; **6**, 249.

Messiah of a new revelation, woman is a, **2**, 125.

Metallic taste of articles written at so many guineas a sheet, **4**, 8.

Metallic tractors, **9**, 15.

Metastasio, **4**, 41.

Metropolis must drain lesser places of talent and wealth, **1**, 127.

Mettray, reform schools of, **8**, 345 ; Colonie pénitentiaire at, 354.

Mexican war of not much importance, **8**, 6.

Michael, Grand Duke of Russia, **10**, 47.

Microcosm, beginning of life in, **2**, 257.

Microscope, achromatic, the impetus given by its invention to the study of anatomy, **9**, 224–228 ; compound, use of in medicine, recent, 422; not mentioned when author was a student, **10**, 164.

Microscopic photography, **8**, 298, 299.

Middle - aged female, in *The Autocrat*, offended at remarks, **1**, 30.

Middletown, Maryland, streets of, **8**, 35 ; wounded in, 35.

Midsummer, **2**, 225.

Mignonette, **2**, 182.

Milan cathedral, **6**, 260.

Milburn, Rosa, in *Elsie Venner*, **5**, 76; dances with Mr. Langdon, 104 *et seq.* ; her beauty, 231.

Mildmay, Mrs., sister of Lady Harcourt, **10**, 28.

Military men, held in small account in Northern States, **1**, 260 ; record of young men of social position during Civil war proved worthy, 261 ; have an eye for country, **3**, 105.

Millionism, green stage of, **1**, 308.

Milkmen, pumplike movement of their arms, **2**, 156.

Mill, John Stuart, a friend to the North in Civil war, **8**, 99 ; suggests that the rebellion should not be too easily defeated, 101.

Millais, Sir John, **10**, 57.

Millennium, not very real, **8**, 349, 350.

Miller, Hugh, **10**, 188.

Millipedes. *See* Sowbugs.

Milo of Crotona, **1**, 159.

Milton, compared to a pear, **1**, 83 ; his season for writing, **2**, 24 ; kisses given him, 268 ; his "Paradise Lost," **3**, 91, 92 ; believed the moon to affect insanity, **8**, 212 ; quoted, 376, 431; memorial window to, **10**, 205.

Mince-pie, called meat - pie, in rural places, **5**, 97.

Mind : classification of minds, **1**, 1 ; jerky ones fatiguing, 6 ; logical, 14 ; a calm, clear one best basis for love or friendship, 131 ; saturation point of, 133; automatic action of, 134; healthy ones should let lower faculties have exercise, 181; one with thoughts, compared to circus-rider with horses, **2**, 38; those with skylights, **3**, 42; feeders for, 80; different ones move like the different pieces on a chess-board, 220; non-clerical, 257; as affected by age, **4**, 41; the unbalanced mind often fertile in suggestions, 96; where during unconsciousness, **5**, 390–392; wretchedness of one subject to the perpetual interference of another, **6**, 74; bewildered in periods of disturbance, **8**, 78; must have pressure of duties to be healthy, 231; mechanism of, 260–314; and matter, 262–264; duality of, 267, 268; resemblance of mental action to vision, 268; relation between mental action and space, 264–271; relation of mental action and time, 272–301; slang a sign and cause of mental atrophy, 275; duration of associated impressions a possible mental dynamometer, 276; mental action ordinarily automatic may be voluntary, 278; long interval of obscure mental action, in old persons, before a question is answered, 279; coefficient of mental action, 293; mental labor attended by an increased waste, 294; decay of, with age or disease, 296; condition of, under which horrid crimes are committed, 322; qualities of those to which the incredible appeals, **9**, 29, 33; distinction between the vulgar and superior, 211; some are satisfied with the decillionth dilution of proof, 392; argument with certain class of, a lever without a fulcrum, 392; **10**, 172. *See also* Automatism; Brain; Consciousness; Intellect; Memory; Thought; Unconscious mental action.

Mind cure, **10**, 172.

Ministerial veto allowed by Saybrook platform, **8**, 411.

Ministers: an old one on inattention in audience, **1**, 30; emotion of an underpaid minister at surprise party, **2**, 76; barbarisms among, 106; opinions about medicine, 110; should be cheerful, 144; two signs by which it may be known if one is on a safe path, **6**, 157; health of, **8**, 397; take on the character of the popular lecturer, 404; have furnished the highest type of character, 405; work of, not confined to their professional duties, 405, 466; influence of, in politics, 406; aristocratic dignity of, in New England, 406, 407; were prophets, 407, 408; humor in, 409, 410; good to have ancestors among, 410; famous sons of New England, 411; have been republicanized, 412; usually treated with more than respect, 413; intimate relations which should exist between physicians and, 415, 416; a wise one at the sick bed, 415; not prepared for duties till something is known of bodily derangements, 417; hard for, to preach to unbelievers, harder, to empty pews, 418; creed of children of, 421, 422; tried for heresy, 425; were often doctors, **9**, 319, 320, 329, 330. *See also* Clergymen; Preachers; Priests; Pulpit.

Ministration, genius of, among women, **2**, 274.

Minnesota, as a health resort, **9**, 296.

Minorities, rule of, **9**, 207.

Minstrels, Ethiopian, **8**, 72.

Mint, engine at the, **1**, 32.

Miracles, we have witnessed, **4**, 31; said to be wrought by the Roman Catholic clergy, **8**, 402.

Misalliance. *See* Mésalliances.

Misers, visions of, **3**, 255 *et seq.*

Misery, that we smile at, **3**, 84; of semi-provincial fashionable life, **6**; 256.

Misfortune, professional dealers in, **1**, 33.

Misjudgment, liability to, **3**, 255.

Misprints, **1**, 49.

Misquoting, a privilege of talking, **1**, 71.

Missionaries of ablution, **3**, 314.

Mississippi River, **3**, 335.

Missouri, governor of, introduced ordinance for extinction of slavery, 1863, **8**, 90.

Missouri River, **3**, 335.

Mis-spelling of their names very hateful to people, **4**, 311.

Mistress, The, character in *Over the Teacups*, **4**, 45; watchfulness over Delilah, 201, 224; her interest in the "exhibition," 265; her emotion, 268.

Mitchel, Jonathan, **3**, 326.

Mitchell, Donald Grant, **4**, 133.

Mitchell, John K., **9**, 439.

Mitchell, Weir, expression borrowed from, **4**, 28; his treatment of nervous exhaustion, 184.

Mitchell's School atlas, poem worked out by the aid of, **8**, 46.

Mithra, **3**, 326.

Mitscherlich, **9**, 292.

Mizaldus, quoted, **5**, 222.

Mnēmē, river of, **10**, 167.

Model of all the Virtues, in *The Professor*, of many but irritating excellencies, **2**, 70; hatred expressed for her merits, 101; reasons why not lovable, 146–149; returns to boarding-house, 314.

Modern customs, antiquity of many, **3**, 322.

Modern houses afford no opportunities for ghosts, **3**, 23.

Modesty, false, about going to bed, **1**, 208; a Christian virtue, **4**, 195 *et seq.*

Modulated or musical consciousness, **8**, 270, 271.

Molière; his satires on Galenism, **9**, 319.

Mollusk, spawn of, **2**, 257.

Mompesson, Rev. Mr., and wife, **10**, 186.

Monadnock, Mount, 3, 345.
Monarchy, tolerated in an immature state, 8, 79.
Money, the corner-stone of American aristocracy, 1, 260 ; its transforming effects for good, 260; power of, 2, 135 ; nothing earthly lasts so well, 151 ; other things besides money-making and money-spending, 8, 112.
Monks of Mount Athos, 3, 106.
Monoliths, Egyptian, 4, 102 ; 10, 195. See also Obelisks.
Monro, Dr., 9, 412.
" Monsieur de la Palisse," of De la Mon- noye, 2, 231.
Monstrosities, subject to laws, 3, 223 ; the Poet's fondness for, 229 ; fright- ened the New England fathers, 8, 357 ; 9, 280.
Mont Blanc of four score, 4, 27.
Montaigne, on perturbing medicines, 9, 339.
Montefiore, Sir Moses, 4, 199.
Montesquieu, quoted, 8, 395.
Montgomery Place, Boston, 10, 136.
Montmorenci, Constable of France, his armor, 10, 123.
Monuments, Egyptian idea of, 4, 101 ; American, 102 ; some which deform our public grounds, 104; by "wretched widow," 10, 104 ; commemorating the great fire in London, 179 ; to Duke of York, 194 ; to Nelson, 194. See also Bunker Hill monument ; Wash- ington monument.
Moon, boy's idea of, 2, 109 ; as seen through the telescope by the board- ing-house party, 3, 137 et seq. ; life of its inhabitants, 4, 59 ; influence on human beings, 8, 211, 212 ; blindness caused by, 212.
Moon-hoax of 1835, 3, 138.
Moore, Ann, first woman to practise medicine in New England, 9, 317.
Moore, Mrs. Bloomfield, 10, 28.
Moore, Thomas, 3, 313.
Mora, an Italian game, conversation compared to, 1, 15.
Moral faculties influenced by poison of snakes, 5, 225.
Moral hospital, a substitute for a plan of punishment, 8, 344.
Moral idiots. See Imbeciles, moral.
Moral imbeciles. See Imbeciles, moral.
Moral impossibilities, 8, 335.
Moral influences, depressing, the cause of disease, 8, 2, 3.
Moral insanity. See Imbeciles, moral.
Moral left-handedness, 3, 222.
Moral nuisances, 8, 90.
Moral order of things, reason for be- lieving in, 3, 221.
Moral parricide, 4, 248.
Moral reflections, we often find our own anticipated by others, 3, 325.
Moral sense, defective, like lack of ear for music, 8, 81 ; may be paralyzed by passion, 335 ; congenital want of,

shows itself very early, 337 ; zero of, 341.
Moral surgery, its brutality, 2, 114.
Moral teratology, 3, 225.
Morals, mechanism of, 8, 260-314 ; ma- terialism has wrought strange confu- sion in, 301.
Morbid poisons, 9, 54.
Morbus Addisonii, 3, 67.
Mordvinow, Russian admiral, 9, 72.
Morhof, Dr. Johnson's indebtedness to, 4, 160.
Morley, John, on eternal punishment, 4, 253 ; 8, 384.
Mormon gospel, 8, 88.
Morning after a party, 5, 115 ; 8, 213.
Morning-glory, 6, 73.
Morrissey, John, 3, 45.
Morristown revolt, 8, 102.
Mortality, degree of, among patients, not a fair test of physician's ability, 9, 73.
Morton, Thomas, on the water of Massa- chusetts, 9, 321 ; on Dr. Fuller's visit to Gov. Endicott, 325.
Mosaics, broken, dreams like, 4, 68.
Moses, in remarkably good condition for a man of his age, 4 25.
Mother's Secret, A, 2, 127.
Mothers, memory of an old man of a young mother, 2, 183 ; apron strings of American mother made of India rub- ber, 285 ; hardships of, 3, 340 ; their virtues ripen late in their children, 4, 47 ; their influence, 247 ; a true one forbids her babe to be split in halves, 8, 80.
Motion, theories of, 9, 217.
Motives, choice of, 2, 35 n. ; connection of, with determination, 8, 329.
Motley, John Lothrop : poem in his honor, 1, 26; his mot on luxuries of life, 125 ; memories of, 7, 14 ; on the attitude of Europe in Civil war, 8, 98 ; named for his grandfather, 411.
Motor, Keeley's, 10, 28.
Motor impulse, time in transmission of, along the nerves, 8, 272-276.
Mount Auburn, first tenant of, 8, 167.
Mount Holyoke, 5, 42.
Mount Tom, 5, 42.
Mountain, The, in Elsie Venner, 5, 41 ; its gloomy influence, 43, 53 ; Rattle- snake ledge, 43, 141 ; Dudley Venner wanders over its sides, 275, 276 ; the mountain-slide on, after Elsie's death, 463-466.
Mountain-slide, the gradual healing of a sorrow compared to new vegetation over, 5, 280.
Mountains, and seashore, comparative merits of, 1, 263 ; influence of, 5, 42 ; the dateless pyramids of New Eng- land, 8, 256.
Mourning fruit, 1, 307.
Mouse, technical term in pugilism, 2, 280.
Mouth, a man makes his own, 5, 178.

Movement, variations in the rapidity of, 9, 246.

Moving from a house compared to dying, 2, 276.

Mowing, 5, 261.

Moxa, 9, 289.

Mucilage pencil, 10, 202.

Mueller. See Müller.

Muffins, English, 10, 201.

Mug, memory of a bitten, 1, 200.

Muggletonian sect, 2, 294.

Muhlenbein, Dr., 9, 74.

Mulberry mark, 5, 223.

Mulder, his doctrine regarding protein, 9, 237.

Mules, government, serviceableness of, 8, 32, 33.

Muliebrity, 1, 216 ; 5, 126.

Mulier, a pun on, 4, 304.

Müller, Johannes, followed Hartley, 8, 378.

Müller, Julius, on Kant, 8, 377 ; on original sin, 383.

Müller, Max, 10, 79, 89, 90.

Munneche, Dr., of Lichtenburg, 9, 77.

Munroe, Nathaniel, musical powers of, 8, 171.

Murderers : their pious frame of mind at death, 2, 292 ; Dumollard, 8, 44, 341, 356 ; Jarvot, 340 ; Lacenaire, 341 ; Lemaire, 341, 342.

Musa, 1, 249.

Muscarium, home for house - flies, 3, 244 et seq.

Muscles, time of decline of muscular powers, 1, 156 ; rowing gives most labor to, 169 ; important ones, 5, 32 ; involuntary action of, 8, 195 ; action of, after death, 201, 202 ; must be exercised, 202 ; contraction of, 9, 240 ; ciliary muscle, 249 ; excessive development of, 4, 181.

Muse of poetry, 1, 99, 249.

Music, its effect upon emotions and intellect, 1, 132 ; the unfathomable mysteries of, 4, 95 ; affectation in the apparent enthusiasm of many for, 97 ; education necessary to understand the more complex kinds of, 97 ; conditions into which it may bring a sensitive nature, 98 ; can be translated only by music, 98 ; the Volapük of spiritual being, 99 ; a moral safety valve, 5, 341, 419 ; depressing sort, 6, 80 ; indefinable, 8, 271 ; no vocal, is popular that is not written with strict reference to the rhythm of respiration, 319 ; those with no ear for, should speak carefully of, 394.

Music-baths good for the soul, 4, 97.

Music-pounding, 3, 62.

Musical faculty has a little brain of its own, 4, 98.

Musical hullabaloos, 4, 94.

Musician, the, character in Over the Teacups, 4, 52.

Musicians, strange motions of, 1, 85.

Musk-deer, 2, 287.

Musquash Hollow, in The Guardian Angel, 6, 19.

Mustang, Richard Venner's, in Elsie Venner, 5, 158, 162 ; shot dead by Langdon, 370, 380.

Mustard, largely advertised in England, 10, 187.

Mutual admiration, Society of, approval of, 1, 2, 4.

My friend the Poet. See Poet, My friend the.

My hunt after " The Captain," 8, 16-77.

My Lady Bountiful, 2, 231.

" My three companions," paper received by Pansophian Society in A Mortal Antipathy, 7, 96.

Myopes, intellectual, 8, 268.

Myrtle Street, Boston, discovery of, 1, 165 ; garden in, 272.

Mysteries, common everywhere, 2, 257.

" Mysteries of Udolpho," 6, 275.

Mysterious Scandinavian, 7, 60-62.

Mystical remedies, 9, 332, 333, 335.

Nahant, 1, 265.

Nahum, a prophecy of, 4, 216.

Names, uncouth, 2, 95 ; of civic dignitaries, on walls and tablets, 9, 397 ; magic of, 10, 80.

Napier, Sir Charles, 7, 222.

Napier, Dr. R., 9, 354.

Napkin-ring, the, boundary-mark between certain classes, 7, 298.

Napoleon, consoled the Parisians by gilding the dome of the Invalides, 4, 308 ; called the English a nation of shopkeepers, 8, 10 ; his power of sleeping at any time, 231 ; Table-talk quoted on his control over his mind, 299 ; modernizing the political world, 9, 179 ; his mind furnished with drawers, 408 ; exhumation, 10, 96 ; tomb of, 173, 174 ; Barbier's satirical lines on, 173.

Narrow church, 2, 298.

Nasal twang, 5, 128.

Nash, Beau, 10, 107.

Nash, Lonson, sees sea-serpent in 1817, 8, 166, 167.

National Gallery, London, confused impressions of, 10, 151.

National hymn, our, 4, 29.

National Medical Library at Washington, 9, 406.

National sins, Providence punishes, by national calamities, 8, 86.

National thought and feeling, tidal movement of, 8, 83, 84.

National type of humanity, 1, 171.

Nationality of the Two Annexes, in Over the Teacups, 4, 83.

Natural forces well under control of civilization, 3, 271 ; warfare of man with, 4, 54.

Natural man, 3, 234.

Natural nobility, 3, 276.

Natural selection, is the conservative principle in creation, 2, 19.

Naturalists, have no time for friendships, 3, 249.
Nature, is fond of " gift-enterprises," 1, 55; the amen of, is always a flower, 229; leaking of, into cities, 273; fertile in variety, 2, 80; in her mysterious moods, 164; makes no leaps, 167; and grace, 3, 304; study of, its difficulties, 3, 307; her anodyne, 4, 30; development of the forces of, 31; as a nurse, 55; supplied the models for the pyramid and obelisk, 101; deals wisely with the old, 294; pitiless yet pitiful, 295; grotesques of, 5, 266; method of healing, 320; 414; 9, 46; those whom she loves, 6, 209; how studied by the physician and the theologian, 7, 81; hips and elbows and other bones of, 8, 74; sanitary commission of, 90; programme of, in the seasons, 132, 133; three classes of observers of, 133; her answer to man's questions, 158; the end of the show of the seasons, 184, 185; a word and a blow with, when her laws are insulted, 228; most trusted physician, 233; course of, in dismantling a human countenance, 249, 250; laws of, 262; Jonathan Edwards's notion of, 392; prolific and ambidextrous, 420; anticipates the plasterer in fibro-cartilage, 9, 230, the glass-blower in the formation of cells, 233; Sydenham's belief concerning, 268; a caricaturist, 10, 42; fond of trios, 138; does not care to mend old shoes, 183.
— and Art, questions between in the medical profession, 9, 181; definition of the terms, 196.
Natures, changed by foul surroundings, 8, 86; defective and ill-balanced, most subject to force of habit, 226; a good physician, best confessor of nervous, over-sensitive, 416.
Naushon island, 1, 39.
Nautilus, pearly and paper, 1, 97.
Nautilus, The Chambered, 1, 97.
Navy Yard, Charlestown, 1, 206; 2, 3.
Neæra, 1, 105.
Nebuchadnezzar, 10, 152.
Nebular theory, 3, 180.
Necessity, abrogates all rules, 8, 115; Dr. Johnson quoted on, 302; one thing to prove in terms, and another to accept as an article of faith, 303; in spite of the logic of argument for, we believe ourselves free, 381. See also Automatism; Philosophy; Will.
Needlework, Miss Linwood's, 2, 183.
Negative facts, proper interpretation of, 9, 130.
Negative veracity, 8, 164.
Nego quia probatum est, 8, 303.
Negroes, their passion for ornament, 5, 201; age of old black women hard to tell, 238; first regiment of, 1863, 8, 91; good service of, as soldiers, 118.

Neighbor Walrus, his garden, 2, 248.
Nelson monument, 10, 194.
Nerve, olfactory, connection of, with brain, 1, 77; of hearing, 4, 98; 8, 271; that runs to the pocket, 9, 409.
Nerve centres, torture for the, 3, 346.
Nerve fluid. See Nervous system.
Nerve force. See Nervous system.
Nerve-playing, artists in, 1, 129.
Nerve-tapping, 1, 6.
Nervous system, disturbance of, 7, 83, 215; 8, 2; anatomy of, 194-196; connection of thought and emotion with, 262; time in transmission of sensation and motor impulse, 272-276; investigations regarding, 9, 241, 246; singular relations between electricity and nerve force, 246. See also Semilunar ganglion.
Nervous woman, a doctor's knowledge of, 5, 98.
Nervousness, its resemblance to fear, 2, 255.
Nest, the world has a million roosts for a man, but only one nest, 1, 142.
Nettle-rash, caused by eating strawberries, 8, 220.
Neurin, 9, 284.
Neutrality, of Great Britain in our Civil war, 8, 97; there is none for a true American in Civil War, 117.
Nevins, Dr., 10, 18.
" New American Cyclopædia," man who was well read up in first volume of, 1, 143.
New England, women of, 2, 148; large number of crazy people in, 217; effect of its moral atmosphere upon sensitive characters, 242; life in, has an insufficient flavor of humanity, 245; its air better than Old England's ale, 250; the aristocracy of, 5, 13; seaport towns of, 14; Cotton Mather's account of splenetic maladies prevailing there, 6, 156; climate of, trying, 8, 206, 207; always had a yearning for Judea, 310; soil of, does not " laugh when tickled with the hoe," 406; dignity of the clergy of, 406, 407; share of the Mathers in religious history of, 423; malaria in, 9, 324; old houses in, 10, 19; landscape of, 22; geological objects in, 188.
" New England Magazine," first efforts of The Autocrat of the Breakfast-Table appeared in, 1831-32, 1, vii.
New Englanders, many of them hard and unimaginative, 2, 245; demoralized if self-respect is gone, 5, 135; feel at home in London, 10, 205. See also Brahmin caste of New England; Hired-man; Yankee.
New Hampshire, a queer sort of State, 5, 134.
New Haven, 8, 75.
New Ironsides, 8, 22.
New Jersey, a double-headed suburb, 8, 21.

New Portfolio, The, first opening of, 7, 1.
New World, double proportion of oxygen in its air, 6, 221 ; vocabulary of the, 8, 172 ; quietly buying many of the treasures of the Old, 9, 410 ; keeps imagination on scanty diet, 10, 131.
New York, compared to Venice, 2, 85 ; something higher demanded of it, 86 ; streets of, quotation from Knickerbocker's history regarding, 3, 324 ; everybody that lives in, feels that he owns it, 8, 74 ; Central Park, 74, 75 ; arrival at, from England, 10, 181.
New York girl and Boston girl, their conversation, in The Guardian Angel, 6, 269.
" New York Mirror," 7, 4.
New Yorkers, peculiar pronunciation of, 2, 142 ; two, their reminiscences, 3, 330.
New Zealander, Macaulay's, 9, 410 ; 10, 94.
Newbury, doctors of, 9, 326–328.
Newburyport, 5, 14.
Newgate calendar, 3, 222, 265.
Newgate ordinary, 5, 226.
Newman, John Henry, his " Grammar of Assent," 1, 14 ; quoted on unconscious or semi-conscious mental action, 8, 276 ; phrase quoted, 312.
News-boys of Baltimore, wailing tones of, 8, 48.
Newspapers, lying in, 1, 117 ; 8, 89 ; indispensability of, 8, 1, 6 ; comic, 286.
Newton, Sir Isaac, his speech about the ocean, 1, 84 ; his mathematical power, 3, 105 ; inspiration of, 5, 318 ; and law of gravitation, 8, 84 ; time-relation of the sense of vision illustrated by, 275 ; Swift quoted on, 279 ; commentaries of, on the Prophecies, 389 ; statue of, 10, 62 ; engraving of, 72.
Newton, John, 4, 251.
Niagara, a giant's tongue, 4, 214.
Niepce, moving in parallel paths with other inventors, 8, 84.
Night, noises in, 2, 163 ; beauty of, 6, 88.
Nightingale, Mr., his collection of " china," 10, 116.
Nightingale, Mrs., Roubiliac's monument to, 4, 171 ; 10, 62, 120.
Nightingale, Florence, her saying about music, 3, 62 ; quoted on necessity of light to health, 8, 209 ; on color in relation to disease, 211 ; the noblest daughter of the healing art, 9, 181 ; quoted on deterioration in families, 199 ; her skilful nursing, 299.
Nightingales, 10, 179.
Nile, 4, 100.
Nineveh, 10, 123 ; sculptures from, 152.
Ninth son of a ninth son, 9, 5.
" Nishmath Chajim," C. Mather's, 9, 362, 366.
Nitrate of silver for epileptics, 2, 105 ; 8, 190 ; 9, 188, 441.

Nitre, 9, 332.
Nitrogen, its uses on the planet Saturn, 4, 61, 62, 65 ; supplied by food, not by respiration, 8, 216.
Nobility, natural, 3, 276 ; certain titles of, 4, 219, 222 ; untitled, which has the dollar for armorial bearing, 6, 268.
Nobleman, subterranean palace of, 10, 158.
Noises in the night, 2, 163.
Nolan, Captain, at Balaklava, 2, 251.
Nonagenarians, well-known examples of, 4, 26.
Non-alcoholic drunkenness, 6, 158.
Noose, a fearful weapon, 5, 332.
Norman horse, 2, 236.
Normans, in England, 10, 66.
North, The, valor of, 8, 10 ; and South, no difference of race in, 10, 36, 102, 103 ; acquiescence of, 88 ; fanaticism of, fixed the dye of slavery, 88 ; moral uprising of, in 1861, 93 ; virtue and manhood of, 100 ; material power of, 103 ; Southern estimate of, 107 ; wealth of, 112, 113 ; fighting for existence, 116.
" North American Review," 9, 402.
Northampton, Marquis of, his mansion Compton Wynyate, 10, 97.
Northampton, Mass., elm at, 1, 235 ; meadows of, 244 ; experience of, with Jonathan Edwards, 2, 114 ; 8, 391–394 ; natural beauty of, 5, 42.
Northeasterly winds less disagreeable than southeasterly, 10, 39.
" Northern Magazine," 1, 120.
Northern mudsills, 8, 107.
Northerners. See North, The.
Norton, Charles Eliot, 8, 411 ; 10, 183, 185.
Norwalk, railroad disaster at, in 1853, 8, 75.
Norwich, large elms at, 1, 287 ; should be called Norridge, 288.
Nose-ring, 10, 57.
Nostrum, 9, 336.
" Notes and Queries," quoted, 1, 282 n.– 284 n.
" Nothing to Wear," Butler's poem of, 8, 351.
Notoriety, cheap way of acquiring, 4, 86.
Notre Dame, Paris, 10, 170.
Novels, every human being has stuff for one in three volumes, 1, 59 ; first one usually drawn from experience, 60 ; medicated, 3, 26 ; 5, ix. ; 8, 358 ; fate of, 3, 112 ; dangers of, 6, 376 ; "Some experiences of a Novelist," a paper, 7, 108.
Noxious agents, 9, 201, 442.
Noyes, John B., 8, 52
Nuisances, moral, 8, 90.
Number One. See Dictator, the.
Number Five, character in Over the Tea-cups, 4, 48 ; her tact, 50 ; her dream, 55 et seq. ; her voice, 78 ; her treat-

ment of Number Seven, 96 ; her visit to the Professor's laboratory, 144 ; her popularity, 167 ; reads the story of the Terrible Clock, 169 *et seq. ;* discusses the two Annexes with the Tutor, 175 ; her friends also her lovers, 238 ; her readings with the Tutor, 242, 262 ; her affections a kind of Gibraltar, 266 ; growing intimacy of Number Five and the Tutor, 284.

Number Seven, character in *Over the Teacups,* an ingenious man with a brain like a tinder box, **4,** 14 ; the seventh son of a seventh son, 53 ; his plan for a new social arrangement, 68 ; his opinion of poets, 75–79 ; his plan for teaching drawing, 82 ; his opinion on music, 94 *et seq.;* his squinting brain, 99 ; his plan for improving the race, 111 ; his abridged history of two worlds, 117 ; he discourses on cranks, 161 ; talks about himself and his habits, 205 *et seq. :* a poet who does not write poetry, 217 ; his opinion about churches, 258 ; talks of poetry, 279.

Numerical system of Louis, in medicine, **9,** 432.

Nuns inclined to consumption, **8,** 2.

Nursery, America a new, for the race, **2,** 83.

Nutrition, a catalytic process, **9,** 240.

O. T., a boy familiar to the Autocrat's childhood, **1,** 207.

Oak : the horizontal direction of its limbs indicates supremacy, **1,** 232 ; large one at Beverly Farms, 288 n. ; **10,** 48 ; a foliated atmospheric crystal, **2,** 67 ; oaks at Windsor, **10,** 48, 189.

Oath of Hippocrates, the. *See* Hippocrates.

Oatmeal or pie as a national food, **4,** 185.

Obelisks, Egyptian, **3,** 149 ; **10,** 1, 176 ; Nature's anticipation of their form, **4,** 101 ; building an obelisk, 193 ; **10,** 195. *See also* Monoliths.

Obituary, premature, **4,** 135.

Objective projection of intuitions in exalted nervous conditions, **6,** 94.

Obliquity, mental. *See* Squinting brain.

Obscure perceptions. *See* Unconscious mental action.

Observation, different methods of interpreting, **9,** 114 ; false induction from genuine facts of, 186.

Observatory, visit of the boarding-house party to, **3,** 131 *et seq.;* description of, 133 ; solemnity of, 134.

Observer, a mere, too fond of facts, **9,** 384.

Obsolete impressions, in nervous young women, in the dying, and in animals, **8,** 300.

Obsolete self-determination, **8,** 307.

O'Byrne, the Irish giant, **10,** 67, 68.

Occasional poems, **4,** 269, 270.

Occasional talkers, **3,** 266.

Occidental, the, manhood of, based on self-respect, **3,** 270 ; demands of, **8,** 309.

Occupation necessary to health, **8,** 231.

Ocean, two men walking by, **1,** 83 ; mystery of, **6,** 26 ; ocean breeze, 77 ; what it says to the dweller on its shores, **7,** 97 *et seq. ;* its sullen indifference, 251 ; solitude of, **10,** 15.

Ocean cable literature, **2,** 26.

Octavia on hearing Virgil's verses, **3,** 312.

October, **8,** 162.

Octogenarian, how to become one, **4,** 181 *et seq.*

Octosyllabic verse, fatal facility of, **8,** 316 ; correspondence of accent in, with heart pulsations, 320.

Odors, memory appealed to quickly through, **1,** 75 ; power of, in reviving old memories, **7,** 24, 25 ; of various flowers, effect of, in some cases, 89 ; of apples, disagreeable to some persons, 88, 89 ; diffusion of, **9,** 55 ; of drugs on old doctors, 387.

" Odyssey," **3,** 323.

Official smile, **8,** 67.

Old age, forty-five is the starting-point of, **1,** 151 ; Dr. Johnson held that it began at thirty-five, 151 ; sign of, between eyebrows, 152 ; gentle and gradual in its approaches, 153 ; fifty is the childhood of, 154 ; formation of habits a mark of, 155 ; new occupations taken up, 159 ; its effects on beauties, 160 ; no giving up because of, 162 ; the disease of old age, 163 ; neglected pleasures then in reach, 163 ; boating a good exercise for, 163 ; use of spectacles in, 173 ; the heart should not grow cold in, 174 ; an infant's life has the character of a first, **2,** 66 ; appearance of, produced by a few lines in face, 192 ; the Professor's paper on, **4,** 24 *et seq. ;* its tranquillity, 30 ; its cheerfulness, 33 ; its privilege, 34 ; habits its crutches, 37 ; like an opium-dream, 39 ; its religious attitude, 45 ; its memories, 46 ; its charity for the failings of others, 46 ; Wordsworth's picture of, in " Matthew," 48 ; its tender melancholy, 192 ; a pair of spectacles its saddle, 295. *See also* Age ; Longevity.

Old age of the world, the latest days are : the idea to be found in Lord Bacon, Roger Bacon, Seneca, Pascal, Hobbes, Tennyson, etc., **8,** 287, 288.

" Old Blue," **4,** 31.

Old Catholics, **8,** 407.

Old Gentleman opposite. *See* Venerable Gentleman.

Old house, fear of, **2,** 162.

Old Ironsides, **8,** 96.

Old Man, theological term for certain human qualities, **6,** 17.

Old Man, The, dreams, **1,** 68.

Old men, poetry not dead in, **1,** 100 ; distinction between being called *an* old man and *the* old man, 148 ; a person startled when he first hears himself called an old man, 154 ; first children of, **2,** 66 ; tears of, **4,** 30 ; old men know the exceptions, young men know the rules, **9,** 377 ; on the platform at public meetings, 411.

Old people, are monsters to little ones, **3,** 14 ; worth of their reminiscences, 169 ; their feeling that they have outlived their usefulness, **4,** 36 ; have a right to be epicures, 184 ; nature's wise dealings with, 294 ; do not lose their vanity, 295 ; need courtesies, **6,** 18 ; long interval of obscure mental action in, before answering a question, 279.

Old Probabilities, no priest could hold his own against, **8,** 327.

Old Song, The, **7,** 85.

Old World, and New, comparison of their types of organization, **1,** 236 ; evidences of the past in, **2,** 245 ; air of, good for nothing, 249 ; its system one of intellectual locks and canals, 295 ; convenience of living in, **10,** 204.

Old World folks, American feeling about, **2,** 35 ; seem childlike, 36.

Olfactory nerve, connection of, with brain, **1,** 77.

Oligarchy, tolerated as a convenience in an immature state, **8,** 79.

Oliphant, Laurence, **10,** 67.

Oliver, Dr. James, **9,** 336, 404.

O'm, sacred word of Hindoo mythology, **2,** 7, 241.

Omens of childhood, **1,** 205.

Omnibuses, Parisian, **4,** 157.

" *One-Hoss-Shay,*" *The Wonderful,* **1,** 252.

One-man system of teaching, **9,** 286.

One, two, and three story intellects, **3,** 43.

Onion, a communicative vegetable, **8,** 148.

Open fire-places, **8,** 182, 208.

Opening of the Piano, The, **2,** 73.

Ophidians, cannot move eyelids, **5,** 209 ; their friendship with human beings, 220, 224, 397 ; frightful malignity of, 225. *See also* Rattlesnakes.

Opinions, asked for, when praise is wanted, **1,** 294 ; of more value than arguments, **2,** 116 ; if unattacked, beneath contempt, 119 ; right to hold one's own, defended, 123, 124 ; should be freely expressed, rarely defended, **9,** 271.

Opium, **9,** 200, 202, 348 ; Dr. Gallup's opinion of, 259 ; in delirium tremens, 264.

Opium-dream, old age like, **4,** 39.

" Opium-eater, The," DeQuincey's, **2,** 238.

Opium-eating, intellectual, **3,** 99.

Opium of the heart, foxglove called, **2,** 261.

Opposition, success impossible without

it as fulcrum, **6,** 276 ; spirit of, to science, **9,** 97 ; a good mordant, 272.

Oracle, fine thing to be an, **1** 142.

Orange - juice landscapes, Gilpin's, **1,** 232.

Orator, inspiration of the, **8,** 288.

Orchids, pink, **10,** 47.

Order of Things, the Master's specialty, in *The Poet,* **3,** 41.

Organic tendencies. *See* Inherited tendencies.

Oriental, the, manhood of, based on self-abasement, **3,** 270 ; modes of thought of, **8,** 309.

Original sin, congenital sinfulness, **5,** 248, 256 *et seq. ;* we hear little of, **8,** 327 ; Jonathan Edwards on, 372, 382 ; Julius Müller and Prof. Fisher on, 383 ; C. Mather quoted on, **9,** 360. *See also* Automatism ; Heredity ; Imbeciles, moral ; Responsibility ; Sin.

Originality, editors anxious to get, **1,** 290.

Orion, nebula of, **2,** 78.

Ormonde, winner of the Derby, **10,** 33, 36 ; picture of, 40.

Ornaments, personal, as reminders of the New Jerusalem, **3,** 295.

Orthobrachians, **4,** 64.

Osgood, David, **3,** 14 ; **6,** 18 ; carried politics into his pulpit, **8,** 406 ; anecdote of his parish, 408.

Osgood, James R., **10,** 158.

Otis, Dr. G. W., **9,** 426.

Otis, James, **2,** 15.

Ottenheimer, Phillip, **8,** 47.

" Our Sumatra correspondence," **1,** 117.

Outworks to the citadel of belief, the fewer the better, **3,** 319.

Ovarian eggs of future civilization, **1,** 195.

Overcome Family, their rôles in the affecting scene called the " Surprise Party," **2,** 76.

Over-feeding, intellectual, **4,** 148.

Over-medication, **9,** 184, 185, 200, 203, 206.

Overstatements, occasional, to be treated calmly, **1,** 51.

Overvaluation of one's self, **4,** 112.

Owl, **6,** 88.

Oxbow Village, the scene of *The Guardian Angel,* **6,** 1 ; war fever in 1861 in, 385 *et seq.*

Oxbow Invincibles, **6,** 385.

Owen, John, pays a dollar for a red pond-lily, **8,** 153.

Oxford, visit to, **10,** 79–82 ; Bodleian library, 81 ; trees in grounds of Magdalen, 81, 82 ; second visit to, 86–90 ; degree conferred by, 87, 88 ; academic dress at, 87 ; luncheon at All Souls, 89.

Oxford Street, London, **10,** 145.

Oxygen, its use on the planet Saturn, **4,** 65 ; double proportion of, in New World air, **6,** 221.

Oysters, fine social distinction between

"shell-oysters," and the pickled variety, **5,** 109; the sad oyster, **8,** 159, 160; acceptable on board ship, **10,** 14.

Ozymandias, statue of, **10,** 117.

Padded cells for would-be suicides, **1,** 186.

Paddock Elms, **1,** 239; **8,** 163.

Paddy, liability of using the word before Irish gentlemen, **2,** 95.

Paduasoy, **2,** 262.

Paganini, **10,** 5.

Paget, Minnie Stevens, **10,** 47.

Paget, Sir James, **10,** 27, 41.

Pail of water, memory of a white-pine, **1,** 200.

Pain and disease, the accidents of a settled order of things, **5,** 320.

Palaces are artificial caverns, **10,** 20, 48.

Palais Royal, **10,** 174; shops, 175.

Palate bone, **9,** 284.

Paleness of fighting-boy before contest, **2,** 268.

Palgrave, Mr., **10,** 52.

Palgrave, Francis Turner, **10,** 52.

"Palladium Spagyricum," P. J. Faber's, **3,** 27.

Palmerston, once a dandy, **1,** 259.

Pancreatic fluid, **9,** 238.

Panem et Circenses, **8,** 1.

Panic silences, **4,** 84.

Panorama, internal, in a spinster's mind, **6,** 347; of past life seen when drowning, **8,** 299.

Pansophian Society, in *A Mortal Antipathy,* **7,** 38, 94 *et seq.*; Secretary of, etc., 94, 106, 117, 127; papers contributed to, 96, 108, 133, 166.

Pantheon, Paris, **10,** 165.

Panther, sea compared to, **1,** 264.

Pantopathists, **8,** 234.

Panvini, Dr., his experiment in a hospital at Naples, **9,** 78.

Paolo, Kirkwood's servant, in *A Mortal Antipathy,* called Paul, **7,** 50 *et seq.*

Papin's digester, **2,** 149.

Pappooses, **5,** 392.

Parable, of Pharisee and Publican, **3,** 335; of Eden, **8,** 367.

Parabola, **2,** 237; the vital, **7,** 84.

Paracelsus, remedies of, **9,** 319; was a sot, 387; introduced the use of mercury, 443.

Parallax, of thought given by lay sermons, **2,** 7; terrible, between the period before thirty and that after threescore and ten, **9,** 436.

Parallelisms in animal and vegetable life of Old and New World, **1,** 237.

Paralysis, partial, scraping of the toe in, **8,** 127; crossed, of sensation, **9,** 244.

Parang, murderer, **8,** 340.

Parasite, South American, **4,** 92.

Paré, Ambroise, **4,** 189; **9,** 63, 225, 269, 279, 365, 375, 411.

Parenthesis about the mouth in old age, **1,** 150.

Paris, dinners at the Trois Fréres in, **1,** 78; "good Americans when they die go to," 125; church of St. Etienne du Mont in, 280; hospitals and physicians of, in 183–, **9,** 427–438; visit of author to, **10,** 161–178; in the dead season, dull and torpid, 162, 177; Place Vendôme, 162, 173; visit to former haunts, 163, 164, 166; Café Procope and its frequenters, 166–168; pictures in the Louvre, 169, 171; museum of the Hôtel Cluny, 170; Notre Dame, 170; seen in life's morning and in its twilight, 174; restaurants, 174, 175; Palais Royal shops, 175; bridges, 175; three objects always to be met on the Pont Neuf, 175; Champs Elysées, 176; Bois de Boulogne, 176; Place de la Concorde, 176; ruins of the Tuileries, 177.

Parish, Elijah, carried politics into his pulpit, **8,** 406.

Parishioners, not the property of their ministers, **8,** 421.

Parisian omnibuses, **4,** 157.

Park, Edwards A., said to have unpublished manuscripts of Jonathan Edwards, **8,** 428.

Park, Mungo, **7,** 260.

Park Street church, **2,** 11.

Parker, Theodore, took down the bars to new pastures, **8,** 420.

Parkman, Francis, son of a clergyman, **8,** 411.

Parkman, Dr. Samuel, **9,** 210.

Parks in London, **10,** 140, 141.

Parliament, Houses of, **10,** 52 *et seq.*

Parlors, front, **5,** 58.

Paroxysms, emotional, often the basis of religious character, **6,** 194.

Parr, Thomas, **4,** 26; **10,** 10.

Parricide, moral, **4,** 248.

Parry, Sir Edward, **9,** 176.

Parson Turell's Legacy, **1,** 297.

Parsons, T. W., on election days, **8,** 146.

Partridge, cause of poisoning, **8,** 219, 220.

Party, one given by Colonel and Mrs. Sprowle, in *Elsie Venner,* **5,** 85–117; giving one is a formidable matter, 87; is a trial chamber of society, 94; solemnity at, 108; the morning after, 118 *et seq.*; dainties brought away from, by guests, 122, 123; a London, the most formidable thing about it is getting away from it, **10,** 45. *See also* Tea party.

Pascal, story of, told by Abbé Boileau, **7,** 90, 92; quoted on transmissible responsibility, **8,** 303, 304; treated of the duties of the Supreme to a dependent being, 305; parallel between, and Jonathan Edwards, 363–366; greatly influenced by women, 365; one of the noblest sayings of, 369; melancholy of, **10,** 166.

Pason, Samuel, **9,** 337.

Passengers, fellow, to Europe, **10**, 15.

Passing bell, **5**, 454.

Passions, power of, **1**, 132; secret, **2**, 91; the pale ones the fiercest, 268; those which whirl victims to their doom, **6**, 143; moral sense may be paralyzed by, **8**, 335.

Passive cerebration, **3**, 316.

Past, photographs of the, **1**, 242, 243; effect of the, **2**, 246.

Pasteur, visit to, **10**, 171; his patients, 172.

Patch, Samuel, **4**, 156; **6**, 175.

Patent medicines, **8**, 235. *See also* Quack medicines.

Path, the Long. *See* Long path.

Pathological piety, **3**, 303.

Pathology, as part of theological education, **3**, 304; of Giles Firmin, **9**, 279, 280.

Patients, apt to be fools and cowards, **1**, 86; not the property of doctors, **8**, 421; **9**, 390; how to obtain, **9**, 371; shrewd doctor's methods of dealing with, 389; good, 390; what they rightfully expect of a doctor, 434.

Patin, Guy, **9**, 441.

Patronizing manner, **6**, 243.

Patti, **10**, 46.

Paul, or Paolo, Kirkwood's servant, in *A Mortal Antipathy*, **7**, 56 *et seq.*

Paul Veronese, **10**, 20.

Paulus Æagineta, **5**, 222.

Pavements, healthfulness of, **5**, 303.

Payne's "Home, Sweet Home," **10**, 76, 96.

Peabody, George, **10**, 205.

Peaches, dried, **1**, 78; hot-house, **10**, 98; their perfection as fruit, 169.

Peake, the Widow, in *Elsie Venner*, **5**, 140, 455.

Pear-tree, moral, **8**, 147; high-bred, 147.

Pears, men as they mature are like, **1**, 82; city-grown, **5**, 303; a cheek having the tinge of a seckel pear, **6**, 25.

Pearson, Eliphalet, **3**, 13, 18.

"Peau de Chagrin," Balzac's, **4**, 72; **9**, 373; of State Street, **4**, 73.

Pebble, value of, **1**, 84.

Peckham, Silas, and Mrs., principal and matron of the Apollinean Institute, in *Elsie Venner*, **5**, 47, 48; at Colonel Sprowle's party, 92; his nasal twang, 128; makes Colonel Sprowle a bid for the remnants of evening party, 131-133; wants to claim Richard's dead horse, 379; reluctantly permits Helen Darley to visit Elsie, 427-430; tries to squeeze down Helen Darley's salary, 474-479; has to leave town, 484.

Peculiarity, tendency to touch upon another's, **2**, 94.

Pedal locomotive, **1**, 168 n.

Pediculus melittæ, **3**, 74, 75.

Peel, Mr., Speaker of House of Commons, **10**, 52, 53.

Peine forte et dure of a London reception, **10**, 45.

Peirce, Benjamin, **1**, 2 n.; **2**, 49; **4**, 28; **8**, 147; **9**, 285.

Peirson, Dr., of Salem, **9**, 132, 142, 404.

Pelvis, deformed, **9**, 295.

Pemberton, the Rev. Eliphalet, the senior pastor in *The Guardian Angel*, **6**, 16; his noble presence and stern creed, 17; announces the return of Myrtle, 124; receives present of slippers from Myrtle, 335; goes to help announce to Myrtle the decision of Court in her favor, 407 *et seq.*; grows young again, 424.

Pembroke, Earl of, **10**, 110, 123, 125.

Penance, materialism of doctrine of, **8**, 306, 307.

Pendulum, Foucault's experiment with, **10**, 165; Galileo's conception of, 166.

Penhallow, Jacob, a lawyer in *The Guardian Angel*, takes Mr. William Murray Bradshaw into partnership, **6**, 5; Master Gridley gives him important paper in regard to Withers estate, which Bradshaw had improperly withheld, 357 *et seq.*; announces the decision giving the bulk of the Withers estate to Myrtle, 412 *et seq.*

Pens, stylographic, **4**, 298; quill, steel and gold, drink too often, 299.

Pentateuch, first discerning criticism of, by Astruc, **8**, 417, 418.

Penzance, **9**, 296.

Peonies, **2**, 248.

People who are *too* glad to see us, **3**, 334.

"People's Perennial and Household Inquisitor," in *A Mortal Antipathy*, **7**, 132; correspondent of, 132 *et seq.*; his interviewing, 132-140; undertakes to interview Kirkwood, 144.

Pepper, astonishing effects of, as reported in "Our Sumatra Correspondence," **1**, 118.

Pepys, **3**, 276; **10**, 179.

Pequawkett Centre, in *Elsie Venner*, **5**, 22, 23.

Perceptions, easy to calculate the number of possible, in a life-time, **8**, 274.

Perceval, Spencer, **5**, 226.

Percival, James G., **7**, 5.

Percy, Lord, arm-chair in which he used to sit, **2**, 188.

Percy lion at Alnwick, **1**, 281; **10**, 6.

Pericles, age of, common motive and force in, **8**, 84.

Périer, Madame, her memoir of her brother Pascal, **8**, 365.

Peril escaped, makes a great story-teller of a common person, **3**, 266.

Periodicals, of greatest use to doctors, **9**, 401; uselessness of, without indexes, 402-405; writer in, appears, as it were, in his shirt-sleeves, 404; dangers of exclusive reading of, 408.

Periods of disturbance. *See* Disturbance.

Periods of vivid impressions. *See* Impressions.

Perkinism, **9,** 15 *et seq.*

Perkins, Colonel, of Connecticut, **4,** 26.

Perkins, Dr. Benjamin Douglass, **9,** 18, 21.

Perkins, Dr. Elisha, **9,** 17 ; **10,** 58.

Permanent homes, lack of, in America, **3,** 11.

Personal aversions, indulgence in, **3,** 333.

Personal equation, **8,** 272 ; in relation to reading poetry, 318 ; moral, 379.

Personal incidents touch our sensibilities, **1,** 280.

Personality, of the poet, **3,** 109 ; of the writer, impossibility of concealing it, **4,** 20 ; plural, 166 ; as many as eight personalities said to have existed in single female, **6,** 22 ; each one's individual, may not be sole tenant of his corporeal frame, 22 ; often doubled in dreams, **8,** 282, 283.

Peruvian bark, **9,** 348, 366.

Perverse moral choice. *See* Mal-volition.

Perversity, occasional paroxysms of, **4,** 282.

Peschier, homœopathist, of Geneva, **9,** 90.

Pestilence, among the Indians, probably small-pox, **9,** 315.

Peter the Great, frightened when an infant, **7,** 90 ; overcame his terror at the sound of wheels on bridge, 90, 214.

Petit, J. L., **9,** 437.

Petit verre, **4,** 291, 292 ; **10,** 207.

Petroleum, the light furnished by the rocks of Pennsylvania, **1,** iv. ; Saint, gospel of, **3,** 40.

Pétroleuses, **10,** 178.

Pettenkofer, **9,** 413.

Pettingill, Miss Susy, in *Elsie Venner*, **5,** 97.

Petty tyrants, **8,** 86, 93.

Pews and pulpit, relation of, **4,** 248.

Peyer's patches, **9,** 238.

Pfeiffer, Mrs., **10,** 40.

Phacueidoscope, **9,** 249.

Phæacians, resemblance of, to Marble-headers of Ireson's day, **3,** 323.

Pharaohs, **6,** 222.

Pharisee and Publican, lesson of parable of, **3,** 335.

Pharmacopœia, of Giles Firmin, **9,** 280 ; of the 17th century, 331–333 ; the College, 354.

Phelps, Mr., American minister to England, **10,** 28 ; introduced the author to Prince of Wales, 34 ; dinners at his house in London, 37, 50, 51.

Phelps, Mrs., **10** 51, 57.

Phi Beta Kappa Society, dinners of the, **4,** 9 ; Emerson's oration before, 233 ; ribbons of the, **10,** 87.

Philadelphia, main features of, **2,** 84 ; approach to, by water, **8,** 22 ; the natives pretend to know one street from another, 50 ; Quaker element in, 70 ; agreeable impressions of the outside of, 70, 71 ; characteristics accounted for by geographical position, 71 ; Upper Ferry Bridge, 71.

Philanthropist, the, in *My Hunt after "The Captain,"* **8,** 29–43.

Philanthropists, practical, **8,** 34, 35 ; humor in, 34 ; hardest task of philosophers and, 328.

Philipse house, Yonkers, **5,** 144.

Phillips, hanging of, **2,** 3.

Phillips, Grenville Tudor, curious coincidence concerning, **4,** 18.

Phillips, Wendell, uses image of *The Two Streams*, **8,** 46 ; masculine Cassandra, 83.

Phillips Academy, Andover, reminiscences of, **8,** 243–253 ; revisited in 1867, 253–259.

Phillips & Sampson, **7,** 9.

Philomathean Society, banquet at Liverpool, **10,** 180.

Philosophers, class of, who exhibit a small truth bandaged to look large, **2,** 39.

Philosophy, true, and true faith ought to be one, **8,** 312 ; hardest task of, and philanthropy, 328. *See also* Automatism ; Brain ; Environment ; Ideas ; Intellect ; Mind ; Necessity ; Physiological psychology ; Psychology ; Senses ; Time and Space ; Unconscious mental action ; Will.

Phlebotomy. *See* Blood-letting.

Phlegmatic people, inheritance of the world belongs to them, **3,** 41.

Phosphorescence, **5,** 305.

Phosphorus, smell of, **1,** 75 ; relation of, to thought, **7,** 235 ; chemical changes in, **9,** 214.

Photographs, of the past, **1,** 242 ; give features one particular look, **2,** 191 ; development of, **6,** 180 ; instantaneous, **8,** 124 ; microscopic, illustrate the alleged material record of memory, 298, 299.

Phrases, of shrewd doctors, for patients, **9,** 389 ; odd phrases, *see* Words and Phrases.

Phrenology, visit to Emporium, **2,** 195 ; result of examination, 197 ; short lecture on phrenology and its resemblance to a pseudo-science, 197 ; its truth cannot be proved, by reason of the structure of head, 199 ; cases which prove nothing, 200 ; the world's debt to, **5,** 226, 227 ; the first phrenological picture made, **6,** 141 ; a mistake of, **7,** 125 ; a pseudo-science, **9,** 244.

Phryne, **1,** 10.

Phthisis. *See* Consumption.

Phyllum siccifolium, **3,** 240.

Physalia, **1,** 97 n.

Physician in " Arabian Nights," his prescription, **6,** 181.

Physicians. *See* Doctors.

Physiological psychology, growth of, **8,**

329 ; Ribot on, 358 ; has taken up the problem of the will, 378.

Physiology, laws of, not altered by republicanism, **3**, 276 ; its progress by aid of the microscope, **9**, 231 ; its largest truth, 232 ; importance of, 375 ; changes in methods of teaching, 421, 422.

Piano forte players, manners of, **1**, 85.

Pichegru, General, amount of sleep of, **8**, 231.

Pickwick, Mr., **10**, 162.

"Pickwick Papers," **6**, 274, 275.

Picnics, sufficiently depressing, **8**, 219.

Pico della Mirandola, **10**, 124.

Picts, **10**, 114.

Pictured thought, **8**, 269.

Pictures, death-bed, **5**, 296 ; in the Boston Athenæum Picture Gallery, **7**, 3 ; at Blenheim, **10**, 6 ; Grosvenor House, 54 ; one of lady, by Reynolds, 85 ; at National Gallery, 151 ; those at the Louvre recalled, 169, 170.

Pie, the Young Fellow's surmise as to age of, **1**, 79 ; the Autocrat eats too large a piece, 80 ; desponding poetry resultant therefrom, 81 ; as a national food, **4**, 186.

Pied piper of Hamelin, **5**, 10.

Pierce, Ruth, struck dead at Devizes with lie on her lips, **1**, 281 ; **10**, 186.

Pierpont, John, **7**, 5.

Pierrepont, Sarah, wife of Jonathan Edwards, **8**, 365.

Piety, pathological, **3**, 303.

Pig, annual tragedy of the, **7**, 25.

Pig's feet, digestibility of, **8**, 218.

Pigeon, Master, schoolmaster at Pigwacket, in *Elsie Venner*, **5**, 26, 27.

Pighogg, Churrergeon, **9**, 317.

Pigment, dark, of certain animals, **2**, 229.

Pigsty, artistic, called Porcellarium, **6**, 382.

Pigwacket Centre, **5**, 22-24 ; district school of, 24.

"Pilgrim's Progress," **6**, 76 ; quoted, **8**, 48, 388 ; mental condition of Christian in, 416.

Pilgrims of Plymouth, we have a right to be proud of the clergy of, **8**, 404, 405 ; condition of the country on arrival of the, **9**, 314-316 ; their experience with clams, 315 ; mortality of, the first winter, 316 ; glance at the conditions of, 320-324 ; graves of the dead levelled, 325 ; dealing of, with quackery, 328 ; their stern life took the nonsense out of, 363.

Pillar, The Hangman's. *See* Hangman's stone.

Pin, reason of captive preserved by means of a, **6**, 74.

Pindar, his odes were occasional poems, **4**, 270.

Pinel, Dr., **8**, 212 ; **9**, 389.

Pinkney, William, appearance when pleading, **1**, 7.

Pinnikle, Mrs., of the Apex family, in *The Guardian Angel*, **6**, 289.

Pinnikle, Miss Rhadamantha, **6**, 312.

Pinxter Blumejies, **8**, 154.

Piorry, **9**, 437.

"Pious and painefull," **2**, 146.

Piozzi, Madame, **3**, 186, 325 ; **4**, 243, 284.

Piper's "Trees of America," **1**, 236.

Pirates, Danish, skins of, nailed to church doors, **1**, 107.

Piron, **10**, 168.

Pisa, Galileo in Cathedral of, **10**, 166.

Pitch-pine Yankees, **3**, 276.

Pitié, Hôpital de la, Paris, **10**, 164.

Pittsfield, Massachusetts, **10**, 77.

Pius IX., believed by many to have possessed the evil eye, **7**, 65.

Place de la Concorde, Paris, **10**, 176.

Place Vendôme, Paris, **10**, 45, 162, 173.

Plagiarism, disgust for, **1**, 146 ; unconscious, **4**, 153 ; supposed cases of, **8**, 45, 46 ; innocent, 287, 288.

Plague, a word used very vaguely, **9**, 315.

Plainness of speech and manners, **2**, 145.

Planchette, **9**, 368.

Planetary foundlings, **4**, 54.

Planing-mill, resemblance to a bee-hive, **3**, 325.

Plantagenet razor, **10**, 16.

Plantain, **2**, 235.

Plants, cultivation of, **9**, 253.

Plaster of Paris, called "calcined mineral of Lutetia," **2**, 29.

Plasterer anticipated by nature, **9**, 230, 233.

Platform, apostolic old men on the, at public meetings, **9**, 411.

Pleasure of being forgotten, **3**, 161 ; of finding one's own thought expressed by another, **4**, 10.

Pleasures of memory, **3**, 328 ; to the old, **4**, 46.

Plenipotentiary, winner of the Derby in 1834, **10**, 6 ; picture by Herring, **5**, 296 ; **6**, 33, 40.

Pliny, his "Natural History," **5**, 209 ; his horror of quackery, **9**, 191.

Plotinus, **7**, 167.

Pluck, dandies have, **1**, 258.

Plural personality, **4**, 166. *See also* Dual consciousness.

Plutarch, his anecdote of profligate, **8**, 332.

Plymouth, Pilgrims of. *See* Pilgrims of Plymouth.

Po, crossing the, **1**, 279.

Pocahontas, Myrtle takes the part of, in *The Guardian Angel*, **6**, 279 *et seq.*

Pocasset, in *The Guardian Angel*, **6**, 20.

Pocket, not needed by an honest person, **4**, 64 ; nerve that runs to the, **9**, 409.

Pocket-book delusion, **1**, 207.

Poe, Edgar A., **2**, 281.

Poems, changes introduced in one of Autocrat's to suit teetotallers, **1**, 47 ;

each has a soul and body, 99; in green state until long kept and used, 101; parts should be knit together in absolute solidarity, 104; post-prandial kind, 222 : each one represents a great expenditure of vital force, **3**, 97, 98; unpublished, **4**, 87; occasional, 269, 270; unwritten better than written, **10**, 99. *See also* Poetry; Poets; Rhymes; Verse.

Poet, My friend the, on suddenness of lyric conception, **1**, 98; his opinion of rapidly growing towns, 128; a brief poem by, 174; the Autocrat's relation with the Professor and the Poet, 178 *et seq.* ; would have liked woman's praises, 183; his dread of anniversaries, 222; poem by, 223.

Poet, a kind-hearted, modest, genial, hopeful, (Charles Mackay) **1**, 222.

Poet, The, at the Breakfast-Table, **4**, 307.

Poetaster who has tasted type is done for, **1**, 293.

Poetic muse, **1**, 249.

Poetic nature, the real, **6**, 209.

Poetical impulse, external, **1**, 99.

Poetical reputation, desire for, **4**, 74.

Poetry, a luxury, not a necessity, **3**, 100; a matter of heart-beats, **4**, 41; contagious, 50; attenuated volumes of, 76; everybody can learn to make, 77; taught in twelve lessons, 78; its manufacture an important industry, 84 *et seq.* ; true poetry the ashes of a burnt-out passion, 85, 92, 279; common in love letters, 92; unrhymed and unversed, **6**, 208; critical test of, by the stop-watch, **8**, 318; popular, always written with reference to rhythm of respiration, 319; associated with English scenery, **10**, 49, 50.

Poets, love verses while warm from their minds, **1**, 101; moods of, 180; compared to a hand-organ, 181; their stock of tunes limited, 182; water lily the type of the poet's soul, 182; women first to appreciate, 183; poets as creators not frequent, 183; two kinds of, 184; excess of sensibility in, 185; apt to call in stimulation for intellect, 187; more prone to this abuse because mind and body have previously flagged, 191; never young in a sense, **2**, 239; flight unerring like that of goose, 240; find material everywhere, 244; want a home, 246; their inner nature, **3**, 11; their knowledge of the subjects with which they deal, 72, 73; those who never write verses the best talkers, 94; treated as privileged persons, 99; all real ones are artists, 100; concessions should be made to their idiosyncrasies, 101; personality of, 109; their fondness for reading their own compositions to others, 202; their non-clerical minds,

257; length of life among, **4**, 40; they should exalt the idea of manhood, 49; Number Seven's opinion of, 75; the best poets not always appreciated at once, 88; unsuccessful, 88; Horace's counsel to, 89; think themselves different from common folks, 89; one would not make rhymes while his house was burning, 279; nor declaim a versified proposal to his Amanda, 280; depreciated, **6**, 204; capable of divided affection, 214; as natural observers, **8**, 133, 134; mental attitude of, while writing, 286; classified by Akenside, 295; the natural antagonists of religious pessimists, 431; are fond of trees, **10**, 70; understand their own poetry, 70; stained windows in honor of, 205.

Poets' Corner of Westminster Abbey, **10**, 59-62.

Point d'Alençon, **6**, 311.

Poison-cure doctrine of disease, **9**, 256, 257, 262, 266.

Poisoners, painted of dark hue, **2**, 229.

Poisoning, from eating partridge, **8**, 219, 220; from lobsters, clams, mussels, mackerel, 220.

Poisons, morbid, **4**, 54; which may cause human beings to manifest peculiarities of lower animals, **5**, 219, 224, 225; girl fed on, 222; mineral, **9**, 367.

Poissardes of the French revolution, **10**, 178.

Poisson : his "Théorie du calcul des probabilités" has a fishy flavor, **8**, 147; author's recollection of, **10**, 167.

Police, literary, **3**, 152; Turkish cadi's methods might be infused into the management of, **8**, 349; of London, polite, **10**, 192.

Polish lance, **1**, 19.

Political firebugs, **3**, 3.

Political freedom in America is owing to Protestantism, **5**, 253.

Politicians, worn-out, **5**, 165; as doctors, **9**, 345, 384; a lady's dog the bitterest one the author met in England, **10**, 200.

Politics, common people of New England will not stop talking, **2**, 118; Americanized, 207, 208; as a trade, **8**, 81; influence of the clergy on, 406; the muddy sewer of, **9**, 384; not talked of at dinners in England, **10**, 75, 200.

Polkommet, Lord, his way of preparing for a judicial decision, **8**, 290.

Pollard's Tahvern, in *Elsie Venner*, **5**, 65, 85.

Pollock, Mrs., finds author a secretary in England, **10**, 25.

Pollok, Robert, **6**, 206.

Polyandry a normal condition of the church, **6**, 17.

Polygamists, love-letters of, rich in poetical extracts, **4**, 92.

"Poly-Olbion," Drayton's, **4**, 133.

Polyphysiophilosophical societies, **1**, 136.
Pomfret, Connecticut, religious conflict in, **8**, 411, 412.
Ponce de Leon, memory is like the fountain of, **10**, 168.
Pond-lily, **1**, 182 ; a red, **8**, 153.
Ponsonby, Miss, **10**, 186.
Pont Neuf, Paris, three objects always to be met on, **10**, 175.
Pooh-Poohs, tribe of, **8**, 326 ; common-sense as represented by one of the, 351.
Pool, Miss Bella, in *The Guardian Angel*, **6**, 270.
Poole's " Index," **9**, 403.
Poor Gentleman, part often played by the Autocrat, **1**, 43.
Poor Relation, in *The Autocrat* and *The Professor*, takes offence, **1**, 30 ; leaves table suddenly, 86, 101 ; her decorum about " retiring," 208 ; doubts the Autocrat, 262 ; wedding-present given by, 311 ; **2**, 21.
Poor relations, social attentions to, **2**, 140.
Pope, quotation from an epistle of, to Addison, **3**, 111 ; his lines on London monument, **10**, 179.
Popgun, That Boy's, its first appearance, **3**, 63 ; its last appearance, 236 ; its efficiency, 237.
Poplar, a tall, **1**, 232 ; Lombardy, **3**, 19 ; **10**, 191.
Poplars, The, home of Myrtle Hazard, in *The Guardian Angel*, **6**, 6, 21.
Poppy-water, **9**, 361.
Population, of earth-born intelligences, **2**, 107 ; our native, not increasing so rapidly as formerly, **9**, 294.
Porches, provocative of civilities, **1**, 302.
Pork, the only merchantable article a Hebrew is never known to seek profit from, **6**, 272 ; digestibility of, and prejudice against, **8**, 218.
Porphyro and Madeline, **7**, 234, 235.
Porpoises, **10**, 15.
Portents, **9**, 356.
Porter, Dr., of Andover, face " festooned " in wrinkles, **8**, 249.
Porter, Dr., of Conway, prophecy of, **8**, 408.
Porter, Zachary, " Atlantic Monthly " founded at his inn, **8**, 171.
Portfolio, the first, opened more than fifty years ago, **7**, 2 ; the second opened in 1857, 11.
Portland, **5**, 14 ; **8**, 110 ; getting too prosperous, **5**, 15.
Portraits, those necessary to a man of family, **1**, 21 ; in literature drawn too faithfully 61 ; portrait by Titian of young man, in Louvre, 193 ; a lady's portrait with sword-thrust through it, **2**, 188 ; one's own, apt to be a surprise to him, 190 ; artist's method of securing, 191 ; resemblances in, to various relatives, 192 ; that of Leah the witch, 262 ; of ancestors seen in a vision, in

The Guardian Angel, **6**, 91-95 ; of Judith Pride, 182, 183 ; by Reynolds, **10**, 54, 85, 151.
Portsmouth, how not to pronounce, **1**, 288 ; Rockingham House in, **5**, 15.
" Portuguese Sonnets," **2**, 223.
Posey, Susan, in *The Guardian Angel*, **6**, 3, 51 ; her letter to Clement Lindsay, 96 ; Master Gridley warns her not to receive alone the ministrations of the Rev. Mr. Stoker, 145 *et seq. ;* visits his study with Mrs. Hopkins, 152 ; receives Clement Lindsay, 227 *et seq. ;* dusts Master Gridley's books, 369 ; he comforts her in regard to her lost love for Clement Lindsay, 373 ; Lindsay gives her her freedom, 374 ; she and Gifted Hopkins tell their love, 386.
Position. *See* Social position.
Possession, demoniacal, **5**, 396 ; **8**, 357.
Possumus quia posse videmur, **8**, 381.
Post-prandial poems and speeches compared to pulling up flowers by the roots, **1**, 222.
Potato : small ones always get to the bottom, **1**, 291 ; excitement of digging, **8**, 169 ; eye of, 210 ; potato ball, **9**, 275 ; in England, **10**, 201.
Pott, Percival, **9**, 413.
Potter, the ventriloquist, **4**, 77.
Potter, Paulus, **2**, 29.
Poultry Cross, Salisbury, England, **10**, 122.
Poussin, **10**, 170.
Powwows, Indian, **6**, 89.
Powders, sympathetic. *See* Sympathetic powders.
Power, creative, demands freedom from disturbance, **3**, 100 ; feared only when it cannot be mastered, 271.
Powers, active, decay of, welcomed by some, **4**, 39.
Practical men, mistake of, **9**, 176.
Praise, writers given to, as they mature, **1**, 81.
Prayer, folly of, in a shipwreck, **1**, 88 ; for the dying, **2**, 303 ; remarkable gift at, owes much force to a strong animal nature, **6**, 121 ; no doctrine of, an excuse for not using all natural means, **9**, 364.
Preacher, a dull, from hearing no sermons might lapse into heathenism, **1**, 29 ; has his hearer's head in chancery, 413. *See also* Clergymen ; Ministers ; Priests ; Pulpit.
Preble, Fort, twenty buccaneers lodged in, by Portland men, **8**, 110.
Precedents : when old ones fail, we must make new, **8**, 115.
Preface, difference between first and second, **2**, viii. ; three great ones, **9**, 310.
Prejudices, their value, **3**, 6 ; intellectual irritation produced by rubbing against other people's, 6.
Prelude, **1**, 296.

Pre-natal influence, **5**, x.

Prentiss, Dame, **1**, 200; **8**, 239.

Preparation-jar, doctor's, the true monumentum ære perennius, **5**, 215.

Prescriptions, medical, not always founded on experience, **9**, 175; as heirlooms, 335, 336; familiar Latin of, 394.

President of the United States, **2**, 115; supposed case of one who is not a gentleman, 141; every American-born husband is a possible, **5**, 172.

President's Old Arm-Chair. See *Parson Turell's Legacy.*

Press, the great gland of the civilized organism, **4**, 148; impossibility of keeping up with the, 151.

Presumptions, half our work in life is to overcome, **4**, 284; of vast importance in medicine and law, **9**, 202.

Previous state of existence, **1**, 73, 74.

Pride, Judith, a beautiful ancestor of Myrtle Hazard, in *The Guardian Angel*, **6**, 15; marries "King David" Withers, 25, 93; portrait of, 182, 183; her bracelet, 186, 218, 241, 261, 277, 312, 315.

Pride, false, in a woman, **1**, 271; spiritual, warning against, **3**, 336.

Priesthood, its teaching through ignorant centuries, **4**, 40.

Priestley, Dr., **4**, 155; **10**, 27, 29, 55, 73, 171, 199.

Priests, notions of human destiny derived from, **5**, 325; ministers and, **3**, 125; **8**, 402; dead for the Protestant world, 402; Dr. Arnold's definition of a, 403; power of a, in sorrow, suffering, and death, 403. *See also* Clergymen; Ministers.

Primroses, **10**, 18, 124, 191.

Prince, Rev. John, opposed to comets, **8**, 357; early student of science, 409; attacked Prof. Winthrop on the subject of earthquakes, **9**, 355.

Prince, Thomas, **3**, 121.

Prince-Rupert's drops, certain literary celebrities compared to, **1**, 38.

Princes, making persons feel at ease a special accomplishment of, **10**, 35. *See also* Albert Edward; Albert Victor; Christian.

"Princess, The," Tennyson's, quoted, **8**, 292.

Princesses. *See* Christian; Louise; Wales.

Princeton College, Scotch theological thistle always flourished at, **8**, 394.

Principle, maintained against obvious facts, **1**, 56; dying for, higher than scolding for, **2**, 121.

Prior, Matthew, breathed more quickly than Spenser, **8**, 319.

Prisoners, companionship found by, in a flower or an insect, **6**, 75; Confederate, **8**, 36, 37, 58–61; unfair to make speeches to, 59. *See also* Criminal.

Prisons, defects of, **8**, 345; reform of, 353–357. *See also* Crime; Criminal.

Private journal, extracts from the Autocrat's, **1**, 246.

Private property in thought, **3**, 303.

Private theatricals, **1**, 43.

Privileged class of gentlemen and ladies, inevitable, **2**, 134.

Prize-fighters with iron pots on their heads, knights called, **2**, 135.

Probabilities provided with buffers, **1**, 56.

Prodigal son, sermon on, **2**, 117; consolation of the parable, 302.

Professions, Coleridge advised literary men to have one, **1**, 179; **8**, 231; digging a moat round their corporations, **2**, 11; knowledge cannot be limited by, 14; the learned, 105; a master of one, must have learning, **9**, 400.

Professor, The, at the Breakfast-Table, some verses by, **1**, 26; on hiring an earthquake, 72; gets abused, 81; letters from autograph hunters, 90; his detection of youth who broke his night lamp, 108; returns home from a gathering of "the boys," 120; irritable at being called an old man, 148 *et seq.*; his paper on old age, 150–174; describes his boating, 163 *et seq.*; his fleet, 164; his boat, 168; the Autocrat's relations with the Professor and Poet, 178 *et seq.*; his poem *The Two Armies*, 225; his house, 241–243; his poem *The Deacon's Masterpiece*, 252; under chloroform, 295 *et seq.*; other mention of, 194, 195, 196; appears as character in *Over the Teacups*, **4**, 24; talks about music, 98; Delilah cuts his hair, 201; his personality, 306 *et seq.*

Professor, The, in *Elsie Venner*, his uneasiness in regard to wording certificate for Bernard Langdon, **5**, 16 *et seq.*; his letter to Langdon in regard to curious cases of moral perversion, etc., 221–228; his advice to Langdon to strike for best circle of practice, 482, 483.

Professor's Story, The, original name of *Elsie Venner*, **5**, vii.

Professors, tend towards conservatism, **2**, 14; a good thing to get rid of old, **9**, 423; chair of, an insulating stool, 426; of medicine in Paris, 427–437.

Profligate, a, made virtuous by a fall, **8**, 332.

Prologue to private theatricals, **1**, 45.

Pronunciation, peculiar, in New York, **2**, 142.

Proof-sheets, caution about, **1**, 49.

Prophecy, the best sort of, **8**, 13; of New England ministers, 407, 408; of M. Babinet on the destruction of the earth, 425, 426.

Prophet of evil, dreadful business of being, **2**, 252.

Proposal, woman's premonition of coming, **6**, 323.

Proprieties of life, as observed by Anglo-Saxons in the XIXth century, **8**, 67.

Proselytes, cause of reproaches, **8**, 419.

Protein, Mulder's doctrine concerning, **9**, 237.

Protest of the Province of Massachusetts, **8**, 85.

Protestantism, no rest for it until it gives up its legendary anthropology, **2**, x.; the having no woman to be worshipped makes it unpoetical, 178; the business of dying not so well understood in, as by Roman Catholics, **4**, 250; America owes its political freedom to, **5**, 253; largely a matter of race, 317; its false shame in regard to spiritual needs of the sick, 450; its failure to provide for those who worry about their souls, **6**, 29; the confessional not unknown in, 160; it means "none of your business," 404; the priest is dead for, **8**, 402; a long process to republicanize, 404; many compartments in the fold of, 419; vital division of, 430, 431. *See also* Religion; Roman Catholic Church.

Prout, Dr., **9**, 215.

Proverbs, remembered by their jingle, **9**, 287.

Providence, Rhode Island, high tide at, in 1815, **8**, 164.

Provincialism, city, **4**, 277; deprovincializing effect of war on, **8**, 10; Continental, as bad as that of Coos county, 11.

Provisional races, aborigines called, **2**, 82.

Psalmody, depressing, **6**, 80; of Scotland, **10**, 86.

Pseudo-science, definition of, **2**, 197; not wholly a lie, 198.

Psora, **9**, 45, 49, 57, 82, 391.

Psychology, investigations in, **4**, 16; moral, **8**, 359. *See also* Philosophy; Physiological psychology.

Psylli, **5**, 225.

Public, addressed as if it were an author's private correspondent, **7**, 12; ignorance and prejudices of, **9**, 416, 417.

Public Garden, Boston, **1**, 273.

Public opinion, the Autocrat's receipt for regulating, **1**, 115.

Publicity often gives a thought mediocrity, **3**, 344.

Publisher, Gifted Hopkins's visit to, in *The Guardian Angel*, **6**, 298 *et seq.*

Pudding-stone, **2**, 256.

Puerperal fever. *See* Fever, puerperal.

Puffing, anonymous, **2**, 75.

Pugilistic encounter, **2**, 279.

Pugilists are "stale" soon after thirty, **1**, 156.

Pugin, **10**, 122.

Pulpit, spiritualism as a Nemesis of the, **2**, 13; and pews, relation of, **4**, 248; **8**, 402–433. *See also* Clergymen; Ministers; Preacher.

Pulse, distinguished by its rhythmical character, **8**, 315; possible influence of, on accent, 319; coincidence between, and number of steps in a minute, 320.

"Punch," **10**, 42, 201.

Punch, whiskey, **2**, 132.

Pundit, his awe of word O'm, **2**, 7.

Punishment, scale of, in law, **8**, 324; Despine argues against capital, 345; too severe, less likely to be inflicted than moderate, 345, 346; secondary, 355, 366.

Punishment, future, **4**, 245 *et seq.*; **8**, 414.

Puns, **1**, 11; Macaulay quoted on, 13; a kind of wit, 50; an indignity to the understanding, 251; specimens of, 251, 252; cant or slang worse than, 256.

Pupil of the eye, simile of the mind of the bigot to the, **1**, 144.

Purgatory, doctrine of, among New England Protestants, **4**, 244.

Puritan exclusiveness, **4**, 194.

Puritans, we have a right to be proud of the clergy of, **8**, 404, 405.

Purpose, need of a strong, **8**, 115.

Put not your trust in money, but put your money in trust, **1**, 49.

"Putnam's Magazine," **7**, 10.

"Putney," the hymn, **6**, 81.

Pyramids, preferable to railroad village, **2**, 246; model of, furnished by Nature, **4**, 101; common motive in builders of, **8**, 84; of Darshour, **9**, 230; decussation of, **9**, 243.

Pythoness, in Lowell Street, **9**, 367.

Pyx, a quartz, **4**, 164, 165.

Quack medicines, demand for, **9**, 186. *See also* Patent medicines.

Quackery, dropped in real danger, **8**, 232; danger in employing, 237; the vulgar ones become atrophied, **9**, 301; the Pilgrims' way of dealing with, 328; all but immortal, 367; of our own time, 368.

Quadrupeds, learned, **8**, 91. *See also* Animals.

Quaker element in Philadelphia, the, **8**, 70.

Quality, the definition of, **2**, 133; quality-ladies preferred, 136.

Quantity, false, the use of a, a fatal misstep for public men, **1**, 110.

Quaritch, Bernard, his collection of rare books, **4**, 115; visit of author to his shop, **10**, 146–149; extracts from his catalogues, 148, 149.

Queen of Sheba, **3**, 322.

Queens of England. *See* Anne; Bloody Mary; Victoria.

Queenstown, **10**, 18.

Querulousness in disease, **8**, 28.

Questions, submitted to the Professor, **2**, 203; tendency of aged or disordered persons to repeat, **8**, 296; old, incidentally settled in the course of new investigations, **9**, 242.

Quetelet, meteorological tables of, **8**, 134, 184.

"Qui a bu, boira," **8**, 340 ; **9**, 424.

Quincy, Josiah, 1772–1864, **4**, 27.

Quincy Market, **2**, 196.

Quinnepeg Pond, in *Elsie Venner*, **5**, 47.

Quintain, riding at the, **2**, 120.

Rabelais, **10**, 128.

Rabelais Club, **10**, 59, 198.

Rabies humana, a Parisian distemper, **10**, 172, 173.

Race of life, **1**, 95 *et seq.*

Races, higher, sympathies go with, **1**, 66 ; recognized inequality of, the corner-stone of the Southern dispensation, **8**, 87.

Rachel, ophidian head of, **5**, 225 ; Fechter's estimate of, **7**, 243 ; her magnetism, 244.

Racing, not republican, **1**, 34 ; records of, 36. *See also* Derby ; Horses.

Rack, **2**, 207. *See also* Torture.

Radcliffe, Dr., **9**, 386.

Radnor, Earl of, **10**, 121.

Railroad, intoxication of travel on, **8**, 18 ; magnetizing effect of travel on, 19 ; cars, gambling on, 52 ; cars lighted by candles, 52 ; danger from women who will open windows, 214 ; inspector at station trying the wheels and irons, 260, 261. *See also* Telegraph ; Travel.

Railroad village, attractiveness of, **2**, 246.

Ramsbotham, Dr., **9**, 111, 132, 138, 164, 166.

Ranke, Leopold von, **4**, 27.

Raphael, author, as a child, believed him to be superhuman, **1**, 204 ; early death of, **2**, 157 ; his "Santa Apollina," 178 ; paintings of, mentioned, **7**, 19, 48 ; disinterment of, **10**, 96.

Rarey, M. Despine borrows a lesson from, **8**, 346 ; his method with intractable horses, **9**, 389.

Raspail's proof-sheets, **1**, 25.

"Rasselas," less interesting to the young than "Vicar of Wakefield," **6**, 77 ; recommended to medical students of a philosophical turn of mind, **7**, 168 *et seq.*

Rat, impulse to kill, **5**, 168.

Rathbone, Fred, dealer in Wedgwood ware, **4**, 13, 17 ; **10**, 18, 21.

Rats, Les, des Salons à lecture, **1**, 58.

Rattlesnake ledge, in *Elsie Venner*, **5**, 43 *et seq.*, 141 ; Langdon's visit to, 188-191 ; buried in mountain-slide, 464.

Rattlesnakes, **5**, 43 *et seq.* ; number of rattles indicate age of victims killed, 44 ; Bernard Langdon, in *Elsie Venner*, charmed by one, 190, 191 ; Langdon procures some to study, 207 *et seq.* ; their significance in Nature, 208 ; preserved specimen, 215 ; all animals are panic-struck at sight of, 223 ; influence of their poison over moral faculties, 225 ; their connection with the mystery of Elsie's life, 434, 435 ; not ill-meaning citizens of the universe, **8**, 336.

Razor, the Plantagenet, **10**, 16 ; the Star, 16, 17, 202.

Read, T. Buchanan, uses image of the two streams, **8**, 46.

Reader, the Autocrat would have one to read for him continually, **1**, 63.

Reader, manuscript. *See* Butcher, the.

Readers, every writer of individuality may expect to have one, **3**, 36, 37 ; those who have no libraries of their own, 209 ; new generation of, **10**, 38.

Reading, slackens strength of feeling, **1**, 133 ; for the sake of talking, 134 ; difference between a man's and woman's, 275 ; courses of, **4**, 149 ; Dr. Johnson quoted on, **8**, 270 ; peculiar pleasure of reading in a foreign language, 350. *See also* Books.

Ready-made clothing, a poem compared to, **1**, 67.

Realism, its contributions to literature, **4**, 105 ; to art, 107 ; accusations to be brought against, 109.

Rebel prisoners. *See* Prisoners, Confederate.

Rebellion, War of the. *See* American Civil war.

Receptions, attended in London, **10**, 28, 29, 37, 43 ; official, 43, 44 ; crowds at, 44, 45 ; reception given by author and family in London, 54.

Recognition, grades of, illustrated by supposed meeting of thermometers and barometers, **10**, 142, 143.

Recollections, small store of, essential to identity hereafter, **1**, 209.

Record Office, English, **10**, 56.

Red pond-lily, **8**, 153.

Red republic of letters, **3**, 10.

Red sorrel, **3**, 22.

Rees's Cyclopædia, **9**, 402, 403.

Reflex action of the brain. *See* Unconscious mental action.

Reflex headache, **4**, 129.

Reflex vision, **9**, 248.

Reform club of London, **10**, 198.

Reform schools, **3**, 345.

Reformers, their danger is from the flattery of abuse, **2**, 202 ; bitterness towards, **8**, 90 ; office of, 90.

Regent's Park, London, **10**, 140, 141.

Regicides, John Dixwell, one of the, **10**, 53.

Register of deeds, in *The Poet*, his daily life, **3**, 60 ; his investigations, 168 ; discussion as to whether he is a superfluous person, 170 ; his interest in The Lady, 289 ; the intimacy explained, 289 *et seq.*

Registrar-General, of England, **9**, 104, 111, 169.

Regulus, returning to Carthage, **2**, 122.

Reid, Dr., on moral imbeciles, **8**, 337.

Relatives, opinions of, as to a man's powers, are of little value, **1**, 54 ; apt to hate each other, **5**, 151.

Relics of battlefields repulsive, **8**, 42.

Religion, one's breeding shows itself in his, **1**, 312 ; its currency consists of polarized words, **2**, 6 ; should belong to the common people, 107 ; science not an enemy of, 113 ; women more religious than men, 124, 209 ; time for it to be Americanized, 207 ; genius for, **3**, 128 ; not an intellectual luxury, 190 ; need of, 193 *et seq. ;* does not rid a man of his natural qualities, 304 ; springs from sentiments, **8**, 91 ; what we want in, 401. *See also* Creed ; Clergymen ; Ministers ; Priests ; Protestantism ; Roman Catholic church ; Sermons ; Soul ; Spiritualism ; Theology ; Will.

Religious attitude of old age, **4**, 45.

Religious character, emotional paroxysms often the basis of, **6**, 184.

Religious discussions, worth and dangers of, **3**, 187 *et seq.*

Religious excitement, American climate predisposes to, **6**, 155.

Religious opinions, difficulty of holding one's own, **2**, 92 ; each man has some peculiar to himself, 297.

Religious professions, of criminals of small account, **8**, 340.

Religious spirit, 2, 212.

" **Remarkable judgments,"** quoted from Cotton Mather, **2**, 115.

Rembrandt, 2, 29.

Remedies, uncertain effect of, **6**, 130 ; more eagerly sought than causes of disease, **9**, 195 ; those employed by Gov. Winthrop, 330–335 ; by Dr. Oliver, 336, 337 ; manuscript list of, 339 ; perturbing, 339 ; four great, 348 ; none which have been proved to be useful rejected by doctors, 391. *See also* Disease ; Doctors ; Drugs ; Medicine ; Medicines.

Reminiscences : display of minus quantities in those of old people, **4**, 33.

" **Remorse,"** Coleridge's, quoted, **8**, 355.

Repeating one's self, **1**, 7, 8.

Repetition, liability of, in writing, **4**, 8 ; propriety of, 9 ; self-repetition of startling news in the mind, **8**, 4.

Reply, not equivalent to an answer, **9**, 81.

Reporters, how they make up their reports, **3**, 3. *See also* Newspapers.

Repose, idea of, inseparable from death, **2**, 276 ; necessary to production of beauty, **5**, 124.

Republic of letters, Red, **3**, 10.

Republicanism, does not alter the laws of physiology, **3**, 276 ; levels in religion, **8**, 411.

Republicans, the only true ones in the solar system are the inhabitants of Saturn, **4**, 62.

Reputation, conventional literary, **1**, 38 ;

living on reputation of reputation one might have made, 61 ; poetical, desire for, **4**, 74 ; old, prized in the country, **5**, 165.

Resemblance and identity, distinction between, in homœopathy, **9**, 69.

Resistance, Sam. Adams's word, **2**, 41.

Respectability, the hat the *ultimum moriens* of, **1**, 178.

Respiration, work done in, **7**, 261 ; effect of exercise on, **8**, 229 ; only partly under control, 261, 329 ; distinguished by rhythmical character, 315 ; natural rate of, 316.

Responses in High Church service, **3**, 128.

Responsibility, for imperfect volition, in *Elsie Venner*, **5**, ix., x., xii. ; moral, limits of, 225, 226 ; of the deformed, physically and mentally, 247, 248 ; undue sense of, **6**, 78 *et seq.*, 409 ; transmissible, moral chaos began with the idea of, 303–306 ; transferable, accepted by theology, 325 ; tendency to limit the range of moral, 328. *See also* Automatism ; Crime ; Heredity ; Sin ; Unconscious mental action ; Will.

Responsum Raphaelis, 9, 354.

Rest. *See* Repose.

Retiarius, 5, 332.

Retina, the, and its brain, **9**, 247.

" **Retiring,"** at night, etiquette of, **1**, 208 ; **5**, 339.

Revere, Dr., **8**, 27.

Revere, Paul, **8**, 10.

Reverence, spirit of, should be cultivated in young people, **3**, 195 ; should begin with self-respect, 270 ; unanalyzing instinct of, **9**, 181.

Reverie, state of, creative genius allied to, **1**, 191 ; encouraged by tobacco, **8**, 226.

Reversed current in flow of mind, **2**, 147.

" **Review of Reviews," 4**, 151.

Revival of humanity, 3, 305.

Revivals of religion, under Edwards, **8**, 389, 390.

Revolution, American. *See* American Revolution.

Revolutions are not made by men in spectacles, **9**, 378.

Revolving supernumeraries, in a stage show, people like, **8**, 73.

Rewards of authorship, 3, 160.

Reynolds, Sir Joshua, **2**, 29 ; **10**, 47 ; his " Mrs. Siddons as Tragic Muse," 54 ; picture of lady by, 85 ; portraits by, 151.

Rheumatism, wrapping in a wolf-skin for, **9**, 280 ; carrying horse-chestnut for, 369, 381, 382.

Rhode Island, trees in, **1**, 233 ; greenings, **8**, 163, 164.

Rhymes, 1, 18 ; habit of chewing on, 292 ; paucity of the language in, **3**, 72, 73 ; **4**, 80 ; as a narcotic, **3**, 99 ; and clever writing, capacity for, often mistaken for extraordinary endowment, 155; are iron fetters, **4**, 79; rhyming as an amusement for feeble-minded children, 80; not the private property of a few noted writers, 84; cool off a man's passion, 280; burdens and restrictions of, 313; Gifted Hopkins's, **6**, 200; a common form of mental weakness, **7**, 292 *et seq.* *See also* Poems; Poetry; Rhythm; Verses.

Rhythm, is a tether, **4**, 79; of respiration and pulse, **8**, 315, 316; relation of that of verse to respiration, 316; of disease, **9**, 273. *See also* Poems; Poetry; Verses.

Ribera, Joseph, **4**, 107.

Ribot, Dr., on moral imbeciles, **8**, 358.

Rich people, more apt to be agreeable than others, **2**, 133; their refinement and delicacy, 135; frailties of, **3**, 296; sons of, **8**, 148; restlessness of, 231, 232. *See also* Society; Wealth.

Richard III., **9**, 389; **10**, 120.

Richardson, G. W., **2**, 49.

Richardson, H. H., the architect, **10**, 194.

Riche, Sir Nathaniel, **9**, 341.

Richerand, **9**, 436.

Riches. *See* Wealth.

Ricord, the Voltaire of pelvic literature, **9**, 255, 437.

Ridiculous, sense of the, dangerous for literary man to indulge in, **1**, 90.

Riding, expense of, **1**, 166; gives the pleasure of governing another's will, 167; graceful, **5**, 149, 181, 182; makes men imperious, 150. *See also* Horses.

Riedesel, Baroness, Hessian prisoner in Revolution, **10**, 105.

Riffelberg, Mark Twain's ascent of, **10**, 103.

Rigby, Dr., on puerperal fever, **9**, 159, 162, 164–166.

Right and wrong, standards of, not uniformly applicable, **5**, 246; eternal struggle between, **8**, 14.

Right-handedness, cause of, **8**, 268.

Right of reëntry released, case of, **3**, 293.

Ring, once property of a Salem witch, **2**, 9; one found by Thaddeus M. Harris, D. D., **3**, 15; ring of Thothmes III., 111.

Riolanus, **9**, 95.

Rip Van Winkle, **6**, 275.

Ritchie, Mrs. Anne (Thackeray), **10**, 40.

River, like a soul, **6**, 74; its solace to Myrtle, in *The Guardian Angel*, 75; what it says to its human companions, **7**, 99; its egotism, 251.

River of Life, dreamed of by the dying, **2**, 277.

Rivers, Lord, **9**, 23.

"Roba di Roma," Story's, **7**, 65.

Robert, of the multitudinous buttons, **10**, 73, 135.

Roberton, Dr., on puerperal fever, **9**, 124, 132, 138, 139, 158.

"Robinson Crusoe," **6**, 76.

Robinson, Dr., of Andover, **3**, 332; **8**, 257.

Robinson of Leyden, **2**, 174.

Roby, Joseph, **1**, 245 n.

Rockingham House, Portsmouth, New Hampshire, **5**, 14.

Rockland, the scene of *Elsie Venner*, **5**, 41, 55.

Rockland Fusileers, in *Elsie Venner*, **5**, 287.

"Rockland Weekly Universe," newspaper, in *Elsie Venner*, **5**, 158, 165, 220, 363.

Rockport, Massachusetts, horse-chestnut at, **1**, 289 n.

Rodgers, Professor William B., **9**, 248.

Rogers, Samuel, **3**, 330; **4**, 157, 264, 270.

Rolfe, Benjamin, shot by Indians, **8**, 252.

Roman baths, at Bath, **10**, 106.

Roman Catholic chapel, in *Elsie Venner*, **5**, 64, 150.

Roman Catholic Church, its adherents looked upon by Protestants as spiritual larvæ, **2**, 242; its consolations, 291; its members understand how to die better than Protestants, **4**, 250; **8**, 403; its membership largely a matter of race, **5**, 307; Brownson's faith in, 324; **8**, 420; Dr. Kittredge's opinion of, in *Elsie Venner*, **5**, 406, 407; its doctrine of invincible ignorance, 456; recognizes the class whose engrossing thought is their own welfare, **6**, 29. *See also* Protestantism; Religion.

Romance, materials for, in boarding house, **2**, 94.

Rome, age of enlistment in ancient, **1**, 151; the world's mistress in her stone girdle, 280; battle of three-hilled city against seven-hilled city, **2**, 78; active mind of century tending either to Rome or Reason, 123; age of, 245; evacuation of, by the French in 1876, **8**, 406.

Romulus, **2**, 82; and Remus may have imbibed wolfish traits, **5**, ix.

Room, difficulty of leaving a, **1**, 17.

Roosts, the world has a million for a man, but only one nest, **1**, 142.

Roscoe, William, Irving's emotion on seeing, **10**, 52.

Rose, The, and the Fern, **4**, 118.

Rose water, homœopathically used, **9**, 66.

Rosebery, Lady, reception by, at Foreign Office, **10**, 43–47.

Rosebery, Lord, **10**, 29, 34.

Roses, **1**, 227, 229; **8**, 146, 148, 149, 150, 153; antipathy for, **5**, 443.

Rossetti, Miss, alludes to caterpillars in her poems, **8**, 153.

Rothschild, Lady, **10**, 37, 46.

Roubiliac, his monument to Mrs. Nightingale, **4**, 171 ; **10**, 62, 120 ; busts by, 77.
Rouget de l'Isle, **4**, 86.
Rousseau, J. B., **10**, 166.
Rousseau, Jean Jacques, effect of the past upon, **2**, 246.
Rowens, Major Beeri, deceased husband of the Widow Rowens, in *Elsie Venner*, **5**, 286.
Rowens, Widow, in *Elsie Venner*, her tea party, **5**, 286-328 ; her charms as a widow, 288, 289 ; feels that she could be induced to be Mrs. Dudley Venner, 289 *et seq.* ; her library, 296, 297 ; becomes Mrs. Pickins, 484.
Rowing. *See* Boating.
Roxbury pudding-stone, **2**, 256.
Royal Academy exhibition, **10**, 151.
Royal College of Physicians, London, **9**, 20.
Royal College of Surgeons, **10**, 67.
"Royal George," Cowper's, **1**, 281.
Royal touch, **9**, 3, 354, 413.
Royce, Professor, **4**, 16.
Roze, Marie, in "Carmen," **10**, 73.
Rubens, **10**, 170.
Rubila, a secret remedy, **9**, 335.
Rubinstein, **10**, 55.
Rudolph, the headsman, **1**, 46.
Rue, antipathy for, **5**, 443.
Ruffian, stage, at boarding-house table, in *The Autocrat*, **1**, 53.
Rukers, Thomas, maker of steel-chair, **10**, 128.
Rule, Scotch gardener, **8**, 148.
Rum, offensive misuse of the word, **1**, 190 ; old Medford, **7**, 275, 276 ; smell of, in haying time, **8**, 154.
Rumford, Count, his "Of the Pleasure of Eating," **8**, 363.
Rummel, writer on homœopathy, **9**, 76.
Rumrill, Deacon, in *The Guardian Angel*, **6**, 147, 149 ; entertains Clement Lindsay as a boarder, 225 *et seq.* ; returns "Ivanhoe" as a sinful work, 376.
"Run down," different meanings of the phrase, **7**, 82.
Rush, Dr. Benjamin, **7**, 172 ; **9**, 180, 181, 192, 292, 384.
Ruskin, his aversion to a country without castles, **3**, 11 ; **10**, 131 ; too ill to receive author, **10**, 90, 185 ; St. Ruskin read with reverence, 127.
Russell, incendiary, **8**, 351.
Russell, Mr., American consul at Liverpool, **10**, 18, 180.
Russell, Henry Sturgis, **2**, 166.
Russia leather, smell of, in nice books, **1**, 23.
Russian ambassador, author occupies his seat in House of Commons, **10**, 65.
Rustic fence, best thing between Philadelphia and New York, **8**, 72, 73.
Ruth, **6**, 123.
Rutter, Dr., on puerperal fever, **9**, 123, 124, 143.
Ruysch, Dr., **9**, 227.

Sabbath, Puritan, **1**, 212 ; word misused for Sunday, **2**, 312.
Sabbath-day pressure, **6**, 20.
Sabbath face, mournful suggestions of, **2**, 215.
Sacrifice that may be demanded by the Civil war, **8**, 14.
Saddle, the true seat of empire, **5**, 150.
Saddle-leather, preferable to sole leather, **1**, 166.
Saddle-leather skin, **5**, 286.
Saint Anniversary, the patron saint of America, **8**, 361.
Saint Anthony the reformer, **2**, 202.
Saint Botolph's daughter, **8**, 75.
Saint Étienne du Mont, church of, in Paris, **1**, 280 ; **10**, 164.
Saint-Hilaire, G.: his "Teratology," **8**, 358.
Saint Martin, Alexis, with an accidental side-door to his stomach, **8**, 218.
Saint-Martins-in-the-Fields, **10**, 194.
Saint Paul's Cathedral, epitaph of Wren in, **9**, 396 ; effect of dome of, **10**, 150.
Saint Petroleum, gospel of, **3**, 40.
Saint Valentine's day, **8**, 135.
Sainte-Beuve thinks science has destroyed faith, **8**, 401.
Sainte-Foix, **10**, 166.
Saints, three among women to one among men, **2**, 121 ; the greatest, may be a sinner that never got down to hard pan, **6**, 355.
"Saints and their Bodies," paper by T. W. Higginson, referred to, **1**, 163.
Sal volatile, its uses, **6**, 344.
Salaam of East-Indian children, **10**, 57.
Salamanders, human beings are all, **8**, 199.
Salem, mean annual temperature, **8**, 134 ; Village, **10**, 130 ; witchcraft, *see* Witchcraft.
Salesman, character in *The Poet*, **3**, 60 ; why he does not talk more, 204, 205.
Salic law, **6**, 369.
Salisbury, England, a week in, **10**, 108-132 ; Cathedral, 108, 109, 118, 119, 121, 129, 130-132 ; Close, 108, 109, 113, 121, 122 ; epitaph on native of, 110 ; spire, 117, 118, 131 ; monuments, 119, 120 ; formerly unhealthy, 122 ; memories of week in, 131, 132.
Salisbury Crags, **10**, 85.
Salisbury Plain, **10**, 111 ; larks of, 191.
Salmon, Dr., **9**, 414.
Salt fish, constant diet of, compared to fixity of opinions in some people, **2**, 93.
Sampson, Deborah, **6**, 76.
Samson, carving of, under pulpit, **10**, 164.
Samson's Ribs, part of Salisbury Crags, **10**, 85.
Sanborn, F. B., on prison reform, **8**, 353, 354, 356.
Sanchez, Father Thomas, **1**, 252.
Sanctorius, **9**, 413.
Sanctum, a doctor's, **5**, 215.

Sandys, Dr., **10**, 78.

Sanitary map of every State in the Union needed, **3**, 280.

Sanitary science, **9**, 352.

Santorini's laughing muscle, **1**, 194.

Sappho, **3**, 110.

Saqui, Madame, **4**, 42.

Saracens, Southerners the, of the 19th century, **8**, 106.

Sargent, John, **10**, 151.

Sarum, Old, England, **10**, 110, 111, 122, 123.

Satisfaction, in theology, **8**, 371.

Saturation-point of individual minds, **9**, 392.

Saturday Club of Boston, **1**, 2 n., 63; **7**, 10; **10**, 2, 62, 133.

Saturn, its appearance, **4**, 60; atmosphere, 61; metals, 62; great industrial product, 63; women, 63; government, 62, 63; no looking glasses there, 64; perfect equality there, 62, 65; its reformers, 64; life somewhat dull in, 65; dislocation of the lower jaw common in, 65; recreations in, 65.

Saturnians, **4**, 62–66.

Saul, **5**, 170.

Saunders, Cortland, **8**, 68, 69.

Saurin, **10**, 166.

Savage, Thomas, number of doctors in his "Genealogical Dictionary," **9**, 316, 317.

Savary, his "Letters on Egypt," **5**, 225.

Savate, French method of boxing, **2**, 53.

Saving one's bright thoughts, **1**, 27.

Savonarola, subject of poem at Oxford, **10**, 89.

Saxon race still trodden down by Normans, **10**, 66.

Saybrook platform, ministerial veto allowed by, **8**, 411.

Sayings, old, not to be trusted, **4**, 176.

Saymore, Mrs., in *Elsie Venner*, frees her mind as to the Sprowle family, **5**, 84.

Scale of measurement, among Americans and English, **10**, 143, 144.

Scandinavian of mysterious origin, **7**, 60–62.

Scarabee, in *The Poet*, **3**, 49; receives a visit from the Master and the Poet, 238 *et seq.*; absorption in his studies, 244; his resemblance to his beetles, 248; prefers spiders to men, 250; his gift to Scheherezade, 348.

"Scarlet Letter," Hawthorne's, **7**, 7; **8**, 18.

Scars, change little through life, **8**, 298.

Scenery, English, poetical association with, **10**, 49, 50.

Schehallion, **6**, 323.

Scheherezade, in *The Poet*, her personal appearance, **3**, 52; her stories, 53; her unfriendly critics, 83; she looks at the double-star, 140; her sympathy for the Young Astronomer, 141; the lessons in astronomy, 234 *et seq.*; her conspiracy

with That Boy discovered, 236; change in her manner, 297; effect of absence of mind upon her stories, 300; effects of the Young Astronomer's poem upon her, 313; abandons story-writing, 346.

Schenckius, **9**, 410.

Schliemann, **10**, 152.

Schneider, Mr., teacher in Apollinean Institute, in *Elsie Venner*, **5**, 166.

Schoenbein, **9**, 292.

Scholars, great men not commonly great, **1**, 132; scholar's coat of one, **6**, 113; first scholars, **7**, 174; one should not be in a hurry to part with his books, **9**, 408; library of one, 409.

Scholastic teaching, **9**, 273–311.

School-girl's letters, superlatives in, **8**, 361.

Schoolhouse, New England, **5**, 29, 30.

Schoolmistress, in *The Autocrat*, turns pale at a remark of Autocrat, **1**, 32; appears to blush, 107; her valuation of truth, 117; the Divinity Student reads over her shoulder, 135; Autocrat notices her paleness, 202; says "bedtime" and not "retiring," 208; kisses the keepsake of the Old Gentleman opposite, 211; praised by John the young fellow, 219; Autocrat's first walk with, 239; he writes pensively, 246–248; the Autocrat's last walk with, 270–277; she promises to walk the *Long path* with Autocrat, 277; sensation among boarders at her choice, 304; like Queen Esther, 308; her wedding-presents, 311; given away by the Old Gentleman, 313; referred to in *The Professor*, **2**, 309.

Schoolmistresses, **10**, 41, 42.

Schwann, his theory of cell-formation, **9**, 232.

Science, certainty of, has no spring in it, **1**, 56; grand airs of, 179; not the enemy of religion, **2**, 113; and common sense, **3**, 120; the disturbing facts of, 180 *et seq.*; change of feeling regarding these facts, 181; free discussion of, 182; humility of, 185; Dr. Johnson's estimate of scientific men, 263; and imaginative art, distinction between, **4**, 108, 110; is knowledge, **5**, 318; Nature loves men of, **6**, 209; attitude of modern, **8**, 310; the thought of God discovered by man, 331; men of, the natural antagonists of religious pessimists, 431; scepticism of, **9**, 181; the topography of ignorance, 211; the piece-meal revelation of the plan of creation, 251; as an aid to medicine, 274–277, 289, 290; medicine the most difficult, 384.

"Science mousseuse," **8**, 274.

Scientific men. *See* Science.

Scientific periodicals, value of, in inverse ratio to their age, **9**, 401.

Scientific wrappers, **3**, 123.

Scotland, **10**, 6, 7, 85, 86; psalmody of, 86. *See also* Edinburgh.

Scott, Thomas, his "Commentary," 6, 233, 235; portrait of, 376; his indebtedness to Matthew Henry, 8, 385.

Scott, Sir Walter, confused with Thomas, the commentator, 6, 225 *et seq.*, 233, 235, 247; his "Ivanhoe" regarded as a vicious work, 376; his "Antiquary," 10, 113.

Scottow, J., quoted, 9, 324.

Scraping floor with chair, effect of, 1, 50.

Scribblers, anonymous, 2, 118; feed on each other, 4, 24.

Scrofula, cure of, by royal touch, 9, 3, 354, 413.

Scudder's pond, 8, 153.

Sculpin, a nickname for the Little Gentleman, which see.
— the fish described, 2, 2.

Sculptor, ancient, 6, 253.

Scurvy, 9, 267; effect of, on the Pilgrims, 9, 323.

Sea, odors of, 6, 77; always busy with its own affairs, 8, 256; anxiety at, unavoidable, 10, 15.

Sea-anemones, 2, 145.

Seabury, Samuel, 9, 341.

Seafoam biscuit, 10, 201.

Séances, 10, 172.

Seaport towns of New England, 5, 13, 14.

Sears, J. Montgomery, 10, 179.

Sea-serpent, 8, 167, 168; horse mackerel taken for, 2, 257.

Seashore compared with mountains, 1, 263.

Seasons, The, 8, 132–185.

Seckel pear, cheek having the tinge of, 6, 25.

Second childhood, counterpoised by a first old age, 2, 66.

Second natural birth, 2, 243.

Second sight, 2, 250.

Second thought, 8, 289.

Secondary lives, 6, 94, 219.

Secretary, young lady, procured for author while in England, 10, 25.

Secrets, verse a proper medium for, 1, 60; any one's is open, if waited for long enough, 2, 90; intimation of a great, among many persons, 177; it is not the secret of love, 180.

Sectarianism, banished by war, 8, 11.

Sectional divisions, Washington warns against the danger of, 8, 85.

Sects, exchanges between, should happen often, 8, 419; bearing of, toward each other, 4, 196.

Seed, Southern, in Northern soil, 2, 242.

Seed-capsule of thought, 1, 200.

Selborne, England, 10, 104, 186.

Self - abasement, Oriental, 3, 270; 5, 247; 8, 309.

Self-assertion, ladies have little, 2, 136.

Self-consciousness, 1, 193.

Self-deception possible at threescore and ten, 4, 31; a system of, the disgrace of medicine, 9, 265.

Self-depreciation, 4, 112.

Self-determination. *See* Will.

Self-esteem, audacious, is imposing, 1, 10.

Self-forgetfulness, 6, 150.

Self-government, the natural condition of adult society, 8, 79; meaning of, 92.

Self-inspection, perpetual, leads to spiritual hypochondriasis, 8, 397.

Self-interest, 7, 272.

Self-love, 7, 138.

Self-made men, 1, 19; 9, 407.

Self-quackery, 9, 12.

Self-repetition. *See* Repetition.

Self-respect the basis of reverence and Occidental manhood, 3, 270.

Self-torture, 5, 170.

Self-trust, faith means, 2, x.

Self-unconsciousness of individuals and of families, 1, 55.

Self-valuation, 4, 112; 8, 233.

Selfishness, disguised, as a part of doctrine of depravity, 5, 258; children at first purely selfish, 321; care for one's own welfare hereafter, is a supreme form of, 6, 30.

Semilunar ganglion, 8, 27, 55.

Seminaries, called young-lady-factories, 2, 239.

Seminary clock, at Andover, 1, 287.

Senate-chamber of the United States, violence in, 8, 86.

Senile dementia, 5, 473; of civilization, 2, 11.

Sensation, time in transmission of, 8, 272–276.

Sense of superiority to our fellow-creatures, 3, 273.

Senses, education begins through the, 1, 117; condition of, in excitement or trouble, 8, 18, 19.

Sensibility, excess of, in poets, 1, 185.

Sentiment, for flowers, 1, 229; defended, 2, 124; Christianity full of, 302; Christ's life animated with, 313.

Sentimental journeys must be made alone, 8, 254.

Sentimentality better than affectation of superiority to human weakness, 3, 136.

Sentiments, as motives of action, 8, 91.

Separation, social, incompatibility of interests a sufficient warrant for, 7, 299.

September gale of 1815, 8, 163, 164.

Sermons, effect upon hearers, 1, 29; one projected by Autocrat, 8C, 174; hearers of, entitled to opinions on theology, 2, 111; a few famous, 117; one on the dangers of beauty, by Mr. Stoker, in *The Guardian Angel*, 6, 124; his famous sweating, fainting, and convulsion-fit ones, 158. *See also* Lay sermons.

Serpents. *See* Snakes.

Servants, one of the serviceable, red-handed, broad - and - high - shouldered type, **1**, 99 ; in former days, **7**, 249, 285, 286.

Servetus, name of, might call up unpleasant recollections, **8**, 417 ; came near anticipating Harvey, **9**, 179 ; damaged by fire, 366.

Serving-man, New England, **5**, 134–138.

Sets in fashionable girls' school, **6**, 268.

Seven-branched golden candlestick, **3**, 332.

Seven wise men of Boston, sayings of, **1**, 124.

Seventeenth of June, why memorable to author, **10**, 75.

Seventh son of a seventh son, **4**, 53, 205 ; **9**, 5.

Sewall, Mr., vice-consul at Liverpool, **10**, 18, 180.

Sewall, Samuel, **3**, 14.

Sex, shows itself in the moral perversions of hysteria, **8**, 339.

Sextons, cheerful people, **2**, 312.

Shabby gentility betrayed by the hat, **1**, 178.

Shadoof, **4**, 207.

Shaftesbury, Earl of, his description of Henry Hastings, **4**, 27 ; cured by Locke, **9**, 344.

Shakers, **4**, 68.

Shakespeare, a Folio copy of, with flakes of pie-crust between leaves, **1**, 79 ; reading of, by different minds, 133 ; on the effect of the moon on the insane, **8**, 212 ; "Hamlet" quoted on slang, 275 ; "Macbeth" quoted on the memory, 297 ; "Hamlet" quoted, **9**, 376 ; "Henry IV." quoted, 382 ; mentions cuckoo, **10**, 50 ; house at Stratford, 91, 130 ; Memorial buildings, 94 ; new epithets applied to, 95 ; why his remains are not disturbed, 95, 96 ; First folio, 149.

Shaving made easy by Star razor, **10**, 16, 17, 202.

Shawl, blanket, **1**, 19.

Shawshine River, **8**, 251, 258.

Shearer, Deacon, in *Elsie Venner*, **5**, 326, 474, 484.

Sheep-stealer's fate, **1**, 282–284.

Sheffield, Massachusetts, elm at, **1**, 235.

Sheldonian Theatre, Oxford, **10**, 88.

Shell, murmur of, **6**, 77.

Shell-fish, very minute eggs of, **2**, 257.

"Shell-oysters," **5**, 109.

Shelley, quoted, **2**, 239 ; **10**, 18.

Shelter, most rudimentary forms of, **8**, 180.

Shenstone, quoted, **3**, 328 ; his "Warmest welcome at an inn," **8**, 20; epigram of, **10**, 69.

Shepard, Thomas, feared for the future welfare of unborn babes, **8**, 304 n. ; teaching of, quoted, 308.

Shepherd of Salisbury Plain, **10**, 111.

Shimei, as critic of supposed lecture, **2**, 120.

Shimmenses of Boston, **10**, 73.

"Shipman" of Chaucer, **9**, 376.

Ships, Autocrat's fear of, **1**, 205 ; promise of one to him in boyhood, 207 ; one drawn by tug, compared to husband and wife, **2**, 289 ; of war, cost of, **8**, 8.

Shipwrecks, men are cowards in, **1**, 88.

Shirley, James, **3**, 110.

Shock, serious effects of sudden, **7**, 92.

Shoes, cost of, in war times, **8**, 60.

"Shoo-fly," some notes of, borrowed from Beethoven, **8**, 287.

Shop, displaying perennial articles for sale, **2**, 231.

Shop-windows, in London, **10**, 144, 145 ; in Paris, 175.

Shopping, **10**, 159.

Shortening weapons lengthens boundaries, **1**, 19.

Shovel, Sir Cloudesley, **4**, 296.

Shrewdness of men who live with horses, **8**, 63.

Shrine of female saint, **10**, 156.

Shriver, General, of Frederick, **8**, 25, 48.

Siamese twins, **3**, 223 ; **7**, 33.

Sibyl, young daughter of Lord Rosebery, her letter to Queen Victoria, **10**, 29.

Sick, the, are sensitive and fastidious, **9**, 386.

Sick rooms, conduct of the underbred in, **2**, 144.

Sickness. *See* Disease.

Sidney, Sir Philip, **10**, 124, 125 ; portrait of, 126.

Sierra Leone, life of native of, **1**, 302.

Sight, unusual remedy for failing of, **1**, 173.

Signatures, doctrine of, in medicine, **9**, 360.

Sigourney, Mrs., **1**, 8.

Silk dress, dried-leaf rustle of, **6**, 152.

Silliman, Professor, **4**, 16.

Silver, family, **5**, 198 ; nitrate of, for epilepsy, **2**, 105 ; **8**, 190 ; **9**, 188, 441.

"Silver threads among the gold," Italian version of, **4**, 123.

Similia similibus curantur, **9**, 42, 51.

Similitudes and analogies, infinite ocean of, **1**, 84.

Simonides, **3**, 110.

Simultaneous intellectual movement, **8**, 84.

Sin, has many tools, **1**, 125 ; first act of, 209 ; an old, dead, in secret drawer of soul, **2**, 91 ; a function, not an entity, **3**, 306, 307 ; congenital sinfulness, **5**, 248, 256 *et seq.;* Doctor Kittredge's view of, in *Elsie Venner*, 324 ; fruit of, is a harvest of crime, **8**, 86 ; in punishing crime we do not punish, 360 ; the subject of justice, 369. *See also* Automatism ; Guilt ; Heredity ; Imbeciles, moral ; Original sin ; Responsibility ; Will.

Sincerity, dangers of, **2**, 30.

Singers, immediate triumphs of, **3**, 113.

Singing, congregational, **2,** 215; imperfections of, 216; in the head, **5,** 240.

Singletary, Jonathan, witness in the witchcraft delusion, **3,** 326.

Sismondi, **4,** 253.

Sixth Massachusetts Regiment in Baltimore, **8,** 7, 13.

Sixth sense, in women, **2,** 266.

Skeleton, in the Harvard Medical School, **9,** 424.

Skin, human, nailed to church doors, **1,** 107; piece of, determines the perpetrator of mischief, 108; saddle-leather sort common in Englishmen, **5,** 286.

Skipping stones, **10,** 159.

Skull, fractured, cured by prayers and plasters, **9,** 358.

Skunk, pleasant reflections awakened by far-diffused effluvium of, **7,** 24, 25.

Skunk-cabbage, Miss Cooper quoted on, **8,** 139; President Hill quoted on, 141.

Slang, worse than punning, **1,** 256; the blank checks of intellectual bankruptcy, 256; sometimes useful, 257; a sign and cause of mental atrophy, **8,** 275.

Slavery, an organic disease of the nation, **8,** 83; most pernicious effect of, 85; the only cause of division of the country, 87; legitimate effect on the whites, 88; fanaticism of Southerners for, sincere, 105; the mother cause of lesser antagonisms, 117.

Sleep, blessedness of, in grief, **8,** 4, 5; proper amount of, 231; of criminals, 334.

Small-pox, patient suffering with, wrapped in scarlet, **8,** 210, 211; an amiable man rendered quarrelsome by, 332; inoculation for, 418; subject to irregularities and caprices in its transmission, **9,** 107; apparent insensibility to virus of, 118; contagion only one of the co-efficients of, 123; Farr's statement with reference to, 133; goes through same periods of increase and diminution as puerperal fever, 133; havoc caused by, among the Indians, 315; inoculation for, 345–347.

Smalley, G. W., renders valuable aid to the author in great crowd, **4,** 276; **10,** 45; at dinner at Mr. Lowell's, 66.

Smell. *See* Odors.

Smelt, **8,** 181.

Smibert, **2,** 262.

Smile, the terrible, peculiar to self-conscious persons, **1,** 193; those that make wrinkles and not dimples, **3,** 84; without reference to the real feeling, **3,** 44; official, **8,** 67; of a Boston doctor, worth five thousand dollars a year, **9,** 388.

Smith, Dr. Edward, on alcoholic drinks, **8,** 221, 223.

Smith, Mr. and Mrs. Goldwin, **10,** 132.

Smith, Isaac, poorhouse parson, **3,** 16.

"Smith, Captain John, Rescue of," a tableau, **6,** 278 *et seq.*

Smith, Nathan, **9,** 350, 374.

Smith, Samuel Francis, **2,** 50.

Smith, Samuel Stanhope, **3,** 166.

Smith, Soden, curator of the South Kensington Museum, **10,** 157.

Smith, Sydney, surgical operation proposed by, **1,** 48 n.; his sermon on Duties of loyalty, 91; his remark about a false quantity, 110; contrivance in his pasture, **3,** 6; anecdotes of, **10,** 54, 68.

Smith, William, the Yorkshire antiquary, **10,** 196.

Smith, William, LL. D., his "Dictionary of the Bible," **8,** 417, 418.

Smithfield fires, are all out, **5,** 326.

Smithite, Smith is always a, **2,** 297.

Smithson, James, **10,** 205.

Smoking, dangers of, **8,** 225, 226.

Smoky quartz color of running brook, **5,** 46; of a girl's eyes, 51.

Smollett, **7,** 177.

Smyth, Egbert C., **8,** 427.

Smythe, Miss Florence, in *The Guardian Angel*, **6,** 272.

Snakes, intimacies between human beings and, **5,** 207, 224; charmers of, 225. *See also* Ophidians; Rattlesnakes.

Snap in middle of head, **5,** 206.

Snap-weed, seed-capsule of, **8,** 90.

Snapping turtles, **1,** 195.

Sneaking fellows, to be treated with a certain tenderness, **1,** 219.

Snelling, W. J., his "Truth, a Gift for Scribblers," **7,** 5; his anecdote of Black Hawk, 6; his treatment of N. P. Willis, 6; his estimate of contemporary authors, 8.

Snelling, Dr. William, fined for cursing, **9,** 327, 328.

Snuff-taking, **1,** 77.

Snowstorms, date of earliest, **8** 170; old-fashioned, 175; averages of, 175–177.

Soap, perfumed, **2,** 98.

Social compacts, end of, **8,** 79.

Social distinctions, **3,** 57.

Social position, consciousness of, makes people gracious, **1,** 271; intensely real, permanent, and engrossing, **2,** 134; elective character of, 134; settled mostly by women, 134; division of scholars in school according to, **6,** 268. *See also* Society.

Société d'observation médicale, **1,** 2 n.

Sociétés polyphysiophilosophiques, **1,** 136.

Society, tries to grind lives to single flat surface, **2,** 33; high society contains much real equality, 140; heroism in, 140; its love for abundant vitality, 150; has place for every form of talent, 285; ideal state of, life dull in, **4,** 67; puts its maidens on trial in ball-room, **5,** 94; vocabulary of very fashionable, **8,** 274; the greatest need of, at present, 349; must protect itself against the criminally disposed, 359 ; conditions of, their influence on medicine, **9,** 177. *See also* Rich ; Social position ; Wealth.

Society for the propagation of intelligence among the comfortable classes, **2,** 56.

Society of Acclimatization, Paris, **10,** 176.

Society of Mutual Admiration, **1,** 2, 4.

Socrates drinking the hemlock, **2,** 122.

Soil, its effect on character, **3,** 21 ; of England, not worn out, **10,** 188.

Soldiers' graves, **1,** iv.

Solemnity at evening party, **5,** 108.

Solitary confinement, evils of, **8,** 345.

Solomon, **2,** 214 ; temple of, **3,** 332.

Solstice, summer and winter, **8,** 136.

Somnambulism, **8,** 280, 281.

Somnambulist boarder, **2,** 168.

Song for a temperance celebration, **2,** 33.

Songs which bring tears, **4,** 95, 97.

" Songs without Words," **6,** 208.

Soper, Deacon, in *Elsie Venner*, **5,** 92 ; expresses liberal views as to dancin', 95, 96 ; over-indulges in ice-cream, 115–117 ; his caution in regard to Richard Venner, 376, 415.

Sophy, faithful servant, in *Elsie Venner*, **5,** 146 ; her suspicion of Richard Venner, 201, 202 ; consults Rev. Dr. Honeywood about Elsie, 238–244 ; expresses her fears of Richard to Doctor Kittredge, 345–354; tells mystery of Elsie's birth, 434 ; dies on Elsie's grave, 464.

Sorrel, red, **3,** 22.

Sorrow, ornamental, of widowhood, **5,** 288.

Sortes Virgilianæ, **5,** 176.

" Sortie of Gibraltar," Trumbull's picture, **7,** 3.

Soul : souls grown white in holy duties, **1,** 202 ; crippled, 219 ; has a series of envelopes, 241 ; those of women long for atmosphere of affections, 305 ; must look for truth with own eyes, **2,** 6 ; its being of an infinite, instantaneous consciousness, 10 ; a little secret drawer in, 91 ; conception of how one appears, 131 ; thinks to know the body it inhabits, 190 ; disquiet in, 217 ; need of transplanting some souls, 243 ; according to Descartes, is in the core of the brain, 247 ; surrendering itself to spiritual dictatorship, **5,** 253 ; tuning of two souls to each other, 274 ; where is it during unconsciousness, 390–392 ; loving one's own, too well, 415, 416 ; those of young girls, **6,** 73 ; compared to river, 74 ; no age in, 177 ; a book, a child of the, 292 ; a great cause makes great souls, 475 ; man without a soul, *see* Browne, Simon.

Sounds, their suggestiveness, **1,** 211, 212 ; strange effects of, on some persons, **7,** 89.

South Downs, England, **10,** 133 ; its mutton, 133 ; its ancient church, 134.

South Kensington Museum, **10,** 156, 157.

South Mountain, battlefield of, **8,** 37.

Southerners. *See* Confederate states.

Southey, **9,** 409.

Scwbugs, as a medicine, **9,** 333, 361, 362.

Space and time, **1,** 266 ; **7,** 26.

Spagnoletto. *See* Ribera, Joseph.

Sparring. *See* Boxing.

Sparrow, English, **3,** 314.

Spartan boy and the fox, **9,** 388.

Spasmodic cerebral action not clearly an evil, **1,** 189.

Speakers, idiosyncrasies of, **4,** 297.

Specialists, conceit of, **1,** 9 ; are like coral insects, **3,** 78 ; their limitations, 79 ; their value, 82 ; medical, **4,** 125 *et seq.* ; **9,** 352 ; do not be bullied by, **4,** 148 ; they may be bores, 156 ; near-sighted, **8,** 268 ; prefer monthly or annual periodicals, **9,** 401 ; read early medical records, 412.

Specifics, result of the destruction of all, **9,** 184 ; Dr. Gould's hope of finding, for every disease, 443 ; benefits obtained from the proper use of a few, 202, 444.

Spectacles, **1,** 173 ; remarkable powers of reflection of, **6,** 56.

Speech, odious tricks of, must be got rid of, **1,** 110 ; seat in the brain of the faculty of, **8,** 270 ; freedom of, **9,** 206.

Speeches, little value of dying, **2,** 292, 293 ; Gladstone's speech on the Irish Land Bill, **10,** 63, 64 ; one demanded of author, at Cambridge, England, 76, 77 ; one at Edinburgh University, 84.

Spencer, Herbert, **8,** 85.

Spenser, Edmund, **6,** 203 ; breathed more slowly than Prior, **8,** 319.

Spermaceti, **9,** 332.

Spider, the Scarabee's favorite, **3,** 244.

Spigelius, giant folio of, **9,** 279, 411 ; copy of his " Anatomy " in Boston Athenæum, 342 ; made the liver his perpetual memorial, 412.

Spinal cord, **9,** 243 ; irritation of, 389.

Spinney, three Misses, in *Elsie Venner*, **5,** 92 ; elegant manner of eating frosted cake, displayed by the eldest, 108.

Spires, rocking of, **1,** 285 ; of Tewkesbury Abbey Church, **10,** 103, 118 ; of Salisbury Cathedral, 117 ; deflection of, 118 ; of Strasburg Cathedral, 117 ; of Chichester Cathedral, 118.

Spirits of hartshorn, its uses, **6,** 344.

Spiritual consolation, desire for, not to be ignored in the sick, **5,** 449.

Spiritual dictatorship, **5,** 253.

Spiritual doubts, **3,** 148.

Spiritual nature, an endowment like a musical ear, **8,** 394.

Spiritual pathology, **3,** 306.

Spiritual pride, warning against, **3,** 336.

Spiritual standard of different classes, **2,** 121.

Spiritual transparency of golden-blondes, **2**, 229.

Spiritualism, undermining accepted ideas, **2**, 12 ; as a Nemesis of the pulpit, 13 ; has made the destiny of the race a matter of common reflection, 107 ; as a reaction, **9**, 181.

Spiritus vini Gallici, **8**, 47.

Spit-balls, **5**, 25, 30.

Spoken language, plastic, **1**, 27.

Spontaneous generation, experiment in, **3**, 175 *et seq.*

Spores of ideas, **8**, 46.

Sporting man, the virtues of a, **1**, 37 ; deafness in right ear of, **10**, 58.

Sprague's " Annals," stories in, **8**, 409, 410.

Spring, **8**, 132-150 ; astronomical beginning of, 135 ; earliest flowers of, 139-143 ; advent of the birds in, 142, 143.

Spring has comé, **1**, 197.

Springfield, Massachusetts, large elms at, **1**, 235 ; **10**, 81 ; a city among villages, a village among cities, **8**, 76.

Sprowle, Colonel Hezekiah and Mrs., in *Elsie Venner*, give an evening party, **5**, 85-117 ; the morning after, 118 *et seq.;* Colonel shows anger at Silas Peckham's thrift, 132, 133 ; other mention of, 376, 377, 379.

Sprowle, H. Frederic, youngest son of Colonel Sprowle, **5**, 80, 89 ; performs interesting experiment with his ears, 97.

Sprowle, Miss Matilda, daughter of Colonel Sprowle, **5**, 83.

Sprowle, T. Jordan, eldest son of Colonel Sprowle, **5**, 85, 88, 298.

Spurzheim, **9**, 221, 245.

Squinting brain, **4**, 96, 99, 111, 114, 115, 162, 166, 204, 281, 282, 299 ; **6**, 205 ; **8**, 175.

Squirming when old falsehoods are turned over, **1**, 113.

Squirrels eat snakes, **8**, 217.

Stable, aromatic, ammoniacal atmosphere of, **5**, 385.

Staël, Madame de, feelings of, about ghosts, **8**, 429.

Stafford, Edward, manuscript letter of, **9**, 330, 331 ; sovereign remedy of, 331, 355.

Stage army, people compared to supernumeraries in, **8**, 73, 240.

Stage ruffian, character in *The Autocrat*, **1**, 53.

Stafford House, **10**, 53.

Stain, action of, on the Book of life, **8**, 4.

Standard of judgment, **1**, 14 ; of right and wrong, not uniformly applicable, **5**, 246.

Standish, Miles, his defeat of the Indians, **9**, 190 ; his sword, **10**, 123, 124.

Stanley, Dean, **10**, 185.

Stanley, Lady, **10**, 41.

Stanley, Lord, quoted, on prison reform, **8**, 354.

Stanley, Edward, the surgeon, **10**, 7.

Stanley, Hon. Lyulph, **10**, 41.

Staples, Philip, in *Elsie Venner*, **5**, 229.

Star-dust, **3**, 179.

Star-of-Bethlehem flower, **2**, 247.

Star razor, **10**, 16, 171, 202.

Stars, double, **3**, 73, 139, 317, 346 ; nursery legend concerning, 307 ; in a June night, **6**, 88.

Stars and stripes, **2**, 87.

" Stars and the Earth," Eberty's, referred to, **1**, 265.

Startling news, self-repetition of, in the mind, **8**, 4.

Starvation the natural end of tutors, **2**, 62.

Starvation-diet of letting alone, **9**, 393.

"State Banner and Delphian Oracle," in *The Guardian Angel*, **6**, 1 ; Byles Gridley comments on issue of, 3-6, 228 *et seq.;* extracts from, 228 *et seq.*, 416, 419 *et seq.*

State House, Boston, the hub of the solar system, **1**, 125 ; covers less ground than St. Peter's, **2**, 55 ; view from, 217 ; when a man attacks the, there is not much left for him, 281 ; dome of, **4**, 308 ; **10**, 38.

Statistics : function of statisticians, **8**, 133 ; tables of, discussed instead of Divine foreknowledge, 326 ; work of, **9**, 180.

" Statoo of deceased infant," statuette of Cupid mistaken for, **1**, 109.

Stearns, Charles, of Lincoln, **3**, 14.

Stearns, Samuel H., master at Phillips Academy, Andover, **8**, 247.

Stebbins, Abel, the Doctor's hiredman, in *Elsie Venner*, **5**, 134-138 ; reports to the Doctor his observations of Richard Venner, 343, 344 ; foils Richard's attempt to dispose of Langdon, 370-376 ; appropriates Richard's saddle and bridle, 378 ; parleys with the Venners' coachman, 383-386.

Steel chair at Longford castle, **10**, 128, 201.

Steel instrument of torture, **10**, 202.

Steeple of Central Church, Boston, **10**, 193, 194. *See also* Spires.

Stephen, Leslie, **10**, 67.

Stephens, Alexander H., **4**, 19 ; **8**, 87.

Stereoscope, deceptions of, **3**, 219.

Sterling Castle, **10**, 6.

Sterne, **10**, 7 ; Calais suggestive of, 161.

Stethoscope, wrong end used by wise-looking doctor, **3**, 118.

Stewart, Dugald, recognized the ability of Jonathan Edwards, **8**, 362.

Stiles, Ezra, his copy of Plato, **8**, 409.

Stillness, vulgar persons cannot preserve, **2**, 139.

Stimulation, **6**, 249.

Stoker, Bathsheba, daughter of the Rev. Joseph Bellamy Stoker, in *The Guardian Angel*, **6**, 12 ; her appearance, 13 ; her devotion to her mother,

149 *et seq.;* her religious character, 194 ; marries Cyprian Eveleth, 428.

Stoker, the Rev. Joseph Bellamy, junior pastor, in *The Guardian Angel*, **6**, 3 ; surprise party at his house, 4 ; his excessive interest in Susan Posey, 98 ; his sermon on the Dangers of Beauty, 122 ; Master Gridley warns Susan against going to his study alone, 145 ; his invalid wife, 147 *et seq.;* his intense spiritual interest in the pretty members of his flock, 147 ; Mrs. Hopkins and Susan visit him, 152 ; his three sensational sermons, 158 ; begins to exercise his fascinations upon Myrtle, 159 *et seq.;* Myrtle is warned from him by Master Gridley, 175 ; receives a curt note from her, 191 ; preaches his convulsion-fit sermon, 192 ; is seriously injured by falling of sounding-board, 420 ; tenderly cared for by his wife, 424 *et seq.*

Stokes, Professor Sir George G., **10**, 75.

Stomach, involuntary motions of, **8**, 195 ; and the tongue, **9**, 189.

Stone, Col. W. L., **9**, 287, 288.

Stone, in a field, effect of overturning, **1**, 111 ; with whitish band, **2**, 247 ; a large, to keep wolves from graves, 263 ; **8**, 166.

Stone cutter, Number Seven's respect for a, **4**, 215.

Stonehenge, **10**, 110–114 ; *The Broken Circle*, a poem on, 111–113 ; literature of, 113, 114 ; probable way in which the large stones were moved at, 114.

Stoops, charms of, **2**, 224.

Store-room, dark, **2**, 188.

Storm, equinoctial, in *Elsie Venner*, **5**, 459 *et seq.;* September gale of 1815, **8**, 163, 164. *See also* Snow-storms.

Story's " Roba di Roma," **7**, 65.

Story-writing for support, **3**, 53.

Stoughton University, in *A Mortal Antipathy*, **7**, 36.

Strabismus, cerebral. *See* Squinting brain.

Stranger, who came with the young fellow named John, in *The Autocrat*, his remark about Boston State House, **1**, 125 ; attentive to Landlady's daughter, 307.

Strangling, one cannot accomplish by force of will alone, **8**, 261.

" Strap," the word suddenly spoken to suspected deserter, a means of recognition, **1**, 107.

Strasburg, Cathedral at, rocking of spire of, **1**, 285 ; **10**, 117 ; statue of, in Paris, 176.

Stratford on Avon, **10**, 6, 60 ; visit to, 91–97 ; some boys questioned about, 92, 93 ; Shakespeare Memorial buildings, 94 ; hot days at, 187.

Stratification of the currents of thought, **4**, 166.

Strawberry, **8**, 151, 153, 154, 220 ; **10**, 169.

Streets, of Boston and New York, **3**, 324 ; in England, **10**, 192.

Striking-in of thoughts and feelings a bad symptom, **1**, 134.

Strong, the, hate the weak, **2**, 19.

Struggle for life, **4**, 55.

Struldbrugs, Swift's account of, not very amusing reading for old people, **4**, 36.

Stuart, Gilbert, his paintings, **1**, 22 ; **7**, 3.

Stuart, Moses, striking figure of, **8**, 249.

Stupidity often prevents insanity, **1**, 42.

Stylish women, **2**, 155.

Stylographic pens, **4**, 298.

Submission to intellectual precedent, **5**, 417.

Submit, epitaph of, at Dorchester, **8**, 166.

Success impossible without opposition as a fulcrum, **6**, 276.

Succory, **2**, 234.

Sue, Eugène : " chourineur " in his " Mysteries of Paris," **8**, 340.

Suffering, professional hardness to, **2**, 263 ; may cure ignorance, does not change the moral nature, **8**, 307.

Sugar-bowl, the poetical, **4**, 75, 93, 117, 119, 285.

Suicide, feelings which conduce to, **1**, 186 ; averages of methods of committing, **2**, 166 ; as a recreation among the inhabitants of Saturn, **4**, 65 ; family of a suicide, punished, **5**, 228 ; rarely carried out by those who have a natural outlet of verse, **6**, 232 ; the number to commit, under given conditions may be predicted, **8**, 327 ; induced by religious excitement, 390, 416.

Sulky, a doctor's, **5**, 139 ; its meaning, 140.

Sullivan, John, his charm of manner, **1**, 21 n.

" Sumatra correspondence, Our," **1**, 117.

Summer, persons in easy circumstances suffer from cold in, **1**, 256 ; description of, **8**, 150–161.

Summer residence, comfort essential to enjoyment of, **1**, 265.

Summer schools, **9**, 287.

" Summons, a, for sleepers," sermon, quoted, **2**, 117.

Sumner, **1**, 2 n.

Sumter, Fort, in 1861, **6**, 385 ; **8**, 94, 95 ; meaning of the attack on, 114, 116.

Sun, slight effect of, on iceberg, **2**, 288 ; course of, through the signs of the zodiac, **8**, 135 ; rising and setting of, in Boston, 135, 136 ; chemistry of its light, 210 ; benefit of sun-bath, 209, 212, 213.

Sun and Shadow, **1**, 41.

Sunday, Autocrat shows his respect for, **1**, 174. *See also* Sabbath.

Sun-day Hymn, **2**, 319.

Sunflower, and yellow birds, **8**, 150 ; her passion for her god, 209.

Sunsets in Boston, **2**, 82.

Superfluous people, **3**, 170.

Superior men not debarred from admiring each other, **1**, 3.

Superiority to our fellow-creatures, sense of, **3**, 273.

Superlative, American love of the, **4**, 104 ; in school-girls' letters, **8**, 361.

Superstitions, of children, **1**, 205 ; author confesses to have, **2**, 186 ; no logic in, 270 ; not easily banished, **3**, 328 ; crowded out by civilization, **4**, 254, 255 ; medical, **9**, 187, 188, 206, 380, 442 ; light shed on, by the prevailing treatment of disease, 314 ; possible influence of the union of theology and medicine on, 320.

Surface-Christianity, good breeding is, **2**, 133.

Surgeon, hardness in a, **2**, 263 ; a tenderhearted one, 264.

Surgery, moral, its brutality, **2**, 114 ; invokes the aid of all mechanical arts, **8**, 313 ; specialties in, 352 ; in the Civil war, 352 ; extraordinary success in, achieved by Lawson Tait, **10**, 99, 100.

Surprise-party, **2**, 75 ; **6**, 4.

Susquehanna, the, **8**, 49.

Sutherland, Duke of, **10**, 53, 54.

Suwarrow, **5**, 216.

Swans, taking one's geese for, **1**, 273 ; stately, **2**, 236.

Swanwick, Miss Anna, **10**, 40.

Sweating gold, fable of the Jews', **2**, 163.

Swedenborg, if he did not bring a new revelation, infused new life into the old ones, **8**, 308 ; his doctrine of " correspondence," **9**, 408.

Swellings cured by dead man's hand, **2**, 246 ; **9**, 360.

Swift, author unconsciously hits on an idea of, **1**, 146 ; as Cadenus, **2**, 89 ; mischance of reading some of his poems, **4**, 109 ; outraged decency, **7**, 177 ; quoted on witty sentences, **8**, 275 ; on Sir Isaac Newton, 279, 280 ; " Journal to Stella " quoted, 284 ; quoted on his own genius, 296.

Swift, Zephaniah, struggle of, against the powers of the clergy, **8**, 411, 412.

Swimming glands in blood, **2**, 58.

Swinburne, his epigram on Carlyle, **10**, 139.

Swinnerton, John, **9**, 357.

Swords, Roman and American, **1**, 19 ; naked, King James's fear of, **5**, 222, 223.

Sydenham, recommended Don Quixote to medical student for professional reading, **7**, 162, 167, 168 ; **9**, 293, 354, 399 ; applied Hippocrates' doctrine, **8**, 233, 234 ; an " old school " physician, 236 ; his probable diagnosis of case of Christian in " Pilgrim's Progress," 416 ; his prescriptions, **9**, 268 ;

and the Pharmacopœia, 281 ; quoted, 292 ; what he did for medicine, 343, 344 ; works of, thrown away on Cotton Mather, 359 ; prescription of roast chicken, 363 ; still authority on male hysteria, 413.

" Syllabus of errors," **8**, 407.

" Sylva Novanglica," book desired with, that title, **1**, 236.

Symbols, reverence for, **2**, 292 ; a comfort, **5**, 254.

Sympathetic powder, Digby's, **9**, 8 *et seq.*, 206, 279 ; **10**, 58.

Sympathy, of surgeons compared with that of theologians, **2**, 263 ; brings unexpected friends, **3**, 154.

" Symphony concert " of conversation, **4**, 52.

Symplocarpus. *See* Skunk cabbage.

Symptoms, cultivation of, **4**, 187.

Synod of Boston, 1680, **3**, 368.

" Syntax, Dr.," may have been written to make fun of Rev. Wm. Gilpin, **1**, 231.

Systematic knowledge, involves much that is not practical, **9**, 284–291, 372.

Tableaux at Madame Delacoste's school, in *The Guardian Angel*, **6**, 278.

Tablets, story of the boy devoted to, **8**, 182, 183.

Tadema, Alma, **10**, 67.

Tadpoles, effect of dark upon, **2**, 242.

Taglioni, **3**, 95.

Tail, a giant's, **4**, 154, 155.

Tailor, English, **10**, 145.

Taine, quoted on Cowper, **8**, 397.

Tait, Lawson, his great services to surgery, **10**, 99, 100.

Talby, Dorothy, **9**, 356.

Talent, a little, makes people jealous, **1**, 3 ; and genius compared, **2**, 240 ; society has place for every form of, 285.

Talipes varus, **2**, 9.

Talkative, Mr., his place in society, **4**, 156.

Talkers, the real, with fresh ideas and good warm words, **1**, 143 ; apt to say unwise things, **2**, 18 ; the best are poets who never write verses, **3**, 94 ; lovers as, 95 ; occasional talkers, 266 ; good talkers apt to be bores, 301 ; **4**, 83.

Talking, uselessness of, with some women, **2**, 274 ; its value in helping us find out ourselves — not other people, **3**, 2 ; it should be governed by the way in which others will understand it, 4 ; conditions of good, 45 ; philosophy of, 46 ; without words is half the conversation of women, **6**, 9 ; one of the two accomplishments common to mankind, **8**, 121 ; talking machines, 122 ; persons who do the most, do not always think most, 289. *See also* Conversation.

Talking dynasty, **3**, 263 *et seq. ;* **9**, 302.

Tamaracks, **6**, 88.

Tar-baby, in the negro legend, **9**, 422.
Tar water, Bishop Berkeley's, **9**, 12 *et seq.*
Tarantism, Tarantula, **7**, 178 *et seq.*
Tart, national with English, **10**, 201.
Tartarus of the heathen world, the hell of the church of to-day, **4**, 254.
Tartini's "Devil's Sonata," **2**, 308; **8**, 283.
Tassels, concealed in some households, in brown linen bags, **5**, 86.
Taste, nerve of, has no immediate connection with brain, **1**, 77.
Tastes, natural, have a basis beyond the reach of will, **8**, 261.
Tate, Nahum, eulogy of his masterpiece, **8**, 294.
Tate and Brady, **10**, 86.
Taylor, Bayard, **3**, 325.
Taylor, Jeremy, his tolerance, **3**, 191; quoted on constant decay and renewal of the body, **8**, 199, 200, 266; quoted on theophobia, 305; quoted on godly fear, 398.
Taylor, Rebecca, **9**, 306.
Tea, influence of the afternoon or evening cup of, **4**, 7; effects of excess of, **8**, 224; afternoon, a necessity in London life, **10**, 25; a cup of, at the right moment, 26; strength of, in England, 28; served at theatre, 68.
Teachers, the dullest of, **9**, 288; intercourse of, with students, 393, 394; special gift of those born for, 425; those of one's youth outgrown, **10**, 164.
Teacups do not hold so much as coffee-cups, **4**, 21.
Teakettles, death of children from drinking hot water from spouts of, **2**, 166; **8**, 327.
Tea-party, at Widow Rowens's, in *Elsie Venner*, **5**, 286–328; the seating at the table, 299, 300; maxims for, 301, 302.
Teapot, literary, **1**, 62; history of one which belonged to Instructor Flynt, **4**, iii.
Tea-table, an overloaded, **5**, 301.
Tears, and laughter, **1**, 90; old men's, **4**, 30; caused by music, 95, 97; the sweet tribute of feminine sensibility, **6**, 366.
Teeth, **2**, 46; article of a supposed medical creed concerning, 111.
Teetotalism, tweaking the nose of, **4**, 292.
Teetotaller's changes introduced in one of the Autocrat's poems, **1**, 47.
Telegraph and railroads, the nerves and muscles of the country, **8**, 7.
Telepathic toothache, possible existence of, **4**, 17.
Telescope, in the mall on Boston Common, **4**, 305; Herschel's, **10**, 6.
Temperance, excess better than hypocrisy, **2**, 33; and longevity, **4**, 184; the first necessary habit of a doctor, **9**, 386. *See also* Intemperance; Intoxication; Teetotalism; Wine.

Temperance celebration, song for, **2**, 33.
Temperature, healthy degree of, **8**, 208; clothing should be adapted to sudden changes of, 227, 228; of Windsor Castle at 65°, **10**, 48.
Temple, Sir W., favorite herbs of, **9**, 360.
Temple, the, London, **10**, 153, 154.
Temple bar, London, **10**, 150.
Tempora mutantur, etc., amendment of, **8**, 175.
"Ten Great Religions," J. F. Clarke's, **4**, 196.
Tendencies, inherited. *See* Heredity.
Tennent, Rev. Wm., trance of, **2**, 178.
Tenniel, **10**, 67.
Tennyson, as an example of longevity, **4**, 41, 292; his "Day Dream," quoted, 287; his "Princess," quoted on woman's logomachy, 292; his "Walking to the Mail," quoted, 308; difficulty of reading his "Maud" aloud, 318; his "In Memoriam," **6**, 223; quoted, 432; the greatest lay-preacher, 432; some of his contemporaries, **10**, 44; visit to, 68–71.
Tennyson, Mr. and Mrs. Hallam, **10**, 69, 71.
Tennyson, Lady, **10**, 68, 69.
Teratology, the science of monstrosities, **3**, 223 *et seq.*
Terburg, **10**, 170.
Terence, quoted, **6**, 174.
Terms, medical, definition of some, **9**, 196.
Ternham, Nicholas de, **9**, 320.
Terrible Clock, The, Number Five's story of, **4**, 169.
Terrible people, women take to, **6**, 159.
"Terrible Tractoration," **9**, 20.
Terror, The. *See* Vincent, Lurida.
Terror, death from, **7**, 91.
Terry, a detective, in *Elsie Venner*, **5**, 162.
Terry, Ellen, **10**, 30.
Testimony of the dying to be received with caution, **2**, 292.
Tewkesbury, excursion to, **10**, 103; its Abbey church, 103, 118.
Thacher, Dr. James, his biography of doctors, **9**, 352.
Thacher, Thomas, both doctor and minister, **9**, 329.
Thackeray, **6**, 226; **10**, 35, 107.
Thames, Britons' stockades in, **2**, 245; Embankment, **10**, 136, 159.
Thanks after meat in England, **10**, 78, 130.
Thanksgiving, **8**, 154, 169, 170.
That Boy, in *The Poet*, **3**, 7; his method of interrupting a tiresome conversation, 63; his conspiracy with Scheherezade discovered, 236; his friend Johnny, 281.
Theatre-goers, their stories more vivid than those of men with other experiences, **3**, 330.
Theatricals, college, **2**, 17.

Theft and perjury in the Cabinet of the United States, **8**, 86.

Theile, **9**, 220.

Theologians, their sterner beliefs soften in later years, **4**, 39 ; Nature studied by, from below upwards, **7**, 81.

Theology, most people have had a professional education in, through hearing sermons, **1**, 29 ; that which makes life hopeless is brutal, 42 ; recent great changes in Protestant, **2**, ix.; comparative, as necessary as comparative anatomy, **3**, 149 ; must be studied through anthropology, 183 ; education in, should include pathology and toxicology, 304 ; atmosphere of, its change in thirty years, 306 ; practitioners of, who like to treat morbid states of mind, **6**, 144 ; and medicine, **7**, 81 ; **9**, 319, 320, 358 ; development of the nictitating membrane by students of, **7**, 81 ; little more than traditional anthropology, **8**, 324 ; lent the devil to the lawyers, 324 ; violates the law of homology, 325 ; whence its dogmas, 357 ; giving place to anthropology, **9**, 417. *See also* Infant damnation ; Punishment, future ; Religion ; Transmissible responsibility.

Theonomy, **9**, 417.

Theophobia, **8**, 305.

Theophrastus, **4**, 190.

Theories, usually in sets like chamber furniture, **8**, 217 ; old, must get out of the way of the new generation, **9**, 430.

Theriaca Andromachi, **9**, 282.

Théroigne de Méricourt, **8**, 338.

Thimble-riggers, **10**, 32.

Thinking, the epidemic of, **3**, 269. *See also* Thought.

Thinking-cell, an egg the best form for, **3**, 105, 106.

Thirst, in torture, **2**, 305.

Thirty-nine articles, summarily disposed of, **8**, 420, 421.

This is it (a prologue), **1**, 45.

Thomas, Edith, **4**, 206.

Thomas, Francis, **2**, 49.

Thompson, Dr., of Middletown, **8**, 33, 44, 45.

Thompson, Sir Henry, **10**, 68.

Thompson, Rev. William Hepworth, **10**, 72.

Thomson, Alexander, **9**, 220.

Thomsonism, **9**, 367, 414, 415.

Thoreau, mentions houses buried by snow, **8**, 175 ; recognizes the necessity of shelter in winter, 180 ; on pickerel fishing, 181 ; in his hovel at Walden, 183.

Thornton, Abraham, claims wager by battle, **2**, 106 ; **4**, 13.

Thornton, Arabella, Portia-like daughter of Judge Thornton, in *Elsie Venner*, **5**, 102 ; her opinion of Richard Venner, 178–181 ; talked of as suitable second wife to Dudley Venner, 281.

Thornton, Judge, in *Elsie Venner*, **5**, 102 ; advises Colonel Sprowle on a matter of propriety, 106, 107 ; talks of Richard Venner, 178–181.

Thoroughbred, a, should not be called a "blooded" horse, **1**, 37.

Thothmes III., ring of, **3**, 111.

Thou, J. A. de, preface of, **9**, 310.

Thought, may be original though often uttered, **1**, 7 ; saving bright thoughts, 27 ; conversation shapes, 27 ; moves in cycles, 73 ; a real one knocks the wind out of somebody, 113 ; occasional desire to stop the wheels of, 186 ; uttered, is like an excretion, 196 ; seed-capsule of, 199 ; the excretion of mental respiration, **2**, 24 ; runs in layers, 37 ; scheme of movement of three independent consciousnesses in one mind at once, 37 ; continuity of thought and action, 38 ; mind among thoughts compared to circus rider with horses, 38 ; a word the saddle of, 38 ; recurrence of same thoughts, 56 ; multitude of, compared with blood globules, 59 ; how one is helped to get at one's own, **3**, 1, 2 ; loss of its original form, 2 ; some kinds like the blind fishes in the Mammoth cave, 2 ; one feeds on another, 2 ; mediocrity often given it by publicity, 344 ; pleasure of finding one's own expressed by another, **4**, 10 ; attrition of, 11 ; stratification of the currents of, 166 ; does not flourish in inhospitable soil, 281 ; a fine flow of, checked by a goose-quill, 299 ; the best, done unconsciously, **6**, 404 ; relation of phosphorus to, **7**, 235 ; a boy finds his materials for, in simple sources, **8**, 251 ; mechanism of, 260–314 ; flow of, like breathing, 261 ; observation only extends to, as connected with the nervous system, 262, 263 ; mental cud sometimes lost, 267 ; have we a field of ? 269 ; worded thought, 270 ; underground workshop of, 278 ; some never emerges into consciousness, 282 ; radical change in, produced by slight material cause, 284 ; develops with the growing brain, 289 ; automatic, continuous flow of, largely peculiar to the female sex, 290 ; induced current of, 292 ; not a physical force because it cannot be measured, 295 ; perpetual metempsychosis of, **9**, 372.

Thought-sprinklers, **1**, 27.

"Thoughts on the Universe," Byles Gridley's unsuccessful book, in *The Guardian Angel*, **6**, 42, 43 ; quoted by William Murray Bradshaw, 50, 237 ; second edition suggested by publisher, 298, 366 ; a "thought" for new edition, 354 ; proposal for new edition, 402 *et seq.;* specimens of some "thoughts" with notes of revision, 404 *et seq.;* large-paper copy of, 430 ; occasional quotations from, 23, 174, 175, 205, 291, 404–406.

Thrale, Mrs. *See* Piozzi, Mrs.
Thread of a discourse lost, **4**, 297.
Three Johns, The, **1**, 53.
Three-hilled city, battle of, against the seven-hilled city, **2**, 78.
Three maiden sisters, the book of, **2**, 230.
Three wrinkles, the, between eyebrows, **5**, 87.
Three-story families, **5**, 293.
Three Words, The, **2**, 180.
Threshing old straw, **4**, 10.
Throat-distemper, **9**, 347, 348.
Thumb-nail used in measuring cloth, **6**, 207.
Thumb screws, **2**, 207.
Thunderbolt, **8**, 155, 156.
Tiber, **2**, 246 ; **3**, 332.
Ticknor, George, next door to being son of a clergyman, **8**, 411.
Tidal movement of national thought and feeling, **8**, 83, 84.
Tige, Abner Briggs's dog, in *Elsie Venner*, **5**, 35, 38.
Tiles, pictured, **5**, 144.
Tilley, Edward, "sounded" with cold, **9**, 316.
Tillotson, Archbishop, **5**, 412 ; his opinion of the Athanasian creed, **8**, 420.
Time, threatens with the sand-bag oftener than with the scythe, **4**, 30 ; annihilation of, by great events, **8**, 13 ; the great physician, 233 ; relation of mental action and, 272–301 ; cannot be magnified, **9**, 250.
Time and space, **1**, 266 ; **2**, 39 ; **7**, 26.
Timid and doubting ones. *See* Weak souls.
Tinnitus aurium, **2**, 240.
Tissues, rending, cry of, dear to woman's ear, **6**, 347.
Titian, his portrait of young man in the Louvre, **1**, 193 ; his pictures at Blenheim, **10**, 6 ; his "Young Man with glove," 170.
Titles, the Poet's passion for, **3**, 274 ; American appetite for, **4**, 222, 231 ; Americans shy of confessing the impression made by, **10**, 21 ; sound of, pleasant, 121.
"Titmouse," Emerson's, quoted, **8**, 179.
Titus, arch of, **3**, 332.
To the Eleven Ladies, **4**, 43.
Toads, remedy prepared from, **9**, 262, 280, 331.
Tobacco, called the Great Vegetable, **1**, 101 ; its stain may strike too deep into character, 103 ; men tire of, **2**, 137 ; and longevity, **4**, 184 ; as a relief from trouble, **6**, 249 ; and health, **8**, 225, 226.
Tobacco-stopper, owned by the Autocrat, **1**, 102.
Tocqueville, A. de, on slavery in the United States, **8**, 85, 93.
Tokens of regard, gratitude of author for, **1**, iv.
Tolerance, feeling of, **5**, 168.

"Tom Jones," **2**, vi.
Tomato, **9**, 275.
Tomcod, **8**, 181.
Tongue, the, and the stomach, **9**, 189 ; tongue-scraper, 189.
Tonnellé, Dr., **9**, 106, 123, 163, 165.
Too Young for Love, **4**, 202.
Toothache, telepathic, possible existence of, **4**, 17.
Topping, Miss Berengaria, in *The Guardian Angel*, **6**, 272, 287.
Tornado, Great, of 1851, **8**, 156 ; September gale of 1815, 163, 164.
Torquay, **9**, 296.
Torque, golden, worn by Elsie Venner, **5**, 99, 159, 358, 457.
Torture, implements and methods of, **2**, 207 ; thirst excited by, 305 ; for the nerve-centres, **6**, 346 ; an old-fashioned form of argument, 380 ; in witchcraft, by miniature figures, **8**, 95 ; steel instrument of, **10**, 202. *See also* Rack.
Torturing instinct, **1**, 129 ; **2**, 95.
Tournelle, the, **8**, 346.
Tower, Euthymia, in *A Mortal Antipathy*, known as "The Wonder," **7**, 41 ; her athletic feats, 41 *et seq.* ; graduates at the Corinna Institute, 77 ; contrasted with Lurida Vincent, 145 ; Dr. Butts calls upon her, 186 *et seq.* ; first meeting with Maurice Kirkwood, 189 ; is eulogized to Kirkwood, who resolves to speak with her, 253 ; her leading characteristics, 254 *et seq.* ; her meeting with Maurice Kirkwood, 261 *et seq.* ; rescues Kirkwood from death by fire, 270 *et seq.* ; visits him during his recovery, 278 *et seq.* ; is engaged to become his wife, 282.
Tower of London, encounter of the author with baboon there, **10**, 5, 150.
Townley, Mr., **3**, 213.
Towns, esteem in which each is held by its inhabitants, **1**, 126.
Townsend, Colonel, his power to suspend the action of his heart, **7**, 237.
Townsend, Mr., **10**, 67.
Townsend, Solomon Davis, M. D., **2**, 264 n.
Toxicology as part of theological education, **3**, 304.
Toy, French, directions for using gently, **1**, 80.
Traceries in margin of drawing-book, **2**, 234.
Tracts, religious, **2**, 110.
Training, effects of prolonged, **8**, 230.
Trains to dresses, vulgar misuse of, **2**, 154.
Traitor at home, the, **8**, 89.
Traits, ancestral, in embryo, **6**, 26 *et seq.*
Trajan, column of, **10**, 156.
Trance, **2**, 237 ; mostly peculiar to women, 238 ; instance of, 267.
Transmissible responsibility, moral chaos began with the idea of, **8**, 303 ; accepted by theology, 325. *See also*

Automatism ; Heredity ; Responsibility ; Sin ; Will.

Transmission of qualities. *See* Heredity.

Transmutations, chemical, **9**, 215.

Transparency, spiritual, of golden-blondes, **2**, 229.

Transplanting, necessary for souls as for plants, **2**, 243 ; of ideas, **3**, 146.

Transportation of criminals, **8**, 345.

Trap set by authors to get book-sellers' advertisements, **3**, 302.

Travel, certain principles to be assumed in, **1**, 278 ; emotions excited by, not those usually to be expected, 280. *See also* Railroad.

Travellers of advanced years, **10**, 206, 207.

Travelling companions, **8**, 19.

Treadwell library, **9**, 398.

Treason, **8**, 9.

Trecothicks, the, in *Elsie Venner*, **5**, 102.

Tree-wives, the Autocrat's, **1**, 230, 233.

Trees, in New England, **1**, 230 ; endowed with life, but not with love, 231 ; mother-idea embodied in each kind, 232 ; an immense one, 234 ; title of a desiderated work on, 236 ; queer shapes of foliage, 266 ; ages of, as shown by rings, 286 ; grafted, **3**, 165 ; the real, live underground, **4**, 212 ; their tails, 213 ; forest, **5**, 67 ; always talking, 185 ; struck by lightning, **8**, 156 ; in England, **10**, 22, 189-191 ; the soothing companionship of, 69, 70 ; Tennyson's, 69, 189. *See also* Apple trees ; Beeches ; Elm ; Hawthorn ; Hemlock ; Horse-chestnut ; Larch ; Lindens ; Lombardy poplar ; Maple ; Oak ; Poplar ; Tamaracks ; White ash ; Wild cherry ; Willows ; Wych-elm.

" Trees of America," Piper's, **1**, 236.

Trepan, **9**, 326.

Trephine, **9**, 326.

Treviranus, **9**, 226.

Triads, adjectives used in, **1**, 85.

Trial by battle, **2**, 106 ; **4**, 13.

Triangulation of characteristics of a family, **5**, 271.

Trifle, a confection, **5**, 110.

Trigamy, seemingly advocated in the Bible, **2**, 5.

Trilobites, **2**, 94 ; **5**, 238 ; **6**, 275.

Trinity College, Cambridge, **10**, 77.

Trinks, Dr., of Dresden, **9**, 85.

Trios, Nature fond of, **10**, 138.

Tripe, begged for by Katharine in " Taming of the Shrew," **8**, 194, 195 ; digestibility of, 218.

Tripod of life, the brain, heart, and lungs, **2**, 260.

" Tristram Shandy," **6**, 275.

Triumph of Song, one of Gifted Hopkins's poems in *The Guardian Angel,* **6**, 302, 367.

Triumphs, immediate, of singers, **3**, 113.

Trivial indispositions, **8**, 2.

Trois Frères, restaurant in Paris, dinners at, **1**, 78.

Trombone, playing the, with a book, **4**, 295.

Tropics, recollections of, **6**, 26.

Trot, picture of a, **2**, 165.

Trotting horses. *See* Horses.

True Knight of learning (toast to Motley), **1**, 27.

Trumbull's " Sortie of Gibraltar," **7**, 3.

Trunk, arrival of, before a guest, **5**, 156 ; old, in garret, **6**, 37, 360 ; old-fashioned, 295 ; its contents, 296 ; a spinster's, 352 *et seq.*

Truth, primary relations with, **1**, 14 ; compared to a cube, 116 ; each soul must look for, with its own eyes, **2**, 6 ; is tough, 109 ; iconoclasm, only way to get at, 117 ; private property in, 295 ; lost in its own excess, **4**, 110.

" Truth, a Gift for Scribblers," W. J. Snelling's, **7**, 5 *et seq.*

Tubercles, patient knows what it means to have, **9**, 389.

Tug, ship drawn by, compared to husband and wife, **2**, 289.

Tuileries, ruins of, **10**, 177.

Tulpius, **9**, 410.

Tunes, dismal, **6**, 80.

Tuning of two souls to each other, **5**, 274.

Tupper, his " Poems," **1**, 16, 311 ; large sales of his " Proverbial Philosophy " in America, 261 ; Tupperian wisdom, 271 ; a poet whom it is unnecessary to mention, **5**, 58.

Turk, Maelzel's, **2**, 16.

Turkish ambassador to England wins a pool at the Derby, **10**, 37.

Turner, **10**, 151.

Turtle, and his shell, **2**, 28 ; snapping, **6**, 19, 125.

Tussaud, Madame, **10**, 178.

Tutor, a, starvation his natural end, **2**, 62.

Tutor, the, in *Over the Teacups,* **4**, 49 ; a philosopher and a poet, 50 ; talks over the two Annexes with Number Five, 175 ; reads Italian with Number Five, 242, 262 ; their increasing intimacy, 283 *et seq.*

Tutor, the Latin. *See* Latin tutor.

Twelve - syllable verse, unphysiological construction of, **8**, 317.

Twentieth century, we are only getting ready for, **8**, 350.

Twins, in *The Guardian Angel,* adopted by Mrs. Hopkins, Byles Gridley's fondness for, **6**, 47, 97 ; named by Byles Gridley, 52, 53 ; their play with him, 108 ; Cynthia Badlam's mysterious interest in, 169 *et seq.* ; they receive the benefit of the bequest left by Cynthia Badlam, 426 ; their names changed, 427 ; baptized, 429.

Twins, in the birth of thought, **2**, 56.

Twitchell, Dr., **9**, 353.

Twitches, which women give when they drive a horse, **5**, 93.
Two Armies, The, **1**, 225.
Two-story gentility, **5**, 57, 58, 293.
Two Streams, The, **2**, 153 ; alleged plagiarism in, **8**, 45.
Two-tined forks, persons born with, in their hands, **9**, 429.
Tyburn, awkward burning at, **1**, 33.
Tydeman, Bishop, **9**, 320.
Tyler, John, **8**, 32.
Tyndall, **10**, 2, 57.
Types, of organization in Old and New World, **1**, 237 ; of men and women, repetition of, met in England, **10**, 196.
Typhoid fever, **7**, 203 *et seq.*, 261 *et seq.* ; **9**, 266.
Typhus syncopalis, **9**, 203.

Ugly Things, Old Sophy's expression for rattlesnakes, in *Elsie Venner*, **5**, 354, 434.
Ulmus Americana. *See* Elm.
Ultimum moriens of gentility, the hat is, **10**, 193.
Ulysses, **3**, 323 ; **9**, 376.
Umbrella in London and Paris, **10**, 187, 188.
Unbeautiful women get more lovers than the beauties, **5**, 126.
Uncomfortable people, finally take spite against themselves, **2**, 272.
Uncommon sense, **5**, 396.
Unconscious cerebration. *See* Unconscious mental action.
Unconscious mental action, Leibnitz on, **8**, 276, 278 ; Hartley on, 277, 278 ; instances of, 278–284 ; mystery of, exemplified in act of mental association, 285, 286 ; connection of motive and determination an expansion of the doctrine of, 329 ; growth of knowledge of, 378, 379 ; study of the individual reduces his acts more and more to, 379 ; our knowledge concerning, still in its infancy, **9**, 246. *See also* Automatism ; Guilt ; Heredity ; Philosophy ; Responsibility ; Sin ; Theology ; Will.
Unconsciousness, where is mind or soul during, **5**, 391, 392.
Under the Violets, **2**, 253.
Underbred people, their conduct towards the sick, **2**, 144.
Underground workshop of thought, **8**, 273.
Underhill, Captain, **9**, 334.
Undertaker, the young, a character in *The Professor*, **2**, 312, 318.
Undertakers, cheerful people, **2**, 312.
Undervaluation of one's self, **4**, 112.
Underwood, Dr., on diseases of children, **9**, 116.
Underwood, F. H., consul at Glasgow, **10**, 84.
Ungifted, the, in literature, **1**, 292 ; the case of X. Y., a "cheaply - got - up youth," 292.
Unguentum armarium, **9**, 6, 206.

Unicorn's horn, **9**, 341.
Unintelligent Me, **9**, 376.
United Fraction of America, **8**, 104.
United States, one people in the whole country, **8**, 10 ; political condition of, July 4th, 1863, 81 ; asked to commit suicide by the South, 94 ; resources of, 111 ; an organic whole, 116. *See also* American Civil war ; American Revolution ; Confederate States ; North.
Universities, English, **9**, 277.
University of New York, reports of the Regents of, **8**, 184.
University towns of England not to be compared, **10**, 82.
Unloved, great procession of the, **1**, 305.
Unprofessional experimenter in medicine, **9**, 380.
Unwise things apt to be said by talkers, **2**, 18.
Unwritten answers to correspondents, **4**, 310, 311.
Upham, C. W., of Salem, **9**, 357, 358.
Upper Ferry Bridge, Philadelphia, **8**, 71.
Uranus, darkness beyond the orbit of, **8**, 84.
Urn in which The Teacups put their unsigned poems, **4**, 75, 93, 117, 119, 285.
Usher, Archbishop, precise date of creation given by, **2**, 113, 210 ; **8**, 132.
Uwins, T., engraver, **2**, vi.

Vaccination, **9**, 54, 69, 96, 349 ; **10**, 172.
Vagabonds : queer, old, rum - scented, good-for-nothing, lazy, story-telling, half-vagabonds, **5**, 47.
Valentine, Basil, **9**, 366.
Valerian, for hysterics, **1**, 70 ; **6**, 171.
Vampires, invalid, **4**, 183.
Van Buren, **9**, 287, 288.
Van Deusen, Miss Matilda, afterwards Widow Rowens, in *Elsie Venner*, **5**, 288.
Vandalism in burial grounds, **1**, 239.
Vanderpoel, Dr., **9**, 255.
Vandyke, **10**, 123.
Vane, Sir Harry, **10**, 121.
Vanity does not die out of the old, **4**, 295.
"Vanity of Human Wishes," Johnson's, quoted, **10**, 80.
Variety, Nature fertile in, **2**, 80.
Varolius, **9**, 412.
Vassall house, Cambridge, **10**, 105 ; Vassall tablet, Cambridge, **8**, 161.
"Vathek," Hall of Eblis in, **1**, 247.
Vatican council of 1870, **8**, 407.
Vaughan, Mrs., of Beverly, **10**, 29.
Vaughan, Petty, **10**, 4, 7.
Vaughans, the, in *Elsie Venner* **5**, 102.
Vauxhall Gardens, **10**, 5.
Veal, a disturbing food to many, **8**, 219.
Vegetation, forcing its way into cities, **1**, 274 ; frozen interregnum in, **8**, 179 ; breathing process of, 200 ; food for, 202 ; fertilizer of the human body, 216.
Vegetables, in Galen's system, **9**, 318.

Vegetarians, **8**, 217, 218.

Velocipedes, **1**, 168 n.

Velpeau, **9**, 428, 429.

Vendôme column, **10**, 173.

Veneering in conversation, **1**, 143.

Venerable Gentleman, the, in *The Auto-crat* and *The Professor*, **1**, 3 ; fond of common sense, 14 ; recalls poetry of his boyhood, 99 ; his white hat is rudely treated, 177 ; forgets his French, 178 ; fond of reminiscences, 208 ; displays a keepsake of early romance, 211 ; wedding gift from, of Cashmere shawl, 312 ; gives Schoolmistress away, 313 ; mention of, **2**, 21, 318.

Venesection, **9**, 258. *See also* Blood-letting.

Venice, New York compared to, **2**, 85.

Venison, digestibility of, **8**, 218.

Venner, Catalina, dead mother of Elsie, in *Elsie Venner*, **5**, 148, 179, 434, 459.

Venner, Dudley, father of Elsie, in *Elsie Venner*, at Col. Sprowle's party, **5**, 97 *et seq. ;* his grief and care for Elsie, 153, 154 ; his relation to his daughter, 270–278 ; his lonesomeness, 279 – 284 ; tells his love for Helen Darley, 467 *et seq. ;* married to her, 483, 484.

Venner, Elsie : physiological basis of story of *Elsie Venner*, **5**, vii., ix. ; supposed sources of, ix., x. ; not adaptable to dramatization, x., xi.

— the character : first mention of, **5**, 52 ; her appearance, 77, 78 ; at Col. Sprowle's party, 99 *et seq. ;* her home, 141–145 ; her strange habits, 146 ; her disappearances, 146, 147 ; one of her wild dances, 147 ; influence of Mr. Langdon upon her character, 184 ; saves Langdon from rattlesnake, 191 ; her strange perversions of character, 192 *et seq.;* Old Sophy's anxiety for, 241–244 ; her restlessness in the midsummer, 261 *et seq. ;* her room, 266–268 ; watches Langdon and Letty Forrester, 308 *et seq. ;* Sophy tells the Doctor that no one must marry her, 349, 350 ; her method of revenge on Richard, 360, 361 ; goes to the school after the assault on Langdon, 393–399 ; attends church, 413–418 ; asks Langdon to love her, 422, 423 ; her sickness, 424 *et seq. ;* Helen Darley comes to nurse her, 431 *et seq. ;* Sophy tells the mystery of her birth, 435 ; Langdon visits her sick bed, 446 – 448 ; her death, 453, 454 ; her burial, 456–459.

Venner, Richard, cousin of Elsie, in *Elsie Venner*, his childhood, **5**, 150 – 153 ; returns on a visit, 155 *et seq. ;* gets restless, 159 *et seq. ;* begins to form plan to marry Elsie, 197 *et seq. ;* examines Elsie's vacant room, 264–268 ; grows jealous of Langdon, 267 *et seq. ;* practises with lasso, 332–334 ; his jealousy and plottings, 334–342 ; speaks slightingly of Langdon to Elsie, 360, 361 ; tries to lasso Langdon, but is

foiled by Abel Stebbins, 369 *et seq. ;* leaves the town forever, 377, 378.

Ventilation, **8**, 213, 214 ; **9**, 195.

Venus, transit of, **4**, 305.

Venus of Milo, **7**, 235 ; **10**, 177.

Veratrum viride, **9**, 264, 265, 295, **296**.

"Verdant Green," **1**, 257 ; **5**, 88.

Vernon, Fortescue, **3**, 29.

Veronese, Paul, **10**, 20.

Verse, seeming antiquity of good verses, **1**, 31 ; unpublished, 40 ; **4**, 87 ; the proper medium for secrets, **1**, 60 ; abstinence from writing, the mark of a poet, 201 ; writers of, presumably inferior persons, 292 ; commonplace, quality of, **4**, 77, 313 ; over-production of, **6**, 307 ; physiology of versification, **8**, 315–321 ; relation of structure of, to rhythm of respiration, 316 ; "fatal facility " of octosyllabic, 316, 317 ; heroic, 317 ; fourteen-syllable and twelve-syllable, 317.

Verses, to author at Cambridge University, by Mr. Heitland, **10**, 79 ; at annual meeting of class of 1829, 111. *See also* Poems ; Poetry ; Rhymes ; Rhythm.

Versipelles, **5**, 222.

"Vertical railway," **8**, 74.

Vertigo, caused by corned beef, **8**, 219.

Vesalius, **2**, 29 ; **4**, 123 ; **6**, 141 ; **9**, 178, 220, 279, 411, 412, 423.

Vessels, collision of, **2**, 56.

Veto, ministerial, allowed by Saybrook platform, **8**, 411.

Viaticum, blessing of, unknown to Protestants, **8**, 404.

"Vicar of Wakefield," **6**, 275.

Vice, more contagious than disease, **8**, 345.

Vicissitudes of old families, **5**, 11 *et seq.*

Victoria, Queen, exhibits herself to the public, **1**, 303 ; as Princess, in 1834, **10**, 5 ; a child's letter to, 29 ; her birthday, 43 ; author invited to meet her at garden-party, 185.

Vieille fille fait jeune mariée, **6**, 422.

Vieussens, Raymond, **9**, 221, 245.

Villages, have the conceit of great towns, **1**, 128 ; attractiveness of a railroad village, **2**, 246.

Vincent, Lurida, in *A Mortal Antipathy*, her characteristics, **7**, 40 ; coxswain of the Atalanta, 47 ; stratagem by which she wins the boat-race, 51, 52 ; graduates from the Corinna Institute, 77 ; Secretary of the Pansophian Society, 94, 127, 128 ; thinks of studying medicine, 104, 125 ; resolves to discover Maurice Kirkwood's secret, 120 ; is convinced that Kirkwood is suffering from the bite of a tarantula, 176 ; writes him a letter, 194 ; is dissuaded from sending the letter, 199 ; letters to Mrs. Kirkwood, 283, 290 ; gives up the idea of becoming a doctor, 283 ; her views on homœopathy, 284 ; delivers a lecture on quaternions,

291 ; engaged to a clergyman with a mathematical turn, 301.

Vinci, Leonardo da, **9**, 248.

Vinegar Bible, many people get their Scripture from, **5**, 326, 474.

Violence in the United States Senate-chamber, **8**, 86.

Violins, their pores full of music, **1**, 103 ; fifty-eight pieces in, 104 ; a Guarnerius, **2**, 308.

Viper, not so bad as a child in Edwards's theology, **4**, 249 ; **8**, 393.

Virchow, his theory of cells, **9**, 252.

Virgil, **2**, 61 ; **3**, 312 ; **5**, 176 ; **8**, 369.

Virginia adventurers, **10**, 149.

Virginia's death, **2**, 60.

Virtue, Jonathan Edwards's notion of, **8**, 373.

Virtues, the negative, lead to emaciation of character, **1**, 262 ; of common humanity, **3**, 306.

Virtuoso, **9**, 409.

Vis Platonica or Baconica, **8**, 295.

Visceral conscience, **9**, 337.

Vision, resemblance of the act of intelligence to that of, **8**, 268 ; time-relation of the sense of, 275 ; reflex, **9**, 248 ; physiology of, 249.

Visiting, breakfast least convenient time for, **10**, 25.

Visitors, ceremonial inclined plane for getting rid of, **1**, 17.

Visscher, Cornelius, **2**, 29.

Vitality, fashion full of, **2**, 136 ; fondness of society for, 150 ; expended upon a poem, **3**, 97, 98 ; excess of, 334 ; the ascending and descending scale of, **9**, 198.

Vitriol, blue, **9**, 10.

Vocabulary, stirring up a writer's unsanctified, **4**, 8 ; the lover's, 91 ; English and American compared, **8**, 172, 173 ; of some very fashionable people, 274.

Voice, generally disagreeable sound of American voices, **1**, 213 ; sweet voices of German women, 215 ; muliebrity and femineity in, 216 ; of a little child in hospital, 216 ; in heaven, 217 ; people never hear their own, 217 ; potent influence of a child's, **2**, 45 ; mysterious woman's voice heard in night, 174 ; proves to be a violin, 308 ; influence of, **4**, 178 ; not under control in sudden and sharp sensations, **8**, 330.

Voiceless, The, **1**, 306.

Volapük of spiritual being is music, **4**, 99.

"Voleur," the branding mark of the galleys, **1**, 106.

Voltaire, called "wicked Mr. Arouët," **2**, 69 ; Jonathan Homer's external resemblance to, **3**, 15 ; his chapel, 193 ; compared with Erasmus and Rabelais, **10**, 128 ; mentioned, 72, 166, 168.

Voluntary actions, automatic actions of the secondary kind *may* be, **8**, 278, 281 , governed by impulses from obscure sources, 315 ; seeming contingencies of so-called, matters of certainty, 326, 327 ; special actions to produce a certain effect are neither ordered nor noticed, 329, 330 ; apparent, in exceptional natures, really automatic, 330. *See also* Automatism ; Mal-volition ; unconscious mental action ; Will.

Voting, independent, **2**, 207.

Vox humana of the organ, **2**, 308.

Voyage across Atlantic, **10**, 3, 11, 13–18.

Voysey, Rev. Charles, **10**, 197.

Vulgar people. *See* Underbred people.

Vulgarity, expressions of, **1**, 28 ; making believe to be what you are not is essence of, **2**, 154 ; every people has its own forms of, **4**, 223.

Wager by battle, **2**, 106 ; **4**, 13.

Wagon, an old broken-down, **4**, 208.

Waking, pain of, in trouble, **8**, 5.

Wales, Prince of, **10**, 34, 35, 46.

Wales, Princess of, **10**, 34, 46 ; the author writes in her album, 55, 56.

Walker, the hygeian humorist, reasons for not washing his face, **1**, 192.

Walker, Dr. James, **4**, 34 ; **8**, 363.

Walking, arm against arm, **1**, 18 ; action of legs in, 72 ; attractions of, 165 ; riding and rowing compared with, 167 ; against the wind, **4**, 187 ; physiology of, **8**, 121–131 ; one of the two accomplishments common to mankind, 121 ; machines, 122, 129–131 ; rhythm of, 124 ; a perpetual falling with perpetual self-recovery, 127 ; one is shorter while walking than at rest, 128 ; impossible to walk in a straight line blindfolded, 128 ; amount of, for exercise, 228, 229.

"Walking to the Mail," Tennyson's, quoted, **8**, 308.

Wall-flowers, kindness to, **2**, 140.

Wallace, Dr. Clay, **9**, 249.

Wallop, Lady Camilla, **10**, 86.

Walpole, Horace, his story of Pope, **10**, 34.

Walpurgis night, **2**, 164.

Walrus, Neighbor, his garden, **2**, 248.

Walshe, Dr. Walter Hayle, **10**, 157, 198.

Walton, Izaak, remark of, on the pike, **8**, 283 ; his "Life of George Herbert," **10**, 127.

Walton's "Polyglot," **6**, 263.

War, is only organized barbarism, in opinion of many of the youth who enlisted in American Civil war, **6**, 411 ; war-fever, **8**, 3, 4 ; passion of Revolutionary times, 7 ; teachings of, 8 ; vices and virtues discovered by, 9 ; deprovincializing effect of, 10, 11 ; the mint for coining the world's history, 13 ; a just, the last link in a chain of impulses from God, 92 ; is a child that devours its nurses, 114 ; what it means, 116 ; effect of, on doctors and surgeons, **9**, 363. *See also* American Civil war ; American Revolution ; Confederate States ; Mexican war ; North.

War of 1812, **10**, 184.

War of Secession. *See* American Civil war.

Ward, Mr., vicar of Stratford-on-Avon, both clergyman and physician, **8**, 406 ; **9**, 319, 320.

Ward, Gen. Artemas, **3**, 28 ; the old gambrel-roofed house, his headquarters, **7**, 30.

Wardian case, the atmosphere is a, **8**, 200.

Ware, John, **9**, 299, 351.

Warfare of man with natural forces, **4**, 54.

Warming-pans, useful in the West Indies, **4**, 231.

Warren, the two doctors, **9**, 350.

Warren, John C., **9**, 252, 304, 421.

Warren, Joseph, **2**, 15 ; **3**, 28 ; **7**, 30 ; **8**, 13 ; **9**, 350.

Warrington, Dr., statements of, in regard to puerperal fever, **9**, 145.

Warwick, **10**, 6.

Washington, his "Farewell Address," **2**, 87 ; headquarters of, at Yonkers, **5**, 144; foresaw the danger of sectional divisions, **8**, 85.

Washington elm, **3**, 19.

Washington monument, **4**, 102, 103 ; **10**, 195.

Washington pie, **4**, 186 ; **10**, 201.

Washington Societies, **2**, 87.

Wasp, sloop-of-war, expected return of, **1**, 206.

Watch, meddling with hair-spring of, **2**, 43.

Watch-paper, the Old Gentleman's tender memories connected with, **1**, 211.

Watching with the sick, **2**, 272.

Water, in the treatment of gunshot wounds, **9**, 205, 270.

Waterhouse, Dr. Benjamin, **5**, 165 ; **9**, 309, 349, 438 ; **10**, 157.

Watering-pot, Number Five's, **4**, 218.

Waterlily, the type of the poet's soul, **1**, 182.

Waterloo, Wellington's laconic description of, **10**, 55 ; mound at, 195.

Watson's lectures, **9**, 116.

Watt, Mr., and Mr. Watts, confusion of names of these two gentlemen in London, **10**, 158.

Watts, Dr., **5**, 57 ; **6**, 207.

"Watts and Select Hymns," **6**, 202.

Waves, remote sound of, **1**, 213.

We will not speak of tears to-night, **2**, 77.

Weak, hated by strong, **2**, 19.

Weak constitution and devout disposition, correlation between, **3**, 303.

Weak souls, we should try to judge them fairly, **8**, 79 ; agitation of great questions necessary to win over, 80.

Wealth, durability of, **2**, 151 ; foolish talk about, 152 ; rapid redistribution in America, **5**, 21 ; obligations of, **7**, 32 ; proper purpose of, **8**, 113.

Weapon ointment, **9**, 6–8.

Weapons, nations to be judged by length of, **1**, 19.

Weather-gage of patients, **9**, 287.

Webb, Colonel, owner of Newstead Abbey, **10**, 57.

Weber, Messrs., on walking, **8**, 122, 124.

Webster, Daniel, Olympian brow of, **8**, 83 ; had to change size of hat every few years, 289 ; his comparison of himself with other orators, **9**, 396 ; parody of his speech about Hamilton, 403.

Webster, Noah, his "Unabridged" criticised, **2**, 40 ; his spelling, 41 ; gratitude owed him, 44.

Wedding, spectators at, **9**, 370.

Wedding-presents to the Autocrat and Schoolmistress, **1**, 311.

Wedmore, Mr., **10**, 153.

Weeds, not too humble for artist's eye, **2**, 234.

"Week in a French Country-House," **3**, 161.

Weeks, Master, of Pigwacket Centre District School, in *Elsie Venner:* his unsuccessful struggle with Abner Briggs, Jr., **5**, 24–26.

Weight, Englishman's and American's ways of estimating, **10**, 143.

Weinzäpfli, his jump at Berne, **1**, 281.

Welch, Mr., of Pomfret, reply of, to Z. Swift's attack, **8**, 412.

Welfare, care for one's own, a supreme form of selfishness, **6**, 30.

Well, drying of, previous to mountain-slide, **5**, 461, 462.

Well-sweep, the old-fashioned, **4**, 207, 208.

Wellington, his gentleness in later years, **1**, 82 ; said his dandy officers were his best, 258 ; his laconic description of battle of Waterloo, **10**, 55.

Wells Cathedral, **10**, 186.

Wens, cured by a dead hand, **9**, 360.

Wentworth, Miss Dorothea, married to the Rev. Jedediah Langdon, in *Elsie Venner*, **5**, 11.

Were-wolves, **5**, 222.

Werner, **9**, 222.

Wesley, John, **2**, 110 ; **7**, 196.

West, Benjamin, **7**, 3.

West Boston bridge, **8**, 178, 181.

West India goods, **5**, 81.

Westbury, England, white horse on hillside, **10**, 108.

Westminster, Duke of, Eaton Hall, seat of, **10**, 20 ; his stables, 21 ; as winner of Derby, 32.

Westminster Abbey, **10**, 4, 29 ; visit to, in company with Archdeacon Farrar, 59–61 ; Poets' Corner, 59, 60 ; impresses one as overcrowded, 60 ; the dust of, 62.

Westminster Catechism, **8**, 432.

What we all think, **1**, 146.

Wheat harvest, in New York, **8**, 154.

Wheatstone, moving in parallel path with other inventors, **8**, 84.

Wheel, an extraordinary product of genius and skill, **4**, 208 *et seq.*

Wheelock, President, **6**, 162.

Whewell, Dr., **4**, 164, 165.

Whipping, may drive a child to obedience, not to virtue, **8**, 306; may, under certain conditions, be useful to the insane, 356.

Whips, fascination of, for youth, **3**, 273.

Whiskey, Scotchman's usquebaugh, nationalized, **8**, 223.

Whiskey punch, **2**, 132.

Whisper, articulation without bleating, **8**, 122.

White of Selborne, **8**, 133, 183; **10**, 104, 186.

White, Kirke, **1**, 185.

White, Sir W. A., degree conferred on, at Cambridge, **10**, 75.

White ash, **5**, 439; its effect upon Elsie, in *Elsie Venner*, 440, 443.

White-man's foot, Indian name for plantain, **2**, 235.

White-pine Yankees, **3**, 276.

Whitefield said sermon was good for nothing until preached forty times, **1**, 139.

Whitman, Walt, **4**, 234, 235.

Whittier, **4**, 41, 292; **7**, 5; influence of, on the inherited beliefs of New England, **8**, 432; his "The Minister's Daughter," 432; favorite tree of, at Danvers, **10**, 69.

Whitwell's Cephalic snuff, **5**, 165.

Wibird, Mr., former partner of lawyer Penhallow in *The Guardian Angel*, **6**, 349.

Wicks, three, to lamp of life, **2**, 260.

Widows, a woman marked by nature for one, **5**, 288; easy-crying, take new husbands soonest, **6**, 230; Indian summer of serene widowhood, 348; monument erected by a wretched, **10**, 104.

Wife. *See* Wives.

Wigan, Dr., his theory of the brain, **1**, 74; on duality of mind, **8**, 267, 268.

Wigglesworth, Michael, case of infants in his "Day of Doom," **8**, 304 n.; quoted, 372; both doctor and minister, 406; **9**, 329.

Wight, Isle of, **10**, 68; luxuriance of, 69; places of interest, 71.

Wigs, of the New England clergy, **8**, 407.

Wild, Miss Virginia, the second wife of Jeremy Withers, in *The Guardian Angel*, said to have had Indian blood, **6**, 25.

Wild cherry, **5**, 47.

Wild creature, a, dormant in each heart, **2**, 94.

Wilde, Oscar, and wife, **10**, 28.

Wilkes, John, his saying about cutting out the handsomest man, **2**, 89.

Wilkins, Lieutenant, of the 20th Massachusetts, **8**, 26.

Wilkinson, Thomas, complained of, for practising medicine contrary to law, **9**, 317.

Will, compared to a drop of water imprisoned in a crystal, **1**, 86; limitations of, 89; misunderstandings in regard to its limitations, **2**, 34; bias decides choice of, 35 n.; steps from one moving thought to another, 39; who determines the self which is self-determining, **4**, 312; lacks control of voluntary determinations, **5**, 220, 225, 226; habits take place of self-determination, 252; all large views of mankind limit our estimate of its freedom, 317; doctors perceive its restraints, 323; limitation of self-determination of, **6**, 131; seat of the, **8**, 271; freedom of, 302, 303; is anything but free, 327; connection of motive and, 329; test of free, 333; no proper exercise of free, in passion, 335; the sense of duty a necessary condition for the exercise of free, 335, 336; belief in free, will remain, 359; Milton's fallen angels puzzled over free, 376; similes of Hobbes and Leibnitz on, 377; belief in the freedom of, itself a powerful motive, 381; our knowledge concerning the, still in its infancy, **9**, 247. *See also* Automatism; Guilt; Heredity; Mal-volition; Necessity; Original sin; Philosophy; Responsibility; Sin; Unconscious mental action; Voluntary actions.

Will, making a, **6**, 30.

Willard, Samuel, **9**, 356, 366.

Willett, Henry, of Brighton, England, **10**, 18, 47, 90, 186.

William the Conqueror, **10**, 66.

William III., **9**, 3.

William IV., **10**, 5.

Williams, Dr., on iritis, **9**, 255.

Williams, Colonel Elisha, **3**, 331.

Williams, Roger, practiced medicine, **9**, 329.

Williams, Stephen W., **9**, 352.

Williams the oculist, **9**, 87.

Willis, Dr., **9**, 412.

Willis, N. P., **1**, 259; **4**, 147; his resemblance to Hippolytus in the picture of Hippolytus and Phædra, **7**, 4; the most prominent of the young American authors about 1830, 5; quoted on east wind, **8**, 151; found ale a kindly "thought-stopper," 223.

Willow whistle, **8**, 140.

Willows, **1**, 288; **10**, 190.

Wilson, Dr., of Harrisburg, **8** 53, 54.

Wilton, seat of the Earl of Pembroke, **10**, 110, 116; pictures at, 123, 124; sculpture at, 124; lovely maidens at, 124; where Sidney wrote his "Arcadia," 124.

Wind, walking against the, **4**, 187; voices of the, **6**, 88; bloweth *not* where it listeth, **8**, 327.

Wind Clouds and Star-Drifts, **3**, 144, 172, 197, 230, 258, 285.

Windermere, **7**, 104.

Windsor, England, **10**, 6, 47; the Castle, 47, 48; the Park, 48; cuckoo heard at, 50.

Wine, of the ancients, **1**, 66; a specific against dull dinners, **2**, 32; its use should be open, 33; famous vintages of, **3**, 102; lying delusion of, **5**, 278.

Wink, called a palpebral spasm, **2**, 14.

Winning post of human life, a slab of white or gray stone, **1**, 96.

Winslow, Dr., **9**, 412.

Winslow, Mrs., descendant of Ann Holyoake, in *The Guardian Angel*, **6**, 23.

Winslow, Edward, and Massasoit, **9**, 189; on the roses and grapes of Massachusetts in 1621, 321; on the climate, 322.

Winslow, Jakob Benignus, mural tablet of, **1**, 280.

Winsor, Justin, **9**, 416.

Winter, **8**, 175–185.

Winthrop, Prof. James, **3**, 224; **9**, 355.

Winthrop, John, Governor of Connecticut, medical practice of, **9**, 330–335; an amateur practitioner, 337; his yellow salve, 342.

Winthrop, John, Governor of Massachusetts, **3**, 224; medical entry in his Journal, **9**, 313, 314; on scurvy among the Pilgrims, 323; doctor and lawyer, 330; sends for East-Indian bezoar, 340; his "Life and Letters" and his "History" cited, 356–358.

Winthrop, John, F. R. S., **9**, 335.

Winthrop, Robert C., **10**, 34.

Winthrop, Theodore, and the Eighth Massachusetts regiment, **8**, 10.

Winthrop, Waitstill, **9**, 335.

Wisdom, often learned by folly, **2**, 13; leaks into books, **3** 302.

Wiseman, Cardinal, **9**, 4.

Wiseman, Dr., **9**, 354, 413.

Wit, its essence is in a partial and incomplete view, **1**, 50; dangers of a reputation for, 91.

Witch, portrait of, **2**, 262.

Witch-hazel, the first spring flower, **8**, 140.

Witch Hill in Salem, **9**, 230.

Witchcraft, Calef's book on, **2**, 8; souvenir of, 9; repeal of statutes against, 106; clergymen rejoicing in the delusion, 122; Salem, **3**, 326; **9**, 357; torturing b⸱ miniature image, **8**, 95; murders for, largely attributable to the clergy, 414; agency of the Mathers in the delusion of, 423.

Witches' Hollow, in *The Guardian Angel*, **6**, 88; vision seen by Myrtle in, 91–95.

Witch-marks, **2**, 262.

Withers, Jeremy, son of "King David," in *The Guardian Angel*, **6**, 25; married again Miss Virginia Wild of Indian ancestry, 25; his daughter became mother of Myrtle, 26.

Withers, "King David," **6**, 15; married Miss Judith Pride, a famous beauty, 25.

Withers, Major Gideon, father of "King David," **6**, 24, 92.

Withers, Malachi, **6**, 1; son of Jeremy, 25; his miserly traits, 27; hangs himself in garret, 34 *et seq.*; his estate settled in favor of Myrtle Hazard, 412 *et seq.*

Withers, the Hon. Selah, founder of the Poplars, **6**, 21; his wife, Ruth Bradford, accused of witchcraft, 24, 93.

Withers, Miss Silence, her advertisement for her missing niece Myrtle, **6**, 6; her appearance, 13; her wrong theory of bringing up a child, 30; sense of "responsibility" for Myrtle, 78; receives calmly the decision of court as to Withers estate, 409; is happily wedded to an ex-missionary, 422.

Withers Homestead. *See* Poplars, the.

Wives, "married maids-of-all-work," **1**, 43; the marrying of three, seemingly advocated in the Bible, **2**, 5; faithful little wife of a genius compared to tug drawing tall ship, 289; Bishop Hall prefers nature before grace in the election of one, **3**, 304; **6**, 195; preferred at the piano rather than at the dissecting-table, **4**, 225; wife of a worldly man, **6**, 255; duty of a doctor's wife, **7**, 93.

Wolff, **9**, 83.

Wolseley, Lord, **10**, 44.

Wolverton, Lord, **10**, 31.

Wolves, great stone on graves to keep ⸱hem away, **2**, 263; **8**, 166; men with natures of, **5**, 222.

Woman's rights, **3**, 246.

Woman's voice, heard in the night, **2**, 174; proved to be a Guarnerius violin, 308.

Womanhood, youthful, a garden-bed of, **4**, 267.

Woman-tamers, **5**, 10.

Women, advice to young, **1**, 49; delicacy in dealing with, 80; excellent instrument for a nerve-player, 129; their praise a poet's reward, 183; ill-bred ones morbidly sensitive to polite admiration of men, 194; all men love all women, 220; all women love all men, 221; to love one in particular we must first get her image through pinhole, 221; finest specimens attract those who can afford luxury of beauty, 260; should be true as death, 271; wrong pride indicates low and bad blood in, 271; those who have weighed all life can give, 276; some are mechanical talkers, **2**, 30; can keep their minds detached from their talk, 31; creation of, 50; judicial character not captivating in, 101; three saints among, to one among men, 121; the Messiah of a new revelation, 125; they mostly settle matters of social position, 135 ; intellectual process should not be too evident in, 147 ; brain-women do not interest like heart-women, 148 ; elegance of, 150 ; stylish, 155 ; the men whom they marry, 157 ; their choice of love, 159 ; love-magnets, 160 ; their effect upon men, 177 ; faces sometimes portray a great secret, 178 ; often their one secret is " I love you," 180 ; more religious than men, 209 ; effect of genius in, 241 ; subject to atrophy of heart, 249 ; immovability of some, 274 ; some good ones have no right to marry perfectly good men, 287 ; happiness of marriage of women of genius with truthful, simple men, 287 ; as listeners, 3, 90 ; their desire to please, 91 ; in social life, 94 ; their compassion for suffering, 141 ; need faith more than men, 186 ; power of adapting themselves to changing standards, 189 ; belief of, in the love-cure, 272 ; on the planet Saturn, 4, 63 ; their love-letters, 92 ; as doctors, 131 ; 9, 299 ; as book - tasters, 4, 157 ; do not bear transplanting, 177 ; penetrating quality of the voices of many Northern, 178 ; their atmospheric rings, 286 ; education of, 288 ; they grow old in a more becoming way than men, 293 ; intoxicating effect of, 5, 104 ; over-womanized woman, 105 ; unmanageable kind, 169 ; many tortured by a neuralgic conscience, 170, 171 ; often reject men because they love them, 181 ; have an instinctive tendency to use unlawful means to redress wrongs, 193 ; pathos of those who are unsought, 230, 231 ; a woman always a daughter to man who loves her, 282 ; power of healing sorrow of an early love, 283 ; those to be feared who cannot find utterance in words or song, 341 ; flat - patterned kind, 342 ; their faith, 391 ; know the meaning of love, 469 ; talk without words is half their conversation, 6 10 ; take to terrible people, 159 ; apt to be hysterical when a young minister is about, 171 ; tell their love in many forms, 223 ; love the conquering party, 230 ; to many, the most pathetic image in the world is of themselves in tears, 267 ; decant their affection from old bottles into new, 296 ; their premonition of coming proposal, 323 ; cry of rending tissues dear to their ear, 347 ; fondness of fashionable sort for discovering social diamond in the rough, 6, 285 ; fear of, by young men, 7, 245 ; ideals of, 259 ; of Maryland, compared with Yankees, 8, 32 ; breast of, the cradle of pure and holy sentiments, 91 ; borrow half their tenderness from maternity, 92 ; conscientiousness of, 93 ; sacred office of, 112 ; endure exposure far better than men, 215, 216, 227 ; need more or purer air than men, 216 ; born

atmospheric reformers, 216 ; law that governs clothing of, 227 ; automatic, continuous flow of thought peculiar to, 289 ; logomachy of, 290–292 ; milk in veins of, sweetens acrid doctrine, 422 ; as advocates of Perkinism, 9, 27 ; breeding and nursing period of American, 295 ; never know who are their contemporaries, 10, 44.
Wonder, The. See Tower, Euthymia.
Wonderful " One-Hoss-Shay," The, 1, 252.
Wood, Charlotte Ann, school-girl, in Elsie Venner, 5, 51, 71, 76.
Woodbridge, Benjamin, grave of, 1, 239.
Woodchuck, 6, 88 ; one which used to listen to piano, 8, 271.
Woodcock, Elizabeth, buried under the snow, 8, 175.
Wooden houses, a better kind of wigwam, 10, 20.
Woods, Dr., of Andover, looked his creed, 8, 250.
Woods, life in the, 5, 185 et seq.
Wood-sleds, creaking of, on the snow, 1, 212.
Woodville, Dr., 9, 115.
Woodward, Dr., on the influence of the moon on the insane, 8, 212.
Wool, General, at Baltimore, 8, 24, 48.
Woolner, busts by, 10, 77.
Worcester, Massachusetts, 8, 76.
Worcester's Dictionary used instead of Bible to take oath upon, 3, 8.
Words, poetry of, 1, viii. ; plasticity of spoken language, 28 ; a word the saddle of a thought, 2, 38 ; worth of, 41 ; words not looks win women, 89 ; mean little as compared to features, 181 ; certain short ones like Japanese toys, 3, 89.
Words and phrases. Namely :
Æolipile, 1, 118.
Æstivation, intramural, 1, 263.
" Allgermine Zeitung," so printed in the " Banner and Oracle," 6, 3.
Androgynous, 10, 12.
Bathycolpian Here, 1, 71.
Belluses, 5, 119.
Bibliothecary, 10, 147.
Blair-ing one's conversational style, 1, 40.
Blo'monje, 5, 110.
Bo'kays, 2, 185.
Boiled-parsnip blonde, 6, 259.
Bonnet, to knock hat over a man's eyes, 5, 332.
Bread-basket, technical term in pugilism, 2, 280.
Bulbous-headed fellows, 1, 7.
C-spring shay, riding to heaven in a 6, 170.
Calenture, 1, 245.
Camphire, 6, 296.
Carapace, 2, 28.
Cherry-pictorial, 2, 132.
Conversational soprano, 1, 214.

Crispations, **10**, 117.
Cuss, **2**, 21.
Cymbal, a genus of doughnut, **6**, 231.
Damsels (meaning damsons), **6**, 231.
Deodand, **1**, 12.
Donated, **6**, 4.
Down-East, **5**, 13.
Dynamometer, **2**, 93.
Edulcorated, **2**, 62.
Epeolatry, **2**, 117.
Eudiometer, **2**,72.
Féeest (New York dialect for "first"), **6**, 269.
Frût-cake, **5**, 121.
Fust-rate, **1**, 28.
Geoponic eyes, **5**, 166.
Golden cheese, a million of dollars is a kind of, **5**, 2.
Great Vegetable, the, (tobacco) **1**, 101.
Haälth, **5**, 92.
Haousen, in New England, for houses, **10**, 160.
Haŏw, **1**, 110 ; **2**, 44.
Holme, **10**, 103.
Huckleberry districts, **6**, 202.
Humph ! **6**, 16.
Interpellations, **10**, 88.
Kerridge, **1**, 109.
Kiss-your-brother, no galvanism in, **5**, 389.
Lady-baskets (crinolines), **1**, 19.
Lahcóon, **5**, 299.
Ligate, **9**, 302.
Loaned, for lent, **5**, 90.
Loggerheads, **5**, 66.
Luniversary, **1**, 49.
Lyceums, **5**, 281.
Marangs, **5**, 110.
Melasses, **1**, 67.
Millionocracy, **5**, 2.
Mistress Quicklyisms, **10**, 38.
Mizzourah, **1**, 138.
Molossa's (molasses), so spelt in Mather's "Magnolia," **1**, 67.
Mouthable, **10**, 71.
Muséum, **2**, 97.
Musidora-ish, **6**, 213.
Natur' and Grace, **6**, 226.
Omniverbivorous, **1**, 257.
Palpebral spasm (a wink), **2**, 14.
Papaä, **6**, 274.
Pätridges, **5**, 120.
Patulous fage, **1**, 244.
P'dóose, **5**, 81.
Pimpant, **2**, 136.
Pleasing vegetables, elms called, **1**, 236.
Polyphlœsbœan, **1**, 83.
Popped, a hat sat down upon, **1**, 178.
Porcellarium, **6**, 382.
Port-chuck, an inhabitant of Cambridgeport, **1**, 177 ; **8**, 240.
Psychometers, **6**, 157.
Pugil, **1**, 77.
Quadrumanous rough (a baboon), **10**, 5.
Remember of, **1**, 109.
Saäs-plates, **1**, 308.

Sahtisfahction, **1**, 109.
Screeching Indian Divell, **5**, 43.
Sense, all sorts of, but common sense, **6**, 40.
Shooing hens, **2**, 248.
Slack-water period of prosperity, **5**, 11.
Slippernoose, **5**, 373.
Snappin' turkles, **5**, 384.
Spine of the back, **6**, 420.
Spotting, through blinds, **5**, 298.
Squirt, college boy's term, **3**, 252.
Srub, **5**, 111.
Stoppin' at, **1**, 109.
Sternutation, **1**, 118.
Stillicidium, **1**, 80.
Straightened (said of the dead), **5**, 455.
Straw in the bung-hole of the universe, **2**, 24.
Super-septuagenarian, **10**, 206.
Tabullo (tableau), **1**, 138.
Thank-you-ma'ams, in the road of life, **6**, 170.
Thunder-and-lightning women, **5**, 292.
Tire of all creation straightened out for a crowbar, **1**, 125.
Understatement, slight habitual, **5**, 9.
Vaandoo, **5**, 83.
Verbicide, **1**, 11.
View, ability to pronounce, a test of Brahminism, **5**, 482.
White plague of the North (consumption), **5**, 140.
Woman, the, who "calc'lates" is lost, **1**, 49.
Yallah dog, **5**, 35.
Yes ? a vulgarism in conversation, **1**, 18.
Wordsworth, his "Boy of Windermere," **2**, 160 ; **8**, 18 ; seems to have solved some of the great secrets of life, 180 ; his picture of old age in "Matthew," **4**, 48 ; use of facts of observation by, **8**, 134 ; "fingering slaves" of, **9**, 366 ; his lines about cuckoo, **10**, 50, 52 ; the region made sacred by, 186.
Work, as a means of deadening the sensibilities, **6**, 250.
Work-knowledge is in the senses, **9**, 377.
Working-people, bravery of, **8**, 10.
Works of art in the Professor's room enumerated, **2**, 29.
World, not yet ripe, **1**, 24 ; the real, is within to those who love, **6**, 411 ; the latest days are the old age of the, **8**, 287 n., 288 n.
World & Co., **6**, 261.
World-tamers, **5**, 10.
Worship, companionship in, **4**, 258 ; meaning of the word translated, **8**, 309.
Worthylakes, grave of the, **2**, 3, 306.
Wounded, the, at Antietam, **8**, 29, 30 ; at Middletown, Md., 35, 36.
Wounds, heal by God's presence, **5**, 316 ; treated with Weapon ointment, **9**, 6 ; with Sympathetic powder, 7.

"Wreck of the Medusa," Géricault's, **10**, 16, 170.

Wren, Sir Christopher, and the law of gravitation, **8**, 84.

Wright, W. Aldis, **10**, 75, 87.

Wrinkles, cheapest coat-of-mail against Cupid, **2**, 223; the three, between eyebrows, **5**, 87.

Writers are like lovers, **3**, 35. *See also* Authors.

Writing, with feet in hot water, **1**, 7; like shooting with a rifle, 28; drudgery of, **3**, 299; by the column, **4**, 8; charm of, consists in its surprises, 298.

Writtle, William, murderer, **5**, 224.

Wrong, first act of, **1**, 209.

Wych-elm, **10**, 81.

Wylie, Sir J., on disease caused by lack of light, **8**, 209.

Wyman, Dr. Jeffries, **3**, 178; **10**, 183.

Yale College societies, **6**, 270.

Yankee appellations, **2**, 95.

Yankees, a band of gypsies, **2**, 246; pitch-pine and white-pine, **3**, 276; personified in Silas Peckham, in *Elsie Venner*, **5**, 48.

Year 1809, birth year of Gladstone, Tennyson, Darwin, and the author, **10**, 44.

Yes, we knew we must lose him, **1**, 26.

Yonkers, Philipse house at, **5**, 144.

York, Archbishop of, **10**, 54.

York, Duke of, monument to, **10**, 194.

York, England, fine breakfast at, **10**, 82; cathedral, 83.

Yorkshire, **10**, 6.

Yorkshire groom, his fight with a sophomore, **2**, 53.

Young, Edward, **4**, 49.

Young, Dr. Thomas, **10**, 2.

Young America, let him roll! **4**, 238.

Young Astronomer, the, in *The Poet*, devotion to his work, **3**, 59; his loneliness, 140; his poem, 144, 172, 197, 230, 258, 285; gives Scheherezade astronomy lessons, 234 *et seq.*; changes his seat at the table, 235; tells Scheherezade the story of Andromeda, 317.

Young days, boasting about, **4**, 32.

Young Doctor, the, in *Over the Teacups*, **4**, 51; talks about family doctors, 124; also about medical specialists, 128; his admiration for Delilah, 224; seeks advice from Number Five, 240; his out-of-town patient, 261; takes the two Annexes to the "exhibition," 264; his engagement to Delilah becomes known, 270.

Young fellow. *See* John.

Young Girl. *See* Scheherezade.

Young-lady-factories, boarding-schools called, **2**, 239.

Young Lady, who has come to be finished off, **1**, 10.

Young men, letter of advice to one, **1**, 289; American, opportunities of, **2**, 283; beauty of Greek, 283; courage of, **5**, 10; may get to highest level by ten years of unflagging labor, 20; restless when on their good behavior, 158; young men know the rules, old men know the exceptions, **9**, 377.

Young people prefer the thoughts and language of their own generation, **4**, 7.

Young surgeon, old physician, **3**, 119.

Young women. *See* Women.

Youth, flakes off like button-wood bark, **1**, 153; degeneracy of American, 170; and age are something in the soul, 199.

Youthful womanhood, a garden-bed of, **4**, 267.

Zaehdarm, Philippus, **4**, 27.

Zekle and Huldy, **10**, 49.

Zend Avesta, quotation from, **3**, 326.

Zephyr, **10**, 39.

Zimmermann, his "Treatise on Solitude," **1**, 6 n.

Zipporah, practice of, **9**, 313.

Zodiac, signs of, sun passes through, **8**, 135; in almanacs, 186.

Zola, **4**, 107 *et seq.*, 251; **7**, 177.

Zwingli, **8**, 84.

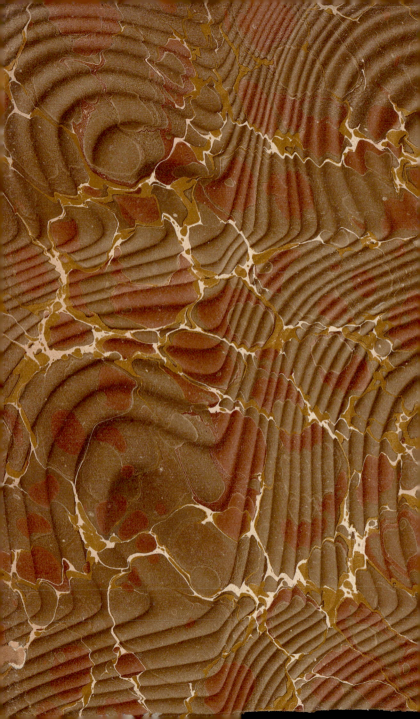